ABOUT THE AUTHOR

Economist Robert H. Nelson has been a Visiting Scholar with the Brookings Institution, the Woods Hole Oceanographic Institution, and the Political Economy Research Center. He has written widely on economic and environmental issues including *Zoning and Property Rights: An Analysis of the American System of Land Use Regulation* (MIT Press), *The Making of Federal Coal Policy* (Duke University Press), and articles in *Forbes, The Wall Street Journal, The Washington Post, The Journal of Economic Literature, Policy Review,* and many other publications. He resides in Chevy Chase, Maryland.

REACHING FOR
HEAVEN ON EARTH

REACHING
FOR
HEAVEN
ON
EARTH

The Theological Meaning of Economics

Robert H. Nelson

Rowman & Littlefield Publishers, Inc.

ROWMAN & LITTLEFIELD PUBLISHERS, INC.

Published in the United States of America
by Rowman & Littlefield Publishers, Inc.
8705 Bollman Place, Savage, Maryland 20763

Copyright © 1991 by Rowman & Littlefield Publishers, Inc.

British Cataloging in Publication Information Available

Library of Congress Cataloging-in-Publication Data

Nelson, Robert H. (Robert Henry), 1944-
Reaching for heaven on earth : the theological meaning
of economics / Robert H. Nelson.
p.   cm.
Includes bibliographical references and index.
1. Economics—History.   2. Economics—Religious
aspects—History.   3. Economic history.   I. Title.
HB75.N428   1991
330—dc20   91–11446 CIP

ISBN 0–8476–7664–1 (alk. paper)

Printed in the United States of America

∞™ The paper used in this publication meets the minimum requirements of
American National Standard for Information Sciences—Permanence of
Paper for Printed Library Materials, ANSI Z39.48–1984.

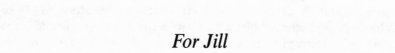

For Jill

Contents

Foreword

In ancient rhetoric the foreword, or exordium, was supposed to establish *ethos,* the valued character of the speaker. A listener needs assurances from the beginning that a speech is worth listening to. Readers of books are like that, too. But an economist, like a cynic, is someone who knows the price of everything and the value of nothing. Robert Nelson and I are both economists. How is one cynic to establish the valued character of another?

The answer, I think, is to note that we are both part of a turn in economics away from cynicism and toward value. The cynics, who leave value aside, are giving way. Economics, like the analytic philosophy with which it shares much, has spent five decades separated from the rest of the culture, looking down with a cynical sneer on theology and literature and other matters of value. If an economist wants to sneer at an argument he will often say, "That's rather *theological,* isn't it?" (The other sneer-words are "philosophical" and, compliments of 1930s positivism, "metaphysical.")

Yet old Adam Smith was first of all a professor of moral philosophy, who thought his book *The Theory of Moral Sentiments* (1750, 1790) was as valuable as *The Nature and Causes of the Wealth of Nations* (1776). John Stuart Mill, besides being the leading economist of his age, was moral and political philosopher. Yet the worldly philosophers commenced after Mill to withdraw from morality. By 1900 the *Dictionary of Political Economy,* under the heading "Morality," could formulate the profession of economics in a way few economists would now dispute:

> The relation of morals to economics is often misunderstood. Political economy is, properly speaking, a science rather than an art. It aims in the first instance at the explanation of a certain class of facts. . . . The special knowledge of economic facts possessed by the economist may enable him to give valuable advice on economic questions, but this, strictly speaking, is not his business. His business is to explain, not to exhort. It is therefore beside the mark to speak of economists, as such, preaching a low morality or rejecting morality altogether.

The economist was to be seen as a man of business, not a preacher. He sold Gradgrind facts, not the mere theological and philosophical and metaphysical preaching of morality. In 1900 the word "preaching" already sneered, as teenagers sneer at their parents' preaching.

The *Dictionary* claims too that the economic facts are Science rather than morality or art. By 1900 the specialization of "Science" in English to mean "lab-coated and quantitative" had already been accomplished. (Consult the first edition of the *Oxford English Dictionary,* sense 5b, first cited in this "modern use" in 1867, which the *Supplement* of 1933 describes as by then "the dominant sense in ordinary use.") No other language did it. The science word still means just "disciplined inquiry" in French, Italian, Spanish, German, Polish, Turkish, Korean, Hindi, Tamil, and others, as it did in English until the middle of the nineteenth century. A German speaks of *die Geisteswissenschaften* to signify what we call the humanities. When an Italian mother brags about her studious boy, *"mio scienziato,"* she means he studies hard in school, not that he wears a lab coat and deals in the observable implications of higher order theories. The peculiarly English and recent definition has made it easy for economists and their imitators (economics is mainly an English science) to suppose that a science could have nothing to do with morality or theology or the meaning of life.

It would be a strange economics, of course, that did not treat at least the pursuit of happiness and consequently the morality of getting more in this earthly life. Economics has a branch called "welfare economics" into which moral questions have been diverted since the coming of scientism. The graduate schools in economics teach that economists need merely to distinguish positive against normative, "is" against "ought," the way things are against how they should be. It is a 3×5-card theory of ethics, conveniently brief, antiquely positivistic.

The sole moral judgment an economist is supposed to be able to make is a wholly uncontroversial one: if every person is made better off by some change, the change (which is then called "Pareto optimal") should take place. Even philosophers like John Rawls have adopted the notion of Pareto optimality, trying in the economist's manner to pull a decently detailed moral theory out of a hat. Welfare economics has shown some stirrings of complexity in moral life, as in the works of the economist and philosopher Amartya Sen and a few others. But most economists continue working the magician's hat. The hat does not contain a living theory of moral sentiments; mainly this welfare economics is Victorian utilitarianism stuffed and mounted and fitted with marble eyes.

Nelson's book insists on giving the stuffed parrot back to the pet store. Nelson is what is known in the trade as a "policy analyst." Though trained in economics, he uses the economics for practicalities. He therefore knows a dead bird when he sees one. Though trained technically like the rest of us, he is not concerned primarily with matters of pure theory, that is, what can be drawn out of the hat if you assume you have one filled with birds.

Economics and theology are opposites, right? Wrong, says Nelson, leaning against the European presumption since Goethe and Coleridge. Economics and theology look to modern eyes like strange partners. Nelson makes it work, showing in detail that theology has always had its economic double. Like Thorstein Veblen long ago he takes seriously a favorite turn of the newspaper columnist, that economics is mere religion. Voodoo economics. He takes it seriously by going further, knocking the "mere" out from the front end of the expression. Religion, he notes, is not mere. It is what we make of life. Economics, according to Nelson, is the religion of the ordinary.

Nelson detects two traditions in religion, which he calls the Roman (in both the ancient and the Catholic sense) and the Protestant (in both the Calvinist and the rebellious sense). The issue between them has always been the perfectability of humankind. Moderation, prudence, courage, and justice, the four natural virtues, are especially admired by Romans. By their works ye shall know them. On the other hand the three theological virtues, faith, hope, and charity, are especially Protestant. Amazing grace, how sweet the sound, that saved a wretch like me. On Sunday even Catholic Americans partake of this Protestant spirit. But the rest of the week, surprisingly, we Americans are Roman citizens. As Nelson puts it, "Of all nations, the United States exhibits a characteristic national outlook that matches most closely the Roman tradition. Americans typically believe that reason guides the world, showing a deep faith in progress." An American soldier in the Gulf, when asked whether he hated the Iraqi enemy, said, "No, of course not. I reckon I'm here to do a job and so is he." A centurion standing uneasily between Jesus and the Pharisees could not have better expressed the attitude of Rome.

Rome under the Republic had a civic religion, consisting of the reading of entrails and other sensible precautions. The civic religion of the modern world is social engineering, which depends on similar techniques of divination. The religion promises material salvation, restoring the Garden of Eden and yielding, as Nelson points out, a spiritual salvation. For better or worse, economics is the theology of the modern religion.

Though Nelson does not hold much with social engineering, he by no means disdains religions, spiritual or secular. Religion is not something that can be dispensed with. Nelson does not believe that religion is past. The popular notion is that modernization has overthrown religion. The notion is mistaken, though secular intellectuals from Voltaire to the average reader of the *New York Times* have believed it fervently. "Modernization theory" is among the less substantial achievements of the social sciences, claiming on no good grounds that medieval peasants were very different from you and me. We need religion just as much as our ancestors did. The most modern of nations—I mean America—is among the most religious, draping the exercise of national power in religious symbolism, going to worship on the Lord's day in numbers that would appall the average Frenchman. We moderns continue to need a religion of the Judeo-Christian sort, with its progress and its salvation. "The twentieth century has seen a revival of the wars of religion," says Nelson. Yes, and we fight under the banners of economic theologians.

Nelson believes that our civic religion needs renewal, and finds the renewal in a combination of left and right, the environmentalists and the libertarians. Both are suspicious of the established church. Nelson recommends a Protestant variety of churches in our secular religions. The variety would give people a free choice of economic regime. Unfashionably, he preaches "tolerance of diverse economic theologies."

One can see the unfashionability of it all by contrasting Nelson's small-is-beautiful recommendations with those of the economic bishops, for example Robert Reich, a policy analyst at the Kennedy School of Government at Harvard. Reich has recently sounded the alarm against what he calls "secession" by the educated classes. What worries him is that taxable income will move out from under the taxing authority, disabling the government from making a community. By contrast, Nelson views secession as just the ticket, the most basic of political and religious rights. Only an established church views the splintering of religious power with alarm.

The economist Albert Hirschman speaks of three social mechanisms, "exit, voice, and loyalty." If you don't like the environmental policies of your town you can love it or you can leave it, exercising *loyalty* or *exit;* or else you can go tell City Hall, exercising *voice.* The Roman tradition in social thinking, represented by Reich on the left and by George Will, say, on the right, wants to create new reasons for loyalty, blocking the exits. The Protestants—or the ecumenical Rome of Vatican II—regards exit as making for a freer world.

Nelson's argument rings true, in its history and in its policy. Economic thinking does run parallel to theological thinking. In a sense well beyond the journalistic sneer, economists of all stripes are theologians. One among numerous clinchers for his historical argument is that many of the Progressives around 1900 in the United States were the sons and daughters of clergymen. They replaced their fathers' theology with a new one. As well they might, for it has ever been so.

I can assure you that Nelson is a surefooted guide to economics, from which I gather (without claiming the *ethos* to speak on such matters) that he is also a good guide to the theology. He strides confidently through economics from Aristotle to the latest Nobel Prize, pointing out along the way the political philosophy from Plato to Nozick and the theology from Paul of Tarsus to the modern masters. He brings the great tradition of Western thought into conversation with the mundanities of the market.

When attempting such a survey it is easy to trip. Nelson does not. And when talking about money and morals in the same breath it is easy to be partisan, but Nelson is not. Smooth-tempered even when disagreeing with Plato or Augustine or Marx, he summarizes them for his own uses fully and accurately. It is an astonishingly clever performance.

It is more than clever, though; it is educational. A student of religion will find here lucid descriptions of the economics most relevant to theology. A student of the economy will find discussions of the philosophers and theologians most relevant to economics. Most people are satisfied to remain ignorant of the other. Nelson asks why people are so resistant to economic thinking, a question which has often occurred to me. When I remark that a serious social thinker must understand economics, my colleagues in political science or sociology laugh nervously. When money is talked about at all, people laugh. But the situation is no better on the other side. When one suggests to the priests of the modern civic religion that they might study theology, they merely grin stupidly and go on with their econometric spells.

I do not know how much economics the average student of religion knows. Judging from the recent Bishops' Letter, not much. But I am sure that economists know nothing about theology. They need an education—and have the characteristic flaw of the ignorant, which is to deny that becoming educated is worth the effort. After Nelson, no excuses. The theologian who thinks that a dimly remembered Marxism is all he needs to know of economics, or the economist who thinks that religion is merely what's left over when science has done its job, no longer has an excuse. Read Nelson, and repent.

Nelson provides a way for those bleared with trade to see their place in the Western tradition. He moves freely between church and market, Tillich and Schumpeter. The result is an open road between the two halves of the culture, humanism and science. Getting the two parts of the culture long separated to talk to each other is a noble undertaking. Nelson believes, astonishingly, that they can actually learn from each other.

The book marks the end of modernism in economic thinking, namely, the strange notion that fact and value live in different universes. Maybe in God's eyes they are separate. In our universe here and now they live together. "To abandon the scientific method . . . is to undermine a basic faith of the American welfare state, a faith as deeply embedded in Western civilization as the Roman tradition of thought." Nelson speaks of a "postmodern economic theology," by which he does not mean any of the alarming things that you may have gathered about postmodernism from the popular press. He means merely that a science like economics must entail values like theology. "The new world of the welfare state and of economic pursuits would have to be placed within the context of a broader understanding of the meaning and purpose of human existence." Modernism has led economists over the past century to ignore the context.

The one way to push the argument a little further is to doubt that science and religion were ever far apart. Isaac Newton saw God's plan in the universe, and would not have seen it without a theological motive. It is that mad modernist notion that science and humanism are split. Nelson says modestly that his book is "historical," not "scientific." But his argument says that the two should not be put in separate boxes. In 1946, at the height of modernism, the philosopher of history

R. G. Collingwood put the matter well: "Scissors-and-paste historians study periods; they collect all the extant testimony about a certain limited group of events, and hope vainly that something will come of it. Scientific historians study problems: they ask questions, and if they are good historians they ask questions which they see their way to answering." Nelson is a scientific historian of religion and economics, who shows that a policy science must deal with meaning and statement together. The journalists like to say that the scientific claims of economics have crumbled (they have always said it, from 1800 to the present). That is not the point. The point is that science is humanistic, all the way down.

DONALD N. MCCLOSKEY

Preface

Some years ago, I began writing about the advisory role of economists in government.[1] I concluded, as a number of others have, that economists do not do in practice what they preach.[2] Economists are not neutral technicians who provide a tool for implementing values and basic beliefs supplied by others. They do not keep themselves separate from politics, confining their efforts to matters that can pass a strict scientific test.[3] To observe these rules would be extremely confining, precluding economic inputs in many areas where economists actively and routinely participate in current social debate.

Instead, as many others also have, I concluded that economists are actually strong advocates for a particular way of thinking about the world.[4] Without some lens or filter, the events of the world would seem mere chaos and confusion.[5] Economics provides a way of ordering, interpreting, and giving meaning to events. Moreover, economists do not offer their perspective from a disinterested and passive stance. Rather, many of the most accomplished are firmly convinced and seek to persuade the rest of the world that the economic way of thinking is the best way.[6] Economists over the past 30 years have in fact had considerable success in this regard, introducing the use of economic analysis into many new areas of government such as national defense, education, health, and the environment.[7]

As economists have made contributions in areas such as these, they have often been surprised by a critical reception. Many of the fiercest policy debates have concerned matters not of economic detail—where disagreements had been expected—but of the basic acceptability of the economic view of the world. The influence of economics has been

opposed by proponents of other outlooks who resist the invasion of
the market, of efficiency, and of economic tests into particular areas
of social concern.[8] These opponents find that the way of thinking of
economists violates beliefs that are dear to them.[9]

This resistance raises a practical question for an economist: How
might it be said that the economic understanding of the world is
actually better than some other understanding? The old orthodox
answer of the economics profession would be to deny the validity of
the question, asserting that economics makes no such claims and limits
itself to technical and value free matters. However, if this answer is
rejected as both inaccurate in practice and flawed in principle (as I am
far from alone in doing), the matter must be pursued further.[10] A
second answer might be that economics is a true science and that the
scientific method—if perhaps reflecting certain values—has already
amply proved its merits. Yet, aside from the question of whether
science is value-free or not, the scientific accomplishments of economics to date must be rated as modest—certainly a disappointment in
comparison to the expectations of the past. There is today not only
widespread public skepticism concerning the scientific claims of economics, but many doubters among economists as well.

Yet, if the scientific claims of economics are in question, why should
society today regard with favor the strong conviction of many economists that they have a better way of thinking about and understanding
the world? If economics is not so much a matter of providing practical
answers to well-defined problems, and instead seeks to provide the
very framework for social thought, why should society pay close
attention—as it often does—to the advice of economists? From where
or what does economics derive its legitimacy in social policy debate?
These questions formed the starting point for this book.

My inquiry took what for many economists may seem a surprising
direction—into matters of theology. Yet, perhaps this direction should
not seem so surprising. In the past, belief systems were almost always
grounded in religion. In the broadest perspective, theology gave the
meaning of human existence and the context in which events should
be interpreted. Theology established the legitimacy of social institutions, and of the people whose task it was to develop and frame these
institutions. Perhaps the modern age has been naive in believing that it
is different in these respects. If economics offers a way of thinking
about the modern world, and if economics gives legitimacy to many
modern institutions, the question arises whether in some real sense
economics might offer a modern theology.[11]

This possibility is further suggested by the widespread use of religious metaphors to describe the messages of contemporary economics and the behavior of members of the economics profession.[12] Economics has been said by many observers to exhibit "scholastic" tendencies; economists are said to be a contemporary "priesthood"; and the assumptions of economics are said to be beyond refutation and more in the nature of a "divine revelation." Regarding one heated policy dispute, a recent commentator asserted that "the best analogy I can suggest is to the clash between the established Catholic church and the Protestant dissidents in Reformation Europe"[13] Still, while use of such religious metaphors is commonplace in describing the contemporary economics profession, it is rare to find the suggestion that economics literally offers a theology.[14] To the contrary, economics is generally regarded as dealing with the mundane and the ordinary, rather than the spiritual and transcendent parts of life. Economics is—most current economists would say—merely the study of what works and what does not work in organizing society efficiently and in achieving various output and other practical goals that society might set. An economic theology in a literal sense might therefore seem implausible.

Yet, the possibility of an economic theology cannot be dismissed so easily. Even if economists do in fact devote most of their efforts to practical problems of economic organization, the possible existence of an economic theology is a matter of the theological significance of these efforts. If economic success is widely seen as playing an important moral and inspirational role in the affairs of man, then economic advice may become a form of theological prescription. There may be powerful faiths that are contained in the preachings of modern economists, even though these faiths may mostly be left implicit, and even though many economists may not be aware of them.

Indeed, as this book will explore, the history of the modern age (dating from the Enlightenment) reveals a widely held belief that economic progress will solve not only practical but also spiritual problems of mankind. Material scarcity and the resulting competition for limited resources have been widely seen as the fundamental cause of human misbehavior—the real source of human sinfulness. For holders of this conviction, to solve the economic problem would be, therefore, to solve in large part the problem of evil. Karl Marx was only one of many social thinkers of the modern age to preach that, when the problems of food, shelter, and other physical requirements of life are solved, humanity will then finally be free to realize its full emotional and natural potential. In short, for many faithful of modern economic theologies, economic progress has represented the route of salvation to a new heaven on earth, the means of banishing evil from the affairs of mankind.[15]

As guides to show the way along this route, economists then became logically the priesthood best suited to lead their fellow men and women. The answer given to questions concerning the legitimacy of the economic way of thinking has been the following: Since economists have been widely seen as the possessors of the knowledge to gain a heavenly future, for the faithful of this conviction economists have been the proper heir to the legitimacy of earlier priesthoods. Indeed, this book will argue that the prominence of economists in society today and the leading advisory role awarded to economists in government still depend on a widespread faith in the transforming powers of economic progress. Large numbers of average Americans continue to believe that economic growth offers an answer not only to the material but also to the much deeper needs of mankind.

To be sure, contemporary economists may to some extent be living off the borrowed capital to be found in the preachings of earlier social thinkers. Many economists, like many other American intellectuals, are no longer prepared to defend the redeeming consequences of economic progress, at least with any great enthusiasm. Instead, there are numerous signs that the environmental movement and an emerging environmental theology will in the future offer a powerful challenge to modern economic theology.[16] Instead of a path of economic abundance, many people today are renouncing the products of modern science and economic organization and looking to the natural world as the valid source of renewal.[17]

The *Los Angeles Times* thus recently celebrated the twenty-fifth anniversary of the Wilderness Act of 1964 in phrases that were evocative of language not so long ago directed to the transforming powers of economic progress. The editorial told readers that, in creating wilderness, "the bottom line here is . . . wonder and human renewal." There was seen a need for places where Americans can "experience the grandeur and sublimity of nature that is unaffected by man. They can look in the waters of a mountain lake and see themselves in new ways. They can witness the world anew."[18] William McKibben, author of a much acclaimed recent book arguing for much stronger protections for nature, comments that there is a "crisis of [traditional religious] belief" in the current age but that "many people, including me, have overcome it to a greater or lesser degree by locating God in nature."[19] Another current observer notes the "redemptive spiritual themes implicit in the environmental movement.''[20] Until fairly recently, the counterparts to the environmentalists of today were much more likely to find their path to salvation in Marxism, socialism, American progressivism, or one or another form of modern economic theology.

It is perhaps easier to define a theology when it is under challenge. It has been said that the question of the existence of God became a basic concern of medieval theologians only after grounds for serious challenges emerged. Perhaps modern economic theology is more readily identifiable, and its tenets easier to bring into focus today, because the benefits of modern economic progress have now come to be more widely questioned. This book thus also evolved in part from a conviction that the economic way of thinking is increasingly being challenged and that this challenge is fundamentally a theological challenge. Then, if this assessment is correct, and if economists hope to engage in a constructive dialogue with their critics, they may be compelled to enter into a realm with which most are unfamiliar—that of theological analysis and inquiry.

Hence, it may be important to ask what the theological content of modern economics is. Or, more accurately, what are the theological contents of the many different schools of modern economics, which often differ significantly in their fundamental assumptions and beliefs? My method of inquiring into these questions will primarily be historical. This book will attempt to set modern economic theology in the context of a much longer history of theology, a large part of which is noneconomic.

The inquiry will reveal what at least for many economists may come as a distinct surprise. Economic theology is less novel in its tenets than most modern economists (including myself not so long ago) have supposed. The outward form of economic theology is, to be sure, a sharp departure from Judaic, Christian, and other theologies that preceded the modern age. But a deeper examination reveals that the underlying contents of modern economic theology closely follow in the line of main theological traditions of the West.

These traditions originate in Judaic and Greek sources, which thus represent the real beginnings of modern economic theology. In the modern era, just as earlier faiths offered a number of competing paths of salvation, modern economic theologies have offered many competing routes of economic progress and hence of an earthly salvation. Indeed, in a number of areas the disagreements among modern economic theologies will be shown to reflect with remarkable fidelity specific points of theological disagreement that were fought out earlier among Judeo-Christian theologians.

In its approach, this book is based on the method of history. I make no claims that I am engaged in a scientific undertaking. In history, there is only one outcome and there is no opportunity to conduct experiments under varying conditions. Rather than the scientific method, the method of history is in large part the art of persuasion. In history, the best test is whether readers are convinced: Does the historical interpretation illuminate and make more comprehensible the events of the past and the present? Success in this regard is not to be judged immediately, but only after ample discussion and after the critics and the skeptics have had their day.

I should also emphasize that this book is not primarily concerned with the empirical investigations, theories of economic behavior, or other tasks that in the normal course of events occupy the great majority of the efforts of current economists. Many economists today explore mathematically the logical consequences of varying economic assumptions and structures of models. Economists gather facts and figures on economic trends and undertake empirical investigations to discover regularities in economic behavior. The mathematical and statistical methods employed in these tasks are often the same as those used in the physical sciences. Much as the duties of a parish priest may be well removed from theology, an individual economist can full well carry out these tasks without any deep concern for—or even awareness of—the tenets of modern economic theology. Rather than these tasks, this book addresses the "value-foundations" (as an economist or other social scientist might put it) on which the very existence, social legitimacy, and central advisory role (that of the priesthoods of old) of modern economics rests.

Some current economists may acknowledge a pervasive element of theology in past economics and perhaps even in some cases underlying contemporary economic arguments. Yet, it may be suggested that economics is not inherently a theological subject, but one that has often been misused and distorted for unscientific purposes. Properly purged of these influences, economics can and should become the valid science to which it has long aspired. In my opinion there may be some merit in this view; this book does not necessarily lead to a contrary conclusion. Some readers might chose to view the book as a history of the long-standing misuse of economic science. The laws of supply and demand are not a matter of theology. Yet, such a view also seems to me seriously incomplete and in many ways misleading. An economics that limited itself to strictly scientific elements would have been and would still be cautious, hesitant, retiring—a pale imitation of minor significance as compared with the central role economists and the economic way of thinking have played in the modern age.

Other readers may accept that the very way of thinking of economics inevitably reflects numerous value assumptions and that economists are effectively proponents of these values. Yet, they may also reject the characterization of a "theology" in the literal sense of this book. It is commonly believed that a true theology must address mortality and involve some expectation of life after death—a feature that economics clearly lacks. The economic way of thinking also lacks some other features that have commonly been associated with Western religions. In describing economics as a "theology," I am using the term in the sense that economic theology offers a set of principles and understandings that give meaning to, define a purpose for, and significantly frame the perception of human existence. A number of theologians have understood theology in this sense, as when one writes that to describe a secular outlook as a religion "is no mere figure of speech. One's religion is whatever serves as one's ultimate source of meaning."[21] Similarly, I have also rejected several suggestions that the economic way of thinking might better be described as a "philosophy." For me, the term "theology" more precisely suggests a system of thought that is a source of fundamental meaning and purpose.

The types of questions raised in this book will, I believe, receive increasing attention in the years to come. The modern age is the product of beliefs that came to the fore in the late seventeenth and eighteenth centuries, shaping the basic thought of the Enlightenment.[22] Rejecting what were seen as the deceptions of previous centuries, the Enlightenment believed in the pervasive application of science to all aspects of life, the certainty of eventual scientific success in these efforts, and the assurance of a resulting steady progress of mankind.[23] However, in the twentieth century the destructive power of nuclear weapons, two terrible wars of worldwide scope, the Holocaust, Siberian prison camps, and a number of other baneful events have gravely challenged these suppositions.[24]

Economists along with other social and political thinkers nevertheless remain grounded in the modern outlook that has not changed greatly since the Enlightenment. The economics of today still offers essentially a Newtonian mechanics whose framework was largely in place by the early nineteenth century. In the late twentieth century, however, it seems likely that the next century will seek to develop new

ways of thinking to reflect in many respects a less optimistic view of
the powers, the meaning, and the consequences of science. The leading
model of science has itself changed drastically from the age of Newton
to the age of Einstein—another twentieth-century development of
fundamental importance that has yet to be fully felt in mainstream
economics, politics, and social science generally.

In the last chapter of this book, I depart from the mode of historical
analysis and venture a brief sketch of what a future world based on a
"postmodern" economic theology might look like. This projection is
guided by my reading of strong trends—both organizational and theological—of the late twentieth century that have only begun to be
reflected in the political and economic structures of our day. A postmodern world is likely to combine both greater worldwide coordination
and control in some respects and yet also to involve a strong movement
toward decentralization of political authority. The casualty may be the
nation-state as we now know it, which may not be necessary to meet
economic needs but instead serves above all a military purpose that
one can hope will be increasingly outmoded in the nuclear age.

To venture into the large questions addressed in this book can be an
intimidating prospect. I take comfort in the thought that, while no one
person can ever be entirely qualified to answer them, they must
nevertheless be addressed in some fashion. A person trained as a
theologian would have many advantages, but—as I hope to demonstrate in this book—economics has been central to the most influential
forms of theology of the modern age.[25] In this respect, having a
professional background—as I do—in economics, I also have an important asset for the study of contemporary theology.[26] My hope is
that this book will reach an audience not only of economists, but of
other social scientists and theologians as well. To the extent that I have
succeeded in shedding new light on the close ties between economics
and theology, this book is potentially of interest to a wide readership.[27]

I would not have been able to write this book without much assistance from others. I spent almost one year as a visiting scholar at the
Brookings Institution in 1986–87. The book was begun then and largely
completed during a four-month stay as a visiting senior fellow at the
policy study center of the Woods Hole Oceanographic Institution. My
colleagues were patient with what must have seemed an ambitious
undertaking, one that might well be distracting from the more immediate, more manageable, and perhaps more profitable tasks to which I
might have been devoting my efforts. Needless to say, I bear sole
responsibility for this book and its contents.

I owe large debts to many individuals. James Broadus, Robert Crandall, Ted Heintz, Porter Hoagland, Marshall Rose, and Martin Smith all made essential contributions to the arrangements that made it possible for me to write this book. Jean Briggs, Robert Davis, and Carl Spector offered valuable comments and, equally important, strong encouragement at early stages of the writing. Arjo Klamer and Robert Lerman provided valuable critiques at a later stage. Others who made helpful comments include Donald Bieniewicz, Gene Bardach, William Dennis, Paul de Vries, Ted Heintz, Paul Heyne, Loren Lomasky, Peter May, James Michaels, Claudia Mills, Robert A. Nelson, Mancur Olson, John Schefter, Richard Stroup, Jeffrey Wasserman, Aaron Wildavsky, and Jon Wisman. The typing of the manuscript was done by Ilana Gordon, Ella Johnson, and Karen White. I thank all of them for their help.

The Message of Modern Economic Theology

One of the important developments of post–World War II economics was the "Coase theorem," which spawned a whole school of writings on property rights.[1] Yet, few economists know that the very option advocated by Ronald Coase—the making of monetary payments for damages done to another party—also has a long history of study in Jewish rabbinical writings. In the Middle Ages, "although the halakhic sources accepted the idea that it is possible for the individual to set aside his opposition to a plant that is causing him damage in exchange for a monetary consideration, this did not apply when the damage was to one's health."[2] A rabbi of the sixteenth century discussed how he was asked to resolve "the question . . . concerning the butchers who have bought from the neighbors the right to build an abattoir."[3] The rabbi went on to rule that this particular market transaction was not binding on the neighbors under Jewish law.

Many environmental economists today are similarly involved in public debates as to whether the "right to pollute" is properly a salable right; most economists favor such a right, but also encounter strong opposition among members of environmental groups. Indeed, economists today make pronouncements on the desirability and social legitimacy of many economic practices. They seek to persuade government leaders to design the institutions of society in accord with the prescriptions of an economic way of thinking. The governing principle informing these verdicts is usually the following: Does the proposed action serve to advance overall economic efficiency and the long-run productivity of the national (and world) economy? If the priests of old usually asked whether an action was consistent with God's design for the world, in the message of contemporary economics the laws of economic efficiency and of economic growth have replaced the divine plan.[4]

Economic commands have taken the place of the divine intent in other respects as well. For many modern men and women, the power to eliminate evil in the world is no longer a divine prerogative, but is instead primarily a matter of eliminating economic scarcity. If all important material needs could be fully satisfied—economic theology preaches—then the main cause of past wars, hatreds, and other banes of human history would be ended. There would be far less basis for envy, jealousy, and other sources of evil thoughts and actions. People could live in a happy harmony and devote themselves to the higher and finer things of life.

One influential deliverer of this message was John Maynard Keynes, whose economic prescriptions helped to shape major elements of the twentieth-century welfare state. Keynes offered a happy vision of a society in which stable economic growth could be maintained—a goal now attainable because Keynes had supplied the knowledge to tame cyclical disruptions of the market. Worldly-wise and cynical though he often was, Keynes was nevertheless on occasion the deliverer of a prophetic message. At the conclusion of *The General Theory of Employment, Interest, and Money*, he stated that in the long run the following of his prescriptions would "mean . . . the euthanasia of the cumulative oppressive power of the capitalist to exploit the scarcity-value of capital"—and effectively the end of class conflict, which would yield a new era of social harmony and well-being. The current economic system was thus for Keynes a "transitional phase" after which "much else" will also "suffer a sea-change."[5]

In other writings, Keynes elaborated on this vision. He suggested that economic growth was proceeding rapidly enough that for practical purposes an end to scarcity and a transformation in the human condition might be as near as a few generations away. It was not too soon to begin thinking about a new era in history in which the pursuit of self-interest and other unattractive features in human behavior would no longer need to play the large role that had thus far been a regrettable necessity.

I see us free, therefore, to return to some of the most sure and certain principles of religion and traditional virtue—that avarice is a vice, that the exaction of usury is a misdemeanour, and the love of money is detestable, that those [who] walk most truly in the paths of virtue and sane wisdom [are those] who take least thought for the morrow. We shall once more value ends above means and prefer the good to the useful. We shall honour those who can teach us how to pluck the hour and the day virtuously and well, the delightful people who are capable of taking direct enjoyment in things, the lilies of the field who toil not, neither do they spin.

But beware! The time for all this is not yet. For at least another hundred years we must pretend to ourselves and to every one that fair is foul and foul is fair; for foul is useful and fair is not. Avarice and usury and precaution must be our gods for a little longer still. For only they can lead us out of the tunnel of economic necessity into daylight.[6]

The belief in the redeeming power of economic progress has extended far beyond members of the economics profession. Indeed, it is only because this belief has been so widely held that economists have had such a central role in modern society. Many physical scientists, for example, have been motivated in their research efforts by the conviction that improved scientific knowledge and resulting technological advance are critical to the increasing material productivity of modern society. A leading contemporary physicist thus observes that many scientists have dreamed of "a golden age of bliss in which nobody would have to suffer or go hungry any longer. The golden age, which earlier philosophies and religions set in the past or in heaven, was moved to the near future and on earth. . . . Progress in science and technology would abolish need, and moral progress, based on absence of need, would abolish evil."[7]

Similar thoughts have not been far from the minds of many practical men of affairs who have guided the welfare state. When the Ford Foundation was established in the late 1940s, its founders commissioned a study to help set future funding directions. In supporting a major commitment to economic (and other social science) research, the study expressed the conviction that "not until the physical requirements of life and good health are well met may men progress toward the fullest realization of their mental, emotional and spiritual capacities."[8] For the Ford Foundation, the goal of economic development was not primarily "increased want-satisfaction." Rather, the foundation officials hoped to provide "a means to other ends"—such as the elimination of "one cause of war" and the establishment of a "prerequisite to political stability at home."[9]

As chairman of the Council of Economic Advisors, Walter Heller in the early 1960s promoted the "Kennedy tax cut" as a way of stimulating more rapid growth in the U.S. economy. Heller was motivated by a belief that for the individual "abundance enlarges his options, his meaningful freedom." Growth and prosperity made it possible to "battle the tyranny of poverty for some without wrenching resources away from others" and to obtain "the resources needed to achieve great societies."[10] The vision of progress based on material advance has been challenged vigorously in recent years in the United States, but still exerts a powerful influence. The *New York Times* recently observed with respect to one environmental controversy that there was still a "vocal segment of the population for whom development [has] assumed the significance of a spiritual quest."[11]

Evidence of such a faith abounds in popular culture. Among many examples that could be given, a recent *Time* article examined the growing provision of day-care, granting of maternity leaves, sharing of jobs, and other steps being taken by companies to accommodate changing family circumstances of employees. In explaining why these trends should be further encouraged, *Time* suggested, first, that market competition would compel companies to meet the demands of their employees: "If they are not satisfied, they may just look for work elsewhere." Second, the new work practices made it easier for parents "to raise healthy, happy children," which would help to ensure "the quality of the next generation of workers" and in this way represented "a critical investment in America's economic future."[12] As regarded by *Time*, social legitimacy was not a matter fundamentally of the health and happiness of the children for their own sake. Rather, it was derived from economic arguments and especially from the fact that the health and happiness of children would contribute to the continuing economic progress of American society.

Poverty, material deprivation, and economic scarcity are—to be sure—not the sole causes of past human conflict and misbehavior. Another fundamental cause has been ignorance; men have fought because they had disagreed violently. And in the message of economic theology, these disagreements have been due to a failure of rational understanding. Indeed, as the world becomes more rational, a new era of harmony and mutual cooperation will be possible. It will fall to economists above all to demonstrate that a fundamental underlying rationality does in fact guide individual and social behavior.

Admittedly, all the social sciences have played important roles in the twentieth century as architects of the rational faith that helps to sustain the welfare state. A contemporary philosopher notes that the modern age as a whole has tended to be "absolutely confident in the unlimited power of (its) Reason."[13] Yet, social scientists outside economics in recent years have begun to have more doubts. Today, it is the members of the economics profession who offer the strongest assurances. Economists argue that—beneath the surface of what often appears to be widespread ignorance, miscalculation, and self-deception—there are in fact deep and powerful forces at work that obey rationally discoverable laws.[14] In *The Economist's View of the World*, Steven Rhoads observes that "economists think of themselves as the spokesmen for facts and rationality. . . . They think most noneconomists would agree with them," if only they would take the time and trouble to understand the rational explanations provided by economists.[15]

Economists thus take it as an article of faith that the behavior of individuals is not random but follows definite directions that are grounded in the rational. Similarly, in society as a whole, happenstance seemingly plays a large role; but economists assure others that, beneath the great surface disorder, the outcomes of history are not accidental. Instead, they follow a path guided by reason and reflecting a long-run rational order. Human reason in principle is capable of discovering the direction and the meaning of social events. Indeed, the rate of social progress is, in the end, a matter of the rate of advance of rational knowledge.

Amartya Sen comments that, while economists have more than one definition of rationality, one of the "predominant methods" equates rationality with "maximization of self-interest."[16] Contrary to widespread belief, the fundamental importance of self-interest for economists is not that it enables them to make claims to possessing special insight into the psychology of human motivation. Rather, the deeper importance of self-interest is that it opens the path to reaching a rational world. If individuals behave in a self-interested way, it becomes possible to build consistent and systematic theories of rational behavior for them and for society as a whole. Self-interest thus is not a crass and selfish motive but, paradoxically, a necessary quality of human behavior if men and women are to enter onto a path toward a greater future rationality and, in its perfection, a future heavenly peace and harmony on earth.

The Nobel prizewinning economist Herbert Simon has observed that the "classical theory" of economics, based on the assumption of self-interest, yields a condition of "omniscient" rationality—a quality formerly attributed to God, but now to be created in the world through the workings of the economic forces of self-interest. The rational economic model is, moreover, a world that is "strikingly simple and beautiful."[17] A fellow Nobel prizewinner in economics, George Stigler, describes another heavenly characteristic: the "utter dispersion of power," creating a state of true social equality for all. Under the assumption of perfectly free markets and perfectly self-interested behavior, power is "annihilated . . . just as a gallon of water is effectively annihilated if it is spread over a thousand acres."[18] If the current sinful state of human affairs involves the coercive exercise by some human beings of power over others, economists offer mankind a way to a future world in which all relationships will be based on voluntary consent and a perfect harmony will be achieved. In short, to encourage self-interest is not to encourage divisions and coercive measures within humanity; it is instead to establish a necessary condition for reaching an existence of perfect equality and rationality—essential elements in reaching the future heaven on earth promised by modern economic progress.

Other economists—especially in other times—have seen a different rational path to an earthly heaven. For them, society was envisioned as a large mechanical system to be centrally planned by scientific knowledge. Each person would have his proper place in this grand social mechanism, determined by science. As scientific knowledge advanced, the social system could be made to function ever more smoothly, efficiently, and productively—yielding ever-continuing economic progress. For economists of this conviction, self-interested behavior was not helpful, but was instead a disruptive force; thus it was not "rational" but "irrational" to be self-interested. Indeed, to be rational for these economists was to reject selfish motives and to work together supportively with fellowmen for the great long-term gain that all could eventually share.

The Swedish economist and democratic socialist Gunnar Myrdal thus believed that in the welfare state of the twentieth century men and women were learning to be more "economically rational." By this, Myrdal meant that they were abandoning old attitudes favorable to laissez-faire and to self-interested behavior that could now be seen as "traditionalistic, strongly inhibited by existing taboos." As more rational outlooks had spread in the welfare state, however, the groundwork was laid for "the trend towards intervention and planning in the Western world." Regrettably, in the international arena there still existed a strong "irrational" and self-interested side to human behavior. But here as well, as mankind learned to behave more rationally, international behavior also would come to be based more and more on "friendliness and mutual consideration, and that we should all cooperate to our mutual advantage." The whole world would eventually see the light by means of the "rationalistic education [that] is our faith."[19]

As employed by economists, the term "rational" thus shows wide variation with respect to substantive content. Yet, there is one fundamental consistency: "Rationality" for modern economists is a term of moral approval. Amitai Etzioni recently commented that in economics there is an "implied value judgment of the merit of acting rationally" and that in the assumption that "individuals 'must be' rational" there is a closely associated conviction that behavior of this kind must be "basically morally correct."[20] If earlier eras spoke of a person acting justly or being good, in the message of economic theology much the same meaning is conveyed when it is today said that someone is acting or being "rational."

The moral approved is derived from the ultimate transcendent purpose in economic progress. To put mankind on the path of economic growth is not merely a matter of satisfying personal urges and physical desires; it is also to follow a route that leads eventually to the spiritual fulfillment of mankind. Indeed, in the message of modern economic faith, progress is the mechanism by which sin can be eliminated from the world. To eliminate sin has been throughout Western history the path of moral behavior. In short, if what is rational is what yields economic progress, and if economic progress will eventually abolish human sinfulness, then it follows directly that to behave rationally must be to obey the highest moral commandment of mankind. Economists in this regard follow in a long line of priests and preachers in the history of theology.

Despite the fact that economists often disagree in practice on what is rational, almost all are convinced that the same rationality must apply to all people in all places. Since rationality is the basic term of ethical approval, the whole world therefore is subject to a common moral standard. As economic truth is spread to all nations, the world can become a single harmonious community bound together by this common rationality and morality.

The belief that there is one rationality, and that all human beings are ultimately guided by the same rational laws, has yet another consequence of fundamental significance: All humanity throughout the world must be created equal. There are none who are so enveloped in darkness that rational behavior is beyond their capacity. In practice, pervasive irrationality may be found in the world, but to behave rationally is potentially within the reach of all mankind. In short, if to be irrational is to be possessed by the modern equivalent of evil, there are none who are condemned permanently to live in sin. Salvation requires only proper education and the making of a commitment to live by the light of rational knowledge. If Christian missionaries once traveled the world with a message of hope, new missionaries who deliver the good news of the possibility of economic progress, rational knowledge, and human redemption are needed today. Organizations such as the Peace Corps and the various international development agencies have been created to serve such a role.

Finally, if the elimination of economic scarcity will bring the arrival of heaven on earth, all people in every nation will be saved in the same way and will some day share the same heaven. If religion is concerned above all with the path of salvation and the ultimate prospects of mankind, all human beings will be followers in the same worldwide theology whose message is contained in the economic preachings of the twentieth-century welfare state.

Economists as Theologians

As the priest of this economic theology, economists today properly sit at the centers of power.[21] They have no personal wealth, lands, empire, or military supporters to give them influence. Their influence is rather a moral authority—the power to dispense legitimacy in the contemporary welfare state. Government acts that advance the economic progress and the rationality of society receive the blessings of economists; those that impede progress are deemed illegitimate. Social institutions outside of government are similarly scrutinized and judged. Presidents and prime ministers may often ignore the pronouncements of their economic advisors—as kings and lords of old often neglected their priestly advisors—but they should do so knowing they are impeding the ultimate destiny of mankind.

Thus, the governors of states are today widely seen as judged by history. Those modern leaders who have genuinely contributed to the economic progress of mankind will receive a favorable verdict in history. Those condemned will instead have obstructed the laws of growth and economic development, thereby serving to perpetuate economic scarcity—which is the fundamental cause of humanity's current condition of strife and misbehavior.

Economic theology did not become the preeminent theology of the twentieth century for trivial or unimportant reasons. Indeed, by the predictive standards of past religious prophecy, the economic prophets of growth and development have fared exceedingly well. Near the end of the twentieth century, even the poorer citizens of nations within the developed world can live at a standard that exceeds in many respects that of kings and queens of not very long ago. Modern economies have distributed medicine, transportation, communications, and other miracles of science throughout the world. For millions (perhaps billions) of human beings, the material circumstances of life may well have surpassed even many of the hopes of a few centuries past for heaven on earth.

Yet, despite this vast abundance created by the combination of modern science and economic organization, the preachers of economic theology today find themselves encountering a growing skepticism.[22] Economic growth was not to be an end in itself, but the means to a more important goal: the saving of souls. The history of the twentieth century has shown, however, that the powers of modern economic organization and technology can also be used to create a hell on earth. The Holocaust has become the most powerful symbol for the twentieth century of the enduring malevolent forces in human motivation, the potential for cruelty and violence that still lurks in many men and women, despite all the vast economic gains that have gone before. The potential actions of misguided and evil human beings in possession of nuclear energy now instill the fear that a divine wrath such as Noah witnessed could once again descend on all the earth—a retribution for the misdeeds of modern men.

As a result of the skeptical climate of today, not many economists are so bold as to state publicly a strong conviction that economic growth will soon transform the human condition. Yet, many economists still commit their life work to discovering the keys to economic progress. A vast body of economic research is undertaken to probe the decision making of individuals and to investigate the workings of economic laws. Underlying much of this effort is still the implicit expectation not only that economic progress will make people feel better, but that it will bring closer a day when strife, conflict and other pervasive misdeeds of the past will have many fewer grounds for existence. Indeed, if economic rationality should actually come to prevail throughout the world, men and women everywhere could hope to share in a happy enjoyment of the earth's bounties—the Garden of Eden restored by the knowledge of modern economics.

Without some such set of convictions, a number of fundamental questions would arise for which the economists of today would have difficulty providing satisfactory answers.[23] Does the process of economic growth actually have no end—supplying ever greater amounts of goods and services to satisfy an insatiable appetite, while still leaving the basic human condition little if at all affected? If so, could this mean that economic development is really a treadmill, like an arms race yielding current winners and losers but no permanent gain for mankind? If the process of economic growth and development is ever to be brought to any closure, how might this stage of history be recognized other than by the ending of conflicts over property and related human strife?[24]

Many of the best-known economists of the past would not have been troubled by these questions, because for them the transforming quality of economic progress was a matter of sure faith. If this certainty has admittedly been lost for more than a few economists today, it is still a critical tenet of the economic faith not only of many economists but of a significant part of the general public in the late-twentieth-century welfare state.

Modern Economic Theology and Institutional Religion

A faith in human progress—that human existence has a definite direction, and that history embodies movement toward an ultimate resolution—has ancient origins. Such beliefs made their appearance long ago in the Judaic faith in one omniscient and all-powerful God who created all the world in a single act, and in this act imposed a grand design. Christianity departed little in this regard from its Judaic origins, but instead saw the arrival of Christ as the true moment of the revelation of the divine intent for history. In modern economic theology, the divine intent is revealed at a still later date: the discoveries of modern science and technology, which—combined with economic knowledge to make efficient use of these discoveries—have illuminated the path to a new heaven on earth.

The future world promised by modern economic theology also bears close resemblances to descriptions offered by Christian writers over the years to help the faithful to visualize a future heavenly existence. Thus, many Christians have believed that, following the second coming of Christ, there will be a period of 1,000 years during which "peace and righteousness" will reign on earth. This will be a time when, as one Christian writer described it, "nature will also share in the millennial blessings by being abundantly productive."[25] Other Christians ("postmillennialists") have believed this heavenly period is already arriving and that the future on earth will be characterized by "prosperity" and the solution of many "social, economic and educational problems." Yet another group, "amillennialists," have faith that there will be "a future, glorious and perfect kingdom on the new earth in the life to come" that will last indefinitely.[26] It will offer an existence of complete "happiness" and "joy."[27] All this is certain because, since the coming of Christ, people of faith could know that "history is not meaningless but meaningful. Though we are not always able to discern the meaning of each historical event, we know what the ultimate outcome of history will be. We eagerly look forward to the new earth as part of a renewed universe in which God's good creation will realize finally and totally the purpose for which he called it into existence."[28]

In offering similar visions of a heavenly future, in preaching the equality of all mankind, and in still other fundamental ways, modern economic theology represents a continuation in a secular form of the Judeo-Christian heritage. While few economists have acknowledged or paid much attention to this continuity, the connections between secular beliefs and traditional religious convictions have attracted greater interest among a number of theologians.[29] Richard Neuhaus has observed that many secular systems of belief offer "salvation" and that "our secular contemporaries . . . give other names to their sacred world: Western civilization, rationality, liberal values and the such. But for all of us there is a sacredness to the ordered world of meaning. On the other side of order—political, economic, intellectual, and emotional—is death and damnation."[30]

It is an observation made with increasing frequency by scholars in many fields that the core of modern thinking originated in the theological heritage of the West. One authority recently commented that the "major ideas" of the Enlightenment "are for the most part secularized religious concepts."[31] A theologian, Arend van Leeuwen, observed not long ago that the Enlightenment "understanding of history was typically apocalyptic, . . . from the darkness of the past to the light of the present and to that golden age of reason which was about to dawn in the not distant future." It is not only the thought of the Enlightenment but also "modern nationalism, democracy, liberalism, capitalism and socialism, the concepts of modern science and the rise of modern technology" that are "the 'secularized' products" of the Western religious heritage.[32]

These "revolutionizing forces," whose influence has spread around the world in the modern age, "ultimately derive their impetus from that particular history which reaches out from Zion to the very ends of the earth." In the biblical telling there will be "a new paradise . . . the good life and the true life at peace with him, for the whole earth." Today, much the same promise is offered by "modern Western civilization"; in this new form the earlier religious origins have been " 'submerged', . . . coming now to the non-Western nations in the guise of 'secularism' and incognito so to speak." Institutional religion has become a "greatly reduced, weakened and divided Church," but its heritage has remained far stronger, now having entered a new "phase of its history" that has taken the form of a "victorious 'secularized' civilization."[33]

Van Leeuwen was not content, however, to leave the maintenance of the Judeo-Christian heritage to the deliverers of a modern economic message. Thus, he concluded that the contemporary theologians of institutional religion must develop a new economic vision that recognizes explicitly the biblical connections. As he put it,

> It serves only to show how morally confused and theologically blind the Christian Church is, if she is content to proclaim that 'man shall not live by bread alone," when in point of fact Christianity itself has come perilously close to toying with the miracle that commands the stones to become bread. The Old Testament promises an earthly shalom—that life in the good land where 'you shall eat and be full' (Deut. 8:10). In the new Jerusalem the leaves of the tree of life shall be for the healing of the nations (Rev. 22:2). Next to our concern to banish the possibility of a global atomic war comes this struggle for a higher standard of living; it is this which will more and more predominate in the history of the present century. It is a prime duty of the whole Church to think out afresh the perils and the promise which this involves. . . . What we now most desperately need is a clear theology of "materialism", a theology of wealth.[34]

An American Protestant theologian, Willis Glover, offers a related diagnosis. The Enlightenment was a "spiritual movement of great depth and power" in which "the transcendent God was abandoned; but the biblical understanding of man and of the world . . . was retained." In particular, one finds from the Enlightenment onward the secularization of the "belief in the purposeful providence of God in history moving toward the eventual redemption and perfection of man." The historical process is "deified" as part of the "secular millennarianism" that has characterized the entire modern age.[35]

Disagreeing in one fundamental respect with van Leeuwen, Glover argues that the modern faiths are more than a disguised and secularized restatement of the Judeo-Christian heritage. They are instead in his view a brand new religion—the gravest challenge to the institutional Judeo-Christian faiths of the past since the emergence of Islam in the seventh century. With the creation of this "fourth biblical religion alongside Judaism, Christianity, and Islam," and as Western civilization encompasses the entire globe, most of the world may soon be able to trace its religious heritage to the land of Israel.[36]

On the Roman Catholic side, John Courtney Murray—perhaps the most important U.S. Catholic theologian of the twentieth century—finds a "secular substitute" installed in the modern age for "the Christian tradition." The "laws of nature," which the Enlightenment saw guiding the affairs of mankind, were a secular understanding of the "natural law" teachings of medieval Catholicism. In the Roman Catholic tradition there is a long-standing faith in a basic "human inclination to act according to reason." Indeed, if rationality is for the economists of today effectively a standard of virtue, the Catholic church has preached for a much longer time that "to act against reason is . . . to sin."[37]

Murray finds in Christianity a strong conviction that "Eternal Reason" enters the "stream of history as its Redeemer" and one of the worthy products of reason is "the rationalization of human society." In this Christian tradition, "all that is good in the order of nature and of human and terrestrial values 'merits' doing, and that the doing of it can be meritorious, salvific of the doer." There is no unbridgeable chasm between heaven and earth; indeed, the earth is headed "for a transformation. There will be a new heaven and a new earth; and those who knew them once will recognize them, for all their newness."[38] In the modern age, however, it has become technological advance and economic progress that for many will merge heaven and earth—no longer a matter dependent on divine intervention.

If the Judeo-Christian message has often assumed secular forms in the modern age, the transition from the earlier religious forms of the West did not occur without great stresses and strains. Institutional religion in many cases fought bitterly to resist the intrusion of modern ideas. But as early as the late nineteenth century, the social gospel movement had captured much of American Protestantism. This movement preached a secular message—indeed, essentially a message of salvation by economic progress—from the pulpits of institutional Christianity. By the 1950s, observers were noting that "the secularism that permeates the American consciousness is to be found within the [Protestant and Catholic] churches [and Jewish temples] themselves" and that there exists a "general framework of a secularized religion embracing the great mass of American people."[39]

A few religious leaders sought to stand against this trend; Pope Pius XII thus spoke in 1950 against the "heresy of action" by which "the world can be saved by . . . external activity."[40] In the United States, however, few were listening. The Roman Catholic church itself would soon move on to a greater accommodation with modern beliefs in Vatican Council II. In the past two decades, one expression of economic theology—liberation theology—has become the message of a vocal segment of Roman Catholicism in Latin America.[41] In short, while there are still important pockets of "fundamentalism," economic theology and institutional religion are today thoroughly intermingled; organized religion is itself infused with secular themes of earthly salvation through economic progress.

One might note that this outcome would seem to raise some grave issues for the institutional churches and their theological leadership. If salvation in the modern age has in fact come to be seen widely as achieved along the path of economic progress, then the historic messages of the Bible and of institutional religion might seem to have much less to say. It might be easy to conclude that the valid study of religion consists of the study of the laws of economic growth—that is, the study of the prescriptions of modern economics. The real priests of the modern age might not be the priests and preachers in the pulpits of institutional religion, but the members of the economics profession (along with other social scientists). In placing an economic priesthood near the centers of government decision making, perhaps modern society effectively recognizes that it is the economic priesthood on whom the future redemption of mankind really depends. By contrast, institutional religion today often seems relegated to the margins. Institutional religion is honored and given important ceremonial functions, but in most areas is not expected to provide significant theological leadership of American society.

The American exclusion of religious representatives from many key social decisions is frequently said to reflect a division of responsibility in which institutional religion addresses matters of ethics, the hereafter, and the content of faith, while economists and other expert professionals take care of the practical mechanics of a complex modern society. However, social scientists such as Charles Lindblom have emphasized for some time that any social dichotomy between value decisions and implementation decisions is unworkable in practice and untenable in concept.[42] It is in the practical details—contemporary students of politics and administration now widely argue—that the values of society are in significant part shaped. In contemporary society, therefore, economists will have a major input not only in matters of material production but in shaping ethical character—perhaps even more than any of the recognized priesthoods of institutional religion.

Historically, a large number of early social scientists had fathers who were Protestant ministers. Woodrow Wilson, who started his career in political economy and was an early president of the American Political Science Association, was the son of a Presbyterian minister. In the late nineteenth century Harvard, Princeton, and other leading American universities shifted their efforts from educating the future clergy of the nation to educating the future social scientists and other professional experts.[43] Perhaps it was a recognition—although seldom stated as such—of changing theological realities in American life. As expectations of salvation came to be seen as more and more a matter of economic progress on earth, theological interest shifted away from traditional subjects to the social (and physical) sciences.

Today, however, there are indications that this trend could be turning the other way.[44] This book itself reflects a wider recognition that major theological elements are contained within economics (and other social sciences). If the social sciences have sought to base their claims for social authority on their use of the scientific method, these claims are now seen increasingly as a fragile, perhaps crumbling foundation. A number of people, including a small but growing number of economists, reject the scientific claims altogether. It is becoming evident that a large element of faith has sustained the social role of the economics profession. To believe that the path of economic progress is the road to spiritual fulfillment is an act of faith. The message that mankind is rational and that reason will ultimately prevail in the world is no less grounded in faith. If science does not provide the answers, then to ask why someone should subscribe to these beliefs is to raise questions that are ultimately theological.

Partly because the benefits of economic progress are today being more widely questioned, economists may in the future be required to give greater attention to the fundamental assumptions that underlie their activities. This task may involve the study of the place of modern economics in the history of Western theology. It may require making arguments that are developed in theological terms and in a theological framework that is at present unfamiliar to most economists. In the future there may be grounds for greater cooperation and dialogue among economists and theologians. One aim in writing this book has been to provide some further basis for such an undertaking.

The Study of Modern Economic Theology

To say that modern economic theology develops a secular understanding of Judeo-Christian theology is to speak in broad categories. In the modern age since the Enlightenment, there has been not one economic view, but many. The prescriptions for the proper route of economic progress, ideas regarding the speed with which progress can occur, the roles of reason in achieving progress, and all manner of other subjects have often differed significantly. Much the same can be said with respect to the path of salvation as explained by very diverse banches of Judeo-Christian theology over the centuries.

While the modern secularization of the Judeo-Christian tradition has been frequently noted in a general way, what has received much less attention is the great extent to which earlier theological controversies within Western religion have been secularized to become specific disagreements within modern economics. If there have been Christian theologians such as Martin Luther who earlier minimized the role of reason in finding the path to salvation, there have been economists in the modern age—Karl Marx the most important—who have similarly minimized the role of rational arguments in the economic evolution of society. If there have been many Christians who believed that heaven would arrive on earth in a sudden burst, there have also been modern economists—again, Marx the most important—who have similarly prophesied an apocalyptic culmination of economic progress.

Indeed, Marxism has differed from the rationalist economic theology of the twentieth-century welfare state as much as the Protestant Reformation differed from the Roman Catholicism of the late medieval period. The distinguished American (in his early years German) theologian Paul Tillich once rated Marx "the most successful of all theologians since the Reformation."[45] In the Western tradition, the impact of Marx is comparable to that of Luther and the Reformation on the medieval Christian world. It was in a Marxist version that Western European religion first conquered Russia, China, and other important parts of the world. The Marxist faithful proved no less willing than earlier Christian martyrs to give their lives for the cause of economic progress.

As Christians earlier battled over points of theology, in the modern age there have been competing schools of economic faith. Marxism was for some of these schools a vile heresy, one that must be stamped out at almost any cost—as Marxism so regarded them. The twentieth century has seen a revival of the wars of religion, now fought among men often inspired by Marxist, fascist, capitalist, and still other messages of economic salvation. The modern repetition of the religious past has sometimes extended beyond the contents of theology to include the actual events of history as well.

A conviction that the world is rational, that rational laws underlie events, and that human reason can apprehend these laws has origins well before Christianity. It is in part a derivative of Greek philosophy—notably Aristotle—as subsequently incorporated and embodied in a Christian tradition of which Thomas Aquinas is the best-known defender. A less optimistic view with respect to the rational qualities to be found in human affairs also has antecedents before Christianity. In Greek philosophy such views can be found in Plato, who spoke of men living in permanent illusion, as though seeing mere false images projected on the walls of a cave. Within Christianity, the Platonic philosophy strongly influenced the theology of Augustine in the fifth century. In turn, after the late medieval Catholic church departed from Augustine in a number of respects, the Augustinian vision was strongly reasserted by Martin Luther and the Protestant Reformation. Luther denounced Aquinas for what he regarded as the worldly and corrupting rationalism that his thinking had promoted in the Roman Catholic church.

Aquinas and Luther are central figures in two religious traditions that theologians and intellectual historians have seen as deeply embedded in Christianity and the thought of Western civilization more generally. From a Protestant viewpoint Tillich saw a dialogue between two "great lines of thought" that run through the history of the West. One of these traditions moves from Augustine to Martin Luther to Friedrich Nietzsche, characterized by its putting "will in the center, and the intellect as a secondary force." A second line of thought runs from Aristotle to Aquinas to the Enlightenment to the logical positivists and analytical philosophers of the twentieth century, all of whom have a basic outlook that "means putting intellect . . . as the decisive thing in man."[46] A central disagreement between these two traditions is the role of reason—"intellect"—in human affairs. The economists of the welfare state today carry on the tradition that sees the role of reason as more powerful and in a more favorable light.

From a Catholic perspective, John Courtney Murray finds a similar division into what he describes as the "two tendencies" that have interacted throughout the history of the Christian faith. One is characterized by a pervasive sense of "sin as a permanent human fact that casts a shadow over all human achievements" and undermines the role of reason. There is little prospect of rational progress in the world because "the divine promise is not of peace but of the sword." The products of economic exertions or of rational thought yield little benefit because "there is a Principle of Evil abroad, an enemy of human nature, who can organize even the good that men do into a pattern of evil, sow tares among their wheat and send fish of poisoned flesh into the nets which they let down to gather food for mankind." This tradition, which Murray labels as one of "contempt of the world," instead looks to the hereafter and to a divine act of intervention as the only possible source of lasting change in the human condition.[47]

By contrast, there is another basic tradition in Christianity of "affirmation of the worldly." It seeks to "lead men to the life of reason" and "humanizing action [that] is participative in the action of Christ." It involves a "humanism [that] appeals to history and sees in history a manner of law." Among the "Christian achievements" are included "the creation of a temporal order of justice and civic fraternity." This tradition emphasizes that "Christianity released man from a Greek bondage to history and its eternal cyclic returns. It taught him his own uniqueness, his own individual worth, the dignity of his own person, the equality of all men, the unity of the human race."[48]

The modern age has not ended the interchange between these basic ways of thinking, but has instead channeled it into new and secular forms. As Tillich indicates, the scholarship of the twentieth century finds critical antecedents to the Enlightenment in theological developments of the late medieval period from 1100 to 1300. It was in this period that Aquinas and other medieval theologians argued that God had made a rational world and that it was the duty of men to exercise their powers of reason to discover the laws of this world. As one current historian of science explains, "it was this same [medieval] faith that sustained the patient, tireless, arduous and difficult researches of Copernicus, Brahe, Kepler, Galileo, Huygens and Newton"—the scientific inspiration for the Enlightenment.[49]

There has been less scholarly effort given to identifying the secular followers in the Christian tradition of Augustine and the Protestant

Reformation. A few writers, however, have noted the resemblances between Calvinism and the social Darwinism of Herbert Spencer— human existence in each case consisting of a competitive struggle for economic and other success and thereby to enter the ranks of the elect.[50] Important similarities have also been found between the concept of alienation in Marx and a similar Lutheran and Calvinist outlook with respect to the sinful and depraved condition of human existence since the fall of man.[51] A significant Puritan quality has been detected in the thought of Freud. Spencer, Marx, and Freud are further linked by the common Darwinist and evolutionary framework to their thought.

Indeed, as this book will argue, the theological tradition of the Protestant Reformation receives a modern restatement in the Darwinist thought of the late nineteenth and early twentieth centuries—a time when the influence of Darwin shaped much of Western social thinking. Darwinist theories typically saw life in harsh terms, as a demanding battleground where ony the strongest and most capable would prevail. It was not unlike the world of Calvinism, and still earlier Augustine, where it was said that God had decreed that "many are called, but few are chosen."[52] That Marx also fundamentally belongs to this tradition was suggested by a recent student of Augustine: "The Augustinian philosophy of history, a story of the long struggle of the City of the Saints against the City of the Damned, will hardly sound strange to ears accustomed to hearing—in what is at bottom only another and more secularized version of that philosophy of history—of the long struggle of the 'toiling masses' against the 'oppressing classes.' "[53]

The twentieth century eventually rebelled againt the harshness of the Darwinist outlook, much as the Enlightenment had earlier found the pessimistic Lutheran and Calvinist visions of depraved humanity too oppressive to bear. The twentieth century architects of the welfare state have returned instead to the rationalist and utilitarian tradition of the Enlightenment, of Aquinas, and of Aristotle. The welfare state has been built on a powerful faith in the role of human reason in shaping events for human betterment, following along a continuing path of economic progress.[54]

Adam Smith was the first and Keynes the most recent of the great figures of modern economic theology. In between, there have been Bentham, Saint-Simon, Comte, Marx, Spencer, and (for reasons to be examined) Freud. Other modern writers have offered influential visions of the future, but it is above all the modern economic theologians who have laid out the most inspiring plans, the decisive road maps, and the most powerful prescriptions by which the modern age has sought eventually to bring scarcity to an end, to abolish property and government, and to bring about a new era in human affairs—in short, to set events on a course of progress to arrive at heaven on earth. Figures 1 and 2 show where the economists of the modern age fall within the two central philosophical and theological traditions of Western history.[55]

To be sure, in locating major figures of modern economics within these traditions, a perfect fit is not to be expected. To say that Adam Smith or John Maynard Keynes belongs to the Roman tradition is not to say that elements of Protestant pessimism and skepticism of the

Figure 1

Great Figures in the Roman Tradition

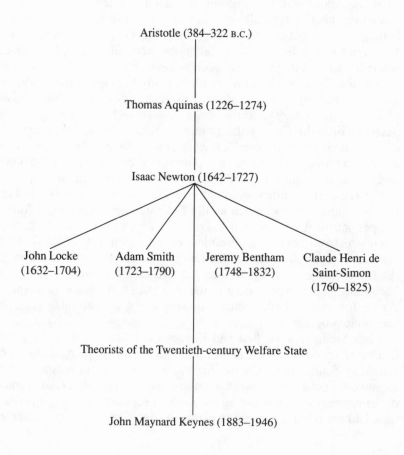

Aristotle (384–322 B.C.)

Thomas Aquinas (1226–1274)

Isaac Newton (1642–1727)

John Locke (1632–1704)   Adam Smith (1723–1790)   Jeremy Bentham (1748–1832)   Claude Henri de Saint-Simon (1760–1825)

Theorists of the Twentieth-century Welfare State

John Maynard Keynes (1883–1946)

Figure 2

Great Figures in the Protestant Tradition

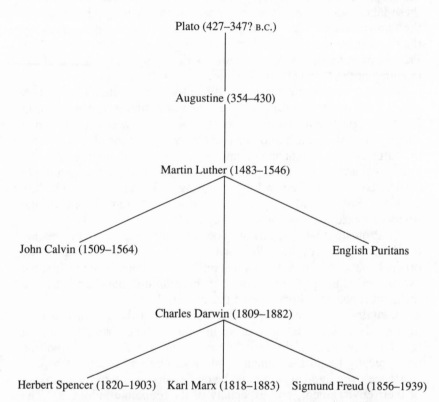

Plato (427–347? B.C.)

Augustine (354–430)

Martin Luther (1483–1546)

John Calvin (1509–1564)

English Puritans

Charles Darwin (1809–1882)

Herbert Spencer (1820–1903)   Karl Marx (1818–1883)   Sigmund Freud (1856–1939)

powers of rational thought cannot be found in their thinking. Similarly, if Marx and Freud fundamentally see mankind as deluded and human thought as subject to irrational influences (the product of underlying realities that yield a false superstructure of human illusion), there are ways in which Marx and Freud see rational forces as exerting a powerful influence in the affairs of mankind. It should not be expected that the characterizations of individual thinkers developed in this book will hold true for every statement made by these leading figures of Western theological and intellectual history. The purpose here is to capture the essence of the way of thinking of the figures examined and the distinctive elements of their thought that characterize their influence on Western history.

Selecting convenient descriptive labels for the two central traditions examined in this book posed some difficulties. In the end, the label "Roman" was finally selected for the tradition shown in Figure 1 and the label "Protestant" for the tradition shown in Figure 2. Both of these labels serve usefully as reminders of the theological heritage of the two traditions.[56] The medieval Roman Catholic church sustained the theology of the "Roman" tradition for several centuries, while the Protestant Reformation offered perhaps the strongest statement of the theology of the "Protestant" tradition.

There are several further justifications for this selection of labels. A strong faith in a world driven by reason and natural law was found in Stoic and other faiths that had many important followers in the Roman Empire. The Roman tradition has generally been associated with a set of attitudes such as reliance on law, a central source of authority, and a practical and pragmatic approach to life—all of which are commonly associated with the Roman Empire during its better periods. The late medieval Roman Catholic church was an institutional heir to the Roman Empire in these and other key respects.

The Protestant label seems apt not only with respect to the specific theology of the Protestant Reformation, but also with respect to the original source of the term "Protestant"—the "protestors" against the established church. The members of this tradition have tended to be the great rebels of history against the evils of their times. This tradition has contained many of the greatest idealists, but the contrast of very high ideals with the actual state of human existence has also made it the source of much of the deepest pessimism. The Protestant tradition has typically found the human condition to be one of alienation—an existence lived by men who must be deeply distrustful of their reason, of their environment, and especially of its economic influences. The Protestant tradition is the source of much of the antagonism to the economic way of thinking found throughout history. Those segments of contemporary environmentalism that renounce the products of modern industrial civilization as sinful, and that seek a return to an earlier and happier state of nature, echo outlooks that are characteristic of this tradition.

It must be admitted that the use of the Roman and Protestant labels has some drawbacks when it comes to the current period. The theology of the institutional Protestant churches of today largely falls within the Roman tradition, reflecting the extensive penetration into mainstream Protestantism of an optimistic and rationalist outlook since the Enlightenment.[57] The mainstream Protestant churches of today have in large part abandoned the theology of the Protestant Reformation, leaving this tradition more often to assume secular forms in the modern age. To add to the potential confusion, the theologies of Pope John Paul II and of his leading advisor on theological matters, Cardinal Joseph Ratzinger, are closer to the original beliefs of the Protestant Reformation than are most of the mainstream Protestant churches of today.[58] The Roman Catholic church in our day has taken the lead in sounding alarms against possible baneful consequences of modern trends—a role that fell to Protestantism four and five centuries ago.

This last observation, however, suggests a final benefit of using the Roman and Protestant labels—which is to highlight the great changes that have taken place over the years within the various segments of institutional Christianity. These changes have tended to be obscured by the use of the same Catholic and Protestant identification for what can be much different church beliefs at different times. As used in this book, the terms "Roman" and "Protestant" at least achieve a consistency with respect to the main tenets of theological belief, if not always describing well what the actual institutional churches of these names have believed in each period.

In summary, a main goal in this book will be to connect modern economic thought to the history of Western theology. I will seek to show not only that modern economic thinking is a secularization of the Judeo-Christian tradition in a general sense, but that it recreates many specific theological controversies of the Western religious heritage. Modern economic theologies have been a radical departure from earlier faiths in outward form, but far less in theological content. The economic way of thinking in the twentieth-century welfare state derives its basic social legitimacy not as a form of science (where its claims are dubious), but from a theological tradition. The authority of current economics is the authority of the Roman tradition.

Part I

The Origins of Modern Economic Theology

Chapter 1

The Early Roman Tradition

In his intellectual history of the United States, the American historian Paul Carter observes that "America's revolutionary leaders and state-makers constructed a government for which Rome was the primary blueprint." The "founding generation . . . reached across the centuries to the forms of classical government and the remembered destiny of Rome."[1] This image would recur throughout American history; in the progressive era one historian wrote that "an American understands easily the workings of the old Roman State because he is a citizen of a state based on the same principle."[2] Recently, a Washington sage observed that the American experience was "a steady, long, praise-worthy rise to eminence in the world almost unequaled since Rome."[3] Carter writes that "the essence of the liberal tradition" in the United States has been "the willed selection of republican government, imag-ined metaphorically as Roman."[4]

Parallels with ancient Rome are found beyond the form of govern-ment. If Rome took its ideas from Greece, and applied them to build great cities and the most powerful state of the ancient world, the United States has had a similar relationship with Europe. The terms "rational," "practical," "moderate," and "common sensical" are widely applied both to Rome and to modern America. Both Rome and the United States were built on the rule of law, to a degree shared by few other societies. If Roman influence spread throughout and shaped the ancient world, the United States has often had a shaping influence in the contemporary world. It was the first modern nation to put democracy into full practice; developments in Western Europe since World War II, and more recently Eastern Europe and other nations around the world, suggest that in this key respect the U.S. example is still spreading over the globe.

The history of Western civilization thus shows some striking continuities between ancient Rome and twentieth-century America. Significant continuities can be found not only with respect to outward aspects of life but also in the way of thinking about the world of many leading citizens. Between Rome and the United States, this way of thinking also achieved a high point in the theology of the late medieval Roman Catholic church and in the thought of the Enlightenment. Although economists today typically make claims to be practitioners of the same methods as the physical sciences, these claims are misleading. As later chapters will examine, the basic outlook of economists actually owes less to modern physics than to an older tradition of thought. If American economists today make their most important contributions to public life by pressing a basic way of thinking (and implicitly, an economic theology), the importance of Rome in its history has led me to label the tradition in which most current economists follow as the "Roman" tradition.

The Roman Outlook

At the heart of the Roman tradition of thought is the conviction that there exist rationally grounded laws of nature and that mankind is both ethically bound and has strong practical reasons to behave in accordance with these laws. Thus, the "all-pervading idea . . . of a cosmic-and-ethical system of natural law," explains one contemporary authority, is central to "Thomism, as in the . . . Aristotelian and Stoic philosophies, and as again in the later, liberal philosophy of the eighteenth-century Enlightenment."[5] In ancient Rome, the natural-law foundations of Stoicism helped to make it "the fitting creed of the best citizens of a universal empire; . . . it introduced a cosmopolitan and humanising spirit into the minds of practical citizens, who were engaged in the work of administering and interpreting the law of the Roman world"[6] At the center of the Stoic faith was the conviction that

"Nature" . . . is objective reason; it is, as with Aristotle, the divine element in the Universe. The reason of the individual man is only a partial manifestation of it: his reason is a divine element in him, and it is in virtue of this divine element in him that man can understand the reason that is in the Universe and can live the life according to Nature. Thus reason is not something that separates the judgment of one man from that of another. The appeal to reason is an appeal to the common reason of mankind. Human laws and institutions, therefore, are no longer despised as merely conventional. They are a realisation, however imperfect, of the law of Nature which is behind and above them.[7]

As Greek influence spread, the Romans justified their laws not by the coercive authority of the emperor or of any other man, but by their grounding in the laws of nature. Since the workings of nature were guided by principles accessible to reason, as Cicero so famously wrote, "right reason is Law."[8] Indeed, in Cicero one finds "the first distinct formulation of the law of nature, in that very form in which it survives in modern thought."[9] The deep respect for the rule of law was one of the most important legacies of ancient Rome and is a characteristic feature of the Roman tradition.[10]

Another distinguishing quality of ancient Rome was the practicality and common sense that helped the Romans to achieve daring military conquests and to build great cities. If Roman thought was not innovative, it tended to be worldly and outward looking. In the Stoic understanding, all men shared the same qualities of reason, and since reason was the unique element in man, all men must be fundamentally equal to one another. The Stoic Roman emperor Marcus Aurelius could thus enthusiastically declare himself a follower of the teachings of the former slave Epictetus. Stoic beliefs would have the important implication that the same system of law was suitable for all societies, capable of guiding governments and peoples throughout the world.

The Roman legal and other outlooks were particularly suited to the task of governing an empire. A small city-state might thrive under a system of personal ties and informal understandings, but the administration of diverse and far-flung territories demanded more formal structures such as the law provided. In a large empire, the prospects for sound government will also be improved by an empirical attitude that favors the assembly of facts and figures and seeks the conduct of systematic investigations before taking action. In the governing of broad regions and diverse peoples, a tolerance for individual differences is a desirable trait. A utilitarian attitude that each man should be permitted to pursue happiness according to his own vision will avoid conflict and encourage acceptance of central authority. The worldly-wise will further recognize that, while men throughout history have found many paths to happiness, probably the majority have sought the good life and to do well in the possessions of this world. The maintenance of individual property rights is an asset both in stimulating prosperity and in preventing undue quarrels and conflicts.[11] Indeed, such outlooks and attitudes were not only found widely in ancient Rome, but are characteristic of a number of other successful empires and large states. They have been found most recently in the United States in the twentieth century.

If Rome administered the first large empire of Western civilization, a second great unifying force in the direct line of Western history—and heir in many respects to the Roman Empire—was the Roman Catholic church. The Catholic church rose to a height of authority in the twelfth and thirteenth centuries when, it is no great exaggeration to say, a Roman theocracy covered much of Europe.[12] Despite a popular impression to the contrary, this second era of Roman dominance also frequently exhibited characteristics of devotion to law, worldliness, empiricism, openness, utilitarianism, practicality, and respect for property. These features run through the thought of Thomas Aquinas, the greatest spokesman for this second Roman era, whose writings would later come to be regarded as the orthodoxy of the Roman Catholic church.[13]

Aristotle is the first and Aquinas the second great representative of a tradition of Western thought that was then to achieve another high point in the Enlightenment and that finally today exerts a dominant influence in the twentieth-century welfare state. Figure 1.1 shows some of the views that are characteristically found in the members of what I have labeled the Roman tradition. To be sure, no one thinker exhibits all these beliefs at all times. Aristotle, for example, is typically Greek in seeing the people of other societies as barbarian inferiors and in finding, as well, inherent differences within humanity that justify slavery and an inferior status for women. Stoicism does not readily yield a belief in social progress. Aquinas is willing to condemn heretics to die, if they persist in challenging overtly the authority of the Roman Catholic church. Yet the more remarkable feature is the degree to which the central figures of this tradition, often separated by 1,000 years or more, display a consistency with its characteristic outlooks.

Aristotle, Aquinas, and other leading figures of the Roman tradition, for example, exhibit a similar outlook with respect to the means of improving the human condition. Human betterment becomes a matter not of transforming the basic nature of man, but of steady investigation, patient study, and gradual improvement in knowledge. Human advance is achieved by realizing a potential that already lies within mankind and that must be discovered by systematic rational inquiry.

Figure 1.1

Characteristic Views of the Roman Tradition

1. The world is rational; nature, including man, is guided by the dictates of reason.
2. The material and external world are the original and fundamental reality— not the world of the mind and ideas.
3. Men are in principle capable of discovering and understanding the rationality of human existence.
4. Systematic scientific investigation is required to uncover the rational laws of nature, demanding careful research and studies.
5. Progress is found in gradual movement toward a natural and rational destiny.
6. Valid law is natural law, which should govern humanity.
7. Justice is what is rational, which is common to all.
8. Because all humanity shares the same reason, all men are fundamentally equal.
9. Life is lived to achieve happiness; a utilitarian goal is appropriate for mankind.
10. Society is an organic community steered by government for the common good.
11. Private property is a beneficial instrument of the common good.
12. It is natural and just to pursue one's own self-interest.
13. The poor are deserving: Society has the strong obligation to support them as fellow members of the community.
14. Wisdom is found in moderation.
15. This-worldly, commonsensical, and pragmatic attitudes best serve the needs of humanity.

The leading figures of the Roman tradition have not been the great revolutionaries of history, but men who typically saw moderation as a virtue and favored an incremental process of human development.

One of the great debates running through the history of philosophy and theology is whether the initial reality of human existence lies in the world of ideas or in the external world. Aristotle, Aquinas, John Locke, and other central figures of the Roman tradition come down squarely on the side of the external reality. Using sight, hearing, and other senses, the mind can only form abstractions that are imperfect representations of fundamental building blocks outside the human mind. Although this controversy today might seem an academic or sterile exercise, the various explanations given through the ages have profoundly influenced the course of history. If the deepest reality lies in the internal workings of the mind, the possibilities for a new world can easily come to be seen as a matter of internal exploration of thoughts and of the discovery of truths that already lie within. Progress may be only a matter of human will, contemplation, and mental exertion. A withdrawal from the external world into mysticism and, in the extreme, solipsism may result.

However, if change in the world consists of a process of learning about and adjusting to a fundamental external reality, all men are bound by the requirements of this outside world. Progress consists of better understanding the world in order to behave in closer accordance with its dictates. Rather than an inward turning to the mind, an outward turning to investigate the world with scientific and other methods is encouraged. A sense of human equality is fostered, since all men face the same external conditions and demands; differences among people are not due to innate differences in their inner thoughts (and perhaps moral worth). The Roman tradition has generally shown a common-sensical and empirical outlook and has sought to dampen the many radical schemes for a reconstruction of human existence found throughout history—beginning with Aristotle, who long ago warned against following the revolutionary designs of Plato.[14]

The Roman tradition exhibits a practical and worldly outlook in its characteristic answer to the question: What is the goal of men on earth and what type of life should they live? Throughout history there have been mystics and ascetics who responded by proposing a life of denial and withdrawal from the pleasures of this world. The early Christian monk Simon Stylites achieved his place in history by living at the top of a Middle Eastern column, prostrating himself more than 1,000 times a day—an existence he endured for 37 years. The more orthodox Roman outlook, however, considers the good life to be the natural purpose of human existence. It is natural for men to find pleasure in this world, if not to excess. Indeed, because what is natural is also what is virtuous, there is no conflict between the pursuit of earthly happiness and ethical standards. The Roman tradition thus character-istically adopts a utilitarian outlook that defends the right of men to pursue their own happiness and their own interests, a set of attitudes whose origins are far older than the prominent place they hold in the writings of current economists.

In fact, the basic underlying tenets of the mainstream economics of today still rest fundamentally within the Roman tradition. As Herbert Simon (winner of the 1978 Nobel prize in economics) observed recently, contemporary economists exhibit a sure faith that individual behavior "is objectively rational."[15] Economists believe in an underlying rationality that involves the "right behavior for the actual circumstances: that the world is out there, people see that world accurately, understand that world and adapt perfectly to it."[16] It is not that people always behave in a perfectly rational fashion—any such assertion would be patently foolish—but that perfect rationality sets a standard toward which men are drawn and in fact can be expected to move steadily. In undertaking economic research into the valid principles of individual rationality, the economists of today are searching for the knowledge to make a better world.

Although often left implicit (and sometimes even denied), these convictions are so deeply held by most contemporary economists that in such matters, as Simon remarks, economists "don't talk about evidence at all."[17] Another contemporary economist, Richard Zeckhauser, writes that "should behavior in certain salient areas be found to violate rationality, it will be treated as beyond economics."[18] That is to say, although men often fail to act rationally in practice, this is of no more significance than that actual human law has always fallen well short of the ideal of perfect accordance with the true laws of nature. Hence, the valid task for contemporary economists is to inquire into the correct standard of rational behavior, to uncover what in the historical viewpoint of the Roman tradition is the valid standard of justice and ethical behavior.

A number of contemporary observers contend that the economic standard of perfect rationality is impractical and unworkable. Given information costs, less-than-perfect calculating skills, and other inevitable human imperfections, it is actually more truly rational to make a certain number of errors. The question really being raised in this debate is whether justice and virtue are better defined by what is humanly possible and attainable or by the absolute ideals. Can true rationality (justice) properly include an element of irrationality (injustice)? Zeckhauser finds this contemporary controversy to be "more a debate between religions than between scientific theories."[19] Few contemporary economists know that the stance they take today is in fact consistent with that taken by Aristotle, Aquinas, and other predecessors in the Roman tradition.

Aristotle: The Founding Father

Historically, many Christians have believed that some men are elected to heaven and others fated to hell, an outcome that in their view cannot be affected by human exertions. The arrival of the millennium, the establishment of the kingdom of heaven on earth, and other earthly developments are determined by a timetable that lies in God's hands alone. Many other Christians, however, have seen a much greater role for humanity in influencing its own destiny. Human reason can and should be deployed to comprehend and to improve the conditions of earthly existence. Further, to do so may be to reach for a unification with and for the greater glory of God, because it is especially in reason that humanity has something in common with God. When it is said that man is created in the image of God, it is above all with respect to the rational faculty of man that this is true.

The earliest statements of this second view of the world are not found in Christianity, but in Greek philosophy. Indeed, historically some of the most important Christian thinkers have seen in this pagan source a major threat to the Christian faith and have sought to purge Christianity of its extensive Greek influences.[20] Many other leading theologians, however, have welcomed the Greek influence. For the body of Christian thought that falls within the Roman tradition, it was Aristotle among the Greeks who provided the first definitive and comprehensive system of philosophy.[21] Aristotle's ideas reached Christianity in part through their being spread throughout the ancient world, where they were absorbed into Christian theology. A second important route came through the rediscovery of key lost works of Aristotle—often from Arab sources—in the twelfth and thirteenth centuries. It was in the thirteenth century that Thomas Aquinas undertook the task for which he would be known to history: the creation of a synthesis of Aristotelian philosophy with Christian theology.

Aristotle's writings are described by one modern commentator as exhibiting an "earthy, naturalistic, down-to-earth bias."[22] Another adds that Aristotle favors "the collective judgment of ordinary men, and their 'general bank and capital' of good sense."[23] His writings are systematic and far ranging, making fundamental contributions to Western thought in fields as diverse as ethics, politics, biology, and logic. Aristotle is concerned not only with how the world should be, but also with the detailed empirical study of how it really is to be found. Reflecting a fundamental disagreement with Plato, Aristotle argued that ideas do not exist independently, but that "universals are reached from particulars."[24] When Aristotle undertakes the study of politics, his efforts include the assembly and close examination of 158 constitutions (only one of which, the study of Athens, has survived). In biology Aristotle surveyed and classified numerous species, devoting great efforts to systematic empirical studies. His scientific efforts are commonly regarded as the greatest of the ancient world; in biology they would not be superceded for 2,000 years.[25]

Aristotle exhibited a pervasive faith in the ability of rational elements to move the world. Throughout his writings, movement is always toward the fulfillment of a natural and higher potential. For man, this natural end of existence is described by Aristotle as the fulfilling of a "life of action of the [part of the soul] that has reason."[26] In the *Nicomachean Ethics* Aristotle finds justice and virtue to lie in the attainment of this practical rationality. Each person has different physical endowments, skills, and other individual qualities. It is up to each person, therefore, to exercise his rational faculties—to determine, first, his natural function in life and, second, how this potential within can best be realized.

Admittedly, in prescribing a rational life, Aristotle does not use the term "rational" in the same sense that a modern physicist would. Aristotle means rational more in the sense that a twentieth-century observer might say that it is rational for society to order its rules so as to serve the first person in line first. Moreover, unlike a law of science, this socially rational rule may not be absolute. In a special case, for example, it may also be rational that women and children should enter a lifeboat first. Rationality in each of these cases depends on persuasive explanations that are grounded in the exercise of human reason.

Therefore, although not following strictly the method of modern physics, Aristotle's sense of the word is still the rationality of not only most colloquial speech today, but also the greatest successes of contemporary economics. Despite many protestations to the contrary, the current social sciences are still at heart classificatory exercises based on the application of reason in a systematic way to assemble and categorize facts, figures, and other information. It is rare in economics that a new hypothesis is formulated mathematically and then proved conclusively on the basis of empirical testing.

If the theory of utility lies at the core of contemporary economics, it is Aristotle who argues that "happiness . . . is the end of things pursued in action."[27] To be sure, Aristotle meant happiness in a much broader sense than a narrow hedonism or pursuit of pleasant sensations. But a twentieth-century utilitarian similarly recognizes that utility must be interpreted broadly enough to encompass the accomplishment of a challenging and perhaps even grueling task, the performing of an altruistic act that is part of membership in a community, or actions that yield peace of mind. For Aristotle the purpose of thinking "about action" is its achievement of "truth agreeing with correct desire"—that is to say, a desire for those things that will genuinely make us happy and that must therefore be in accord with our true nature.[28] Among the few economists of recent years to study Aristotle, Emil Kauder writes that for him "economic goods . . . derive their value from individual utility, scarcity and costs. . . . Aristotle had at least some knowledge of the law of diminishing utility." For the next 2,000 years, until at least the seventeenth century, writers on utility "all follow their master, Aristotle, and they do not present any essential new ideas."[29]

Another twentieth-century economist, Stephen Worland, finds that the role of Aristotelian reasoning closely resembles the logic of utility analysis and other current economic reasoning. In Aristotle, the "end is taken as given, and reason comes into play to discern the cause or means that will bring the desired effect about."[30] Aristotle thus states that "the end cannot be the object of deliberation, but only the means"[31]—an approach similar to that of economists today who take the utility function as given, and then devote their chief reasoning efforts to the question of how to maximize the utility. Worland even goes so far as to conclude that "sustained probing of the issue indicates that there is, at ground, a deep and abiding complementarity between the moral philosophy of Aristotle and neoclassical welfare economics."[32] Herbert Simon comments that "the modern usage of rationality is very close to Aristotle's concept of calculative or deliberative intellectual virtue."[33]

Reflecting his characteristic outlook, Aristotle made a pragmatic case for private property that no doubt allows for further refinement but in this instance as well contains the seeds of much later economic views. Almost 2,500 years ago, Aristotle foresaw the importance of questions such as would divide Marxists and capitalists in the twentieth century. Aristotle explained that "in the opinion of some, the regulation of property is the chief point of all, that being the question upon which all revolutions turn."[34] In considering this issue, Aristotle found that proposals to abolish private property—such as Plato had made for his guardian class—failed to take account of the natural propensities of men. As would be the fate of any design that required a violation of the natural human propensity to pursue one's own interests, communal ownership would be doomed to sow discord. Aristotle stated in his *Politics* "how immeasurably greater is the pleasure, when a man feels the thing to be his own; for surely the love of self is a feeling implanted by nature."[35] It must also be recognized as the natural state of human existence that "all, or almost all, men love money and other such objects in a measure."[36] As a consequence, when these laws of nature are neglected, "we see that there is much more quarrelling among those who have all things in common."[37]

Aristotle proceeds further that, in a system of common ownership, "those who labor much and get little will necessarily complain of those who labor little and receive or consume much." Moreover, since "these are only some of the disadvantages," Aristotle concludes that "property should be . . . as a general rule, private; for, when everyone has a distinct interest, men will not complain of one another, and they will make more progress, because everyone will be attending to his own business."[38] Thus, as long ago as Aristotle, economic gains are seen as depending on the incentive to productive effort resulting from the creation of a regime of private ownership. One of the leading economists of the twentieth century, Joseph Schumpeter, stated that Aristotle's arguments "for private property and the family and against communism" sound "almost exactly like the arguments of middle-class liberals of the nineteenth century."[39] More recently, a political scientist has gone so far as to assert that Aristotle's arguments "constitute to this day the ablest defense of private property."[40]

Thus, the distinctive feature of modern economics is not its utilitarian outlook that recognizes the practical benefits of private property. It is instead the far higher regard in which economic activities have come to be held. Aristotle did not link economic progress with human salvation, as the modern age has often come to see the matter. Indeed, Aristotle took an attitude much more common throughout history: that those who engage in trade and commerce are inferiors. They were considered necessary but hardly to be honored. Aristotle even recommended in *Politics* that in an ideal constitution the artisans, merchants, and farmers should be denied full citizenship and the accompanying right to participate in the political direction of the community.

Aristotle also has little or nothing of the modern sense of the workings of the market mechanism, the possibilities for the use of capital, and the crucial role that the charging of interest can play in an economic system. For instance, he condemns usury. This is a view found widely in Western history, expressed a number of times in the

Bible, where as early as Exodus it is said that "thou shalt not be to him as an usurer."[41]

Aristotle views government not as distinct from the community but as an integral element within it. Aristotle's state is much like a large extended family. Membership in such a supportive community is so important that without its assistance and the inculcation of its values the exercise of reason will be impaired. His vision is sometimes described as that of an "organic" politics, one in which there can be no separation of church and state, for example, because the state is a chief expression of the deepest convictions of the citizenry. Aristotle thus stands far from the nineteenth-century classical liberal view of the state as a contractual arrangement among autonomous individuals. He is, however, much closer to the twentieth-century welfare state in which the citizenry must recognize a set of mutual obligations that join them in a national community in the pursuit of the good life for all.

Ever the realist, Aristotle does not get carried away with his idea of a strong community to the extent that he neglects the practicalities of dealing with potentially quarrelsome and fractious relationships among men. He prescribes that "the rule of the law . . . is preferable to that of any individual" and that "in all well-attempered governments there is nothing which should be more jealously maintained than the spirit of obedience to law." The rule of law is preferable to the rule of any man because "the law is reason unaffected by desire" and therefore "he who bids the law rule, may be deemed to bid God and Reason alone rule, but he who bids man rule adds an element of the beast." Aristotle writes that the lessons of experience that are embodied in the "customary law" should govern, not the "written law" that all too easily reflects the views of bookish theorists.[42]

Aristotle also exhibits a pragmatic attitude concerning the importance of material well-being in achieving the higher goals sought in life. He states that "happiness evidently also needs external goods . . . since we cannot . . . do fine actions if we lack the resources."[43] Classical Greek scholar Martha Nussbaum comments that for Aristotle "economic necessity" limits the achievement of "full human excellence," and "some injustice" is inevitably a product of the human deprivation that is found under "existing economic conditions."[44] The role of government ("politics") is to bring about the "good life." In society the degree of "rationality has a material and institutional basis; the cause of ethical defects is not inherent evil, but bad politics."[45] Worland finds that for Aristotle "to disregard the demands of technocratic rationality, to allow inefficiency and waste . . . is . . . a special kind of evil.''[46] Efficiency is much more central to the thinking of modern economists, but for them as well to encourage or permit inefficiency is to be irrational, to exhibit a kind of moral failing. If increased material production and greater social rationality are not for Aristotle the ultimate ends in themselves, the economic theology of the twentieth-century welfare state also sees the reduction of poverty and deprivation as the means to resolve crime, hatred and many other evils of human existence.

In laying out these and many other ideas in a systematic and comprehensive philosophical inquiry into the human condition, Aristotle founded one of the two main traditions of Western thought. Although labeled in this book the Roman tradition, some might suggest that ''Aristotelian'' would be a letter label. One might also say that, despite great differences in time and place, the majority of the economists of the welfare state are today still in a basic sense Aristotelians.

Thomas Aquinas: Christian Apostle of Reason

The Roman Catholic church was the heir to ancient Rome not only in symbolic but in many practical ways as well.[47] Following the conversion to Christianity of the Roman emperor Constantine (said to have occurred in A.D. 312), Christianity gradually became the state religion, with the Roman emperor its official protector and sponsor. After the move of the capital of the empire to Constantinople in A.D. 330, it was an act of a Roman emperor in the fifth century that officially confirmed the bishop of Rome, Leo I, as the head of Western Christianity.

As the eastern and western portions of the Roman Empire gradually drifted apart, the bishop of Rome was left as ''the one and only successor to the authority of the Christian emperors within the West Roman Empire.''[48] The city of Rome, as well as significant additional lands throughout Italy, came to be administered by the Roman Catholic church. When Pope Leo III crowned the Emperor Charlemagne on Christmas Day in the year 800, many saw the pope's action as asserting a line of authority derived from ancient Rome that was his to pass on. Successors of Charlemagne would be known as the emperors of the Holy Roman Empire.

Following the waves of barbarian invasion that swept recurrently through the continent, Europe entered the era of the Dark Ages and of feudalism. It was a period in which the Roman Catholic church was the chief unifying influence, but even the church could not exert much central control. Weakened as it was, the church nevertheless held the responsibility throughout much of Europe not only in spiritual matters, but in providing for education, care for the poor, rules of marriage and family—indeed, for many of the tasks now the responsibility of government in the twentieth-century welfare state. Over time, the skills and ability of the Roman Catholic church to accomplish these social tasks would increase.

From the 11th century onward, a series of strong popes—beginning with Gregory VII—managed to revitalize the Catholic church. Rome asserted a much firmer authority over European life. The church decreed a hierarchy in which the pope, as the conduit for divine truths, stood highest, leaving kings and other secular leaders to rule with the blessing of the church. The Catholic church imposed demands on the faithful for large revenues, which it used for tasks that ranged from the building of grand cathedrals to caring for the less fortunate. By the thirteenth century, the pope was the dominant figure in the European landscape, exerting power throughout the affairs of European states. At the church council held in 1215, the pope was hailed as "lord of the world."[49]

This second Roman ascendancy proved in many respects a boon to Europe. An era of rapid economic growth lasted from the eleventh to the thirteenth century, stimulating the emergence of manufacturing and trade. It was a time when, as one historian writes, "production on a capitalist basis was becoming the driving force of the European economy."[50] Legal and institutional innovations of the period included partnerships, joint liability, double-entry bookkeeping, bills of exchange, and letters of credit. It was also a period of relative peace, as the authority of the Catholic church helped to ensure that squabbles among the faithful did not escalate into more destructive conflicts. Within the broad umbrella of Roman authority, there was a tolerance of many views and outlooks. Paul Tillich comments that "the medieval church was open in every direction and included tremendous contrasts, for example, Franciscans and Dominicans (Augustinians and Aristotelians), realists and nominalists, biblicists and mystics, etc."[51]

Indeed, this was in retrospect a comparative golden age in Western civilization, achieving heights in many areas not to be matched again until the Enlightenment. The population of Europe shot upward from 1000 to 1300, but then did not see similar increases until after 1800. By the estimate of one current historian, the poor were better treated in the thirteenth century than in any subsequent century until the welfare state of our own time.[52]

Such a view of the late medieval era is fairly recent, however, the product of historical scholarship in the twentieth century. Reflecting the long and bitter legacy of Protestant rivalry and a common Enlightenment antipathy toward the Roman Catholic church, many earlier historians offered what are now seen as having been misleading portrayals—including the very use of the pejorative term "Middle Ages." In truth, it would apparently be more correct to say that there were two Middle Ages. The period of the eleventh century through the thirteenth century was a relative high point, followed by another period of European decline (economically, in population, and in other respects) that was not fully reversed for about 350 years.[53]

Much of the foundation for the Enlightenment and for the modern age was put in place in the period from the eleventh to the thirteenth centuries. It was, as one twentieth-century historian now states, "the forecourt of Modern Times."[54] The era's economic innovations were matched by its intellectual dynamism.[55] The shining star of the day was Thomas Aquinas; his leading twentieth-century interpreter, Etienne Gilson, has written that Aquinas "is the first . . . of modern philosophers."[56]

Aquinas was the next great figure after Aristotle in the Western tradition that situates reason in the very core of human existence. According to Gilson, it was the essential view of Aquinas that "to consult reason is . . . to consult God."[57] As seen by Aquinas, and by many others in the Roman tradition, what is natural, what is just, and what is in a man's own self-interest are all identified with what is rational. Nature, justice, and self-interest thus are not in conflict but are bound together in one great purpose of life, which is to exercise and behave in accord with human reason.

As a devout Christian, Aquinas accepts the authority of divine revelation, but in his thinking no conflicts can exist between revelation and reason properly exercised. If such a conflict should appear, then either the human interpretation of the revelatory message must be faulty, or the practical exercise of reason has been deficient. Also, reason is in principle capable of independently discovering everything that revelation has previously made known to man. This all-encompassing scope includes even the existence of God, for which Aquinas supplies five rational proofs. The role of the Roman Catholic church in receiving and confirming revelation is still necessary, however, because most men do not have either the leisure or the desire to live for the perfection of their reason. All human beings, moreover, are fallible, and even the most powerful mind can never be exempt from errors of

reasoning. Divine assistance and guidance thus remain a crucial element in Aquinas's theology.

If the context for Aquinas's writings is Christian, much of the
content is nevertheless Aristotelian. Aquinas sides with Aristotle in
the great controversy that addresses whether the abstract idea in the
mind, or the external material world, is the fundamental reality. Long
before John Locke and many others in the Enlightenment were to
embrace such a view, Aquinas argued that the human mind begins as a
blank slate (a *tabula rasa*) from which ideas are then formed by
abstractions from sensory perception. Aquinas is also one of the
central figures in the natural-law tradition, writing that "a thing is said
to be just, from being right, according to the rule of reason" and thus
"law is in the reason alone."[58]

The advance of Western science owes much to Aquinas's belief that
rational inquiry begins with a study of the facts of the world. Gilson
finds in Aquinas a deep conviction that "wherever Reason can find a
foothold, Faith has no place."[59] God having once designed the world,
for Aquinas he does not now interfere in arbitrary and capricious ways.
Aquinas at times comes close to the deist faith of the Enlightenment,
according to which God at the creation set the world in motion and has
since then caused the rational laws of nature to govern. Men have a
duty and an obligation to press the powers of their reason to their
outermost limits in order to discover the workings of the universe. For
Aquinas men could come to know God better by better knowing the
rational laws that God made. Human progress thus becomes the
advance of knowledge and the forward movement of science. Gilson
comments that Aquinas presents a "scientific and rational" understanding of the world, an understanding that possesses a distinctly
modern flavor.[60]

Reflecting this outlook, American Catholic theologian John Courtney Murray explains that Aquinas is much concerned with "what . . .
man or society [is] to do, here and now, in order that personal or social
action may fulfill the human inclination to act according to reason." In
many cases this requires "a reason that has penetrated and come to
understand the complexities of the developing human situation." The
"political-economic action of society" requires "careful inquiry of the
wise" in order to ensure that guiding principles are "in accord with
reason."[61] One intellectual historian observes that in his writings
Aquinas "attached very much importance to the purely natural and
rational system . . . and in the main appealed only to this part in
discussing the secular or worldly affairs and problems of human, civil

societies, or developing his social, political and economic thought."[62] In the modern age, economists and other social scientists have taken over the fact-finding, investigative, and law-discovering functions that were the responsibility of the priesthood in Aquinas's day.

For Aquinas, as for Aristotle, the broader purposes of life are to be found in a process of self-realization that involves the movement of each person to serve his natural end. Aquinas also follows Aristotle closely in stating that "the last end of human life is bliss or happiness."[63] Schumpeter found a strong "utilitarian streak" that runs throughout the writings of Aquinas.[64] In keeping with his down-to-earth habit of thought—and despite the fact that for centuries many in the Roman Catholic church regarded sexual activities as impure—Aquinas said that sex could be a healthy part of life, remarking that "married friendship is useful, delightful and honorable. . . . It brings the delight of sex and the physical pleasure animals have."[65]

As with Aristotle, the role of material possessions is secondary. Yet, both thinkers regard it as necessary to take care of basic economic needs before the full attainment of wisdom and the finer things in life will be possible. Thus, Aquinas writes that "two things are necessary" for the well-being of the individual: First, one must "act virtuously." Second, a "sufficiency of material goods" is "necessary to virtuous action," and thus "indispensable to well-being."[66] While there has always been a strong strain in Western religion that regards material acquisitions as morally corrupting, Aquinas views economic comfort as an asset in attaining virtue and the deeper satisfactions of life. In the economic theologies of the modern age, such a message would become still more important.

The worldly qualities found throughout Aquinas's thought are exhibited in his analysis of the need for private property, which is for Aquinas "the most advantageous method of securing for the community the benefit of material riches."[67] Giving almost the same arguments made by Aristotle, Aquinas writes that

Two things are competent to man in respect of exterior things. One is the power to procure and dispense them, and in his regard it is lawful for man to possess property. Moreover, this is necessary to human life for three reasons. First, because every man is more careful to procure what is for himself alone than that which is common to many or to all: since each one would shirk the labour and leave to another that which concerns the community, as happens where there is a great number of servants. Secondly, because human affairs are conducted in more orderly fashion if each man is charged with taking care of some particular things himself, whereas there would be confusion if everyone had to look after any one thing indeterminately. Thirdly, because a more peaceful state is ensured to man if each one is contented with his own. Hence it is to be observed that quarrels arise more frequently where there is no division of the things possessed.[68]

Aquinas had a similarly pragmatic view with respect to the merits of the marketplace. With regard to prices—and a number of other matters as well—what is "just" for Aquinas is not so far from what a contemporary economist would say is "efficient" and "rational." The determination of the just price for Aquinas (and most other scholastics) is not based on the amount of labor required or other egalitarian or distributional standards, as was once thought. Although scholarly inquiry continues, this earlier view is now widely regarded as a historical myth.[69] Rather, as the twentieth-century economist Jacob Viner explains, the currently prevailing view is that in scholastic writings "the just price was the 'common estimate,' which was the price that would be reached under normal conditions in a competitive market as a result of the bids and offers by buyers and sellers."[70] Indeed, the equating of the just price with a competitive price extended beyond Christian theology; Ephraim Kleiman finds that in Talmudic literature, as well, the just price "was none other than the going market price" and that "the mainstream of Talmudic thought is thus seen to have favored competition" in determining whether a price was just.[71]

In scholastic economics, the price is said to be unjust in three main circumstances: (1) where the seller is charging different prices to different buyers (what a twentieth-century economist would call "price discrimination"); (2) where the price is the product of collusion among sellers or buyers (thus involving elements of monopoly); or (3) where a famine or other special circumstance has created an emergency condition.[72] In short, with respect to basic conclusions concerning the role of markets, the differences between scholastic views and current outlooks found in the welfare state are greater in terminology than in substance. In the modern era also, governments have frequently intervened to curb price discrimination, the creation of monopoly powers, and large speculative gains in emergency situations (such as the 1970s oil embargoes).

Scholastic economics attained heights of technical economic understanding that were then partially lost and not fully recovered for several centuries. The creation and refinement of utility theory is widely regarded as being among the significant accomplishments of the economists of the nineteenth and twentieth centuries. Yet students of medieval economic writings maintain that this theory originated "much earlier than is generally assumed."[73] A twentieth-century authority in the field of scholastic economics, Raymond De Roover, has found among the scholastic economists "a theory of value, based on utility and scarcity, which is more in line with modern thinking than that of Adam Smith."[74]

One subject on which scholastic economics was less advanced is the charging of interest. Aquinas, like Aristotle, condemned usury. In practice, however, usury came to be widely interpreted by scholastic economists as "excessive" interest. This position is often still taken today, as reflected in many existing state laws that set upper limits on interest rates.[75]

The saving of souls remained the highest priority for Aquinas, and thus there was little social prestige associated with activities in the economic realm. Among these activities, the hierarchy in the medieval mind gave agriculture the highest rank, followed by manufacturing, and last of all trade and commerce. Aquinas saw trade as beneficial where the original party "has bettered the thing, or because the value of the thing has changed with the change of place or time, or on account of the danger he incurs in transferring the thing from one place to another, or again having it carried by hand."[76] However, Aquinas considered it wrong to profit merely by the process of buying low and selling high. Cleverness in financial markets—loaning astutely or trading sharply—was unworthy because the lender or trader did not add to the value of the object but merely appropriated the benefits of labor and other real burdens supplied by another person. Such an act, for Aquinas, bordered on theft and was therefore illegitimate.

While Aquinas defended private property, private rights could never be absolute. These rights existed because they served the needs of the community; the owner of property was in some sense a trustee for his fellowmen. As one historian of medieval economic thought explains, "while the owner of property has . . . an absolute right to the goods he possesses, he must at the same time remember that this right is established primarily on his power to benefit his neighbor by his proper use of it. . . . If the owner of property was withholding it from the community, or from any member of the community who had a real need of it, he could be forced to apply it to its proper end."[77] The acquisition of large property holdings for the mere sake of acquisition alone was "avarice," which was really "a kind of robbery."[78] There was nothing wrong, however, with "ambition to rise in the world, . . . because everyone may rightfully desire to place himself and his dependents in a participation of the fullest human felicity of which man is capable, and to rid himself of the necessity of corporal labour."[79]

In these attitudes of the scholastics, there is a recognition of the merits of the marketplace and the benefits of economic well-being, but also a subordination of economic forces to community goals. Yet, as illustrated in the title of a 1977 book by a prominent contemporary economist, *The Public Use of Private Interest*, the welfare state today also commonly asserts the primacy of the community and justifies private rights by their usefulness and service rendered to the community.[80] The requirement of the scholastics that the private benefits of individual property should be shared with the community is in practice mainly accomplished in the twentieth-century welfare state through income tax and other forms of taxation (which at times in the United States have taken as much as 90 percent on the margin of the money product of the individual's labor).

In setting minimum wages and in regulating monopoly, unfair competition, discriminatory pricing, and other business practices, the welfare state follows precedents that can be found earlier in scholastic standards of justice in the marketplace. Contemporary popular attitudes toward private profits gained through speculation are not much more favorable than the scholastic rejection of income earned without any element of production or distribution. Agriculture is still widely held today in high regard, manufacturing lower, and pure trading (the reaping of "paper profits") on the bottom rung.

All in all, despite the setting within Christian theology, the presence of elements antagonistic to profits and commerce, and great differences in economic circumstances, the surprising feature is the extent to which Aquinas and other scholastics exhibited outlooks that in the twentieth century are still powerful influences in the welfare state. Perhaps the one truly distinctive element of the modern age is the sense of the immense possibilities for economic growth, a matter dependent on the rapid advance of the physical sciences and of which medieval thinkers had little inkling.

The scholastics justified the economic practices of their time as expressions of the natural laws of a rational world. The twentieth-century economists of the welfare state provide much the same justification, if often using a newly scientific terminology borrowed from modern physics. While contemporary economists seek to discover mathematical laws of economic phenomena and thus to demonstrate scientifically the actual rationality of human behavior, economic assumptions in this regard appear to many observers to be more an act of faith—as the rationality of the world can now also be seen to have been a matter of faith for medieval writers. If economists today see social rationality as leading along a path of efficiency, it is a path that, like the medieval injunction to reason, has a moral basis. It is the modern road of salvation, the means of banishing scarcity and thus evil behavior from the world, culminating in an earthly heaven of economic abundance to match the medieval heaven in the hereafter. Despite the fact that most economists deny a theological function, the economists of the welfare state are in truth the most recent of the priesthoods of history to exhibit the characteristic outlooks of the Roman tradition.

There is, however, another great tradition in Western thought: the Protestant tradition. Following the heights reached in the eleventh through thirteenth centuries when a virtual second golden age of Rome was achieved, Europe and the Roman Catholic church entered into a period of sharp decline. This decline would be symbolized by a series of plagues in the fourteenth century, among which the Black Death was only the most disastrous. Men might easily have concluded that they were being punished once again for seeking to put man on the same plane with God, for believing that human powers of reason could shape the world for human betterment. The next great theological development of Western history would reassert a contrary tradition— one deeply skeptical of the powers of human reason and of economic influences. Indeed, Martin Luther and others of the Protestant Reformation would see in the Roman Catholic church, the pope, Thomas Aquinas, the pursuit of the good life, and the Roman tradition the very work of the Devil himself.

Chapter 2

The Early Protestant Tradition

Although the convictions that men behave rationally and that they can shape their fate through reason are central to the welfare state of the twentieth century, there exists another great and opposing tradition. In the roster of the leading figures of Western thought, the names of Plato, Augustine, Luther, Rousseau, Marx, Nietzsche, and Freud all rank at the top of this second tradition. Because it includes most of the great protestors of history—rebels against the injustices and evils of the times—and also because it owes a great deal to the Protestant Reformation, I have labeled this way of thinking the "Protestant" tradition.

The Protestant Outlook

The Protestant tradition is so at odds with the characteristic rationalism of the welfare state that it takes some getting used to. This tradition tends toward what must seem to many of Roman outlook to be a harsh, fatalistic, pessimistic view of life. Compared with the guiding faith of the welfare state, the world of the Protestant tradition often seems a dark and forbidding place. Indeed, many people prefer not to contemplate its characteristic outlooks. The leading figures in the Protestant tradition have for this reason often been radically recast. Marx and Freud—both preachers of a deep human alienation—were widely sanitized by later followers, leaving them defenders of a reasonable, reassuring, and optimistic existence. Even in his own lifetime, Marx himself is said to have quipped that he was no longer a Marxist.

49

Although offensive to the current rationalism and progressive optimism of the welfare state, the characteristic outlook of the Protestant tradition is nevertheless suggested by certain elements of the popular culture of today. Tom Wolfe has written, for example, of the very high death rates among fighter test pilots in the U.S. Navy.[1] Trying to come to terms with their hazardous and unpredictable existence, these pilots wind up believing in a special pilot destiny determined by possession of something called "the right stuff." Some have it; many do not. It is not a rational thing; it cannot be taught; and its absence will be known for sure only if and when death comes. It is the pilot doctrine of predestination, exhibiting a view of man as subject to forces beyond his control or comprehension that is seen by the Protestant tradition as applying much more broadly throughout human affairs.

Matters of personal love have also received a dispensation from the characteristic rationalism of our time. If it is typically believed today that there must be a reason for everything, that people behave rationally, that they act predictably, nevertheless few people believe that these qualities apply to falling in love. Instead, love often strikes blindly and irrationally; it may well come as an unexpected revelation, having little to do with reason. True love is a gift that cannot be willed or planned. In short, in an age of rationality, love is seemingly an exception, an isolated form of mystical experience to which our society still gives full legitimacy and recognition.

In the Protestant tradition, it is not only the testing of new fighter airplanes that is a selective process in which the successful have simply been blessed with a divine grace not of their own doing. Some men have what it takes, and many do not—the latter fated for hell and the former for heaven. The irrational cords touched by love are seen in the Protestant tradition not as an isolated element of human nature, but as a pervasive feature. The Protestant tradition is the tradition of skepticism that human reason can be the instrument of human betterment. Instead, reason is as often the source of illusion. Men come to believe they can master their fate, when in fact they are frequently weak and deluded. Indeed, by its very misplaced confidence, humanity often worsens its suffering and misfortunes.

In the world seen by the Protestant tradition, the influence of the Devil is no mere figure of speech, but a constant reality that is twisting and turning minds, sowing discord, creating pain and suffering—a constant inspiration for sinfulness. Owing to the deviousness of the Devil, the pursuit of rational knowledge is as easily the road to the abysses of hell as it is to the joys of heaven. It was, after all, the conceit of Eve in seeking to eat of the fruit of knowledge that first caused man to be cast out of the Garden of Eden, the moment of the fall, setting loose the forces of evil in this world.

In the Protestant tradition, one finds mankind first existing in a pure, happy, and virtuous state of nature—whether the Garden of Eden or some prehistoric and innocent tribal existence. However, since then it has been the misfortune of mankind to have lost touch with this earlier and happier natural condition. The story of history is one of man's decline from harmony, contentment, and well-being to war, selfishness, jealousy, and other maladies. If the Roman tradition portrays history as a story of human advance, the Protestant tradition sees instead human retrogression. Aristotle, Aquinas, and their heirs have been the great progressives of history, seeing the basic force of movement in the world as toward the realization of a natural and rational potential. An opposing tradition finds a world in which the direction of movement has been away from the happy nature of an earlier time and toward a growing irrationality and corruption of nature.

The Roman and the Protestant traditions do not disagree basically on the ultimate goal. This goal is to achieve a final unification with true and original nature, yielding a state of harmony and innocence that is for both traditions the valid source of human well-being. But in the Roman tradition, it is human action and the exercise of human reason that can move mankind toward the realization of this goal. In the Protestant tradition, men do not have this capacity within themselves. Therefore, hope for the progress of mankind must be found instead in an autonomous force outside human influences—whether this force be divine intervention, an impersonal law of history, or some other outside power.

Furthermore, progress in the Protestant tradition requires a fundamental transformation in the quality of human existence—the making of a whole new man. It is impossible to perfect the current state of mankind, because men have become too corrupted and sinful to offer a satisfactory foundation for gradual improvement. The need for the intervention of an impersonal and outside force reflects the fact that men have fallen into a condition of such deep alienation that they no longer have the capacity on their own to find a route of escape. Alienated from their true reason and from their true nature, men have fallen into a trap in which, like a man drowning in quicksand, they have nothing to grasp and must simply hope for divine or other outside mercy.

This sense of alienation is as central to the Protestant tradition as a faith in reason is to the Roman tradition. Indeed, alienation and reason play obverse roles in these two traditions. In the Roman tradition, it is the power of reason that allows mankind to move toward fulfilling its natural potential. In the Protestant tradition, it is the opposing force of alienation—undermining, distorting, and misleading reason—that creates an insuperable barrier to the realization of true nature. For Augustine, for Luther, and most recently for Marx, alienation supplants reason as the core element in the human condition; it becomes the decisive factor in understanding history.

This tradition of the great protestors of history decries the wickedness, the false pretenses, the self-serving rationalizations, the injustices, the complacency, the banality, and other failings of the times. What is called "rational" by the powers that be is most often not only a distortion of true reason, but one that serves high priests, wealthy aristocrats, rich landlords, oppressive capitalists, and the other favored classes of history. When Luther found the medieval pope to be the anti-Christ, this demonstrated once again the deviousness of the Devil, now sowing his ill deeds in the very church that professed itself to be the bearer of the highest ideals of mankind.

Figure 2.1 shows some of the characteristic views of the Protestant tradition. Figure 2.2 provides illustrative comparisons of the characteristic tendencies of the Protestant and Roman traditions. The differences between these two traditions mean not only differing ways of seeing the world but also differing prescriptions for individual behavior and for social institutions.

Because mankind in the Protestant tradition can escape its state of alienation only by means of a fundamental transformation of human existence, this tradition includes most of the leading revolutionaries of Western history. The Protestant tradition regards a utilitarian attitude—one that seeks the pleasures of this world and the pursuit of happiness—as a banal outlook. Further, the search for pleasure makes little sense when the fate of mankind is assuredly more sin and suffering. The necessary qualities for successful living are not sensitivity and openness. Men instead need fortitude, endurance, discipline, an iron will, and self-mastery. The ascetic outlook, rather than the utilitarian outlook, will stand humanity in the best stead for the future of trials and tribulations that surely lies in store.

Such austerity and pessimism might not be bearable, if there were nothing else to look forward to. But men can be certain that eventually they will be rewarded—or at least some of them. The fortunate will be

Figure 2.1

Characteristic Views of the Protestant Tradition

1. The human condition in this world is deep alienation from original and true nature.

2. Owing to man's corrupted condition, reason is unreliable, often a source of delusion.

3. Existing law is a corrupted product—like reason—of current human depravity.

4. Justice is not to be found in the rational, but in the iron dictates of God or history.

5. The ways of the world are revealed to men not through reason, but through revelation.

6. True progress demands a revolutionary transformation of human existence.

7. The current world is destined for sin; the triumph of virtue must await a heaven in the hereafter or the arrival of an earthly heaven.

8. Mankind is divided among the saved and the condemned, the superior and the inferior groups.

9. Life is lived not for happiness, but for disciplined labor in the service of God or history.

10. Self-interest and economic competition exert an evil influence in the affairs of man.

11. Communal living and common ownership are the highest form of existence.

12. Government, like property, is a coercive social instrument designed to control sinful and unruly natures.

13. The poor are responsible for their fate; society must not coddle them.

14. Moderation is banality; pragmatism is a sign of weakness.

15. The record of history is not progress, but retrogression—the fall of man.

redeemed for their suffering in a glorious and heavenly future. Predestination plays a large part in the thought of the Protestant tradition. It is predestined that the existing state of human alienation will some day be ended, resulting finally in a recovery and reunion with man's original nature. The path lies, however, not in reason and human exertions, but in humility, forbearance, patience, and above all a faith in God, the forces of history, or some other outside power.

Figure 2.2

Illustrative Comparisons of the Protestant and Roman Traditions

The Protestant Tradition

1. The great "protestors" of history against corrupt institutions of society.

2. God and/or history are impersonal, capricious and powerful, beyond human influence.

3. Pessimistic about the rationality of human behavior.

4. Human existence is harsh and cruel; human condition is that of alienation.

5. Other-worldly orientation, looks forward to escape from current sinful life and society.

6. Ascetic attitude that condemns excess of worldly pleasure.

7. Law is the corrupted product of human weakness and frail reason.

8. Promotes fragmentation, sectarianism and divisions among mankind.

9. Government, private property are oppressive, but needed to restrain human sinfulness.

10. Man must recover past golden age, now projected into future.

11. Fomenter of revolutionary change.

12. The poor receive a fate they deserve; charity undermines the will to improve.

The Roman Tradition

1. Current society is imperfect but can offer the good life.

2. God and/or history are reliable, can be partially understood by reason, influenced by human actions.

3. Optimistic about the rationality of human behavior.

4. Human existence offers the good life; many can hope to experience it.

5. This-worldly orientation, seeks practical improvements in current existence.

6. Utilitarian attitude that seeks overall happiness.

7. Law is the noble embodiment of accumulated human wisdom, puts diverse peoples under one rule of reason.

8. Promotes universal church and overall unity of mankind.

9. Government, private property are beneficial instruments of a better life.

10. Goal is greater perfection of the present world.

11. Incremental reformer of current existence.

12. The poor are unfortunate; society has the obligation to support.

If a high regard for the law is a key element of the Roman tradition, the Protestant tradition sees the law in a much less exalted light. Natural law has no great virtue for men living in a state of alienation. If right reason is corrupted by human sinfulness, then law must be corrupted as well. Law is necessary in the Protestant tradition, but is merely a coercive device required to keep wicked men from doing still greater damage to one another. Indeed, all of government is seen in this light, as a sinful product of man's fallen condition. Nevertheless, its decrees must be obeyed until God—or history—finally opens the way to a happier destiny. When the condition of alienation has at last been lifted, laws and governments will no longer be necessary and will disappear. Men shall then do happily and willingly what serves themselves and their fellowmen, all bound together in heavenly lives of joy and harmony.

Private property is seen by the Protestant tradition in much the same light. There is little of the sense found in the Roman tradition that private property rights are an instrument of human betterment, part of a grand design for human progress in this world. Instead, they are a necessary coercive measure for an existence spent among quarreling and thieving men. Without well-defined property rights, conflict and strife in society would be unceasing and intolerable.

Indeed, owing to human alienation, the pursuit of self-interest takes on in the Protestant tradition a much more dangerous quality. Self-interest is not the rational pursuit of the good life—an attitude that results in a predictability and consistency of human actions, creating an environment in which social planning and the achievement of social progress become a real possibility. Instead, self-interest among sinful men all too easily means theft, lying, cruelty, and oppression. To encourage self-interest is to set loose evil and menacing forces in the world. The greatest need of society is not to provide for but to curb expressions of self-interest.

If the Roman tradition sees economic prosperity as a sign of progress, the Protestant tradition sees greater temptations, more frequent opportunities for sin, and a cause of social decline. The Protestant tradition is the prime source of the deep hostility to material advance and economic influences that is a recurrent theme in Western history.

In the Protestant tradition, the characteristic fear of disorder and of the dangers lying in a corrupted human nature all too easily lend themselves to the use of state power to oppress the sinners. The persecution of heretics by Augustine, the authoritarianism of the newly Protestant states of Luther's Europe, the elimination of political dissent in modern communist nations, all have been justified by the necessity to repress fallen and alienated men who otherwise would pose a grave threat to the beliefs and lives of their fellowmen.

The Protestant tradition thus has an ambiguous and paradoxical relationship to individual liberty. As the tradition of protest, it has often served in practice to break men free of the chains of institutional authority. Inspired by the messages of this tradition, millions have given their lives to revolutions that sought to advance the cause of the right to believe as one sees fit. Yet all too frequently, these very liberators have later proven willing, and even anxious, to oppress others who did not see the world in the correct light.

If the characteristic outlook of the Roman tradition is well suited to maintaining the stability of a large empire, the Protestant tradition instead tends to undermine central authority. The Protestant tradition is more likely to result in the joining of men together in smaller communities of the elect. In a world made up of either saints or sinners, the few saints must join together to sustain one another. The early Christian sects of Rome, the many Protestant denominations of the Reformation, and most recently the cells of the communist faithful, all illustrate the tendency to sectarianism within the Protestant tradition.

If reason is dethroned, and instead humanity must live by faith, then men lose a fundamental common bond. In the Protestant tradition, each band of faithful is certain that it knows the one truth to save mankind—a matter not of reason, but of revelation. Yet, absent the unifying element of reason, this has again and again proven to be a different truth for each group. The failure of other people to agree merely serves to confirm that the mass of mankind has fallen into a corrupted condition—one that has warped and distorted their minds.

This characteristic tendency of the Protestant tradition has often paved the way for violence. A few superior men have been blessed to receive the divine truth. The remaining mass of human beings exists in a state of such wickedness that their lives are hardly worth defending. Indeed, their future may well hold eternal punishment; perhaps they should have no claim then to better treatment in this world. The sacrifice of corrupted men may even serve a divine purpose—or in a secular understanding, the laws of history. In short, the sense of a common humanity of the Roman tradition becomes instead in the Protestant tradition a sense of divided humanity. The religious wars of the Protestant Reformation and the two world wars of the twentieth century both illustrate the potential disasters that can lie in this characteristic way of thinking.

Of all nations, the United States exhibits a characteristic national outlook that matches most closely the Roman tradition. Americans typically believe that reason guides the world, show a deep faith in progress, regard the pursuit of self-interest as a natural trait of mankind, perceive property rights as a benevolent instrument of social advance, and generally possess an optimistic view of a rational world. It requires a brave soul in the United States to challenge the weight of such a powerful orthodoxy. Indeed, among contemporary U.S. economists, there may not be even one today who offers a full-fledged statement of the Protestant tradition. There are, nevertheless, a number of elements of this tradition to be found among some of the strong critics of the American welfare state. For example, the winner of the 1986 Nobel prize in economics, James Buchanan, often suggests in his writings that he is a Protestant mentality seeking to break through the shell of a Roman framework imposed by American sensitivities. It is the presence of important elements of the Protestant tradition that gives Buchanan's writings a flavor so distinct from the mainstream of the American economics profession.

Buchanan's stated goal is nothing less than the nonviolent overthrow of the American welfare state. This goal will require, as he states, "constitutional revolution as the only attractive alternative to the [destructive] scenario that we seem bent to act out."[2] The American welfare state simply lacks the "moral-ethical cement" for long-run survival.[3] It is too large and diverse to sustain a sense of communal commitment. As a result, the various constituency groups and individual citizens inevitably come to see the national government as a source of coercive powers to be exploited. Having found a golden goose, the beneficiaries of the welfare state find that its survival suits their respective purposes. Thus, they look the other way when it comes to the pervasive inefficiency and irrationality that are the mark of a large maturing welfare state. This is the age-old hypocrisy of the Roman tradition, when the use of reason is perverted to become the defense of privilege.

Buchanan is searching for a "federal alternative to the enveloping Leviathan. . . . Could a threat of secession now succeed? . . . Who will join me in offering to make a small contribution to the Texas National Party? Or to the Nantucket Separatists?"[4] In such a large nation as the United States, the very existence of "such things as 'national goals,' 'national priorities,' " must be "absurd."[5] Hence, Buchanan wants to break up this cumbersome and ineffective state into smaller units where the undermining influence of selfishness would be more likely to be overcome by a genuine communal loyalty.

Buchanan sees the claim to rational behavior of the welfare state as bankrupt. If an economic priesthood is heavily responsible for the defense of its moral authority, the economists of today are no less corrupted and useless than the priesthoods of old. If Luther once denounced the medieval church, Buchanan now writes that "most modern economists have no idea of what they are doing or even of what they are ideally supposed to be doing. . . . The king really has no clothes." Not only do economists today deal only with "piddling trivialities," but the "empirical work in economics" mostly confirms the obvious and is no more profound than "proving water runs downhill." Modern macroeconomics "is really no theory at all" and has "little predictive value."[6]

Buchanan also rejects the utilitarian rationalism of contemporary economics, asserting that its "utilitarian origins . . . may have come to haunt us and to do us great harm." He states that "what I am objecting to in modern economic theory is . . . its tendency to force all analyzable behavior into the straightjacket of 'maximizing a utility or objective function under constraints.' "[7] To do so robs men of their dignity and of their sense of moral responsibility. The Roman Catholic church of Luther's day had similarly undermined individual responsibility with its doctrine of salvation by good works. In this insidious heresy, an earlier Roman priesthood had neglected the inner content of faith and taught that salvation was a matter of merely following the mechanical rules of the church. Now, the economic priesthood of the welfare state again teaches that human behavior can be reduced to a formula. Men should behave according to a scientific calculation that will yield a maximum of total utility—a prescription that once again leaves no intrinsically human element and is a matter of mere mechanical observance.

Buchanan objects, however, that "choice requires the presence of uncertainty for its very meaning." Yet, lying at the very heart of contemporary economics is instead a "rational ideal" that "eliminates choice." As a consequence, there can be no genuine "moral responsibility for action." As Buchanan says, there is a need for a "sense of 'becoming' as a central part, indeed probably the most important part of life itself." However, the rationalism of current economics, by eliminating the distinctively human traits of volition and will, effectively denies any "central difference between my dog and any one of us."[8]

Buchanan admits that he often has a pessimistic view of life, saying that he is inclined to foresee "doom and gloom." It is also true that "human behavior is erratic, non-rational, and often wholly unpredictable" and that "man may, and does, behave badly by almost any standard, on many occasions."[9] Human sinfulness coexists with the possibility of redemption, however, a process that cannot follow any strictly logical or scientifically calculated answers such as today's economic priesthood seeks to prescribe.

Yet Buchanan appears to believe in progress, does not seem to assign any significant weight to predestination, advocates the freedom to pursue self-interest, and in other respects falls within the Roman tradition. His thought is thus a blend of the Protestant and Roman traditions. Nevertheless, the inclusion of some significant elements of the Protestant tradition has been sufficiently offensive to cause Buchanan for much of his career to be relegated to the fringes of his profession. Other American economists who might have felt an inclination toward the Protestant tradition have usually been more cautious.

However difficult it may be for current sensitivities to accept this way of thinking, over the centuries the leading figures of the Protestant tradition have contributed their full share to the accumulated wisdom of the human experience. The intellectual environment of the welfare state thus might benefit—certainly it would achieve a higher level of intellectual integrity—from a blunter confrontation with the Protestant tradition. Perhaps what we need is a renewed dialogue between these two traditions that have shaped so much of the thought—and inevitably the experience as well—of the West. Indeed, a full coming to terms with the baneful events of the twentieth century, which have revealed a depth of evil previously unsuspected by most modern men, may yet depend on such a dialogue.

It was long ago in ancient Greece that Plato gave the first great statement of the Protestant tradition. Although presented within a framework of brilliantly developed reasoning, Plato's underlying message was one of reason often deceived, of alienation, and of a history of retrogression into sin and corruption.

Plato: The First Protestant

Not long ago Karl Popper delivered a celebrated attack on the veneration typically accorded Plato as a giant figure of Western thought.[10] Popper found, instead, that Plato was the advocate of a social design that "is fundamentally identical with" a system of "totalitarianism." Plato's basic vision was one in which the "Fall of Man" had resulted in "the internal disunion of human nature," manifested as "war, class war, [which] is the father and promoter of all change, and of the history of man, which is nothing but the history of the breakdown of society." Plato proposed a radical reconstruction of society to reverse the fall of man and to lead the way back to an earlier natural condition, a happier existence characterized by a state of "tribalism."[11]

Popper also found that Plato possessed a basic "hostility to reason" and that he "hated" deeply the "equalitarianism and humanitarianism" as well as the "love of freedom" that were emerging in the Athens of his time. To encourage "self-interest and especially material or economic self-interest" was to bring about "internal strife" and "class war." In order to ward off the pernicious effects of the pursuit of self-interest, Plato's solution was a "communism of the ruling class." Indeed, Marxism was merely a "theory revived" from Plato. Both involved an "utter radicalism, the demand for sweeping measures." In essence, "both Plato and Marx are dreaming of the apocalyptic revolution which will radically transfigure the whole social world."[12]

In the *Republic* the story told by Plato is the story of the Protestant tradition—men alienated from original nature by the forces of pride, ambition, and greed. Mankind must therefore seek to recover its true nature in the only way conceivable: a radical transformation of the human condition. Plato is distinguished from other leading figures in the Protestant tradition not so much by the interpretation he gives, as by the equivocation he shows with respect to the ultimate resolution. For Augustine, for Luther, and for Marx, the long-run future is predestined and contains an ironclad assurance of salvation. Whether it will be in this world or the hereafter, mankind can know with certainty that in the long run its condition of alienation will end.

Even without this element, Plato had a major impact on the history of theology. His writings anticipated and then helped shape important portions of the Christian message. In his *Confessions,* Augustine later wrote that, whereas "the writings of other philosophers . . . were full of fallacies and deceit," the books of the Platonists led "in many ways . . . to the belief in God and His word."[13] For the early Christians, these parallels that Augustine saw were so close that a myth developed to the effect that Plato must have had access to and been inspired by

parts of the Old Testament.[14] As Paul Tillich explains, Platonic elements influenced Christianity especially through "the idea of transcendence, that there is something that surpasses empirical reality." Plato
encouraged those later adherents to Christianity who believed "the
material world has no ultimate value in comparison with the essential
world," and who thus embraced an attitude of "trying to get rid of . . .
bondage to the body, and finally reaching an elevation above the
material world. . . . This element was . . . taken into the church, not
only by all Christian mystics, but also by the official church fathers to
a great extent."[15]

While Plato exhibits in his writings the powers of human reasoning
at their highest, these powers are wielded to demonstrate the illusions
and failings of Greece. When it comes to prescribing a better world,
Plato's explanations are less assuring. Tillich writes that, eventually,
"the heroic Greek attempt to build a world on the basis of philosophical reason came to a catastrophic end in skepticism." This failure of
reason yielded "an inner breakdown of all convictions" and led not to
a world of peace, prosperity, justice, and the good life, but "into the
desert with a suit and gown" where "Christian monks" sought respite
from their alienation from the bodily and material world.[16]

If the writings of Aristotle encouraged worldliness, optimism, practicality, common sense, empiricism, and a utilitarian outlook, the
writings of Plato proved more likely to lead to withdrawal, pessimism,
radicalism, revelation, and an ascetic outlook. Philosopher Martha
Nussbaum comments that, whereas Aristotle believed material well-
being to be a necessary precondition for attaining higher things in life,
for Plato the influence of "the appetites" was to create a "constant
very strong incentive to make false judgments about value and worth."
Those who aspire highest should show "disdain for appetitive activity," and instead "each of us should view ourselves as identical with
the intellectual soul alone." The Roman tradition favors the good life
for mankind and thus supports economic advance; in the Protestant
tradition the pursuit of pleasures in life is a dangerous temptation, and
economic advancement a likely corrupting influence. This tradition
tends to reject a utilitarian outlook and, as in Plato, suggests that men
should "dishonor and disregard the bodily feelings" and instead adopt
"asceticism."[17]

Plato's interpretation of history in his *Republic* inaugurates a characteristic tendency of the Protestant tradition—a view that economic
competition, the pursuit of self-interest, and other economic factors
are in large part to blame for the decline of man into degeneracy,

decay, and strife. Thus, as one twentieth-century observer notes, Plato's "entire *Republic* is founded upon an essentially economic theory of society."[18] Plato explains that, in order to "discover how justice and injustice take root in society," one must examine the desire for "luxury" and how even with their basic needs satisfied "some people, it seems, will not be satisfied to live in this basic way."[19] One thing leads to another, and before long "it is the treasure house that ruins this constitution."[20]

The pursuit of luxury not only divides the city-state into warring internal factions, but spurs war among cities. Before men were tempted by material desires, Plato explains that they were able to keep "from begetting children beyond their means." But as more and more goods and services were demanded, the city "must be swollen up with a whole multitude of callings not ministering to any bare necessity." Plato had some understanding of the workings of economic forces in society. Long before Adam Smith, he describes the benefits of the division of labor, owing partly to the "innate differences" among men, "which fit them for different occupations." As a result, "more things will be produced and the work be more easily and better done," when each person does the "one thing for which he is naturally fitted."[21]

In contrast to the outlook of the Roman tradition ranging all the way from Aristotle to current economists, Plato finds the resulting prosperity to be a menace. Because of it, an area "which was large enough to support the original inhabitants will now be too small." It will become necessary "to cut off a slice of our neighbours' territory"; but "if they too are not content with necessaries, but give themselves to getting unlimited wealth," the aggression of one will be reciprocated by the other. The eventual result is predictable enough: As Plato says, "we shall be at war."[22]

Economic forces bring about a move from the first to the second of Plato's stages of history, from a stage of timocracy (or rule by the nobles) to a stage of oligarchy (or rule by the rich). The second stage cannot last, however, because "a society cannot hold wealth in honour and at the same time establish a proper self-control in its citizens." Seeing the rich wallowing in "extravagance" and "riotous living," the "drones and the paupers" will incite a revolution, further aided by the "spendthrifts" among the youthful rich who are jealous of their more successful comrades. All this brings on the next stage in history, which is democracy and is worse yet.[23]

Democracy's disasters lead eventually to the fourth and last stage of history: dictatorship, which at least serves the necessary function of bringing order to the fallen condition of mankind. It is a story that would be repeated by Christianity often over the next 2,500 years—the fall of man from a natural and innocent state into the abysses of an earthly and, for some, eternal hell.

As portrayed in the *Republic,* Plato's hopes for escaping this fate essentially rest on a plan to minimize the role of competitive strivings and self-interest in his ideal state. Among members of the lower class— reflecting their inferior qualities and status—private property and material rewards will be permitted. But among the guardians and rulers, Plato insists that behavior must be motivated "not for some particular interest, but for the best possible conduct of the state as a whole in its internal and external relations." For Plato, it is imperative that the guardians and rulers "not rend the community asunder by each applying that word 'mine' to different things." Hence, houses, lands, wages, all property must be held "in common."[24]

In order to prevent the emergence of a destructive competition to move upward in class, a tight prohibition on movement from one class to another will be maintained. Plato is also concerned that a personal family life and sexual possessiveness would promote internal divisions, again stirring competitive feelings. He therefore proposes a still more radical measure: that wives, and children as well, live in common. In order to accomplish selective breeding, those men of the highest qualities shall be given "more liberal opportunities to sleep with a wife."[25] Children are to be removed on birth from their mothers, who must not know the identity of their child. All this is to be done for the purpose of stamping out so far as is possible all possessiveness, personal ambition, pridefulness, and other qualities of individual self-seeking from Plato's guardian and ruler classes.

There are some forms of competition, however, that Plato regards as necessary. The rulers will be selected through many "trials" and "whenever we find one who has come unscathed through childhood, youth and manhood, we shall set him as a ruler to watch over the commonwealth."[26] This testing process, which requires many years to complete, is specifically designed to weed out all those who lack the necessary self-mastery, who might not place the community above themselves, who might instead succumb to the temptations of personal wealth and power, and who thus would not be fit to rule. The discovery of the rulers is a process of finding those with inborn qualities that cannot be instilled by reason or other methods. The testing process is thus a matter, one might say, of revealing those men of God-given qualities who are predestined to rule—the "elect" of Plato's ideal state. In this respect, as in a number of others, Plato paves the way for Augustine, Luther, Calvin, and later figures of the Protestant tradition.

Plato's design for an ideal state shows remarkable similarities, in fact, to the feudalism that later enveloped Europe during the Dark Ages.[27] Where Plato had required isolated states that would hold their political and economic interactions to the barest minimum, such autarchy was at the very heart of the feudal scheme.[28] If the pursuit of wealth and prosperity had caused the fall of mankind, feudalism hardly felt such economic influences. Moreover, the feudal era faithfully followed Plato's prescription for a society divided into three classes. At the bottom, as Plato had required, were the farmers and craftsmen, now to be found as the serfs and laborers of the manor. A separate class of guardians—the knights—stood watch among the isolated enclaves of feudalism. At the top would be the rulers, those said by Plato to be possessed of the highest qualities of discipline and spirit, people able to see past the illusions of ordinary existence and to participate in the knowledge of the divine. In the feudal era such men destined to rule were the priests, monks, and other clergy of the Roman Catholic church. Not only men, but nuns and other women as well could enter the ranks of the Roman Catholic church, as Plato had prescribed that his ruling class should include women. Finally, and again closely following Plato's prescription for his rulers, property within the Roman Catholic church would be owned in common, and church work done communally and cooperatively.

If the actual world of feudalism during the Dark Ages might not have appealed to Plato himself, this is another characteristic tendency of the Protestant tradition. The actual results of twentieth-century communism probably would not have appealed all that much to Marx. Luther probably did not have in mind the division of Europe into kingdoms that were frequently at war and whose citizens would often come under the thumb of autocratic rulers, now free of restraining influences from Rome. It seems that it is one thing to protest, another thing to build a new world.

Augustine: Theologian of Alienation

Although Plato had already laid out many of the basic themes of medieval religion, and developed a political and economic design that would bear striking resemblances to medieval society, it was Augustine who would provide the decisive Christian formulation in which all this came to pass.[29] Augustine is known to history as the most important early synthesizer of Christian and Greek thought, reconciling Christian theology with Plato, much as Aquinas more than 800 years later would achieve a similarly important reconciliation with Aristotle. As one twentieth-century authority writes, the Augustinian theology became for the medieval era "the Christian form that the great Platonic tradition took in the West."[30] It has been said that Augustine—more than any other person—determined the future of Christianity and, as a result, much of Western civilization as well.

The fall of man, a descent into strife and sin, the necessity of revelation, redemption outside the material world, all these themes could already be found in Plato. They would become in Christianity, however, a world of clearer truths and starker realities. One God, omniscient and all powerful, created the earth in a single act to satisfy his own purposes. All subsequent history is the realization of the divine plan. Christ gave his life in order that mankind might know this plan and thereby obtain the possibility of salvation. A divine justice reigns over the earth, leaving some men saved but many condemned— all this predestined by an omnipotent God. For those who are of true faith, however, God has given the sure knowledge that the fall of man will one day be reversed and the true nature of man restored, leaving mankind to live thereafter in a heavenly state of peace and harmony that yields never-ending happiness, joy, and righteousness.

Yet, if all this is divinely and infallibly revealed, the God of Augustine is in many other respects inscrutable and distant, his ways far beyond human understanding.[31] God is not a friendly helper, but for Augustine the ruthless and imperious lord of the earth. His power can often be exercised in ways beyond comprehension, seemingly harsh, capricious, and cruel. If Plato provided the dominant Greek influence, Paul was the leading Christian influence in the Augustinian synthesis. Paul preached of God "how unsearchable are his judgements and how inscrutable his ways." Try as they might, men are not guided by their reason but, as Paul lamented, "I do not understand my own actions. For I do not do what I want, but I do the very thing I hate." Knowledge of God for Paul is not attained by reason, but by faith, a faith that cannot be willed but must come as a gift of God. Paul also writes of the "wretched man that I am. Who will deliver me from this body of death"—suggesting a dual element in man, a Platonic and later Manichean and Augustinian tendency to view man as possessed by a spirit seeking to do good but undermined by a corrupt body.[32] Indeed, the

Confessions of Augustine read as one long testimony to the truth of the Pauline vision.[33]

For Paul, and then for Augustine, reason is displaced as the central element in man. Since the fall from the Garden of Eden, the powers of reason have been undermined by the effects of human alienation from original true nature. In their current depraved state, men are more likely to be deceived than to be enlightened. Even when the reasoning is correct, there can be little assurance that action will follow accordingly. Augustine thus writes that, "owing to the liability of the human mind to fall into mistakes," the "very pursuit of knowledge may be a snare" to lead men astray.[34] This is very far indeed from the characteristic rationalism of the twentieth-century welfare state.

Though Aquinas would later teach that the follower down the path of reason moves closer to unity with God, Augustine much earlier said that men cannot hope to know God's ways. For Augustine, a God who can be known to mankind is diminished to this extent. Augustine accused his theological antagonists—the Pelagians—of trying to substitute man for God.[35] This is an age-old war within theology: Insofar as reason elevates mankind, divine mystery and inscrutability may be diminished. It would also be at the heart of the charges leveled by Luther against Rome: that the theology of Aquinas had adopted Aristotle and thereby in its worldliness had lost touch with God. In the twentieth century, when the welfare state again rests on a deep faith in the powers of reason, critics such as Buchanan now charge that a life reduced to a rational prescription offers mere banality.

One twentieth-century authority, Jonathan Randall, observes that "Augustinian Christianity" is for the optimistic, rationalist, egalitarian, and progressive outlook of most people today a "very terrible" thing. It is a theology from which in our time "tender minds, weak souls, shrink."[36] It was also, however, the religion of Europe for almost 1,000 years; and in our own day, sensitive men also shrink from the Holocaust and other genocide and mass violence of twentieth-century history. Indeed, for all its seeming remoteness, perhaps only an Augustinian theology can explain what rational explanation seemingly cannot—how some of these events of the twentieth century could have occurred.

For Augustine, questions of economics and politics are a tangential concern, taking a backseat to matters of faith and the fate of men in the hereafter. Augustine writes that "so far as the life of mortals is concerned, which is spent and ended in a few days, what does it matter under whose rule a man is going to die."[37] Augustine himself lived in a time when he was surrounded by social collapse, beginning his great work *The City of God* shortly after Alaric and the Goths sacked Rome in A.D. 410.

There is little sense in Augustine that the political and economic institutions of society exist for human betterment. They are, rather, largely coercive measures necessitated by human sinfulness and by the need to maintain a semblance of order. Some degree of order is all that can be expected in a world where "the evil regard the good" with a "diabolical, envious hatred" and where incessantly "the wicked war with the wicked; the good also war with the wicked."[38] As products of sin, and instruments by which some men assert dominance over others, neither the institution of government nor the institution of property has any proper place in the City of God that is the destiny of the elect. But in the "earthly city"—the ordinary existence of this world—it is necessary that emperors, kings, and other leaders have coercive instruments simply to maintain order.

The moral standing of rulers is, however, regarded by Augustine as little greater than a Mafia don would today possess—the strong man whose dominance enables him to keep control in an otherwise chaotic world. Since the fall of man, real justice has been impossible; yet, as Augustine writes, "justice being taken away, then, what are kingdoms but great robberies? For what are robberies themselves, but little kingdoms?" A government is merely an act of piracy on a grand scale. Augustine suggests that an actual pirate might properly question the head of a great state as to "what thou meanest by seizing the whole earth; but because I do it with a petty ship, I am called the robber, whilst thou who dost it with a great fleet are styled emperor."[39]

The existence of private property is viewed by Augustine in much the same light: There will not be property in the City of God, but in the earthly city it is a regrettable necessity resulting from human depravity. Augustine says that "any who wish to serve the Lord must not rejoice in the private, but in the common. . . . It is because of our private possessions that there are disagreements, enmity, dissension, wars."[40] Yet it is too much to hope that ordinary men will be able to live without the restraints that property rights serve to maintain. For the select group who are to be leaders in the church, however, it is a different matter. One student of early Christian economic teachings explains that for Augustine "the highest order of life on earth is precisely that of those who give up their wealth and choose to live in a monastic community."[41] If the context is now Christian, Augustine's views on property and an appropriate way of living follow closely those developed by Plato in the *Republic*.

The early Christians generally believed that in the original state of nature there had not been any individual ownership or private property. One early Christian, Lactantius, wrote that before the fall "the storehouses of the good literally lay open to all. Nor did avarice intercept the divine bounty, and thus cause hunger and thirst in common; but all alike had abundance, since they who had possessions gave liberally and bountifully to those who had not." After the fall, however, this was no longer possible: "Not only did the people who had a superfluity fail to bestow a share upon others, but they even seized the property of others, drawing everything to their private gain; and the things which formerly even individuals laboured to attain for the common use of all were now conveyed to the powers of a few."[42] As one twentieth-century scholar explains, early Christianity generally believed that "since the Fall [of man] the natures of men, all of them depraved, make necessary instruments of social domination. The division of property which gives some men a power over the lives of others is one such instrument."[43] Augustine thus can defend the ownership of one man by another: "The prime cause, then, of slavery is sin, which brings man under the dominion of his fellow." It is in any case not of great significance because for Augustine "beyond question it is a happier thing to be the slave of a man than of a lust."[44]

Not only property, then, but all the economic motives and interests associated with property—ambition, self-interest, the pursuit of wealth, a taste for luxury—are among the chief corrupting influences of human existence. The characteristic trait of the earthly city is "the love of self," whereas the heavenly city is marked by "the love of God."[45] For Augustine (as one authority explains),

> The present economy is marked by the anarchy of man's lower appetites and an invincible tendency to place one's selfish interests above the common good of society. It is a state of permanent revolt, which has its source in man's initial revolt against God. The prototype of this revolt is original sin, the sin committed by Adam and transmitted in a mysterious way to all his descendants. As a result, the freedom that man once enjoyed in the pursuit of the good has yielded to oppression and coercion. Coercion is apparent in the most typical institutions of civil society, such as private property, slavery, and government itself, all of which are necessitated and explained by man's present inability to live according to the dictates of reason. The very existence of these institutions is a consequence and a permanent reminder of man's fallen condition. None

was part of the original plan of creation and all of them are desirable only as a means of inhibiting man's proneness to evil. The private ownership of temporal goods both gratifies and curbs man's innate and unquenchable greed.[46]

The Roman Empire is for Augustine the great example of the corrupted condition of human existence in the earthly city.[47] Indeed, much as Plato had prophesied, it was the very military and economic success of Rome that proved to be its undoing. As Augustine concludes, "a host of disastrous evils immediately resulted from the prosperous condition of things."[48] Augustine thus is a great historic antagonist not only of the way of thinking of the Roman tradition, but of the qualities of life in ancient Rome itself. His theology vividly portrays the alienation of man from his true nature that is illustrated by the lust and debauchery of Rome. If Plato was pessimistic about the human condition, the alienation described by Augustine is even more deeply embedded, a divinely imposed condition that reduces mankind to helplessness and to pleading only for divine mercy. In strong contrast to the pervasive belief of our own time, reason alone is powerless to relieve men of their earthly misery.

The Augustinian message would be found again at the heart of the theology of Luther and Calvin and then again in the modern age in Rousseau, Marx, and other secular writers. Indeed, the deep desire found in many modern thinkers to abolish government and property follows in the tradition of Augustine. To hope that property can be abolished is to wish for a reversal of the fall of man and a recovery of man's original innocent nature. To hope that government can be abolished is the other side of the same coin. In the nineteenth century the communism of Marx would emphasize one side, the libertarianism of Herbert Spencer the other. If Marxists saw property as theft, the followers of Spencer saw government as piracy—both to be abolished in the secular visions that they now offered of a predestined future City of God on earth. Marx and Spencer were both latter-day Augustinians, fellow members of the Protestant tradition.

Martin Luther: Theological Protester against Reason

The economic and intellectual dynamism of Europe from the eleventh century to the thirteenth century came to an abrupt end in the fourteenth century. The resurgence of warfare and the spread of

disastrous plagues brought on a new "dark age" in European history.
The population of Europe is estimated to have declined by one-third
during this century. New diseases invading from the East had impacts
on Europe in some ways as devastating as the barbarian invasions that
had beset the Roman Empire 1,000 years earlier.

The powerful sense of forward movement was ended. Decline also
set in within the church, as the Roman Catholic clergy turned inward,
becoming more concerned with protecting its own prerogatives. Financial strains shifted church attention from saving souls to matters of
revenue and business. Theology fell from the heights of Aquinas to the
sterile controversies of later scholastics. By the sixteenth century, the
need for church reform had long been evident.[49] Many men, such as
the humanist Erasmus, sought reform through rational means. There
should be a more vital exercise of reason, they said, in place of the
outmoded and self-serving dogmas offered by the Catholic church of
the time.

Martin Luther, however, did not belong to this group. Luther's
diagnosis was more radical. Much as Augustine had seen the Roman
Empire as undermined internally by the very forces of its worldliness
and prosperity, Luther now saw a Europe that had suffered a similar
fate. Instead of God, the Roman Catholic church had turned to money
and the material pleasures of this world. In the Rome of 1517, the
number of prostitutes is said to have exceeded the number of married
women. Reason, and especially Aristotelian philosophy, had sought to
displace God, corrupting the valid faith of an earlier and truer Christianity.

Luther's aim, therefore, was nothing less than a blotting out of
economic and social trends that were already leading toward the
modern age. Trained in an Augustinian order, Luther sought a return
to the true church and the true faith of Paul and Augustine.[50] Theologically, Luther denounced the influence of Aquinas, who represented
the forces within the Roman Catholic church for accommodation with
modern trends. The message of Aquinas that men could know God's
ways through the exercise of their powers of reason was for Luther
anathema. Indeed, any such belief was nothing less than a proposal to
usurp the place of God. Luther suggested burning the books of Aquinas
and decreed that "only without Aristotle can we become theologians."[51]

Luther's outward protest against Rome began when he publicly
pinned his 95 theses on a church door in Wittenberg in 1517. The pope,
when first informed of the dispute, is said to have asked to hear no

more of this irritating "quarrel among monks." The immediate precipitating issue was the sale of indulgences. The purchase of an indulgence was said by the Catholic church to reduce the pains and burdens of purgatory. In the crudest cases, salesmen for the church (such as a Dominican monk named Tetzel, against whom Luther's ire was particularly directed) assured the faithful that "the moment the money tinkles in the collecting box, a soul flies out of purgatory."[52]

Few things could have been more offensive to the tradition of Augustine and Luther. If Augustine had condemned the belief that the righteous behavior of a man could assure him of his salvation, the Catholic church of Luther's time now seemingly proposed—incredibly enough—to sell God's favors, to arrange salvation in exchange for a monetary payment to the church. For Luther, the ever-present corrupting influence of the desire for money was once again demonstrated, now dragging the church itself into the web of iniquity. From a campaign against the sale of indulgences and for other reforms of church practice, Luther pressed onward with the logic of his views, eventually reaching a point where a complete break with Rome could not be avoided.

As developed by Luther, the theology of the Protestant Reformation once again offered the ancient message of humanity alienated from its true nature and from its reason. Luther wrote that each man is possessed by a "willingness and desire to do evil [that] he cannot, by his own strength, eliminate, restrain or change."[53] He preached in his theology that men should "rely on Scripture against all rational arguments."[54] One historian notes that it was an era in which men "turned from confidence in the rationality of the universe to faith."[55] A modern defender of the Catholic religion, the British writer G. K. Chesterton, directed some of his most biting polemical barbs at Luther, accusing him of having "destroyed reason." As Chesterton saw it, the Protestantism of Luther "was itself the death of theology. . . . Reason was useless. . . . Man could not trust what was in his head any more than a turnip."[56] In the words of a leading German Protestant theologian, Ernst Troeltsch, the faith of Luther was "essentially a self-abnegation and submission, a transference of all hope to the blessed world of the hereafter, and a rejoicing of martyrdom in this world."[57] History was to be seen correctly as the story of the fall of man, once again well demonstrated by events that were happening in Rome.

Although such a religion has little good to say about the design of economic and political institutions, it would nevertheless have extremely important consequences in this regard. Luther follows Augustine in seeing government and property alike as coercive measures demanded by the necessity to impose order in an immoral world. Of rulers Luther writes that "they are God's executioners and hangmen, His divine wrath uses them to punish the wicked and to maintain outward peace." God humors them by allowing them to become "rich" and to have "honor and fear," but it is merely a short-lived respite before most rulers will face a long-term resting place that will be much less pleasant.[58] Much like Plato, Luther regards democracy as an invitation to mob rule, saying that "it is better to suffer wrong from one tyrant, that is, from the ruler, than from unnumbered tyrants."[59]

Because fallen men have lost touch with their true nature, the law for Luther can offer no more than "diseased nature," which truly "amounts to mere beggary and patchwork"—although necessarily obeyed even as it is "sick law."[60] Luther warns against the temptation to expect too much from government. The powers of government are always in danger of coming into the hands of the Devil, who is continually on the lookout for opportunities to exploit the weak, to sow discord, and to oppress mankind. The Devil is often devious in this regard, sometimes presenting the most damaging schemes in alluring guises of humanitarian plans for human betterment. Indeed, the greatest threat to humanity may lie in an excess of human pride that causes men to follow their reason blindly. But reason no less than law is "diseased." Luther writes that "the Devil never stops cooking and brewing these two kingdoms into each other," causing humanity to mistake its own sin-infected thoughts and rational plans for the kingdom of God.[61]

Luther follows Plato and Augustine in seeing self-interest, private property, markets, trade—all the economic forces of society—as a pervasive and fundamental influence for sinfulness. The British economic historian R. H. Tawney observes that it was the idea that "all things have their price . . . which gave their most powerful argument to the [Protestant] reformers." Luther was the preacher of a "revolutionary conservatism," reflecting the outlook of a man who "hated the economic individualism of the age not less than its spiritual laxity." Like many before and after, the solution for Luther was a community of the elect: "The Church must cease to be an empire, and become a congregation of believers. Renouncing the prizes and [competitive] struggles which make the heart sick, society must be converted into a band of brothers."[62] In short, the proper goal is—as Troeltsch explains—"a social order which is free from competition."[63]

From the perspective of the late twentieth century, most of the immediate, if not the long-run, political and economic consequences of Luther's message must be regarded as unfortunate. In breaking free of Rome, a vacuum was left in the organization of religion. Luther encouraged the kings and princes of the new Protestant states of Europe to step in. The separation of the church from state power was lost, and the authority of the state correspondingly increased. Luther's theology further encouraged a passive acceptance of the dictates of the ruler.

Indeed, a new wave of petty tyrants emerged across Europe, waving the banner of Protestantism. Total power now resided within the Protestant states of Europe, a precursor to the totalitarianism that would run rampant in the twentieth century—and that some observers, with respect to Germany, would still attribute partly to the legacy of Luther. In Roman Catholic areas, authoritarian measures also spread, being all the more necessary to combat the grave threat now being posed by Protestantism. Instead of the worldly and paternal overseer of all Europe, the Roman Catholic church tended to become defensive; it was now merely one more zealous sect that happened to be the largest church in a Europe divided into many branches of Christendom.

With the decline of Roman authority, there no longer was any higher body to help to settle disputes among states. The normal and inevitable political quarrels and economic conflicts were now inflamed with the passions of religious contention.[64] On many basic questions the Reformation yielded not agreement but, as one twentieth-century theologian has noted, "a spectrum of theories."[65] Consistent with Christian teaching, which has no place for a lasting pluralism of truths, each new branch of Protestantism was sure that it possessed the one valid understanding of God's intent for the world.

In his theology Luther stated that "it is certain and clear enough that it is God's will that the temporal sword and law be used for the punishment of the wicked and the protection of the upright." If Jesus had once said that "blessed are the peacemakers," Luther now pointed out that elsewhere in the Bible Jesus also said that "my kingship is not of this world; if my kingship were of this world, my servants would fight." Luther thus concluded that "war was not wrong."[66] As the divisions within Europe intensified, bloodshed and violence became widespread. Eventually, as one twentieth-century observer writes, "Luther's theory of just war ended in the catastrophe of the Thirty Years' War," a long and bloody struggle between Catholicism and

Protestantism that is estimated to have yielded the death of as much as one-third of the German population.[67]

Although the beginnings of a new rapid growth in industry were evident in Germany and in other countries of Central and Southern Europe in the mid-fifteenth century, this incipient economic boom came to an end as the Protestant Reformation gathered steam. Partly, it was a matter of new competition in mining and in other economic fields from the recently discovered Americas, which tended to shift the focus of European commerce toward the Atlantic. But equally important, as the economic historian John Nef reports, "at the time of the Reformation political considerations frequently outweighed economic" in determining industrial progress, creating a climate that was "on the whole unfavorable to the growth of industrial output." Newly powerful Protestant rulers consolidated their authority by bringing private industry under tighter control. The incessant fighting "became destructive and damaging to heavy industry." Silver production in central Europe fell by two-thirds from the early 1500s to the early 1600s. During the Thirty Years' War in Germany, mining and other industrial activity faced great obstacles. The effects were such that the absolute levels of economic output throughout much of Europe were lower at the end than at the beginning of the seventeenth century. Economically, the conflicts that followed the Reformation had yielded, as Nef states, "a long period of industrial stagnation and even retrogression."[68]

The greatest beneficiaries were England and the northwest coast of Europe. Emerging victorious against the Spanish armada, England was thereafter less affected by the religious warfare enveloping central Europe. Its greater isolation may also have contributed to a greater religious tolerance—an attitude further reflected in a looser regulation of economic and political life. As Nef reports, the English turned away "from warfare and preparation for warfare to peaceful occupations." The English showed a higher regard for the "motives of private profit and of individualism," which elsewhere in Europe Lutheran theology renounced and with which in any case "despotic government was bound to interfere."[69]

Early in our own century, Max Weber published his controversial thesis that the doctrines of Protestantism were what spurred the emergence of capitalism.[70] However, it was only after the period of religious warfare eventually ended, and a new order had begun to emerge, that the way for capitalism was opened. Weber acknowledged that his evidence referred largely to economic gains achieved by capitalism in the eighteenth century and afterward. By then, Protestantism no longer meant the theology of Luther. Indeed, if a Protestant heritage eventually proved to be a strongly encouraging factor for capitalism—as may very well have been the case—this was contrary to the intent of Luther. As Troeltsch observed many years ago, any encouragement to the emergence of capitalism or other modernizing impacts of the Protestant Reformation were "indirect and unconsciously produced effects, nay, even in accidental side-influences, or again in influences produced against its will."[71]

John Calvin: The First Economic Theologian

Weber's studies of the relationship of Protestantism and capitalism were largely based on the theology not of Luther, but of John Calvin. Calvin was the second great figure of the Protestant Reformation. Although the Puritans of England would be the best-known branch of Calvinism, many other Protestant churches as well trace their theological lineage to Calvin.

Calvin's theology closely followed Luther in many respects. It is once again the story of the fall of mankind into a state of deep alienation from original nature. Owing to the pervasiveness of human depravity, there is little hope for rationality or progress in this world. As one twentieth-century authority explains, for Calvin, "the will is enslaved and at enmity with right reason; the reason aims high but is quickly diverted into futility." Given the inadequacy of reason, and viewing the corrupted condition of the existing Roman Catholic church, Calvin finds inspiration in "Scriptural doctrine and the teaching of St. Augustine."[72]

Yet, despite all the common elements with Luther, Calvin reached a surprisingly different conclusion with respect to the correct Christian life. It was a difference, moreover, that would prove to have ramifications of fundamental economic importance. As Troeltsch has written, in economic and political matters, Calvinist theology—further developed by the Puritans—had an "influence on the history of the [modern] world" that was "extraordinarily great."[73]

While Luther created the theological basis for the break from Roman authority, the importance of Calvin lay in his asserting theological grounds for an equally momentous revolution. Calvinism offered a new legitimacy to the aspirations of growing and ever more productive business and merchant groups. With the support of Calvin's doctrines, these groups not only transformed the economic world of Europe, but also pressed political demands that later opened the way for new individual freedoms and eventually for democratic government in the modern age.

Calvinism took hold in places such as Geneva, Antwerp, Amsterdam, and London—not among the poor, but among the business classes in these centers of European trade and commerce. The new Calvinists were worldly men, seen by Tawney as "the most modern and progressive" of their time.[74] For them a deep dislike of economic competition and material prosperity—such as Luther showed—could not have much appeal. Calvinism instead offered a theology that for the first time addressed the economic concerns central to their lives in a way that was direct and realistic. The Roman Catholic church, although its doctrines posed no fundamental obstacle to business, had nevertheless treated the economic side of life as tangential. Moreover, Catholicism was wedded to a scholastic language and framework that by the sixteenth century was out of touch with the world of European business. In contrast, Calvinism offered a directly relevant analysis that in fact prescribed a "society which seeks wealth with the sober gravity of men who are conscious at once of disciplining their own characters by patient labor, and of devoting themselves to a service acceptable to God."[75]

In this respect, Calvin offered a strategy that was at once old and new. Like many monks and other religious ascetics of old, Calvin found the answer to human sinfulness in greater self-mastery, discipline, control, and sacrifice. Calvin then added, however, a remarkable new element. Instead of fleeing into the desert or retreating into monasticism, as the monks of old had done, Calvin now sought to channel the necessity for a life of denial into the productive tasks of society. It was by the unswerving and complete dedication to a business or other "calling" that men could hope to tame their corrupted nature and its unruly urges.

Luther had looked mostly to the external authority of the state to control the many evils lurking within mankind. But Calvin now found this answer insufficient. In addition, he said, each individual has an obligation to achieve self-mastery. Following a tradition as old as Plato, the Roman Catholic church had regarded the great majority of men as incapable of following such a high standard. Only the limited numbers of priests and other leaders within the church were expected to live celibately and otherwise to pledge their lives to sacrifice in the service of God. For Calvin however, this class distinction and the resulting division of society into hierarchical groupings were unacceptable. The priesthood of Calvinism would not be an elect group segregated from ordinary men; the Protestant reformers were much more demanding, seeking, as it was said, "a priesthood of all believers."

All men were now to be equal in a new fundamental sense; all were to live their lives according to the strictest standards of the church. While Catholic priests had selected other priests for leadership positions, the Calvinists now elected their ministers democratically with the participation of the full congregation. Truly equal men should all have an equal opportunity to participate in the governance of the church. A critical step down the path to modern democratic government and to guarantees of the rights of the individual orginates in the Calvinist prescription that no man can be allowed to shirk his full commitment to the priestly service of God.

It was precisely because humanity was so infected with sin, and the need for control so great, that Calvin placed such an emphasis on the need for order and discipline. It was only by powerful exertion, informed by rational intelligence, that human weaknesses and frailties could be overcome and a Christian life lived—especially now that still greater temptations were being faced, owing to the economic advance of the time. Calvin thus preached a doctine of human weakness and irrationality, but the paradoxical effect was to create a social climate that brought "the whole of life and action within the sphere of an absolutely rationalised and systematic calculation." It "scorns all mere emotion and sentiment as idle and frivolous," and by its effects "work becomes rational and systematic."[76] Calvinism in this way gave a powerful if inadvertent boost to the very forces of economic progress that have been seen throughout the Protestant tradition as among the foremost corrupters of mankind. If Calvin could somehow have known this consequence, that Calvinism would in this manner help to pave the way for the modern world, in all likelihood he would have regarded it as a further confirmation of the never-ceasing influence of the Devil, in this case turning Calvin's own message against his very intent.

The new and higher Calvinist demands on each individual also included an obligation that each person must be ultimately responsible for his own answers with respect to fundamental questions of religious belief. All people were encouraged to think more broadly, to ask basic questions, to adopt a more skeptical and analytical attitude in their understanding of the world. For men who were already involved in trade, commerce, and other affairs of the world, it was logical to extend similar outlooks to these practical domains. Such factors helped to spur the rapid advance of European science that followed soon after the Protestant Reformation. The Reformation also broke the viselike grip in which Aristotelian science—which by then had degenerated into rigid dogmas and unchallengeable certainties—was still holding the thought of Europe. Indeed, the stimulus provided by Calvinism and the Reformation to science was the single most important consequence of the Reformation. This development has given the modern age a character unlike any previous era in the history of mankind.

The economic impacts of all these elements—the drive for disciplined self-mastery, the living of a rationally controlled and ascetic life, the concern for the affairs of this world—were made all the more powerful by the particular theology of salvation preached by Calvin. Calvin rejected any thought that men can actually earn their salvation by their own actions. This had been, after all, a basic cause of the Protestant revolt against Rome. Calvin nevertheless argued that successful business results and other worldly accomplishments offer a good indication of the intent of God, that the person successful in his calling is likely among those already predestined to be saved. Indeed, it may be reasonable to believe that worldly accomplishments depend on the same inner qualities of judgment, integrity, and dedication that can be expected among the elect.

Calvin thus wrote that worldly successes are "testimonies of God dwelling and ruling in us . . . fruits of the saints' regeneration . . . proofs of the indwelling of the Holy Spirit and signs of the [saints'] calling by which they realize their election." Although good works cannot bring about salvation, Calvin explained that this does not "forbid the Christian from undergirding and strengthening his faith by signs of the divine benevolence toward him."[77] Hence, as Max Weber emphasized, although economic success and other "good works" must be "useless . . . as a means of attaining salvation, . . . they are indispensable as a sign of election."[78] Even though worldly success was not technically considered a means of purchasing a place in heaven, yet the practical effect for many men was that success in a calling would come to be seen as the terms for salvation. It was, in a way, a return even at this early point in the Protestant Reformation to the Catholic tendency to find salvation in merit and through action—the very outlook that Luther had condemned.

Calvinism in this fashion introduced a whole new outlook into religion. Until then, theologians had almost always seen business, trade, commerce, and other economic activities as lower forms of existence, necessarily undertaken by inferior members of society. For fear of the corrupting influence of money, Plato's guardians, Roman Catholic priests, and other ruling groups were to be kept far removed from the temptations of the economic realm. Now, however—although Calvin still regarded wealth and prosperity as dangerous influences— Calvinism was prescribing that the attainment of wealth would serve as a sign of election and of a superior status. With this doctrine, Calvin became the first theologian to find that the path to salvation can lie along a route of economic advance. Calvin was in this sense the first economic theologian. This is another of the many respects in which Calvinism provided a crucial bridge to the modern age.

Calvinism was still far removed, however, from a utilitarian attitude toward life. The Calvinist view was that "you may labor to be rich for God, though not for the flesh and sin."[79] Hence, for the successful, there should be no special pleasure involved. In a world intended for pain and suffering, questions concerning the distribution of material goods and services are beside the point. By comparison with the Catholic emphasis on special obligations to the poor, Calvinism showed much less interest in their well-being. Indeed, to be poor is to give a strong indication of being a sinner; the poor may perhaps be suffering because of their wickedness—and if so, deservedly.

Such elements of Calvinism and later of Puritanism very likely contributed, as Weber suggested, to the eventual emergence of capitalism. However, since the initial publication of Weber's thesis more than 75 years ago, a debate has raged among scholars as to whether they were the root cause.[80] The majority of scholars seem to have concluded otherwise. Nef, for example, assigns a greater importance to Protestant innovations that pushed the ambitious and talented out of the church and into the affairs of the world, built up the resources of the state by providing major infusions of confiscated church property, and—with the end of celibacy—spurred more rapid population growth. Further counting against Weber is the fact that the industrial revolution of the twelfth and thirteenth centuries had already begun in Europe long before the Reformation. A Swedish economist, Kurt Samuelsson, delivered one of the strongest attacks, asserting that "wherever Weber saw Protestants and the Reformed church, other factors can be found that are far more obviously calculated to promote trade and industry, capital formation and economic progress."[81]

As religious warfare drew to a close in the middle of the seventeenth century, it had yielded a "moral situation [that] was disastrous" and "brought about disillusion and chaos. The form of life became extremely brutal, unrefined and uneducated."[82] As time passed, however, new possibilities appeared. In fact, because the old order had been so thoroughly demolished by the wars and other ravages of the Reformation period, there was a wide freedom to create a new order. The normal institutional constraints had broken down, opening the way for a new intellectual and social vitality and a new burst of economic growth in the modern era.

This was a scenario that would be repeated as well in the twentieth century, when 30 years of war destroyed the old order of Germany, Japan, and other nations, thereby opening the way for the creation of a new order and an economic boom. As a further striking parallel, the wars of the twentieth century were also inflamed by religious passions, if now in a secular form. Perhaps most remarkable of all, it was still the Protestant tradition—now bearing messages in the names of Marx, Spencer, Nietzsche, and other followers of Darwin—that generated the greatest instigators and inflamers of the religious conflicts of the twentieth century.

The Protestant theology of Luther and Calvin offered little in the way of guidance in building the modern world. Fundamentally a protest against looming modern influences, the theology of the Protestant Reformation could hardly serve as a guide for the new order. It was necessary to discover new ways of thinking to guide the advance of science and industry. Indeed, in the late seventeenth and eighteenth centuries this redirection took form in the Enlightenment. Carl Becker has written that the Enlightenment saw itself as having at last swept away "the Christian doctrine of total depravity, a black, spreading cloud which for centuries had depressed the human spirit."[83] Instead of the Protestant pessimism and harshness, the Enlightenment would once again exalt human reason and the power of man to find the path of human progress on this earth.

The Enlightenment was less novel, however, than was supposed at the time and has often been believed since. At heart, the Enlightenment may be seen as a revival of the Roman tradition in Western thought, now newly developed in a secular form. Ironically, if understandably, the Enlightenment was often opposed most strenuously by the institution whose place it most threatened in the Roman tradition itself: the Roman Catholic church. Since the Enlightenment often exhibited a hostility toward traditional Christian beliefs, only much later did the realization set in that the Enlightenment messages had in large part appropriated earlier Christian themes. Moreover, the Enlightenment would not be the only occasion in the modern age when age-old themes of religion were newly stated in a secular form. In many cases it was in one or another of the branches of modern economic theology that the new secular faiths could be found.

Part II

Secularization and the Rise of Modern Economic Theology

Chapter 3

The Roman Church of Newton

In the thirteenth century Thomas Aquinas had argued that men should carry their reason as far as it will go. It is man's duty to inquire into the laws of nature, to discover those underlying principles that cause the universe to be as it is. God created a rational world. Indeed, God created men in his likeness not in the literal sense of outward physical appearance, but in the sense that the rational faculty within man matches the rational order governing the universe. Since this rational order in its perfection corresponds to the reason of God, to reach for the heights of reason is to come closer to knowing God.

The development of modern science did not in any basic way violate these theological precepts. To the contrary, the scientific method offered a new and far more powerful means of employing the powers of reason. Science became in a sense the most powerful theological instrument ever available to mankind, allowing men to approach the divine ground perhaps more closely than Aquinas ever imagined would be possible.[1] It proved also to have consequences probably more momentous than Aquinas could have conceived—and for his medieval Catholic faith, sometimes profoundly disturbing.

Isaac Newton: Messiah for the Modern Age

The decisive figure in the spread of faith in science was Isaac Newton. The key to the power of the scientific method lay in the use of mathematics. Science contended, and then Newton offered extremely convincing evidence, that the laws of nature are mathematical.

The rules of mathematical reasoning could be defined with much greater precision, and the subsequent logical development was exposed to far less chance of error, than for any previous method of reasoning. The use of mathematics also enforced a quantitative and much more rigorous standard in defining the objects of reasoning. Science advanced through an interaction of empirical observation and the exercise of mathematical logic. Observation of the world suggested possible mathematical laws of nature, which were then empirically tested for validation; in successful cases, the laws could be confirmed.

Once the validity of a mathematical law of nature was established, it would hold at all places and at all times. Starting from these validated laws, a development and elaboration of mathematical reasoning could deduce further laws of nature. Assuming the correctness of the original laws and of the mathematical reasoning, the validity of new mathematically derived laws could be known with certainty, even though they might have yet to be confirmed empirically. All this must be true because right reason and the laws of nature are the same—a truth that Aristotle and Aquinas had asserted long before Newton and the practitioners of modern science invested it with a new and much more powerful meaning.

The development of the scientific method thus gave the characteristic tendencies of the Roman tradition a new impetus. The Protestant Reformation had made important contributions to the development of modern science, especially by clearing away Aristotelian and other inhibiting excess baggage of a medieval rationalism that, while once a vital force for scientific progress, had grown inward and defensive. Yet, theologically, modern science is a logical continuation of aspirations that Luther had gone out of his way to condemn. If the Protestant tradition can contribute importantly to science by encouraging rebelliousness and destroying outmoded orthodoxies, it is the Roman tradition that values the scientific endeavor most highly and helps to sustain the institutional environment in which science flourishes best. A leading twentieth-century historian of religion, Christopher Dawson, observes that science falls within "the Catholic tradition, for to the Catholic philosopher no less than to the scientist the progressive *rationalization* of matter by the work of scientific intelligence is the natural vocation of the human mind."[2]

As the Roman tradition regathered its energies, a period of rapid scientific advance occurred in the seventeenth century—indeed a huge and unprecedented leap. If right reason now assumed the form of scientific and mathematical reasoning, the vastly enhanced powers of science opened a new vista in human affairs. The pace of progress could be expected to accelerate sharply. What seemed no more than a wild hope a few centuries before was now suddenly imaginable. Men might truly succeed in gaining a full knowledge of the laws of nature, perhaps even—with good fortune—all within the space of the next few generations.

The future of mankind was no longer limited to slow advance along a road of difficult progress. If the fulfillment of human destiny was the attainment of a true state of nature, and the laws of nature were soon to be revealed by the powers of the scientific method, men might shortly reach the culmination of their fondest hopes. As the contemporary philosopher Isaiah Berlin explains, the thought of the Enlightenment reflected such common elements of faith:

> What science had achieved in the sphere of the material world, it could surely achieve also in the sphere of the mind; and further, in the realm of social and political relations. The rational scheme on which Newton had so conclusively demonstrated the physical world to be constructed . . . could be applied to the social sphere as well. Men were objects in nature no less than trees and stones; their interaction could be studied as that of atoms or plants. Once the laws governing human behavior were discovered and incorporated in a science of rational sociology, analogous to physics or zoology, men's real wishes could be investigated and brought to light, and satisfied by the most efficient means compatible with the nature of the physical and mental facts. Nature was a cosmos: in it there could be no disharmonies; and since such questions as what to do, how to live, what would make men just or rational or happy, were all factual questions, the true answers to any one of them could not be incompatible with true answers to any of the others. The ideal of creating a wholly just, wholly virtuous, wholly satisfied society, was therefore no longer utopian.[3]

Indeed, if the Christian heaven consists of an existence in a true natural state—the natural harmony of the Garden of Eden restored—then the arrival of heaven on earth was regarded as no more distant than the completion of the scientific task already well under way. By discovering the laws of nature and thereby uncovering the rational structure of the universe, men in their new heaven on earth would at last come to commune directly with God. Such beliefs were, as the American historian Carl Becker has written, part of the "religion of the Enlightenment." The new messiah was Newton, the man who had both perfected the mathematical method and shown conclusively how supremely powerful the use of scientific reasoning could be. By his efforts, Newton "ravished the 18th century into admiration." He had "banished mystery from the world by discovering a 'universal law of nature,' thus demonstrating, what others had only asserted, that the universe was rational and intelligible through and through."[4] For many men of the Enlightenment, it was Newton who was now finally showing the true path to heaven and to a final unification of man with God.

As the Christian world believed that history had two categories— before Christ and after Christ—the eighteenth century believed that the Enlightenment would prove to be the new decisive demarcation point for history. Although the Greeks and Romans were admirable in many respects, the remainder of history was largely a depressing tale of myth, ignorance, and superstition. Christianity, at least as practiced over the centuries by most organized churches and especially by the Roman Catholic church, had contributed its full share to human depravity. But Newton had now come to rescue mankind, showing the valid path of escape from wars, misery, oppression, persecution, poverty, and other banes of human existence.

To be sure, there still remained a great deal of work to be done. The message of scientific enlightenment would have to be spread all over the world to all mankind, allowing distant peoples as well to escape from sin and oppression. A massive educational campaign would have to be undertaken, reaching out especially to the poor, the illiterate, and the downtrodden. New missionaries would be sent forth, a new priesthood bearing the messages of science assembled, and all manner of institutional and organizational details accomplished—all for the purpose of spreading the new message of the scientific enlightenment of humanity.

All these momentous consequences followed from the characteristic outlook of the Roman tradition, assuming that the powers of scientific reasoning were as great as the men of the late seventeenth century and then the eighteenth century came to believe. In the twentieth century, it is widely thought that the most important consequence of science has been the vastly enhanced power to control and manipulate nature for human purposes. However, technological applications did not become a decisive feature of science until the second half of the nineteenth century. In the eighteenth century, the effects of science on philosophy and theology were its most important consequences. By changing the way men thought about the world, science instigated political revolutions, remolded economic institutions, and altered the self-concept of the individual and his proper place in history.

To be sure, all this vast change occurred on the scantiest of actual evidence. While scientific reasoning had made great strides in the study of the laws of physical nature, its results in the realms of individual and social behavior, the workings of the mind, and other human fields were very modest. Mathematics proved much more difficult to apply in these areas than had been expected. There were in fact no mathematical laws of society that even remotely approximated the power of Newton's discoveries in physics. The general applicability of scientific reasoning in these other fields and the widespread expectation of successes equal to the physical sciences were not themselves scientific conclusions. They were in fact articles of deeply held faith.

It was, moreover, a faith less novel than the Enlightenment supposed. It was the faith of the Roman tradition, now finding in science a conclusive confirmation of the rational qualities of the world. Although the form would often be secular and in this respect new, the core assumptions of the Enlightenment were old. As a leading twentieth-century authority, Ernst Cassirer, has said, "far more than the men of the epoch were aware, their teachings were dependent on the preceding centuries."[5] The Enlightenment—another twentieth-century observer writes—"transferred to the world the infinite attributes of God and permitted transferring to man God's moral attributes."[6] Still another authority concludes that "the ideals of the Enlightenment were secularized . . . Christian ideals through and through." Christian beliefs were "matched by the new belief that there is no salvation except through the use of reason. Superstition and ignorance became the original sin of mankind."[7]

Indeed, the new scientific faith swept across eighteenth-century Europe and captured its leading minds with all the characteristic fervor and bearing all the marks of the great religious upheavals of old. It was perhaps the most profound challenge to institutional Christianity since Islam had swept across the Mediterranean world 1,000 years before. It was also as a religious revolution that scientific enlightenment would be spread around the world—like many previous religions also imposed, where necessary, by force of European military might. It would be the first religious revolution of history to encompass the globe.

The events surrounding the spread of the religion of scientific enlightenment have shaped the character of the modern age. To study the modern age is not only to study scientific reason at work, but also to study theology. In shaping social institutions and the beliefs of ordinary people, the most important new theologies would be forms of modern economic theology. The most influential theologians would be

Adam Smith, Karl Marx, John Maynard Keynes, and other leading
economic thinkers of the modern age.

John Locke: Theological Bridge to the Modern World

Although Newton wrote a great deal about theology, he had little to
say about politics and economics. These matters were necessarily left
to his disciples. Among them, the eighteenth century recognized John
Locke as the greatest. Voltaire rated Locke more highly than Plato,
while the French Encyclopedia portrayed him as having done for the
"science" of philosophy what Newton had done for the science of
physics. Cassirer writes that Locke's authority on a number of central
subjects "remained practically unchallenged throughout the first half
of the eighteenth century."[8]

Although the early eighteenth century regarded the social philosophy of Locke as a bold new step forward in human understanding, it
would later become apparent that (as the historian R. R. Palmer writes)
the core of Locke's thought was "carried over" from the Middle Ages,
where it had already been "formulated in the 13th century by St.
Thomas Aquinas."[9] John Courtney Murray explains that Locke rede-
veloped "the great political truths that were the medieval heritage"
and reflected "the fundamental positions of the natural-law philosophy
of the state."[10] In the roster of the central figures of the Roman
tradition, Locke follows Aquinas. With Locke, the central themes of
this tradition are formulated for the first time in a modern dress,
suitable for an age in which the scientific method was now seen as
having perfected the powers of human reason.

Locke believes that scientific reasoning can be applied successfully
to virtually every concern of man. He shares with Aquinas the belief
that even the existence of God can be rationally proved. In adapting
this conclusion to a new era, however, Locke now goes further to
declare that the rational proof of God possesses "equal to mathematical certainty."[11] Locke is also a great advocate, like Aquinas, of the
principles of nature law, explaining that "the state of nature has a law
of nature to govern it, . . . and reason . . . is that law." God has created
and put man in the world with "reason to make use of it to the best
advantage of life, and convenience."[12] Locke has no use for the
Lutheran and Calvinist view of reason corrupted and undermined by
the sinful state of mankind. Instead, reason is for Locke the proper
guide to human conduct, the shaper of social institutions, and the

central force for progress. What is just and virtuous for Locke is what is rational. Again adapting an old message to the age of Newton, Locke argues that morality falls "amongst the sciences capable of demonstration . . . from self-evident principles." A science of ethics can even yield results that, like the existence of God, are "as incontestable as those in mathematics."[13] Locke is also a great advocate of human equality, "there being nothing more evident, than that creatures . . . born to all the same advantages of nature . . . should also be equal one amongst another without subordination or subjection."[14]

Locke follows Aristotle and Aquinas in rejecting the independent existence of universal ideas outside the mind. Because at birth the mind is unformed, Locke considers that the development of the mind proceeds entirely "from experience. In that all our knowledge is founded."[15] Locke's psychology of mental development would have a major impact on the political and economic thought of the eighteenth century. If men are largely shaped by their environment, then the many who still had evil thoughts and behaved destructively were not themselves to blame. Contrary to the teachings of Calvin and before him Augustine, the failings of particular men were not considered to be due to some inherent and irremediable deficiency—an original sin predestined for many since the fall—but could be resolved by education and a better life. The achievement of lasting human progress everywhere on earth depended only on the efforts of men to spread the message of scientific enlightenment.

Locke also follows Aquinas—and before him Aristotle—in finding that "nature . . . has put into man a desire of happiness and an aversion to misery; these indeed are innate practical principles which . . . do continue constantly to operate and influence all our actions without ceasing."[16] Ethics are defined for Locke by a utilitarian standard. About 100 years before Jeremy Bentham would develop a comprehensive philosophy based on this principle, Locke argues that an action is good if it increases personal pleasure, while evil conversely diminishes pleasure or causes pain. Locke's approval extends to the pursuit of self-interest. It is too much to expect most men to act against their own interest. Fortunately, owing to the harmonious workings that are inherent to the laws of nature, what is natural and rational to the individual—including the pursuit of self-interest—will also yield the best overall result for society.

Compared with his predecessors in the Roman tradition, Locke gives more emphasis to the role of private property. It is consistent with nature that the products of a person's labor should belong to him or her. If a man takes the trouble to harvest the trees of the forest, it is for Locke natural and right that he should then possess the wood as well. The defense of property rights is also beneficial, as Aristotle and Aquinas had said much earlier, because it spurs productive efforts that lead to increases of output. Locke explains that when property comes into a person's possession the result is "ten times more than . . . yielded by an acre of land of an equal richness lying waste in common." The existence of property rights therefore "does not lessen but increase[s] the common stock of mankind."[17] However, the right of property is not absolute, but constrained by a higher utilitarian standard. A person should have only so much property as he can use and enjoy—or as Locke states, "as much land as a man tills, plants, improves, cultivates and can use the product of, so much is his property."[18]

Berlin writes that Locke "may almost be said to have invented the notion of common sense."[19] Locke also possessed worldiness, empiricism, practicality, and pragmatism—other characteristic qualities of the central figures of the Roman tradition. He was trained in medicine; was an active participant in English politics (forced to flee to Holland for several years in the 1680s); and systematically investigated a wide range of subjects, allowing him to make influential contributions to the history of thought in philosophy, economics, politics, and psychology.

Yet, despite all the debts to Aquinas and the Roman tradition, there is another important side to Locke. He was brought up in a strict Puritan family, at a young age entertaining the possibility of entering the ministry. Locke's thought is characterized by a deep respect for the rights of the individual. This element, while not new to the Roman tradition, was reinforced and altered by the heritage of Protestantism and its characteristic "insistence of the individual that his conscience must not be surrendered to the authority of state or Church."[20]

Protestant individualism was exhibited among the Puritans through an emphasis placed on the "covenant." The Puritans felt a special affinity for the Old Testament, where the Jews had also entered into a covenant with God. Relationships within the church, between husband and wife, between God and man, among businessmen, and in all walks of life were seen by the Puritans as contractual arrangement among freely acting individuals. A contract was, as Michael Walzer comments, "the highest human bond." Contracts must be, one Puritan minister wrote, "a voluntary obligation between persons about things wherein they enjoy a freedom of will and have a power to choose or refuse."[21]

The Puritan theology of a life lived as the fulfillment of a series of contracts would take a secular form in the political and economic theories of Locke. Long ago—Locke argues—men lived without government. Rights to property and other rationally grounded elements of natural law were enforceable by individuals acting alone against one another. This proving a very cumbersome arrangement, men joined together in a social contract to create government for the express purpose of protecting property. Men thus "willingly" gave up their independence in order "to unite for the mutual preservation of their lives, liberties and estates."[22] As the members of a Puritan parish are joined by a voluntary covenant, Locke concludes that government exists at the direction of the citizenry, to serve the needs of the citizenry, and subject to the continuing approval of the citizenry—themes that would have worldwide impact, including a major influence in the founding of the United States and the writing of the its Constitution.

Locke's extremely influential theory of the state as a social contract is, in essence, the Puritan society of covenants in a secular dress. As one twentieth-century commentator explains, the modern theory of democratic government represents a development and enlargement of "the political principles of popular sovereignty which had arisen largely through the Puritans."[23]

The Puritan tendency to see all of life as a contracting relationship extended even to the workings of the mind. Men were beset by urges of all sorts; they must seek to govern their unruly impulses, a process that resembles a series of covenants formed by the competing parts of the mind. The Puritan search for self-mastery is then secularized by Locke to become his famous psychology. Mental processes consist of mechanical interactions within the mind, existing ideas combining and recombining, all the while following laws of mental development that are said by Locke to be as scientific as the physical laws governing interactions among the elements of the solar system.

The Puritans also taught, as Walzer writes, that labor is a highly desirable activity in itself; hard work develops "social discipline and self-affirmation," which in turn yield "an effective guarantee of social order."[24] The high Puritan regard for labor in the pursuit of a calling is secularized by Locke to become the argument that labor is the true source of productive value in society. Locke contends that "of the products of the earth useful to the life of man, nine-tenths are the effects of labor."[25] His theory of property assigns the right to the man who mixes his labor with an object of nature. For Locke ownership of property is not to be distributed equally among men or according to personal need. The distribution should be, rather, on the basis of a higher ethical standard, one that Locke first learned in his Puritan upbringing: the amount of labor expended.

A labor theory of value would be carried forward from Locke to Adam Smith and then to Karl Marx. This theory does not originate, as is sometimes suggested, in the medieval world's idea of the just wage or price. The more worldly scholastics of Aquinas's time considered that the value of a good was to be found in the pleasure and in the utility to be gained from it. The labor theory is, instead, a derivative of the Protestant view that labor in the service of a calling is the highest purpose of earthly existence. The pleasures and enjoyments of this world are to be spurned, according to the ascetic and self-denying mentality of Calvin and his Puritan followers. For them, as would be the case as well for Locke, Adam Smith, and Marx, value must be in proportion to the amount of labor supplied.

The thinking of Locke thus offers a blend of both Aquinas and Calvin. If Augustine brought Plato into Christianity, and Aquinas then merged Aristotle with Augustine, it would fall to Locke to synthesize Aquinas and Calvin. The impact of this grand synthesis would be heightened all the more by one further element. The Puritan view of society as a set of individuals bound by covenant (or contract) bore a distinct similarity to the Newtonian universe in which there were forces of nature governing the interactions of material objects. Newton had discovered a solar system of individual planets, moons, and a sun, all linked together in a mechanical system bound and driven by the force of gravity. Locke portrayed a political and economic world that consisted of independent individuals (once having existed in nature as separate entities) who were now drawn together and linked to one another by the force of self-interest. The Lockian vision of a mechanically ordered society—drawn from a long-standing Puritan heritage—corresponded with remarkable fidelity to the natural world of Newton's great discoveries in physics. Due partly to this fortuitous coincidence, the immense scientific prestige of Newton would be bestowed on Locke's new secularization of the Puritan society of covenants.

Locke had also softened greatly the harshest and most pessimistic elements in Calvin. Instead, Locke set the world of Puritan contracts within the basic framework of the Roman tradition of Western thought. After a century and a half of religious war and destructive passions, the late seventeenth century and then the eighteenth century were ready for a return to the reason, order, stability, moderation, egalitarianism, and faith in rational progress of the Roman tradition.

This era thus embraced Locke with an enthusiasm that would cause later observers to marvel. Indeed, judged strictly as a philosopher, Locke would later be much criticized for omissions, confusions, misunderstandings, and weak reasoning. His brilliance was instead as a prophet, the offerer of a new secular message of salvation. Locke was the first of the great modern secularizers of the Judeo-Christian heritage—itself heavily derived from ancient Greece and Rome. Blending Puritan theology into a framework of Aquinas, Locke provides the decisive bridge into the modern world.[26] As Ernst Troeltsch has said,

> The great ideas of the separation of Church and State, toleration of different Church societies alongside of one another, the principle of Voluntaryism in the formation of these Church-bodies, the (at first, no doubt, only relative) liberty of conviction and opinion in all matters of world-view and religion. Here are the roots of the old liberal theory of the inviolability of the inner personal life by the State, which was subsequently extended to more outward things; here is brought about the end of the medieval idea of civilisation, and coercive Church-and-State civilisation gives place to individual civilisation free from Church direction. The idea is at first religious. Later, it becomes secularised. . . . But its real foundations are laid in the English Puritan Revolution. The momentum of its religious impulse opened the way for modern freedom.[27]

Adam Smith: Founder of Modern Economic Theology

Self-interest as natural and rational, the individual pursuit of happiness, the advantages of property rights, all these and other elements found in twentieth-century economics were already present in Locke. Yet, they still retained a distant quality. The world of Locke is the rural environment of England in the late seventeenth century. The state of nature that figures so prominently in Locke's theorizing is a self-contained community, small enough that contracts can be negotiated among all members by voluntary consent—a world where production is no more complicated than the application of individual labor to land and other natural resources.

By the middle of the eighteenth century, a whole new world was emerging. Population growth would soon explode, as the combined population of England and Ireland grew from about 10 million in 1750 to about 30 million in 1850. The fly shuttle had been invented in 1733, and in the 1760s the spinning jenny was developed. James Watt in 1763 began his work to improve the steam engine, which had been pioneered by Thomas Newcomen in 1703. Watt's engine would soon be applied in factories where textile production could then be mechanized. By 1820, cotton represented 50 percent of all British exports. For this new era, Locke's pastoral society must have seemed increasingly remote.

Significant weaknesses in his logic had also become apparent. Bishop George Berkeley and then David Hume criticized major deficiencies in Locke's epistemology. Despite the parallels that Locke and others of his time were fond of drawing, closer inspection revealed little that was Newtonian about the Lockian system. The scientific method demanded empirical observation, generalization from observation, and then empirical confirmation of mathematical laws. By these rigorous standards, Locke represented no real advance over the reasoning of Aristotle and Aquinas.

The effort to remedy these deficiencies would culminate in Adam Smith. Indeed, Smith would eclipse Locke in influence on the modern age. Edmund Burke commented on *The Wealth of Nations* that, "in its ultimate result, this was probably the most important book that had ever been written."[28] A current observer finds that only Marx's *Capital* has had a "comparable effect" on the modern age.[29] Adam Smith is today often given as a source of authority, approached by many as a figure commanding reverence and awe. If the modern age can be said to have had saints, Saint Adam Smith follows Saint Thomas Aquinas among the anointed of the Roman tradition.

Milton Myers in his valuable study of the development of economic thought leading up to Smith explains that, well before Locke, self-interest had been identified in the seventeenth century by Thomas Hobbes as the basic motive in human existence.[30] However, still very much in the sway of the Protestant tradition, Hobbes saw self-interest as setting loose dangerous forces in society. As Luther and before him Augustine had concluded, Hobbes could see no alternative to the coercive authority of a dictator. The next century, however, would seek to rebut the pessimism of the Protestant outlook and its secular Hobbesian vision.[31]

Early in the eighteenth century, the writings of the third Earl of Shaftesbury provided an influential and newly explicit formulation of the problem of self-interest. Shaftesbury asked directly: Is the pursuit of self-interest compatible with the greater good of society? He states that "every creature has a private good and interest of his own, which nature has impelled him to seek." However, men also have another deeply embedded desire, which is to pursue the "universal good, or the interest of the world in general." The various human drives are seen as interacting within each person as in a grand Newtonian constellation of forces—an "economy of the passions." Reflecting the pervasive Enlightenment view that the operation of natural laws must tend toward harmony, Shaftesbury therefore concludes that "to be well affected towards the public interest and one's own is not only consistent but inseparable."[32]

Another major contributor to this evolving discussion was the theologian Joseph Butler. In *Sermons*, Butler advanced the view that the universe in all its aspects exhibits a well-developed plan. As this plan has been designed, "public and private good" are not only compatible but "mutually promote each other." Indeed, they "perfectly coincide."[33] The poet Alexander Pope would spread a similar message far and wide—that "self-love, the spring of motion, acts the soul; Reason's comparing balance rules the whole."[34]

For the eighteenth century, the solar system became the prevailing model of nature. Many leading thinkers came to believe that in the workings of self-interest they had found the social equivalent of a Newtonian physics. The individual was the fundamental unit of social analysis, corresponding to the planets and moons. The source of energy, corresponding to the force of gravity, was self-interest. As a twentieth-century authority, J. L. Talmon comments, throughout the eighteenth century self-interest was regarded as "the most real and most vital element in man and human relations."[35] To explore the workings of the individual pursuit of self-interest, therefore, was to develop a true physics of society. Self-interest would become, as another student of the Enlightenment writes, the "moral law of gravitation."[36]

Adam Smith's teacher and mentor, Francis Hutcheson, was one of the many who portrayed society in such Newtonian terms. There were two social forces that for Hutcheson were comparable to gravity: (1) the force of benevolence; and (2) the force of "self-love," which "is as necessary to the regular State of the Whole as Gravitation."[37] In society it is as futile to deny the force of self-interest as in nature it would be foolish to deny the force of gravity. If a man should jump off a cliff, he must not hope to find the law of gravity suspended. Those who would propose to suspend the fundamental law of self-interest show no greater common sense with respect to matters of political and economic governance, said Hutcheson and many others in the eigh-

teenth century. It is a view still often echoed in the late twentieth
century.

Smith was also influenced by the physiocrats whom he met in the
several years he spent in France in the 1760s. As the label suggests,
they believed themselves to be the developers of a valid "physics" of
society. It was thus asserted that "all social facts are linked together
in the bonds of eternal, immutable, ineluctable and inevitable laws."[38]
These laws must conform "to the supreme reason which governs the
universe." Government can do nothing beneficial other than to enact
measures that are "declaratory of these essential laws of the social
order." If a government were to do otherwise, it would be as though
the government were commanding a violation of physics—by the
reckoning of the physiocrats, necessarily constituting "insane acts
obligatory upon no one."[39]

Thus, for Claude Helvétius, poorly conceived laws that seek to
override self-interest or other laws of nature are in society the "roots
of its vices." The knowledgeable statesman can, however, "make
virtuous men" by conforming to the laws of nature.[40] Indeed, government can even turn self-interest to public purposes by creating a
system of incentives, involving "proper rewards and punishments by
law"; and thereby a governor can "get men to do anything he deems
good."[41] This concept that self-interest can be manipulated for social
purposes would later assume even greater importance when the
planned use of the "market mechanism" became a central tenet of the
welfare state of the twentieth century.

Despite the frequency with which appeals to the authority of Newton
were made in the eighteenth century, these appeals still had more of a
metaphorical than a genuine scientific quality. They lacked, for example, any real explanation of the physical mechanism by which self-
interest would be transformed into social betterment. The alignment of
social and individual interest must be true almost by definition—a
matter of faith more than any empirical demonstration. To resolve this
problem, a critical step in the development of the physics of society
was taken by focusing on the concept of the division of labor. Self-
interest could now be seen as leading—through the workings of the
marketplace—to a growing specialization of tasks, which in turn would
yield a steadily increasing output of society. There was, moreover,
much empirical confirmation for this hypothesis. The second half of
the eighteenth century was already beginning to exhibit the rapid
economic growth predicted.

The development of this newly powerful theory of the division of labor through the mechanism of self-interest in the market was much more than a matter of mere technical analysis. If this theory could now illuminate the true Newtonian mechanics of society, men would have finally in their possession a proper understanding of the real workings of nature. With a correct knowledge of the actual laws of nature, the valid route to human happiness, the elimination of strife and discord, the path to future social progress—indeed, the very means of achievement of heaven on earth—would be revealed. All these conclusions followed directly from the central faith of the Enlightenment; that to behave in accordance with the laws of nature is to achieve a harmony with the underlying rational structure of the universe. It would be to achieve a unification with what in the earlier Roman tradition had been the rational order intrinsic to God's design for the world. Hence, those men who formulated the principle of the division of labor had good reason to believe, as Myers comments, that they were in fact "Promethius bringing the gift of fire down from the gods to serve the needs of man." Indeed, if mankind acted to bring its actual governing laws and its behavior into conformance with this new scientific discovery of the workings of the market, the result would be nothing less than the "secular salvation of man and society."[42]

With the theory of the division of labor, salvation came for the first time to be associated clearly with the economic progress of society. To reach heaven on earth is to conform as a society to the laws of nature; and now, according to the theory of the division of labor, these laws must have an economic character. For those who subscribed to this new belief, the religion of the Enlightenment became an economic faith. Economics was no longer a lesser branch of theology. Instead, theology at this point assumed an economic content. This was the beginning of modern economic theology.

To be sure, salvation had already been associated with economic success in the theology of Calvin. But for Calvin it was not the success of society but the success of the individual that counted. Moreover, Calvin saw economic success as a likely sign of divine intervention outside any worldly processes of nature—an exercise of God's powers on behalf of those elect who were already predestined. There is an important similarity, nevertheless, between Calvin and the new economic theology of the eighteenth century. In each case, the importance of economic success does not lie in the direct consumption of the goods and services produced. Following the theory of the division of labor, men are not to be saved by the joys and pleasures attending to any outpouring of goods and services. Rather, economic growth is

more in the character of a by-product; it is a demonstration that men
are truly behaving in accord with the laws of nature. To behave in
accord with such laws is for the eighteenth century the true path to the
redemption of mankind. Hence, economic progress is merely a favorable sign, as it were, that men are truly attaining to the heavenly state
of harmony with nature in which the Enlightenment saw salvation.

If economic success was for Calvin a sign of individual election, it
thus becomes for the Enlightenment a sign of a whole society living in
accord with the divine intent. As Paul Tillich has explained, in the
eighteenth century the "principle of a presupposed harmony . . .
produces indirectly what [in an earlier era] was supposed to be produced directly by a divine interference." For the men of the Enlightenment, "supernatural authority was now replaced by the principle of
[the] harmony" of nature. In this way "the idea of providence is
secularized in the Enlightenment." Indeed, "the first clear expression
. . . can be seen in the area of economics. It was expressed by Adam
Smith . . . in his idea of harmony" as found in the hidden hand of the
market, which yields a division of labor without any conscious intent
or plan.[43]

The very first sentence of *The Wealth of Nations*, published in 1776,
reads: "The greatest improvement in the productive powers of labor,
the greater part of the skill, dexterity and judgment with which it is
anywhere directed, or applied, seem to have been the effects of the
division of labor."[44] If Smith did not originate this idea, he put it
together with other main themes of the eighteenth century in a grand
synthesis of unsurpassed influence.[45] Smith's message is still being
heard all over the world, where today it is finding many new converts
to the use of markets and the freeing of private enterprise and initiative.
Smith's grand synthesis would provide the moral authority to sustain
an economic revolution that over the next two centuries—in combination with the technological developments made possible by modern
science—transformed human existence.

In the nineteenth century, as Karl Polanyi has said, the Industrial
Revolution would be guided and sustained by an "economic liberalism" that "turned into a secular religion." Its followers looked to
Adam Smith as the founder, while Malthus, Ricardo, and other disciples provided further elaboration. The new religion "evolved into a
veritable faith in man's secular salvation through a self-regulating
market."[46] If the poor and others were called on to make sacrifices,
these sacrifices were regarded as being in the service of a greater
cause. To behave according to the economic laws of society was not

only to make economic progress, but to come closer to the achievement of heaven on earth. To discover the laws of the market was to learn the divine intent for the world; to obey the laws of the market was to conform to the divine will, to move closer to unification with God. This is the case because, as a contemporary economist writes, "Smith sees the world as the Design of the Deity, a perfectly harmonious system reflecting the perfection of its designer"—a system in which men are commanded to act in accordance with the laws of nature, the most important of them being the law of self-interest.[47]

To be sure, *The Wealth of Nations* exhibited urbanity, worldliness, practicality, and common sense. These qualities had wide appeal in the Enlightenment and helped to bring about the enthusiastic reception the book received almost immediately. Yet *The Wealth of Nations* could not have become a bible of the modern age through these elements alone. The prophetic impact of the book lay in capturing so well the age-old themes of the Roman tradition, now moving past Locke to put them in a language and context still more suited for modern circumstances. It was a message newly appropriate to a period that was seeing significant new mechanical inventions emerging; that was gaining its first glimpses of the powers of mass production; that was beginning to extend a system of trade and commerce to the far reaches of the earth; that was witnessing an increase in the importance of manufacturing and a decline in the role of agriculture; and that was coming to sense that economic change perhaps might soon alter fundamentally the human condition. To all these developments, Adam Smith responded more persuasively and graphically than anyone ever had before.

Many followers would later find in Smith a Newton of economics. Even today economists sometimes exhibit an attitude that, as the founder of modern economics, Adam Smith must be the first to have had the insight that self-interest is the fundamental force in society—just as Newton first grasped the concept of gravity. Smith must have been the first to understand the social mechanics of the workings of self-interest. He is widely seen as responsible for a quantum leap forward in economics, leaving previous economic knowledge behind in the darkness by comparison—as Newton did in physics. The historic record shows little merit in this viewpoint, however. It amounts, rather, to the canonization of a modern saint by a long-familiar process: the glorification of virtues, the neglect of defects, and the reinterpretation of the historic record.

Joseph Schumpeter, unlike most twentieth-century economists, immersed himself in the economic writings of the past—not only the Enlightenment, but earlier centuries as well. An Austrian who later emigrated to the United States, Schumpeter was one of the leading economists of the twentieth century in his own right. Deeply committed to the belief that economics has the full status of a science, Schumpeter judged Adam Smith harshly by this demanding standard. He wrote that Smith's success in *The Wealth of Nations* was in the manner of a "great performance." The book only "advocated the things that were in the offing." As far as technical innovation or the advancement of economic theory, Schumpeter considered that "the *Wealth of Nations* does not contain a single analytical idea, principle, or method that was entirely new in 1776."[48]

Schumpeter assessed Smith's essential significance for economic thought as providing the key "channel through which eighteenth century ideas about human nature reached economists."[49] The prevailing eighteenth-century view, as Talmon phrases it, "declared [self-interest] to be the most important asset for social cooperation. They hailed it as the most precious gift of Nature. Without the desire for happiness and pleasure, man . . . would have never attained his real self-fulfillment." Not only Smith but many others in the Enlightenment believed that "owing to cosmic pragmatism, our courses and interests are so linked up in a higher unity that man working for his welfare inevitably helps others and society."[50]

Schumpeter also found that, rather than representing a bold new advance in scientific understanding, the fundamental tenets of *The Wealth of Nations* were of ancient lineage. He writes that "the skeleton of Smith's [economic] analysis hails from the scholastics and natural law philosophers."[51] Both the ideas of self-interest and the common good were derived from medieval sources, after which they were carried into Locke and then into the 18th century. As Schumpeter explains,

St. Thomas' sociology of institutions, political and other, is not what readers will expect who are in the habit of tracing the political and social doctrines of the nineteenth century to Locke or to the writers of the French Enlightenment or to the English utilitarians. Considering that, in this respect, the teaching of St. Thomas not only was representative of that of his contemporaries but also was accepted by all the scholastic doctors of later times, its main points should be briefly indicated. There was the sacred precinct of the Catholic Church. But for the rest, society was treated as a thoroughly human affair, and moreover, as a mere agglomeration of individuals brought together by their mundane needs. Government, too, was thought of as arising from and existing for nothing but those utilitarian purposes that the individuals cannot realize without such an organization. Its raison d'etre was the Public Good. The ruler's power was derived from the people, as we may say, by delegation. . . . This mixture of sociological analysis and normative argument is remarkably individualist, utilitarian, and (in a sense) rationalist, a fact that it is important to remember in view of the attempt we are going to make to link this body of ideas with the laical and anti-Catholic political philosophies of the eighteenth century.[52]

Besides the theory of the division of labor, Adam Smith is also regarded as a great antagonist and critic of mercantilism. Here as well, Smith was reasserting a tradition of the medieval Roman Catholic church. Another twentieth-century economist, Jacob Viner, writes that

Mercantilism penetrated much less into Catholic than into Protestant theology. Catholic doctrine as such was universalist by tradition, and papal ambitions, ecclesiastical and political, encountered a formidable obstacle in strongly nationalistic policies. . . . Mercantilism, which was nationalist in essence and stressed national objectives as against the moral claims of individuals or other peoples, found an easier entry into the doctrinal teaching of clergymen belonging to the various state-established, state-supported, and largely state-dominated churches of Protestantism than into the corpus of doctrine of the tradition-bound and supranational Catholic Church. Although in its struggle against Gallicanism and Protestantism, the Papacy did not hesitate to make use of national rivalries for power and wealth, it escaped deep entanglement with mercantilism and doctrine, as some of the established churches of Protestantism did not.[53]

Both Smith and Aquinas provide much practical detail, useful advice, and general information about their times. Both lived in periods of economic change when the forces of modernization were taking a large leap forward. Both—despite some doubts and hesitancies—saw these changes in a basically optimistic way. Both developed theologies that served to legitimize the new forces—rather than, as in the "revolutionary conservatism" characteristic of the Protestant tradition, seeking a reversal and a return to a golden age in the distant past. Smith thus states his confidence in the "natural progress of things towards improvement."[54] As a twentieth-century authority remarks, Smith was another of the progressives of history who believed that the future offered "an easier, more cultivated, more rational and secure

life for the generality of mankind." While Smith shares these beliefs
with others in the Roman tradition, he is the first central figure of this
tradition for whom "nature speaks to history in the language of
economics."[55]

   To be sure, as Locke still reflected his Puritan origins, there remained in Smith a substantial legacy of the Calvinist heritage of
Scotland. Labor is good for the soul and thus to be valued for its own
sake—an attitude reflected in Smith's labor theory of value. Smith's
faith in the rational conduct of society is far from complete and is
punctuated by many qualifications and hesitations.[56] Indeed, men on
many occasions do not behave rationally; thus, the great proprietors
of old brought about their own undoing through their "folly" and their
"most childish vanity." If the pursuit of self-interest serves the purposes of society, it is not by the rational intent of the parties involved.
Rather, the seeker of his own gain "neither intends . . . nor knows"
the result achieved. It is thus only through the good fortune of an
"invisible hand" that society achieves an "end which was no part of
[the individual's] intention."[57]

   Smith finds that carefully developed plans designed for public betterment do much less good than the unintended consequences of the
pursuit of self-interest. He thus writes that "I have never known much
good done by those who affected to trade for the publick good."[58]
Even the seeking of greater material possessions—while admittedly
the normal conduct of man—may be irrational, because the rich may
derive little real benefit. At one point in *The Theory of Moral Sentiments*, Smith says that the poor are "in no respect inferior" in the
matters that constitute "the real happiness of human life." Wealth and
possessions yield "a few trifling conveniences to the body" at a price
that includes "anxious attention" and a fear that at any moment these
assets could "crush in their ruins their unfortunate possessor."[59]

   Smith's confidence in human progress ultimately rests not in the
power of human reason, but in the wisdom of nature. Nature has
created a world in which even petty, misdirected, foolish, and frequently irrational men can achieve a happy and productive result.
Nature has, in short, bestowed on little deserving mankind an unplanned and often little comprehended blessing. To realize this blessing, men need only refrain from tampering with the laws of nature, as
these laws are found in the workings of the free market.

   In all of this, there remains an echo of the God of Calvin. The
Enlightenment had no interest, however, in returning to anything
resembling too closely the original Calvin. The eighteenth century

knew full well the consequences that such a course had held for the sixteenth and seventeenth centuries, when religious passions led to war, destruction, and misery throughout large parts of Europe. A rational man—the kind of man prescribed for the "age of reason"—was a happier, less zealous, and (most important) more peaceful man than a Lutheran or Calvinist savior of mankind.

Indeed, the contemporary historian Joyce Appleby has noted that as early as seventeenth-century England the centrality of "self-interest" was declared by many pamphleteers and other writers who saw this motive "as dependable and constructive." Through "economics" a new "rationality" would be possible—a much sought quality in an era just emerging from religious warfare. One conclusion already reached by some in the seventeenth century was that "legislators and policy makers should accommodate normal human drives by relying less upon coercive authority and more upon the manipulation of economic incentives." If this prescription sounds familiar today, one analyst of economic matters had even anticipated Adam Smith's most famous phrase, writing in the seventeenth century that it was the "invisible hand of the market" that determined prices and—without any central direction or control—caused basic social needs to be met.[60]

The encouragement of the pursuit of self-interest thus owed much to the central preoccupation of the Enlightenment with establishing a more orderly world. Albert Hirschman also traces in *The Passions and the Interests* how the pursuit of economic interests came to be seen as a displacement and a substitute for fiercer and more dangerous emotions.[61] This turn toward a more rational and more economic outlook on life would also find favor in the second half of the twentieth century. Like the Enlightenment, this period has also had to contend with the recent experience of religious warfare—if now, warfare resulting from conflicts among secular economic faiths.

Adam Smith envisioned a future world in which every region throughout the earth would be linked to every other region through the workings of the market. Free trade offers the vision of a true global community, all of mankind advancing on a common road of economic advancement. Mercantilism and protectionism asserted the right of a nation or other limited group to pursue its immediate interests, even when the economic productivity of the world as a whole would suffer. In advocating the bringing together of all mankind in one community, Smith exhibited still another of the characteristic tendencies of the Roman tradition. If Aquinas sought to unite mankind under the same God and under the same church authority located in Rome, Smith would now seek to unite humanity with a single worldwide market. If the God of Aquinas had established a rational order of nature common to all mankind, the free market was for Smith no less the expression of a common rational order and a single natural law suited to guide the actions of men all over the earth.

Jeremy Bentham: Guide to Heavenly Happiness

As the nineteenth century commenced, a close inspection could hardly fail to reveal that the faith of the Enlightenment was in some respects being gravely challenged. The promise of Enlightenment thought had been that the natural operation of the forces of self-interest would yield a steadily happier and more harmonious world— one approaching ever more closely the long-sought unification of human actions with the laws of nature. Yet, while the division of labor and other developments were yielding rapid economic growth, it was hardly harmonious or orderly. Indeed, the Industrial Revolution was causing social dislocation throughout England on a vast scale. For all too many people the result of industrialization was proving to be not happiness and well being, but turmoil, degradation, and misery.

Another problem was that, in order to apply the scientific method in a valid way, it was necessary to define the objects of study with sufficient exactness that they could be measured quantitatively. Subsequent empirical observation would then consist of the continuing assembly of numerical data. Newton, for example, had available to him calculations of the precise positions and times of the planets and moons of the solar system. Once the relevant data were available, any proposed scientific law of nature would then have to be confirmed in a specific way: by whether the proposed law was in fact able to predict events. Newton had in this way established his law of gravity, by correctly calculating the positions of the planets and moons.

Yet, applying such a scientific test, little if any of Enlightenment social thought could pass. Despite the explanation of the division of labor, and the many institutional details and economic facts provided by Adam Smith, his entire body of work would have to be rejected by the standards of the modern scientific method. Smith might be more up-to-date and more relevant to eighteenth-century concerns than Aristotle and Aquinas, but his method of reasoning was in truth little closer to the method of Newton than theirs.

There was still another troubling concern. The scientific method was itself only a method of reasoning of unusual power. Nothing intrinsic to the scientific method said that the laws of nature must merely be accepted and could not instead be used for constructive human purposes such as the redesign of property and other social relationships. Indeed, in the physical sciences, mankind was beginning to learn how to use scientific discoveries to build new technology and otherwise alter the physical world. Why should the scientific laws of society not be used in a similar fashion? Would it not make sense to design and perfect a system of social organization, applying the scientific knowledge of society that should soon be forthcoming?

The key figure who would seek to respond to these concerns was Jeremy Bentham.[62] One of the great optimists, rationalists, and progressives of history, Bentham was born in 1748 and lived until 1832, representing the next generation after Adam Smith. Able to see more clearly gaps, weaknesses, and troublesome features in the religion of the Enlightenment, Bentham spread the message of the next great faith of modern economic theology: utilitarianism. In the late twentieth century the economics of the welfare state has modified this faith somewhat, but it nonetheless still traces many of its characteristic beliefs to their first modern statement in Bentham's new science of utility.[63]

The concept of happiness as a basic goal of man not only was widely held throughout the Enlightenment, but was as ancient as Aristotle and others in the Roman tradition. However, Bentham now added a critical new element. As would have to be the case for any science worthy of Newton, the science of utility would be developed with numerically quantifiable elements. Fortunately, as Bentham now argued, the happiness of each man could be calculated exactly and quantitatively by summing the numerical measures of the individual pleasures experienced and then subtracting the pains: "Sum up all the values of all the pleasures on the one side, and those of all the pains on the other. The balance, if it be on the side of pleasure, will give the good tendency of the act upon the whole, with the respect to the interests of that individual person; if on the side of pain, the bad tendency of it upon the whole."[64]

In Newtonian physics, the effect of a force is measured by the change in the object under its influence. If the basic force in society was already agreed on in the eighteenth century, the effects of self-interest had never been measured numerically before Bentham. These effects were, however, now to be seen as the change in total utility resulting from some action. Bentham thus considers that a valid

Newtonian physics for the behavior of the individual has been attained. Individuals are the mass objects in this new social physics; self-interest is the driving force (the source of energy); and utility is the numerical measuring rod. Bentham also believes that the principle of maximizing utility applies equally to social decision making. The total utility of society is simply the sum of all individual utilities. Bentham therefore concludes that in forming government policies "the happiness of the individuals, of whom a community is composed, . . . is the end and the sole end which the legislator ought to have in view." Decisions are to be made according to the principle of maximizing total social utility for "every measure of government."[65]

In this way, Bentham can claim that he has developed at long last the true comprehensive science of society that the world has been awaiting. Moreover, given such a science, it no longer makes sense to speak of natural law or the harmony of nature. There are, to be sure, scientific laws to be discovered that relate individual or collective actions to resulting levels of individual or social utility—the social equivalents to physical laws of nature. However, these social laws are merely practical tools for the precise calculation of utility. The purpose of discovering a new social law is not to enable men humbly to submit to this law's dictates. Rather, the science of utility will provide mankind with the means to calculate levels of utility more easily and with steadily increasing precision, thereby making possible better choices that in fact will yield higher total levels of happiness.

Bentham thus rejects the thinking of most of his predecessors and instead concludes that "there are no such things as natural rights." The very concept "is simply nonsense . . . rhetorical nonsense— nonsense upon stilts." Applying instead a valid utilitarian approach, if a "right" is not "advantageous to society," it should "be abolished."[66] A social right or a governing law can be justified only by showing that its effect on the net happiness of society is favorable. Bentham takes much the same view with respect to any "law of nature, . . . law of reason, right reason, natural justice, natural equity, good order"— dismissing all as mere relics of religion or of a more recent past where true scientific thinking was never fully applied.[67]

Bentham's new science of utility thus sets the stage for a rethinking of tradition, heritage, convention—all the institutions of society that have never before been scientifically justified. A wholesale reexamination of all social practices will have to be undertaken, verifying whether existing laws, regulations, divisions of authority, and other arrangements do in fact contribute to maximizing the total utility of society.

Bentham is confident that much of what government does is based on myth. History is filled with oppressive, parochial, prejudiced, and self-serving actions of ruling groups. Nevertheless—and Bentham has no doubts on the subject—with the new science of utility as a guide, the failings of past governments need not be repeated. As a consequence, he recommends that "the supreme governor's authority . . . must unavoidably, I think . . . be allowed to be indefinite."[68]

Yet, although in principle he grants wide latitude for change, Bentham was no revolutionary. His attempt to develop a valid Newtonian science of society opened up the vista for the reconstruction of society, but personally Bentham was less than a radical. He thus recommends that the "motto, or watchword" of government should be "quietism" and that in the typical case "any interference . . . on the part of government is needless." Like his utilitarian successor John Stuart Mill, Bentham is a prominent defender of individual liberty, arguing that, "with few exceptions, . . . the attainment of maximum [social] enjoyment would be most effectively secured by leaving each individual to pursue his own maximum of enjoyment." Moreover, government infringement on individual freedom causes "pain," which "is the general concomitant of . . . restraint."[69] If Bentham now employs a new utilitarian logic, the ultimate conclusion is not so different from Locke, Adam Smith, or other Enlightenment predecessors. Bentham similarly agrees that private property is desirable and beneficial to society. He explains that "an article of property, an estate in land" is "valuable" because of "the pleasures of all kinds which it enables a man to produce, and (what comes to the same thing) the pains of all kinds which it enables him to avert."[70]

Nevertheless, while opposed to revolutionary change, Bentham does not shrink in many specific areas from the implications of his new science of utility. Liberated from traditional ways, Bentham is in fact one of the leading proponents of reform in English history. In 1948, on the bicentennial of his birth, the *London Times* would say that "Bentham still exerts a posthumous despotism over English politics."[71] More recently, a political scientist remarked that "there is hardly a major reform in British life of the last five generations that does not go back to Bentham."[72]

Seeking the enlightenment of all citizens by reason, Bentham was one of the early advocates of public education. Other of his reform causes included the creation of a public health service, self-government for the colonies, reorganization of the British government, and competitive admissions based on merit to the civil service. Bentham's efforts were important in the establishment of the University of London in 1827. He advocated prison reform and sought curbs on the cruel treatment of animals. He actively promoted religious tolerance and sought an end to remaining legal discriminations against members of the Roman Catholic and other minority religions in England.

Bentham was a strong advocate of government policy making based on systematic investigation of the facts and figures. While the guiding principle was to maximize utility, it was still necessary in specific instances to conduct extensive research and to make detailed calculations. He sought the establishment of the British census, the first of which was taken in 1801. In all these activities, Bentham promoted what he saw as a more rational, enlightened, and scientific administration of government. Typical of his public-spirited and rationalist outlook, Bentham bequeathed his body to the University of London for dissection and other scientific purposes. His skeleton would later be displayed for the public, dressed in his actual clothes.

With Bentham, modern economic theology takes several critical steps toward the characteristic outlooks of the twentieth-century welfare state. His reform agenda includes a number of the accomplishments of the progressive movements of this century. The economists of the welfare state today still conceive individual rationality in terms of maximization of utility. Utility analysis has become much more mathematically and otherwise sophisticated since Bentham's day, but the fundamental concept is not much altered.

Similarly, economists today identify government rationality with the maximization of the total utility of society. The contemporary requirement to maximize benefits minus costs restates in a new language Bentham's prescription to achieve the highest total level of social utility possible. Economists today still seek, as Bentham did, a precise numerical comparison of the utilities (net benefits) of different government actions. Besides benefit–cost analysis, other contemporary tools for more rational government include cost-effectiveness studies, systems analysis, and policy analysis. In the basic commitment to rational government, in looking to facts and research as a basis for decisions, and in other respects, the current schools of public administration and of public-policy analysis carry on in a framework of thought that finds a founding modern statement in Bentham.

Bentham sets the stage in another key respect as well. Like the economists of the welfare state, Bentham exhibits an obvious deep faith in individual and social rationality—a faith that pervades all his proposals for social reform. Yet, Bentham makes the claim that this faith is derived strictly from his newly discovered science of utility. He criticizes the tendency of past thinkers to jump to conclusions about natural law and the role of reason in society; their conclusions were never developed through a process that is rigorously scientific, based on methods best exemplified by Newton. Yet it was apparent almost from the very inception of utilitarianism that Bentham had no more attained to a rigorous science of individual behavior or of social decisions than his predecessors. Bentham's science of utility was on a par with the mathematical certainty that Locke claimed for the science of ethics or the proof of the existence of God. The claim is easily enough made, but the backup is missing. Bentham becomes yet another illustration of a widespread modern tendency to make strong claims for scientific achievements and to renounce the past for failing in this regard, all the while showing little if any greater scientific rigor than before.

Thus, although Bentham outwardly rejects natural law, right reason, and many other characteristic beliefs of his predecessors in the Roman tradition, inwardly these represent the very core of his understanding of the world. Indeed, this combination of outward denial and inward belief did not end with Bentham. Among many others who have followed in Bentham's footsteps, most economists of the late-twentieth-century welfare state have a deep confidence that individuals and society can and do behave rationally. While economists make strong claims to show that this confidence can be established scientifically, and follow Bentham in grounding these claims in a utility analysis, in the end the asserted rationalism of economic man must be judged much more a product of faith than of the scientific method.

With Bentham, the vestiges of Luther, Calvin, and the Protestant Reformation almost disappeared. The Reformation had condemned the Roman Catholic church of its time for teaching that men can earn their salvation by their own efforts—that salvation by good works is possible. The Protestant reformers saw the rational outlook of Aquinas as leading down a path that inevitably must end with man seeking to replace God. Now, however, Bentham was teaching that mankind can choose its own path to a future heaven on earth through the exercise of its own reason. Indeed, the proper path is the one that yields the maximum of pleasure and the minimum of pain. If Calvin had preached that life is meant for suffering, Bentham now taught that general happiness shall be the fate of mankind if only humanity has the wisdom to behave rationally. If the eighteenth century had typically said that men must conform to the laws of nature, Bentham now said that these laws are merely tools made available by modern science for human betterment.

Indeed, Bentham raised for the modern age some of the same questions raised in the waning days of the ancient world by Pelagius—a man of humanitarian and rational outlook similar to Bentham. Augustine denounced the Pelagian heresy that good intent, helpful behavior, and sound morals on this earth will necessarily bring salvation. To argue in this way—said Augustine—is to presume to know, if not to usurp, the ways of God. The Protestant Reformation similarly perceived the beliefs of the medieval Roman Catholic church as the product of a long descent through the Middle Ages back into Pelagian fallacies. Luther said that the pope and the priests of the Roman Catholic church had become the anti-Christ and themselves sought to take the place of God. In the modern era as well, this question would provoke debate, and eventually even great violence. The leading proponent of social Darwinism, Herbert Spencer, regarded Bentham's rationalistic optimism, humanitarianism, and plans for reform measures in much the same light that Augustine had looked on the theology of Pelagius. The laws of social evolution found in a Darwinian world would not yield a fair world filled with reason and happiness; the world portrayed by Darwin was instead often harsh and cruel, rewarding the strong and powerful over the virtuous and the innocent.

If Augustine and Spencer are fellow members of the Protestant tradition, Bentham exhibits the tendencies of the Roman tradition. A utilitarian outlook is as characteristic of this tradition as is a faith in reason, a high regard for law, and a confidence in the future progress of mankind. Emil Kauder explains that following Aristotle, whose "thinking already contained a number of concepts which have since become important elements in the marginal utility theory," the next high point for utilitarianism was around the year 1200. Recognition of "growing complications of market forms and the discussion of the just price" required that Aquinas and his fellow "medieval doctors" address the "Aristotelian instruments" of utility theory. Its next key stage of development was reached when "French, Italian and Swiss authors of the Enlightenment" "perfected this [utility] analysis." The twentieth-century economists of the welfare state represent the most recent stage of utility theory, but they are generally unaware of the ancient lineage—exhibiting the typical modern attitude in seeing few if any lessons to be gained from the distant past. Thus, the economists of today generally know only "the triumvirate, Jevons, Menger, Walras [who themselves] knew only Gossen as their forerunner."[73]

Bentham's philosophy of utilitarianism did not make a sharp departure from the outlook that was already prevalent in the Enlightenment, but it formalized and pressed this outlook to its logical extreme. Talmon comments that for the eighteenth century "the only recognized standard of judgement was to be social utility, as expressed in the idea of the general good, which was spoken of as if it were a visible and tangible objective."[74] Schumpeter observes that "the common good or social expediency of the scholastic doctors was harnessed into a particular shape by the eighteenth century votaries of reason."[75] Its utilitarianism, in short, is one more important way in which the Enlightenment turned away from the Protestant tradition and back to the Roman tradition.

All in all, this is one of the great controversies of human existence. The Roman tradition seeks as a moderate and practical goal that men should live a happy life with material comforts and pleasures. In accepting this view, the pursuit of individual self-interest is a logical complement. The Protestant tradition, however, sees a utilitarian philosophy as a sign of weakness, lack of resolve, and the absence of a deep religious commitment. To pursue mere happiness is not enough; life must be lived for deeper and more heroic purposes. In the Protestant view, a descent into a sterile hedonism is the most likely ultimate outcome of pursuing the utilitarian outlook. Utilitarianism suggests that human beings may have no higher purpose in life than the horses, sheep, and other animals who seek no less their own pleasures.

Death is not to be sought, but the members of the Protestant tradition have on occasion found something to be said for martyrdom, which may offer the highest glory in this world. War and conflict may not be desirable, but they nevertheless have sometimes been seen by members of the Protestant tradition as offering the opportunity for joining with other believers in a great cause—and possibly gaining thereby a heavenly future. In short, the sense of alienation and skepticism toward reason of the Protestant tradition go hand in hand with an asceticism and demand for discipline that is antagonistic to a utilitarian outlook. Such attitudes are found from the Platonism of the ancient world to Augustine to Luther to Darwinist social philosophies of the late nineteenth century such as those of Marx and Spencer. An opposing way of life is favored from Aristotle to Aquinas to the

Enlightenment to the twentieth-century economists of the welfare state.

Claude Henri de Saint-Simon: Messenger of the Gospel of Efficiency

The Enlightenment faith in a natural harmony of social forces would be shaken above all by two revolutions: the French and the industrial. The widespread turmoil, dislocation, and suffering associated with each suggested a need to rethink basic assumptions. Bentham's new philosophy of utilitarianism was one such effort, opening up by its very framework of thought the possibility of social reforms to ameliorate the workings of the free market. A second effort to develop a new physics of society—one that could stand as a worthy successor to Newton—was initiated by the Count Claude Henri de Saint-Simon.

Bentham and Saint-Simon hardly fit the widespread image of the economist as a hard-boiled realist—the exposer and demander of choices among painful trade-offs. Both were eccentric figures who were out of step with many conventions of their day. Yet, between them, they were the source of much of the economic faith of the late-twentieth-century welfare state. If Bentham contributed the utilitarian framework, Saint-Simon prescribed the mission to maximize efficiency. Economics today is still in significant part a legacy of these two attempts made almost two centuries ago to develop a valid Newtonian physics of society.

Saint-Simon was born in 1760 and died in 1825. With him, the line of central figures in modern economic theology shifts from England to France. One of the more unusual figures in the history of ideas, Saint-Simon was possessed on occasion of visions, spent time in a hospital for the insane, suffered from delusions of persecution, and lived several years in dire poverty. While he preached a social existence of reason and scientific order, his own life was often filled with disorder. Yet despite all this, he had a rare sensitivity to some of the main currents of the modern age.[76]

Saint-Simon believed that the eighteenth century had been more successful in destroying the old than it had been in laying the foundations for the new. The Enlightenment had been "critical and revolutionary"; but for the nineteenth century that lay ahead, plans would be needed that were "inventive and organizational."[77] An early effort of Saint-Simon to prepare a plan for the society of the future was based on his conviction that Newton's law of gravitation should provide the central organizing principle. Saint-Simon therefore proposed that there should be created a social organization guided by a new church of Newton to replace the Roman Catholic church. As Saint-Simon explained, under this new organization "all men will work; they will regard themselves as laborers attached to one workshop whose efforts will be directed to guide human intelligence. . . . The supreme Council of Newton will direct their works."[78] This supreme Council should have three mathematicians, three physicists, three chemists, three physiologists, three literary figures, three painters, and three musicians—this order showing the ranking of scientific and thus social authority in Saint-Simon's thinking. There should also be local councils and temples of Newton as part of the comprehensive reorganization of society. Even at this early stage, and in his own odd way, Saint-Simon was anticipating the role that organizations such as the National Academy of Sciences would later play in a secular age.

Saint-Simon would eventually develop his proposals without reference to revelations, churches, and temples. Yet, the early prescription already contained the seeds of his later views. The core idea of Saint-Simon is that scientific reason, when it is fully perfected and applied, will show a right place, a right time, and a right way for every action—indeed for every element in society. For Saint-Simon, society consists of a network of relationships that is like a biological organism, if on a large scale. Hence, science must be applied from on high, reflecting an understanding achievable only at that level. Through scientific expertise it is possible to know how every individual component fits into the larger social system. A scientific elite—the mastermind of society—will be qualified to dispense this knowledge. Saint-Simon's vision of society as one grand scientific system sets the stage for the numerous later interpretations of scientific socialism.

If Bentham focuses on utility and the consumption side, Saint-Simon's attention is directed to questions of production. For Saint-Simon, the relevant Newtonian science "has as its object an order of things the most favorable to all types of production." He explains that this order must also be "the most favorable to society. Here is at once the point of departure and the end of all my efforts."[79]

To be sure, Saint-Simon does not envision a society in the control of its ordinary businessmen, merchants, and traders. What is necessary is that "scientists will undertake a series of works directly intended to perfect industrial arts." The scientifically trained engineer—not the untutored tradesman or businessman—will assume the central role in directing the society of the future. Engineers and expert administrators will coordinate all social responsibilities, ensuring that each person is assigned to duties that best match his or her talents. Saint-Simon believes that "with the perfection of scientific processes" the growing volume of production will steadily enable mankind to "increase its comforts and diminish its physical exertions."[80] The future will hold an ever greater efficiency of industry and an ever greater abundance of output.

As one twentieth-century authority explains, the social organization proposed by Saint-Simon thus offers "a meritocratic elite of intelligence and creativity" that enthrones "productivity, organization, efficiency, innovation, technological discovery."[81] Other social concerns are secondary; property rights, for instance, have no absolute justification. If Bentham can justify property rights only by the net increase of utility, for Saint-Simon property can exist only to the degree that it advances productive efficiency. Saint-Simon is therefore prepared to dispossess those owners of inherited property who lack the scientific skills necessary to make the most efficient use of their inheritance.

As society is more and more organized on the basis of rational efficiency, Saint-Simon sees human conflict diminishing and eventually disappearing. Each person will play a part objectively determined by scientific requirements. Jealousy and envy will be groundless because men will know that their roles are not imposed by other men, but are determined by a scientific imperative. Humanity will attain to a new state of well-being in a truly harmonious order—an order consisting for Saint-Simon of that of a perfectly functioning machine. In his later years Saint-Simon laid out the basic tenets of his gospel of efficiency:

In society which is organized for the positive purpose of increasing its prosperity by means of science, art, and craftsmanship, the most important political act, that of determining the direction in which the community is to move, is no longer performed by men invested with social functions but by the body politic itself; . . . the aim and purpose of such an organization are so clear and determined that there is no longer any room for arbitrariness of men or even of laws. . . . The actions of government that consist in commands will be reduced to nil or practically nil. All the questions that will have to be solved in such a political system, namely: By what enterprises can the community increase its present prosperity, making use of a given knowledge in science, in art, and in industry? By what measures can such knowledge be dispersed and brought to the furthest possible perfection? And finally by what means can these enterprises be carried out at a minimum cost and in minimum time?—all these questions, I contend, and all those to which they can give rise, are eminently positive and soluble. The decisions must be the result of scientific demonstrations totally independent of human will, and they will be subject to discussion by all those sufficiently educated to understand them. . . . just as every question of social importance will necessarily be solved as well as the existing state of knowledge permits, so will all social functions necessarily be entrusted to those men who are most capable of exercising them in conformity with the general aims of the community. Under such an order we shall then see the disappearance of the three main disadvantages of the present political system, that is arbitrariness, incapacity and intrigue.[82]

There remained, to be sure, a difficult question: What would ensure that each person accept his or her one scientifically determined place? However objectively this place might have been decided, Saint-Simon was aware that mankind sometimes exhibited destructive tendencies, once commenting that "society is in a state of extreme moral disorder, egoism is making frightening progress."[83] To counter such forces, men would have to be taught to subordinate their own desires to the greater needs of society. In so doing, society would attain to a condition of ever higher productive efficiency, thereby serving the long-run interests of all men. Saint-Simon professes a confidence that human behavior will be improved in the future by education, scientific enlightenment, and a recognition that a new era in human existence has become possible. All that is required to bring it about is that men should join together in mutual effort and support.

Saint-Simon sees a world emerging in which the central force in society will no longer be self-interest. If the eighteenth century had seen self-interest as the basic Newtonian force in society, in Saint-Simon's view the more vital force is the love of humanity. One twentieth-century authority has observed that "love was the fluid which coursed through the body social, gave it movement and energy. In Saint-Simon's judgment the equal atoms of the eighteenth century worldview were always on the verge of strife; his ideal of love created an organic harmonious whole out of society's vital parts."[84]

In his last years, Saint-Simon came to believe that the transformation in human nature he was seeking could be accomplished only with the aid of religion. Once having offered the world a church of Newton, he now sees a need for a new and revitalized "general and definitive Christianity."[85] This new religion should blend the truths of his new science of society with the power that Christianity has shown over the ages in inspiring mankind. It will be led not by the priests of old, but by a new priesthood: the possessors of scientific knowledge. The proper functioning of society will now require not only the complete coordinization of all industrial parts, but also the education of the citizenry to a proper love of fellowmen. This also will be the task of the priesthood on whom society relies for its direction.

Saint-Simon thus prophesies a new earthly kingdom in which "religious doctrine shall be presented in all the generality of which it is susceptible" and "will regulate alike the action of the temporal and that of the spiritual power."[86] When this kingdom is realized, men can be assured that "the golden age of mankind is not behind us, [but rather] is in the [future] perfection of the social order [and that] our children will arrive there one day." On his deathbed, Saint-Simon states that "religion cannot disappear from the face of the earth; it can only undergo transformation."[87] His followers would shortly announce that in the social order to come "Saint-Simon will be chief of religion, the Pope."[88]

From such eccentric origins came some of the most influential ideas of the modern age. By the mid-nineteenth century, leading French bankers, industrialists, and government officials would declare themselves disciples of Saint-Simon. American progressivism of the late nineteenth and early twentieth centuries would be in essence an updated version of Saint-Simon. The "gospel of efficiency" has been seen by several historians as the essence of U.S. progressive thought. Thorstein Veblen's proposal for a "soviet of technicians," constituting the "general staff of the industrial system" was warmed-over Saint-Simon.[89] Not only intellectuals but practical men of affairs such as Herbert Hoover professed to believe in the "new hegemony of the engineer."[90]

More recently, John Kenneth Galbraith has preached much the same gospel. In the 1950s and 1960s Galbraith wrote approvingly of the dominant role of technocratic elites in American society.[91] Indeed, many institutions of American society today are grounded in ideas that are traceable to Saint-Simon. In the late nineteenth century, the creation of a range of U.S. professional organizations—including the American Economic Association—was designed to provide the technical exertise required for the scientific management of society. American universities abandoned moral philosophy and established specialized departments in many fields to provide the expert knowledge required to move down the road of economic progress.

If the guiding faith of the welfare state is today an economic faith, in many respects it represents an updating of the gospel of Saint-Simon. Introductory economic textbooks typically state that their subject will be the science of achieving maximal efficiency in the use of social resources. A widely held current view is that government economists should regard themselves as "partisan efficiency advocates."[92] Indeed, the broader role of economists today constitutes that of an intelligentsia of social engineers whose mission is to assist in the efficient management of society.

Saint-Simon's historic influence was magnified by the prominence of many of his followers. One of his closest disciples—his personal secretary for a time—was Auguste Comte, who would go on to become known as the founder of sociology. Like many others of the time, Comte was disturbed by social disorders associated with political and economic revolution. The Enlightenment had believed it could show the way to a true harmony of society. However, looking back to the economic thinkers of the Enlightenment, Comte now finds that, "if one considers impartially the sterile disputes which divide them concerning the most elementary concepts of value, utility, production, etc., one may fancy oneself attending the strangest debates of medieval scholastics on the fundamental attributes of metaphysical entities." The economists of the eighteenth century had offered up the "sterile aphorism of absolute industrial liberty," but had failed to provide what could now be seen to be an urgent necessity—a "special institution immediately charged with the task of regularizing the spontaneous coordination." In short, for Comte "the purpose of the establishment of social philosophy is to reestablish order in society."[93]

Comte followed the framework of Saint-Simon but set out to deliver what Saint-Simon had admittedly only promised: a valid science of society. Initially proceeding in a Newtonian context, Comte developed an elaborate mechanics of society. His social physics involved both static and dynamic elements, the workings of these elements following from Comte's proposed laws of social action and reaction. Comte's writings were praised by figures as prominent as John Stuart Mill. The term "positive"—referring to a value-free status said to be attainable by social science—stems from Comte's depiction of intellectual history as an ascent to the ultimate "positive" science of sociology.

Like Saint-Simon, Comte also came in his later years to regard himself as a great prophet—becoming another of what Talmon describes as the "political messiahs" that the nineteenth century spawned in such profusion.[94] Comte envisions a society of the future that will still be based on capitalism, but the controllers of the instruments of production will not be self-seeking profiteers. Rather, they will be skilled administrators, motivated by a spirit of mutual cooperation. They will all follow a central precept of Comte's new message: that men should live for others. All of society will be ordered by the principles of a scientific rationality. A scientific elite will educate all citizens so that they may come to understand, accept, and live by this rational order.

Comte foresaw his new order bringing about an end to economic scarcity. With material needs and desires fully satisfied, mankind would no longer exhibit the "destructive instinct" that had so often characterized human behavior in the past. Previously, the demanding physical requirements of life had exerted an influence that was "doubly corrupting, directly on the heart, indirectly on the mind."[95] Free from physical wants, men would in the future be able to soar to new heights of emotional well-being. It would be a world filled with love and with provision for all the vital needs of mankind.

If in a secular language, Saint-Simon and Comte were in fact prophesying nothing less than the arrival of heaven on earth. The origins of their new religion also were not difficult to discover. Comte himself praised the all-embracing theocracy that he saw in the medieval Roman Catholic church. As had Saint-Simon before him, Comte regarded the scientists of his new social order as the heirs to the Catholic priesthood. The modern church of science would rule not by coercion, but by moral authority—as the Roman Catholic church had once done. If medieval men had seen in the pope and the church the recipients of divine revelation, modern leaders would now obtain their authority through their possession of the revealed truths of science. The scientific understanding of society—its message preached by Comte's new church—would unite all of humanity, just as the medieval Roman Catholic church had.

Comte thus became, as Frank and Fritzie Manuel have put it, the "High Priest of Humanity" in a new "positivist religion." Like others before it, this was one more religion in which there must be "a total loss of personality as man is merged in the perfect transcendent unity of Humanity." Its lineage "ran from the priests of fetishism, through the Catholic Church, to the high sacerdotal authority of the new religion."[96] Indeed, as Thomas Huxley would explain, it was hard not to notice that Comte's new religion of scientific society was in essence "Catholicism minus Christianity."[97]

With Saint-Simon—and illustrated still more graphically by Comte—the Roman tradition assumes once again key elements of the medieval

Roman lineage. The medieval path to salvation has become the modern path of economic progress. The rationalism of medieval Catholicism has become the rationalism of modern physical and social science. The authority of the Roman priesthood is now the modern authority of the scientific expert. The educational role of the medieval monastery becomes the educational role of the modern university. If medieval theology eventually descended to the sterility of scholastic disputation, it is a fate that many see as having once again befallen the Roman priesthood of our day, now in the fields of economics, psychology, and other social sciences.

There is within the secular theologies of the modern age a deep tension. The modern age promises scientific advance not only in the material realm, but in all areas of human affairs. But to the extent that overt forms of traditional religions of the past are adopted, it may seem to belie these very claims. An explicit recognition of close ties to medieval Roman Catholicism, for example, might well be seen as at odds with modern claims for scientific progress in all areas. Therefore, the modern economic theologies typically offer an outward denial of theological content, while inwardly exhibiting the essential character-istics of religion. It is only on unusual occasions that the deeper religious content breaks out into the open. Both Saint-Simon and Comte let down their guard in their old age, when apparently they were less disciplined and less inclined to maintain a false posture. The religious core of their thought then came through explicitly. The result, however, was a discrediting of their own efforts—a lesson that later preachers of modern economic theology would not fail to heed.

In any case, with Saint-Simon, Comte, and other early socialists of the nineteenth century, modern economic theology takes a critical step. In the Enlightenment, the progress of men on earth was still seen as a matter of acting in accordance with the laws of nature: Once the power of science reveals the laws of nature, observance of these laws will lead directly to a heavenly existence. For Saint-Simon and then Comte, the path to heaven now will first take the form of a vast expansion of the productive powers of society. As efficiency attains to ever higher levels, and the output of goods and services becomes ever greater, society will be able to satisfy more and more of its material wants. The practical end of economic scarcity will come within sight. A new era in human existence will have been attained, as for the first time in history there will be no material grounds for fighting and arguing. In short, if evil actions are grounded in poverty and competition for resources, but scarcity is now effectively to be abolished, salvation must be at hand.

The scientific enlightenment of men to the opportunities for economic progress further assures that they will come ever closer together. The vision of the attainment of heaven on earth has the power to inspire the full devotion of all men. Modern economic theology and its gospel of economic efficiency will show the way, if men will but place their faith in its truths. If "rational" and "irrational" defined good and evil for the Enlightenment, a new moral standard now emerges with Saint-Simon—"efficient" and "inefficient." To meet this new ethical standard is, as was the case for many moralities of old, to enter onto the path to salvation and a heavenly future.

The Roman tradition is, to be sure, always confronted by another great tradition of Western thought. The Protestant Reformation denounced the medieval Roman Catholic church for trivializing man and religion. If the medieval Roman Catholic church offered an organic unity of all mankind, men could also suffocate within its theocratic embrace. Now the same confrontation arose in the modern age: If a new scientific priesthood could answer all questions, where did individual exercise of moral choice come into play? To what extent could it be valid for an individual to follow his or her own beliefs in the face of an expert consensus of scientific professionals? Could men also lose their sense of individual dignity and worth within the embrace of a modern church of scientific faith?

A great new protest movement emerged once again against the Roman tradition. The faithful who followed the preachings of this modern movement of protest would be greatly influenced by a new understanding of science—one that by the late nineteenth and early twentieth-centuries had supplanted Newtonian physics in shaping social thought. The Protestant tradition in the modern age would take a secular form now to be found in Darwinist theories of man and society—the various economic theologies of a new Protestant church of Darwin.

Chapter 4

The Protestant Church of Darwin

Although the Enlightenment is known as the age of reason and of faith in progress, there were some discordant notes. David Hume pointed out troubling philosophical weaknesses in the scientific understanding of the period. Enlightenment thinkers such as Locke had taken the successes of Newton and other scientists to reveal a rational order inherent to the universe. Hume, however, observed that in modern science no such assumption need be made nor was there any final confirmation provided. The seemingly necessary relationship of cause to effect was merely a consistent association of one event with another, an association that for accepted laws of science had held up in practice and had been confirmed empirically in every test. Why such relationships existed was not a particular concern of modern science, nor could science offer any guarantee that the current relationships would always hold true.

Hume's analysis raised the possibility of a less comforting and more mysterious world than the Enlightenment took science to have demonstrated. It could be a world where there was no necessary causal relationship between events. There might not be an underlying rational order that governed the universe, ensuring predictability and order. A central concept of the Roman tradition—the idea of natural law—might be little more than a convenient fiction. The world of modern science might be a cold and impersonal world of objects in nature whose relationships were governed not by inherent purpose but merely by mathematical statements that described a consistency of observed association. If the natural harmony of the universe had for the Enlightenment taken the place of God, Hume now suggested a new secular

123

divinity closer to the Protestant tradition. In Hume's thinking the order of nature remained in the last analysis inscrutable, impersonal, and mysterious, beyond full human comprehension. Although Newton had shown the great explanatory power of assuming the existence of gravity, he had, for example, never explained how the force of gravity actually came to be exerted, which remained as much of a mystery as ever.

Hume's was not the only challenge to Enlightenment faith. A still stronger statement of the outlooks associated with the Protestant tradition would come from a man more fundamentally at odds with the convictions of the Enlightenment: Jean-Jacques Rousseau. Rousseau in turn would pave the way for a full-fledged revival of this tradition with the emergence of Marxist, Spencerian, and other interpretations of social Darwinism in the second half of the nineteenth century.

Jean-Jacques Rousseau: The First Modern Protestant

One of the foremost twentieth-century interpreters writes of Jean-Jacques Rousseau that for him "Rome provides the example: the virtuous republic, beguiled by glittering appearances, is doomed by luxury and conquest." The tradition of Rome is also the fate of modern men—a pessimistic message found in Rousseau as early as the mid-eighteenth century, scarcely past the beginning of the modern age. Rousseau's *Confessions* is a brilliant and impassioned "fulmination against reason."[1] Rousseau himself writes that "I would almost venture to say that the state of reflection is unnatural, and that man who meditates is a depraved animal." The Enlightenment confidence in reason and progress is only self-deception. Instead, Rousseau finds that "suspicion, umbrage, fear, coldness, reserve, hatred and treason [hide] beneath that much praised urbanity that we owe to the enlightenment of our century."[2]

Rousseau believes, as Jean Starobinski explains, that there is "a profound connection between the moral problem and the economic problem." Greater scientific knowledge and economic advance have not made men happier or improved the human condition. Instead, "the cost of intellectual and technical progress has been moral degradation." Rising consumption and greater abundance of goods and services have not satisfied men but only whetted their appetites for more. Possessiveness and pridefulness have spread among mankind. The so-called progress of humanity is really a process by which "selfishness perverts innocent love of self, vice is born and society takes shape. And as reason progresses, property and inequality arise, and what is mine is ever more sharply distinguished from what is yours." All this yields an "ever-growing disparity" between "ourselves and our own inner nature."[3]

The story of this growing gap between economic man and true nature is, as depicted in Rousseau, yet another story of human alienation. Originally, men were found in a "state of nature" where they "lived happily in peace." In this state of nature, "appearance and reality were in a perfect equilibrium." However, humanity could not be content with such innocent happiness. Men insisted on pressing forward with their reason, seeking greater knowledge of the world, building cities, organizing economies, creating governments and all the acts that have been so miscast as progress. The result has been, however, an "ever-increasing burden of human artifice" that, together with human pride, have "accelerated the fall into corruption," leaving mankind in a current "vicious climate of mistrust and opacity."[4] The message of Rousseau is, in short, the age-old story of the fall of man from harmony with original nature. It is a central message of the Protestant tradition, found from Plato to Augustine to Luther and now in Rousseau for the first time in a modern translation.

With Rousseau, to be sure, the story assumes a secular cast. As Starobinski states, "Rousseau takes the religious myth and sets it in historical time." The salvation of mankind now will also be a secular affair. Because "the flaws in man's condition are the work of man himself," it is possible for men to "remake or unmake history." Due to the fact that "the introduction of evil into the world is a fact of history, the struggle against evil is a struggle that must be waged in history."[5]

Yet, not finding outside help in God, Rousseau (like Plato) has no sure answer to the fundamental dilemma: How can humanity, fundamentally depraved as it is, hope to succeed in making an escape from its alienated condition? It would fall to Marx, not Rousseau, to assert a secular answer that offered certainty. Men will be saved not by the intervention of God, but by another impersonal power—none other than the forces of economics as they are worked out through the class struggle according to the laws of history.

Rousseau, however, can offer only vague hopes that education will be the salvation of man. Another possibility—also an unlikely route, given the deep roots of human alienation—is revolution. It is nevertheless clear to Rousseau that, however achieved and whatever the actual prospects, a radical transformation of human existence is required. His successors (as has happened all too often in the Protestant tradition) would set out to remake the world overnight. Rousseau's writings were a leading inspiration for the French Revolution—another demonstration of the connection between the Protestant tradition and religious warfare. As Alexis de Tocqueville was already able to see by the 1850s, the French Revolution had sought "not merely a change in the French social system, but nothing short of a regeneration of the whole human race." Its beliefs were "a species of religion," its functioning in many respects that "of a religious revolution."[6]

Rousseau was an anomalous figure in the Enlightenment and its age of reason. A full-fledged revival of the Protestant tradition would await another century. In the meantime, a number of events were occurring to set the stage.

Charles Darwin: Revealer of the Meaning of History

The eighteenth century had looked confidently forward to a newly rational, enlightened, harmonious, and happy existence. The chaotic and violent events of the French Revolution, however, were hardly consistent with this expectation. Another great shock occurred in the economic sphere. Contrary to the assurances of a new era of social harmony soon to arrive, the capitalist system proved an engine of astonishing productivity but also enormous disruption that destroyed as rapidly as it created. Not Adam Smith, not Bentham, not even the nineteenth-century early socialist Saint-Simon managed to forewarn that the Industrial Revolution would have such unsettling consequences. In England this revolution brought, Karl Polanyi finds, "unprecedented havoc with the habitation of the common people . . . Writers of all views and parties, conservatives and liberals, capitalists and socialists invariably referred to human conditions under the Industrial Revolution as a veritable abyss of human degradation."[7] When economists such as Malthus and Ricardo sought to give a rational explanation that might be seen as a defense for these developments, economics would henceforth be tagged as the "dismal science."

If anything, the pace of economic change was even more rapid in the second half of the nineteenth century. It was during this period that the immensely productive marriage really occurred of modern technology with economic organization. One historian reports that production of commodities, foods, textiles, metals, and fuels showed "an astonishing continuity of growth" from 1850 to 1913 and that "the year 1850 was near the beginning" of a period in which the growth of international trade proceeded at a geometric rate. The years from 1851 to 1867 represent "the point at which science established before the public a claim to the leadership of the industrial arts which in the ensuing fifty years was to be made good, especially in chemical, electrical and metallurgical fields."[8] Working conditions were improving and the general standard of living was rising rapidly, but these revolutionary economic changes were also bound to cause widespread social stresses.

Another revolution was brewing in the nineteenth century in natural history. Discoveries of prehistoric fossils and other findings of paleontology were creating an awareness of a much longer and more biologically diverse history of the earth. New and widely read geological, archaeological, and anthropological studies offered a similarly direct challenge to biblical and other long-standing interpretations of history. The ages of the earth, the animal diversity of early times, and many other matters were seemingly much different than a reading of Genesis might suggest.

The pervasive sense of rapid change in the nineteenth century spurred a search for better understanding of change itself. Instead of the Enlightenment search to discover the immutable laws of a single harmonious order, the nineteenth century would be preoccupied with discovering the mechanisms of change. A preoccupation with the laws of history—more than any other feature—characterized the social thought of the century. J. L. Talmon observes that the nineteenth century was marked by an "idolization of History" that is explainable by the "collapse of concrete historic continuity embodied in organized religion, national tradition, local custom and social hierarchies of long standing." Whereas the Enlightenment saw all past history as an unremitting tale of ignorance and woe, in the nineteenth century "history became an ally instead of an enemy, something to be fulfilled rather than overcome."[9]

Writers in the first half of the century such as Hegel and Comte developed theories of the history of mankind as an evolution in human thought. Later theorists would find history driven by events in the physical worlds of biology and of economic affairs. If the nineteenth century was especially concerned with understanding the mechanisms of change, the account given by Charles Darwin would prove the most persuasive of all. Darwin sought to investigate history as a true scientist. By marrying science and history in an age that was desperately looking for historical explanation and that gave enormous prestige to science, Darwin dominated the social thought of the second half of the nineteenth century and then the early twentieth century. Following the publication in 1859 of *The Origin of Species*, the theories of Darwin would have much the same relationship to late-nineteenth- and early-twentieth-century thought that the discoveries of Copernicus, Kepler, Galileo, and Newton had to the late seventeenth and then the eighteenth centuries.

Darwin now gave a convincing and scientific explanation for what the nineteenth century already knew: The static understanding of social mechanics that had been received from the Enlightenment was inadequate and misleading. The message of Darwin was that, contrary to the teachings of Newton's disciples, the laws of nature do not assure a world of harmony. Indeed, the laws of nature guarantee constant change. No species can ever rest secure, because other species are constantly testing its niche in the natural world. Within a species, no individual can be secure, because a new generation is always emerging with new challengers and potentially superior faculties. Life is a never-ending struggle—not only for the birds, bees, and other lower species, but for man himself. In fact, mankind was now recognized as simply another species. Among men, moreover, there must be further competition for dominance, thus helping to improve the quality of the human species and to assure the long-run survival of mankind.

Darwinism was much more than a biological theory. Indeed, as a matter of biology, Darwin's theories would have been an important but far from decisive development in the history of science. Evolution by natural selection was not even a particularly new idea. Philosophers of the ancient world had laid out the basic idea of natural selection as early as the fifth century B.C. A Sicilian, Empedocles, asserted that nature creates many trials and experiments, out of which the most successful survive, resulting in the steady improvement of the species. In ancient Roman times, Lucretius wrote that "many races of living things must then have died out and been unable to beget and continue their breed. For in the case of all things which you see breathing the breath of life, either craft or courage or speed has from the beginning of its existence protected and preserved each particular race. . . . Those to whom nature has granted none of these qualities would live exposed as a prey and booty to others, until nature brought their kind to extinction."[10]

Darwinism thus did not dominate the thought of the late nineteenth century and early twentieth century in the fashion of Newton—as a new scientific explanation that suddenly revealed a previously unimagined order in nature. Darwinian evolution also differed from Newton's theories and from most physics and chemistry in that there were no predictions about the future that could be tested easily—or, often, tested at all. Indeed, Darwinism was not a product of the same scientific method practiced by Newton. Rather, Darwin's ideas had such an enormous impact because they provided by far the most realistic and convincing history of mankind. Darwinism was really a form of history, if perhaps a newly scientific history.

Darwinism met several essential requirements in a way that no other rival historical explanation—Judeo-Christian or secular—could match. First, Darwinism linked the current state of mankind through time to the fossil record of previous human and animal existence, a record that was being rapidly uncovered in the nineteenth century. This record could not in good conscience be denied; yet it refuted previous histories of Christianity, along with most other past historical explanations. Second, Darwinian evolution linked the existence of mankind to the current members of the animal and plant kingdoms, a linkage that an improved biological understanding was making inescapable. And third, Darwinian evolution offered a theory of history that was based on actual events taking place in the physical world. This last quality greatly enhanced its scientific status, because the most important advances of physical science had occurred as explanations of natural phenomena. Following Kant and other thinkers, the nineteenth century had come to understand that the application of scientific methods to the realm of human ideas was more problematic than the Enlightenment had believed.

Also, Darwinism was not just another history relating the activities of rulers and the timing of events—that is, providing a detailed chronology of an age. Instead, Darwinism began its history before human existence, explained the origins of men, and then sought to understand the development of human physical and social characteristics up to the current age. Moreover, it did not attempt this in any detailed and specific way, but as a general concept. Darwinism was not so much an actual history as an explanation or concept of the meaning of history.

It was not the first such explanation. Indeed, a distinctive feature of Judaism, and then of Christianity, was in finding that there is a single clear meaning to human existence, decreed by a single omniscient and omnipotent God. This meaning is expressed through history—beginning with the creation, then the fall of men into sin, the saving of mankind by the sacrifice of Christ, and finally the future unification of men with God in heaven. Any alternative explanation of human history could not be just another dispute over the factual record. It would have to be nothing less than a new religion.

In seeking to rewrite the story of human existence, the nineteenth century set loose a whole era characterized by what Talmon calls "political Messianism," each new messiah presenting a new "religion of History" to explain the meaning of the human presence in the world.[11] Christianity itself was also undergoing rapid change—all these theological developments causing the twentieth-century observer Robert Nisbet to rate the nineteenth century as "one of the two or three most fertile periods in the history of religion in the West."[12] As the developer of the most influential explanation of history of the nineteenth century, Darwin thus becomes the pivotal theological figure of the century as well.[13] Just as the greatest significance of Newtonian physics for the eighteenth century would be philosophical and theological, Darwin's greatest impact on the twentieth century would be in altering the human self-concept.

If Newton's demonstration of the powers of the scientific method had raised confidence in human reason to new heights, Darwinism delivered a sharp blow. Indeed, the Darwinist interpretation of history tended to denigrate the role of reason. In a Darwinian world, the products of rational thought do not have absolute significance because the driving force in history lies not in the world of the mind, but in the biological realities of natural selection. Reason can be a means of discovering and indirectly influencing the workings of biological evolution, but cannot itself directly shape them. In a Darwinist world, rational thought can have ultimate significance only through its effects on human behavior and as these effects themselves are the direct determinants of the biological prospects for evolutionary survival.[14]

To be sure, people commonly believe that their ideas are objectively true. But in a Darwinist world this faith of the common man might just as well be a delusion—perhaps useful in some cases, oftentimes not— by which nature works its biological ways. If reason serves to promote survival, it thereby serves the purpose of human existence; if reason should somehow undermine the prospects for survival, then reason as it is now known will eventually disappear from the earth. All this is decreed by the evolutionary laws of history. The literal merits of the ideas and the reasoning are themselves of little concern. Ideology, religion, morals, and other elements of culture can have an objective significance only insofar as they play a role in the biological result. This conclusion, which is a consequence of the very framework of

Darwinist thought, applies as well to the rational foundations for churches, political parties, governments, and other basic institutions of society.

Such Darwinist precepts apply, for example, to the concept of individual freedom. The evolutionary struggle is waged among social groups and species—not among individuals. Within an organization, individual liberty is like any other idea, element of culture, or institution of society; it is ultimately justifiable in a Darwinist world only if individual liberty in fact contributes to the evolutionary survival of the culture, organization, or species. Thus, Locke's concept of society as a voluntary agreement among freely contracting parties can be assessed only by such a pragmatic standard. If such a belief causes society to function more successfully (even if it is an illusion), it serves the purposes of history (and may well come to be regarded as true). However, any concept that there is an absolute right in nature to personal liberty and private property must be discarded entirely. Indeed, given the absence of liberty in most societies, there are real grounds for questioning whether a commitment to personal liberty contributes much to evolutionary survival.

Because men were said all to possess the same basic faculty of reason, the Enlightenment taught the equality of mankind. In a Darwinist world, however, the framework of evolutionary theory says that men possess different intrinsic capabilities for survival. The very meaning of history is the winnowing out of the superior men—a modern elect who are the survivors of evolutionary trials—and the casting aside of inferior men. Men thus are fundamentally unequal—divisible into categories of those with inner strengths and qualities to be chosen by history, and those whom history will reject.

The Enlightenment had believed that, as Newton's methods of scientific reasoning were applied ever more widely, the progress of mankind would include the knowledge to live ever more happily in close harmony with nature. The Darwinist reading of history offered no such promises. Indeed, every species is destined at some point to be displaced by a new and superior species. Life in a Darwinist world is harsh and cruel. The workings of nature do not in fact tend toward harmony, but toward perpetual strife.

The powers of scientific reasoning demonstrated by Newton had acted to buttress the characteristic outlooks found over the course of 2,000 years of the Roman tradition in Western thought. Now, however, the understanding of history that Darwin revealed had a much different implication. Darwin's theory of evolution acted to support the characteristic outlooks of the Protestant tradition. Darwinism could easily be taken to mean a denigration of reason; a harsh and cruel fate in this world; a fundamental inequality among men; a future of strife and discord; the necessity for individual discipline and self-mastery to survive; the rejection of a utilitarian purpose in life; and a general state of alienation from a happy, innocent, and natural existence. In these respects, Darwinism suggested an interpretation of the meaning of history that followed in the path of Plato, Augustine, Luther, and Calvin. If Darwinism departed somewhat in seeing history as a story of progress, this did not necessarily contradict the pessimistic message of the Protestant tradition, which allowed for circumstances in which divine intervention would reverse the fall of man and offer the prospect of ascending to a glorious and heavenly future.

Darwin himself wrote in *The Origin of Species* about the natural world. However, as with Newton, it would fall to the disciples of Darwin to develop the key theological implications of his work. In matters of modern economic theology, three of these disciples would have an immense impact on the twentieth century. If themselves of Jewish birth, Karl Marx and Sigmund Freud were products of the same German culture that had given birth to the Protestant Reformation. The third disciple, Herbert Spencer, was from another country central to the history of Protestantism: England. Marx and Spencer had developed their basic ideas before *The Origin of Species* appeared. However, both soon proclaimed themselves to be creators of the true Darwinist theory of society—each declaring himself the revealer of the valid laws of social evolution. More important, each of them was regarded in this way by legions of followers who were convinced that they had now discovered the correct scientific explanation of history. Thus, Marx and Spencer—and then Freud in the twentieth century— joined the ranks of the messiahs of the modern age, revealers to men of the true meaning of their existence.

Karl Marx: Descendent of Martin Luther

Martin Luther and Karl Marx arose from similar economic circumstances—periods of rapid change in which those who were threatened or displaced felt strong grievances. The economic historian R. H. Tawney writes of the Germany of Luther's time that, much like the Industrial Revolution confronting Marx in the nineteenth century, there was occurring an "expansion of commerce which brought affluence to the richer bourgeoisie." These economic developments had resulted in "the rise to a position of overwhelming preeminence of the new interests based on the control of capital and credit."[15] The scholarship of the twentieth century has shown what was not well known in Marx's time, and which would not have fit well with his laws of history, that the institutions of capitalism began to emerge even many years before Luther's lifetime. There had been an economic boom in the eleventh through the thirteenth centuries, a falloff for almost two centuries, and then a resumption of economic growth at a rapid pace in the fifty years or so before Luther launched the Protestant Reformation in the early sixteenth century.

The economic conditions to which Luther was exposed have a familiar ring. Laborers of the sixteenth century were "sinking in an ever-expanding morass of hopeless pauperism." The peasants found that they "suffered equally" from disruptions of rural life. The old landowners, too, were losing out before the onslaught of new business and commercial classes. This all produced a "passionate anti-capitalist reaction." One of its activists was Martin Luther, who "hated commerce and capitalism." For Luther, "the exploitation of the Church by the Papacy, and the exploitation of the peasant and the craftsman by the capitalist, are thus two horns of the beast which sits on the seven hills. Both are essentially pagan, and the sword which will slay both is the same. It is the religion of the Gospel."[16]

In the nineteenth century, the gospel of Marx would also seek to slay the dragon of capitalism. Marxism as a gospel has in fact a remarkable resemblance to Luther's message in many other respects as well. The gospel of Luther was in turn drawn heavily from Augustine, who had looked to Plato for much of his inspiration. Now, Marx once again identifies the pursuit of wealth and riches as the source of human exploitation and enslavement. For all of them, the very achievement of economic success splits society into warring factions, causes some men to oppress others, promotes selfishness and self-centeredness, stirs envy and jealousy, elevates pridefulness and conceit, and in other ways as well undermines the moral fiber of a just and virtuous society.

Marx follows Rousseau in giving a secular explanation for the depraved state in which men are currently found. For both, mankind did actually live long ago in a primitive world of communal living arrangements where private property and conflicts among classes did not exist. At that time men were found in a happier condition (although Rousseau is far more effusive in this regard than Marx is). However, mankind could not resist the opportunities for improved technological knowledge, economic growth, and the creation of organized societies. As a result, economic development occurred and, as Marx explains, surplus production became available for the first time. The presence of this extra production beyond essential needs led inevitably to conflicts over its distribution and control. The result was inevitable: the emergence of ever sharper divisions within humanity—the "class struggle." It is the beginning of a new stage of history—the moment of the fall of man, as Marx now develops his new interpretation.

Henceforth, the economic laws of history decree that a deep alienation from true nature will afflict mankind. Isaiah Berlin has remarked that the Marxist concept of alienation is derived from what "Rousseau and Luther and an earlier Christian tradition called the perpetual self divorce of men from unity with nature, with each other, with God."[17] By the nineteenth century, the laws of history had yielded the current stage of capitalism. In the Marxist telling, mankind had now fallen into a virtual hell on earth. Marx thus writes that, "within the capitalist system, all methods for raising the social productiveness of labour . . . transform themselves into means of domination over, and exploitation of, the producers; they mutilate the labourer into a fragment of a man, degrade him to the level of an appendage of a machine, destroy every remnant of charm in his work and turn it into a hated toil; . . . and drag his wife and children beneath the wheels of the Juggernaut of capital."[18] It is a condition in which "man's own deed becomes an alien power opposed to him, which enslaves him."[19] Human misery and depravity are pervasive. According to Berlin, Marx finds in capitalist society a set of ideals that are "worthless and its virtues vices." Men have fallen into a "corrupt, tyrannous and irrational society"—the earthly city of Augustine, now translated to the Darwinist framework of the second half of the nineteenth century.[20]

In the enslaved and alienated condition of men there are, nevertheless, grounds for hope and redemption. The workings of history, as Marx prophesies, result in a spread "of misery, oppression, slavery, degradation, exploitation; but with this too grows the revolt of the workingclass." As this class grows ever more numerous and becomes "disciplined, united, organised by the very mechanism of the process of capitalist production itself," the results "prove incompatible with their capitalist integument." It is at this point of humanity's greatest despair that men will be saved. Due to its own internal contradictions, the entire capitalist system will "burst asunder. The knell of capitalist private property sounds. The expropriators are expropriated."[21]

Marx gave few details concerning the new world to come. Yet men could know that, as Talmon describes the Marxist prophecy, "the reappropriation of the world and the ensuing abolition of self-alienation will engender a sense of supreme self-respect and dignity in man. For it will do away with the enmity between reason and the senses, spirit and matter, theory and practice, the general good and the individual interest." Indeed, for the Marxist faithful the laws of history have predestined with ironclad certainty that in the future "its earth is its heaven."[22] In this new Marxist rendering, the fall of man and then the salvation of mankind are rigorous scientific truths that follow from the laws of social evolution—laws of history no less scientific than Darwin's new theory of evolution.[23]

In the new Marxist gospel the laws of history are, moreover, grounded in economics. The workings of economic forces are responsible for reducing men to an enslaved condition of deep alienation. Nevertheless, even in the very depths of misery, the preconditions of economics for a new era are being met. The looming salvation of humanity and the cataclysmic arrival of heaven on earth will be commanded by the workings of economic forces. Once men reach their earthly heaven, it will be the results of economic advancement that once again ensure their continuing happiness. Marx believes that technology and economic growth will yield a future vast abundance of goods and services—an end to material scarcity—and thus a final end to the original cause of the class struggle. As one authority writes, Marx is convinced that, "if men are divided by scarcity, they would be united by abundance" and that therefore "the inauguration of a new economics . . . will bring on the full perfection of human nature via the transcendence of production for exchange."[24]

With Marxism, in essence, the place of God is now taken by economics. If Adam Smith was the founder of modern economic theology, Marx is the next great prophet. For Smith, salvation was to be attained by living in harmony with laws decreed by an economic deity. For Marx, it is not harmony that is decisive, but the outputs resulting from the workings of economic forces that are themselves redemptive. By abolishing material scarcity, economics can abolish the principal source of the pervasive human misbehavior of the past. It is a tenet of economic theology found not only in Marxism, but in almost all the economic faiths from the mid-nineteenth century onward. It is central to the economic theology of the twentieth-century welfare state. If the vista of a vast outpouring of material production was opened to clear view for the first time in this period, the greatest significance was not a matter of mere want satisfaction, but in altering and redirecting the theological foundations of modern society.

In elevating the economic laws of history to the role of God, Marx modifies but in many respects follows his mentor Hegel. As Paul Tillich writes, "Hegel's interpretation of history is the application of the idea of Providence in a secularized form." History is for Hegel "the self-actualization of the absolute spirit, the divine ground of being itself. This means that somehow everything in history is divine revelation."[25] Marx observed that he was turning Hegel upside down, reversing the roles of mind and matter. If the God of Hegel worked through the spirit and the reason in man, in Marx the dialectical processes of history operate instead in the economic realm of production and distribution.

Good and evil, justice and injustice are determined in the Marxist theology by the laws of economics. That which is just advances the economic forces of history, bringing closer the salvation of humanity. Traditional religion, natural law, right reason, the harmony of nature, all these and other long-standing beliefs of Western civilization are rejected by Marx as mere manifestations—an illusory "superstructure"—of the internal tensions of a particular stage of economic development. Friedrich Engels stated that in Marxism "the demand for final solutions and eternal truths ceases" and knowledge is instead "conditioned by the circumstances." There can be "nothing [that] is final, absolute, sacred" because every idea "loses its validity and justification" when history moves on to "new, higher conditions."[26] Hence, as Isaiah Berlin puts it, in Marxism "the only sense in which it is possible to show that something is good or bad, right or wrong is by demonstrating that it accords or discords with the historical process. . . . All causes permanently lost or doomed to fail are, by that very fact, made bad or wrong, and indeed, this is what constitutes the meaning of these terms."[27]

In the Marxist gospel men therefore do not control or shape their fate by the exercise of their reason. As Marx writes, "it is not the consciousness of men that determines their existence, but, on the contrary, it is their social existence that determines their consciousness." For Marx, the "juridical, political, religious, aesthetic or philosophic" aspects of life are merely "the ideological forms wherein men become conscious of the [economic] conflict and fight it out."[28] Indeed, the great majority of the beliefs of mankind have always consisted of falsehoods, rationalizations, misunderstandings, delusions, and other forms of self-deception. As Engels would later say, the workings of economic forces have so alienated men from themselves that their "reason has become nonsense."[29] Human reason yields merely a "whole vast superstructure" that serves to hide the deeper truths of human existence—a Marxist rendition of Plato's cave of enslaved and deluded mankind able to see only false images.[30]

Marx believed that human equality would reign in the classless society following the communist revolution, but equality was not yet possible in the current state of human degradation. For the time being, government must exist and must sometimes take coercive measures—as Luther regarded it, a regrettable evil required to maintain social order. Existing government is a consequence of the depravity of capitalism, the current stage of history (a stage that is unavoidable, if temporary). Marx regards scornfully those humanitarians of his time—modern-day Pelagians they are—who expect by reason, good intentions, and goodwill to change the world through government or other measures. Due to their shallow and false social consciousness, these humanitarians fail to understand that the condition of human exploitation is so deeply embedded that reason and good intentions alone are powerless to bring about change. The problem of man's alienation from his nature can be solved only by a radical transformation of human existence. Humanity must place its hopes in the economic laws of history, looking once again to find salvation through the intervention of an impersonal force outside human design.

Marx's view of the rationalistic and optimistic outlook of the typical socialist of the nineteenth century is contemptuous. He is more tolerant of Saint-Simon and other early socialist writers—sometimes even expressing admiration for them—because their failings can be understood as an unavoidable consequence of the less advanced economic stage of history in which they lived. Regarding the socialism of his own day, however, Marx derides it as "utopian socialism." Unlike Marx's "scientific socialism," other socialists succeed in providing only "fantastic pictures of the future structure of society." Many socialist thinkers are subject to gross delusions that find expression in a "modern mythology with its goddesses of Justice, Liberty, Equality and Fraternity."[31] The widespread beliefs in "equal right" and "fair distribution" are characterized by Marx as "obsolete verbal rubbish" and in great contrast to his own "realistic outlook," which is grounded in the dictates—however seemingly harsh or unfair—of the economic laws of history. The constant battle against "vulgar socialism" with its "ideological nonsense about right[s] and other trash" took up much of Marx's time and effort.[32]

Engels would remark that he and Marx had "hardly ever involved ourselves in conflicts with individual bourgeois."³³ Such conflict would be senseless, because the progress of the workers could occur "only through internal struggle, which accords with the laws of dialectical development"³⁴ and could eventually be consummated only through a violent revolutionary struggle. Instead of combating capitalists, in the current state of economic history it was necessary to fight a different battle. Engels remarked that he and Marx had "fought harder . . . against self-styled Socialists than against anyone else."³⁵

The Marxist themes of the fall of man; the enslaved, exploited, and alienated condition of human existence; the self-deceiving quality of human reason; government as a coercive measure made necessary by human depravity; the attacks on false humanitarian sentimentality; the need for a fundamental revolution in human existence; final salvation by a predestined act outside human control—in all these and still further outlooks and attitudes, Marx was a close descendent of Martin Luther.

Marx was, of course, raised in the Protestant Germany of Luther.³⁶ His father, while Jewish by birth, had become a baptized Lutheran in good standing. Marx was thus an heir both to the theological heritage of Luther and to the messianic tradition of Judaism.³⁷ This confluence of forces yielded in the fertile religious climate of the nineteenth century yet another momentous Jewish messiah and protestor of history, Karl Marx.

The many remarkable parallels between Marx and Luther extend beyond their theology to their personal characters, economic attitudes, and actual social impacts—many of them unintended. Tawney writes of Luther's personality in terms of "capricious volcano," "impetuous," "fury," "little mercy," and "dogmatic."³⁸ It was Luther who had denounced "the murdering thievous hordes of peasants" who dared to depart from his own revolutionary prescriptions. Luther suggested that the appropriate disciplinary action was for the authorities to "stab, smite and slay all you can."³⁹ A contemporary of Marx said of him that "I have never seen a man whose bearing was so provoking and intolerable. . . . Everyone who contradicted him he treated with abject contempt."⁴⁰ The resemblance between the two protestors was apparent to contemporaries, one of whom warned Marx against following the example of his "compatriot Luther."⁴¹

Marx and Luther reacted similarly to the common economic circumstances in which they found themselves—periods of rapid economic growth and emerging capitalism. Tawney's characterization of Luther is no less true of Marx: "It was this doctrine that all things have their price . . . which gave their most powerful argument to the reformers. . . . Luther, who hated the economic individualism of the age not less than its spiritual laxity, is the supreme example."[42]

For Luther (no less than for Marx), the social institutions and culture of his time are the works of alienated men, and thus must inevitably be flawed and delusory. As Tawney describes his outlook, Luther felt an alienation from a "society of men" that he perceived as a "chaos of brute matter, a wilderness of dried bones, a desert unsanctified and incapable of contributing to sanctification." The common outlook of Luther and Marx is also illustrated by their shared contempt for the law. Luther speaks of "the tedious, stale, forbidding ways of custom, law and statute." His attitude was often one of "contemptuous dismissal of law and learning" and that "the world of institutions and law [is] alien to that of the spirit." Luther repudiates the entire "visible and institutional framework" of the medieval Roman Catholic church.[43] As Isaiah Berlin comments, Marx is no less dismissive in his time with respect to the "ideas, values, laws, habits of life, institutions . . . the whole purpose of which is to prop up, explain away, defend . . . privileged, unnatural, and therefore unjustified, status and power."[44]

Luther and Marx share a contempt for disinterested intellectuals, who value thought above action. Tillich comments that ever since Luther's harsh attacks on Erasmus there has been "a break between Protestantism and humanism which has not been healed to the present time." In the case of Luther, he "could not stand Erasmus' . . . lack of passion towards the religious content, his detached scholarly attitude towards the contents of the Christian faith."[45] Marx had a similar attitude toward the contemplative intellectuals of his time. His gravestone in Highgate Cemetery in London contains this epitaph: "The philosophers have only interpreted the world in various ways. The point, however, is to change it."

Luther and Marx have what must seem to the Roman tradition in many ways a deeply pessimistic outlook. Life is tragic, not fair—at least until God or history one day intervenes. Luther attacks the comforting reassurances of the Roman Catholic church that persons of virtuous behavior can contribute to their own salvation—that salvation can be influenced by good works. The same criticism is found in Marx's denunciations of the "utopian" socialists of his time, regarding them as persons who are too weak and too lacking in courage to confront the harsher realities of human existence. The monastic orders, charitable practices, and other institutions of the medieval Roman Catholic church are all condemned by Luther in a style of attack that

Marx almost seems to emulate three centuries later in denouncing the institutions of bourgeois society.

Luther and Marx are each preachers of a fundamentally ascetic attitude toward life. The pleasures of this world undermine for Luther the commitment to a life devoted to God, while for Marx they undermine the commitment to a revolutionary fulfillment of history. For both, the utilitarian attitude is the antithesis of the deepest religious sensibility, which involves self-sacrifice and immersion in a cause. Luther and Marx both see the highest calling of mankind in labor. In a depraved world, the act of producing, which is at least good for the soul, exceeds in moral standing the act of consuming. Anticipating the Marxist view that mankind must look to the workers for its salvation, Luther believes that "the labor of the craftsman is honorable, for he serves the community in his calling; the honest smith or shoemaker is a priest."[46]

By contrast, it was not only Marx but Luther as well who believed, as Tawney comments, that "international trade, banking and credit, capitalist industry, the whole complex of economic forces . . . belong in their essence to the kingdom of darkness." Luther's theology seeks "rules of good conscience in economic matters," which will require "an immense effort of simplification," the result of "a tragic struggle which results between spirit and letter, form and matter, grace and works."[47]

Tawney finds in Luther "the father of all later revolutions."[48] Karl Popper attributes to Marx a "moral reformation" that, in its impact on the modern age, may be "compared with Luther's influence on the Roman Church."[49] Marx would be a major prophet of the Protestant church of Darwin, promoting a second great reformation—now in a secular and Darwinist dress.

The social consequences of Luther's efforts were remarkably similar to the historical role that has been played by Marxism in the twentieth century—in many ways regrettably so. Luther and Marx were both vague about what should replace the established institutions that they sought to overthrow. Partly because there were no plans, whenever a revolution actually occurred there was a great vacuum that in each case turned out to be filled frequently by the powers of the state. Lutheran and other Protestant faiths became the state religions of petty tyrants throughout newly Protestant Europe. In the twentieth century, the Marxist faithful of Russia, China and other countries throughout the world ripped apart the social bonds of quasi-feudal societies. Marxism thereby paved the way for the ruthless exercise of power by newly powerful modern tyrants. In both the Lutheran and Marxist cases, men more attuned to a new age often did in fact assume the reins of power. This came at the cost, however, of destroying restraints and protections that had existed in the customs and traditions of the previous society.

By undermining the unity of Europe and letting loose new religious hatreds, Luther set the continent on a path to religious warfare, culminating in the disasters of the Thirty Years' War in the first half of the seventeenth century. Now, Marx, Spencer, and other leading figures of a second reformation would again set Europe on a path to a new thirty-year war, experienced this time in the first half of the twentieth century. Conflicts among Marxist, fascist, and other followers of modern economic theologies helped to spur the twentieth-century wars of religion. The modern wars were in fact consistent with and often justified by the Darwinist vision of a world of unremitting competitive struggle, battle to the finish, and survival of the fittest. In bestowing a religious sanction on the law of the jungle, the new economic theologies of the age of Darwin bear much of the responsibility for the calamitous results.

Although the basic content of Marxism was worked out well before the publication of Darwin's theory of evolution, the first volume of Marx's most famous book, *Capital,* appeared eight years after *The Origin of Species.* In his own view, Marx regarded himself as a follower in the path of Darwin. In *Capital,* Marx sought to do for social evolution what Darwin had just accomplished for the natural order—to examine systematically and in great detail the workings of the evolutionary process. Marx even wrote to Darwin proposing that *Capital* should be dedicated to him, although Darwin declined the offer. The Marxist interpretation of history did in fact bear a remarkable resemblance to the meaning of history found by Darwin. Millions of followers would invest Marxism with all the authority of modern science—much as many social thinkers of the Enlightenment had the authority of Newton bestowed on them. At Marx's funeral in 1883, Engels eulogized that

> Just as Darwin discovered the law of the evolution of organic nature, so Marx discovered the evolutionary law of human history—the simple fact, hitherto hidden under ideological overgrowths, that above all things men must eat, drink, dress, and find shelter before they can give themselves to politics, science, or religion or anything else, and that therefore the production of the material necessaries of life and the corresponding stage

of the economic evolution of a people or a period provides a foundation upon which the national institutions, legal systems, art and even the religious ideas of the people in question have been built, and upon which, therefore, their explanation must be based.[50]

Marxism thus is a religion that denies the significance of religion. Paradoxically, there is no better testimony to the contrary view than the history of Marxism itself. Further, Marxism as a religion has fundamentally conservative aims—conservative in the sense of issuing a moral condemnation with respect to the economic impacts of industrial advance, the rapid spread of new technologies, and other consequences of modernization. If Marx in some measure legitimized these consequences as a necessary economic stage of history, it was nevertheless a stage to be escaped as soon as possible. Moreover, the future sought by Marx was not a projection of existing modern trends, but a call for the reversal of these trends in order to discover a more innocent and natural existence. It was in truth a call for the recovery of the natural harmony of original creation in the Garden of Eden.

Yet another paradox of Marxism is that, despite its fundamentally negative view with respect to modern developments, the actual effects of Marxism have in many cases been to accelerate the forces of modernization. This is a paradox frequently noted with respect to the Protestant Reformation of Luther as well—the acceleration of change despite the Protestant wish to return to the innocence of the distant past. Marxism has in practice overthrown ruling aristocracies, large landowners, business elites, and other wealthy and privileged groups. In this respect it has often advanced—at least initially—egalitarian trends of the modern age. The heirs to Marxism often turned to large bureaucracies and to scientific planning and management as the necessary instruments of managing a communist state in which private ownership has been largely abolished. Although Marxism has advanced such trends in many parts of the world, these results were not the real aim of Marx. Indeed, Marx would very likely have renounced many of the twentieth-century consequences of Marxism, perhaps even seeing in them an inferior and debased relative of capitalism.

In short, the theology of Marx himself must be sharply distinguished from the preachings of his Marxist successors and from the actual results achieved when Marxists have assumed power in the twentieth century. Marx must bear significant responsibility for the twentieth-century consequences of his message, but for indirect reasons—not because he sought these consequences himself. If Marx was seeking to show the path to heaven on earth, his efforts have instead served to demonstrate that a misconceived theology can yield (for some at least) a hell on earth.

Given the Marxist interpretation of history, it has often been considered something of a mystery that Marxism should have achieved its first great successes in Russia—among the most feudal and economically backward nations of Europe. How could a whole economic stage of history—supposedly an iron necessity of Marxism—have been skipped over? Understood theologically, however, what happened is less mysterious. In Marxism, Russian intellectuals could find a new faith that was superficially modern and scientific yet in fact appealed to a long-standing Russian skepticism with respect to rapid technological change, industrial advance, and other Western developments. If the market, competition, efficiency, and other elements of economic progress provoked in the Russian population a deep ambivalence (as they still do today), Russians discovered in Marx a man whose message expressed a similar and thus congenial ambivalence.[51]

By contrast, of all nations the United States welcomed the forces of modernization and economic transformation most openly. Marxism was therefore likely to have little appeal in the United States, as events would show. Instead, it was in the form of the evolutionary theories of Herbert Spencer that the Protestant church of Darwin would achieve its greatest successes in America.

Herbert Spencer: Heir to John Calvin

Herbert Spencer is seldom read today, and most contemporary economists know little about him. He is, nevertheless, a central figure in the history of economic thought. Over much of the world in the late nineteenth century, Spencer was regarded as among the foremost philosophers, easily surpassing Marx in reputation and visibility. Spencer's philosophy of social Darwinism became the public philosophy of the United States for several decades. As late as 1905, Justice Oliver Wendell Holmes felt it necessary to remind his colleagues that the U.S. Supreme Court had not been created to implement the theories of Herbert Spencer.[52]

While Marxism appealed to economically backward and less modern societies, Spencer was received with the greatest enthusiasm in the most economically advanced nations, especially England and the United States. Leading U.S. industrialists such as James J. Hill,

Andrew Carnegie, and John D. Rockefeller declared themselves loyal followers of the gospel of Spencer. Historian Richard Hofstadter remarks that American businessmen found Spencer "congenial to their thinking"; the very framework of his thought "seemed to portray the conditions of their existence"; in Spencer they found someone who blessed "the outlook of a business civilization."[53] Spencer's message was that, left to its own devices, business would provide more and more goods and services and an ever higher standard of living, eventually attaining to a new earthly heaven. Thus, the business and commercial classes were the instrument of an economic progress that would yield the eventual salvation of mankind.

In such respects, Spencer followed not Luther, but Calvin. Calvin had similarly appealed to the citizens of Geneva, London, and other leading centers of European business and commerce; the attraction of Calvinism was greatest among the commercial classes that were most receptive to the new economic forces. Calvinism produced a spirit that, as Tawney observes, was "intensely practical" and took "acceptance of the realities of commercial practice as a starting-point." The effect of Calvinist theology was to grant "admission to a new position of respectability of a powerful and growing body of social interests." For these interests Calvinism "taught them to feel that they were a chosen people, made them conscious of their great destiny in the Providential plan and resolute to realize it."[54] Much the same types of people 300 years later would find the message of Spencer very congenial.

The theologies of Luther and Calvin, despite their much different appeals, had a common core that reflected basic tenets of the Protestant Reformation. Spencer and Marx are known to history as proponents of diametrically opposing economic systems—Spencer of laissez-faire capitalism and Marx of communal ownership of all resources through the instrument of the state. Nevertheless, the bitter conflicts between capitalism and communism have obscured a common theological core. Spencer and Marx are coreligionists no less than Luther and Calvin—both members of the church of Darwin, both understanding the world in terms of the evolutionary laws of history. For both, the decisive elements in history are found in economics. For Spencer as well as for Marx, economics provides the central meaning and direction to human existence. For both, in short, economic forces assume the very role of the divine.

Spencer and Marx furthermore agree in seeing history as a process of stages. Starting from a primitive natural existence, the forces of social evolution bring men together into organized society. Spencer finds the earliest stages of social organization to be characterized by military concerns and political relationships based on social status— qualities still found, for instance, in medieval feudalism. Evolutionary forces then yield the next major stage in Spencer's interpretation of history: the industrial state, which is characterized by economic concerns and relations among individuals based on contract. The emergence of capitalism is, for Spencer as well as for Marx, the result of the economic workings of history.

Spencer hardly had a rosy view of human existence in a capitalist world. He observes that capitalism is itself a "state of transition" that must be "an unhappy state." Men are surrounded by "all these evils, which afflict us." In the current stage of capitalism, "misery inevitably results from incongruity between constitution and conditions." The laws of social evolution mean for Spencer that "humanity is being pressed against the inexorable necessities of its new position—is being molded into harmony with them, and has to bear the resulting unhappiness as best it can." This is a characterization with which Marx would have found little fault.[55]

It is not only the poor who suffer in the capitalism described by Spencer; the competitive struggle requires constant vigilance and discipline throughout society. There is little place for the enjoyment of the good life. Instead, life is lived for hard labor and productive accomplishment, even among those blessed with the greatest advantages. Spencer's followers in the United States, as Hofstadter observes, were "much concerned to face up to the hardness of life, to the impossibility of finding easy solutions to human ills, to the necessity of labor and self-denial and the inevitability of suffering."[56]

There is, however, hope for a better future. Indeed, as Spencer prophesies, the laws of social evolution decree that mankind is on a course of "progress towards a form of being capable of a happiness undiminished by these drawbacks." There is a heavenly concluding point to evolutionary progress and "it is in the human race that the consummation is to be accomplished." It is thus foreordained that "the well being of existing humanity, and the unfolding of it into this ultimate perfection, are both secured by that same beneficent, though severe discipline, to which the animate creation at large is subject . . . a felicity-pursuing law which never swerves" from its course.[57]

Thus, as foreseen by Spencer, a future perfection on earth will be the final outcome—indeed, little different from the final destiny prophesied by Marx. For Spencer as well, the evolutionary struggle will cease; the behavior of men will become more loving and generous, in harmony with true nature; and material abundance will render possessions of private property superfluous. In the promised land of both Spencer and Marx, the fall of man from the Garden of Eden is to be reversed, the coercive power of the state will wither away and individual behavior will be motivated by altruistic concerns. All this follows scientifically from the evolutionary workings of the Darwinian forces of economic history.

Marxism is, however, a theology of the apocalypse. History will reach a climax—heaven will arrive on earth—at the moment of a grand and final cataclysmic struggle between the agents of capitalism and the working class. For Spencer, the attainment of a heavenly state on earth occurs through a gradual evolutionary process. This is an issue that has in fact long divided Christianity as well—some theologians ("post-millennialists") believing that the millennium is already arriving gradually; others that it will come in a sudden and short-lived future burst of divine intervention.

Although the stages of evolutionary progress are similar in Marxism and Spencerianism, the social group that serves as the chief instrument of salvation differs sharply. Marx portrays the workers as the vanguard of history, the class whose actions are responsible for bringing on the millennium. For Spencer, it is the business and commercial classes who have the decisive saving role. This particular difference would have a powerful effect in determining the particular social groups to whom Marx and Spencer would appeal.

The economic forces of history impose demands that in Spencer's message are no less impersonal and commanding of obedience than the economic forces described by Marx. The competitive laws of survival of the fittest decree, and men must simply obey. Hence, as Spencer believes, "the conscious control of societal evolution" is "an absolute impossibility, and . . . the best that organized knowledge can do is to teach men to submit more readily to the dynamic factors in progress." The products of human reason can at best be a "lubricant, . . . not a motive power in progress: it [knowledge] can grease the wheels and prevent friction but cannot keep the engine moving."[58] There exists a deeper reality to life—controlled by underlying economic factors—that is beyond influence through government programs and policies or other exercises of rational planning.

Nevertheless, as Spencer finds, there are many men who believe that "by due skill an ill-working humanity may be framed into well-working institutions." But this optimism is "a delusion." For Spencer, "no political alchemy" is possible; progress can be attained only through following unalterable economic commands. If men should stray too far from this path, their punishment will be severe; they will fall into an earthly hell of "grinding tyranny," "despotism," and "enslavement" under the hand of oppressive government—in all likelihood under a socialist government offering the false (if tempting) path of a rational design for progress.[59]

All manner of social reform is thus rejected by Spencer. He opposes even public education and public health measures as undermining the workings of the survival of the fittest. In Spencer's dark view, if men are not sufficiently capable to live without government assistance, then the laws of social evolution decree that "they die, and it is best they should die."[60] Although there are many men "who have not the nerve to look this matter fairly in the face," by their very weakness and lack of courage they endanger the future progress of humanity.[61] The illusory superstructure of religion, ideology, and other false beliefs that Marx speaks of becomes in Spencer the numerous delusions involving government plans for social reform. The minds of "political enthusiasts and fanatical revolutionaries" are always active, but by their efforts to devise new government programs and other social improvements they merely "bequeath to posterity a continually increasing curse."[62] For both Spencer and Marx, the exercise of human reason can at best marginally alter a short-run course that has already been determined in the long run. Spencer thus shares with Marx a dismissal of socialist and other humanitarian reformers of the day. For both, humanitarian measures are likely to be counterproductive, undermining the economic laws of history and hindering the long-run evolutionary advance.

Since the laws of economics take the place of God in the theologies of both Spencer and Marx, to follow an economic imperative is to obey a divine command. The difference between good and evil follows directly. The operative standard of good is whether a specific action can be said to advance the evolutionary direction of economic laws. Conversely, evil is to be recognized as an action whose consequences will act to obstruct the laws of history. All these elements—the laws of history beyond human influence, the distrust of the powers of reason, the necessity of current human misery, the scorn for rationally devised reforms, the antagonism to humanitarian measures, the rejection of good intentions—are not only common to Spencer and Marx, but are characteristic outlooks of the Protestant tradition.

Moreover, such beliefs follow from the very framework of Darwinist thought. When Darwin showed that an evolutionary understanding can be applied to all the plant and animal world, it seemed to confirm for many that the correct interpretation of human existence must certainly be Darwinist. The resulting view of man and history was radically altered from the optimistic rationalism of the Enlightenment. If the first Protestant Reformation of Luther and Calvin had been directed against the medieval Roman Catholic church, the second reformation of Marx and Spencer would make the Roman church of Newton the object of its scathing attacks.

The ties between Calvin and Spencer extend well beyond their common theological encouragement of (and granting of legitimacy to) the world of business. Spencer preached that it is the rich who are the agents of forward advance in history. The economically successful members of society thus are, as one twentieth-century commentator explains, "the elite, the saints of the new religion" of social Darwinism. Successful industrialists, merchants, and other businessmen "had proved their native superiority by their survival value. This will be recognized as the Puritan [and Calvinist] idea of 'election' in modern dress."[63]

For both Spencer and Calvin, the poor—by their failings—give strong evidence of having sinned. For Calvin, hell lay in store in the hereafter for the wicked of this earth. Spencer's intended destiny for the poor is a virtual hell right here on earth. Society is for Spencer filled with "unhealthy, imbecile, slow, vacillating, faithless members." The existence of these depraved individuals calls for a "purifying process" by which "the multiplication of its inferior samples is prevented." Men must look to the "same beneficence which brings to earthly graves the children of diseased parents, and singles out the low-spirited, the intemperate, and the debilitated as the victims of an epidemic."[64]

Moreover, any attempt to make earthly existence less oppressive is both unwise and futile. Spencer thus writes that there is "bound up with the change [of progress] a normal amount of suffering, which cannot be lessened without altering the very laws of life." Moreover, as fear of eternal damnation once induced men to respect the laws of God, the fear of an earthly hell is now a necessary element in making men comply with the laws of economic progress. The adoption of ameliorative measures such as the poor laws merely "further retards" the evolutionary advance of mankind "by checking the production of commodities, and indirectly by causing a retrogression of character, which painful discipline must at some future day make good."[65]

Tawney observed of Calvin that "the basis of his whole scheme was the duty of industry and the danger of relaxing the incentive to work."[66] Indeed, the way of life favored by Calvin is essentially that of Spencer. As Tillich comments, for Calvin the "summary of the Christian life is self-denial." Calvinist theology yields an "inner-worldly asceticism" that produces an attitude of "sobriety, chastity and temperance" and of "profit through work." Much like Spencer 300 years later, the result is steady human progress by rational discipline and control: "For Calvin the Christian life is a line going upward, exercised in methodical stages."[67] Hofstadter would comment with respect to the American followers of Spencer that "theirs is a kind of naturalistic Calvinism in which man's relation to nature is as hard and demanding as man's relation to God under the Calvinistic system."[68]

As in Calvinist theology, Spencer's beliefs yield a paradoxical understanding of the role of reason in human affairs. The humanity of Spencer no less than Calvin has fallen into sin. Spencer writes of "the love of power, the selfishness, the injustice, the untruthfulness" of the men of his time and that "with the existing defects of human nature, many evils can only be thrust out of one place or form into another place or form—often being increased by the change."[69] Yet, Spencer urged a fierce discipline and rational intelligence on the part of his followers. Anything less would be dangerous in a harsh world where only the fittest will survive. Thus, like Calvin, Spencer offers a theological message of fallen, futile, and diverted reason; yet this message serves in practice to create a highly rational outlook among those who turn to social Darwinism for the explanation of their existence.

On the surface, Calvin and Spencer differ sharply in one key respect. Spencer is the most prominent libertarian in the history of economic thought—a man once described as having a "lifelong maniacal hatred of state power."[70] Calvin, by contrast, saw the necessity of a comprehensive system of social control. Yet, even here, Spencer is in some sense an heir to Calvin. In the Protestant theology of Calvin, men must have the freedom to determine their relationship with God by themselves and without the church as an intermediary. Now in the gospel of Spencer, men must be free to make their own contribution in their own way to economic progress. For Spencer the route of economic progress is the very path to salvation. The individualism of Calvinism in the relationship of man with God thus becomes in a secular dress the message of laissez-faire economics and Spencer's right of the individual to pursue economic progress as he or she sees fit.

In the popular mind of late nineteenth-century America, it was

Spencer—and not Adam Smith—who provided the leading statement
of laissez-faire economics. Most professional economists, however,
continued even then to look to Adam Smith and the classical liberal
heritage—although Thorstein Veblen would remark in 1900 that there
were important ways in which many of the "later economists of the
classical line are prone to be Spencerians."[71] Free-market economics
today almost entirely neglects Spencer. The economic faith of the
twentieth-century welfare state is a rationalist faith of the Roman
tradition. The pessimism, alienation from reason, and general harshness of the Protestant tradition are far from the characteristic outlook
of the welfare state. By contrast, one observer has written of "the
wonderful world of Adam Smith," a place much more attractive to
contemporary sensibilities.[72]

Nevertheless, Spencer played a prominent part in the development
of modern economic theology. Many of the most important events in
the development of the large business corporation and of the industrial
system of the twentieth-century owe a large debt to Spencer. It was
above all the economic gospel according to Spencer that blessed these
events with theological legitimacy in the late nineteenth and early
twentieth centuries.

By the mid-twentieth century, the social Darwinism of Spencer lay
buried beneath the wreckage of two world wars, Nazi atrocities in the
name of a competitive struggle, and other strong suggestions that a
Darwinist world of the survival of the fittest might be unfit for human
existence. The torch of Protestant individualism would now pass to a
third key figure: Sigmund Freud. Freud is best known to the world as
the founder of the science of psychoanalysis.[73] However, Freud's
diagnostic skills and curative powers as a doctor of mental health may
in the end be rated by history as well below his influence on political
and economic affairs. Freud was fundamentally concerned with this
question: How do instinctively aggressive and self-gratifying men adapt
to the necessity of living together in a society that necessarily imposes
significant restraints? The proper relationship of the individual and
society is a matter central not only to psychology, but to politics and
economics as well.

Sigmund Freud: Modern Prophet of Puritan Individualism

From the standpoint of a valid Darwinist science, there were grave
flaws in both Marx and Spencer. The role of Freud would be to rectify

these flaws through a radical recasting of evolutionary thought. For instance, in nature the mechanism of selection of the fittest is worked out through a gradual process of trial and error. There was no place in Darwin's world for the sudden and cataclysmic overwhelming by one species of all others, as Marx had prophesied for the proletariat. Even if a spontaneous rise to dominance of this kind might be biologically possible, there must be a specific mechanism explained or at least postulated to account for the sudden creation of dramatically improved competitive qualities in the dominant species. Such a mechanism, however, is nowhere to be found in Marx's vision.

The social philosophy of Spencer might seem on the surface to be closer to a valid Darwinist science. Yet, Spencer's theories grounded evolution in the world of economics, whereas in a valid Darwinism evolution should be grounded in the biological world. Survival of the fittest does not necessarily mean survival of the richest. Rather, it would have to mean in the long run precisely those species and those individuals that are most successful in passing on their genetic inheritance. A man who skips marriage and family—living in monklike asceticism but totally committed to business and commerce—could well be a Spencerian triumph and yet a reproductive and thus evolutionary failure. Perhaps men (if not women) might better pursue their long-run survival in a Darwinist world by seeking to maximize the number of reproductive acts. The larger the number of children begotten by a man, the greater will be the chance that his genes survive in history. Indeed, such a form of success would maximize his part in the survival of his species and, in this way, in the evolutionary progress of mankind. If for Marx it was the mass of proletariat, and for Spencer it was the corps of successful businessmen that had been the elect class of history, now in a valid Darwinist science there might have to be a new elect group—the most successful reproducers and thus genetic survivors.

It followed, therefore, that in a Darwinist science of human behavior the force most favored in nature should be a sexual force. It would be contrary to nature—indeed, would defeat the very survival of the species—that the pursuit of this basic drive should not yield pleasure. Hence, a vital source of happiness would have to be found in the release of sexual energy. Since this is also the act by which the new elect of history may be determined, it would follow that survival, happiness, and salvation may all be bound together in the sexual act. It is a familiar formula—modified here merely by the substitution of reproductive success for economic success, and the replacement of sexual energy for economic self-interest as the basic motivating force in nature. Freud becomes in this respect a twentieth-century follower in the footsteps of many earlier economists.

The expression of sexual urges, like the pursuit of the economic motive of self-interest, is a social act that is necessarily subject to social constraints. No one man can be the father of all children, just as no one man can possess all wealth. Thus, sexual acts must occur in a social system in which men can compete with one another within acceptable bounds to maximize the opportunity to procreate. If the field of economics was created to study the competition of individuals pursuing their economic self-interest, a new form of social competition would now in a Darwinist world be more fundamental to the laws of society. The science of Adam Smith and of Spencer would have to give way to a new science based on a more fundamental motive for competitive human behavior: the sexual motive. In short, the central place of economics in modern thought would have to be superceded by the science of psychology of Sigmund Freud—as many followers of Freud in fact do believe.[74]

The starting point for Freud was, as he would later write, a recognition that "love strives after objects, and its chief function, favored in every way by nature, is the preservation of the species." Freud therefore "introduced the term 'libido' " in order to "denote the energy" and the expression of "instincts" associated with the drive to reproduce and thereby to preserve the species. For Freud, it was only natural that for each man "sexual (genital) love afforded him the strongest experiences of satisfaction, and in fact provided him with a prototype of all happiness." A man would find it necessary "to seek the satisfaction of happiness in his life along the path of sexual relations and that he should make genital eroticism the central point in his life."[75]

In a competitive world, however, there is always a possibility that an attempt to release sexual energy will have painful results when "a stronger person will show his superiority in the form of punishment." Freud's early psychoanalytical studies viewed neurosis as "the outcome of a struggle between the interest of self-preservation and the demands of the libido, a struggle in which the ego had been victorious but at the price of severe sufferings and renunciations." The need to limit sexual competition among men was seen as explaining much of the character of social institutions. Later in his studies, Freud would direct more of his attention to the many ways in which "civilization has to use its utmost efforts in order to set limits to man's aggressive instincts and to hold the manifestations of them in check."[76]

The underlying internal system that regulates the reconciliation of competing individual psychic needs is often described by Freud in economic terms. He thus writes that "happiness . . . is a problem of the economics of the individual's libido." A successful psychic life consists of a "balance of power" among the parts of the mind, requiring negotiations and mutual accommodations. In some cases "a great economic disadvantage" can occur when the superego becomes too powerful—thereby causing psychological stresses and strains. Similarly, society is filled with sexual and other instinctual demands and the guiding principle in "civilization is obeying the laws of economic necessity" in fulfilling these diverse needs.[77]

It has often been observed that, despite all Freud's emphasis on sexual expression, his own life had a Puritan quality. Freud's economic model of the workings of the mind is one of these ways in which he exhibits a Puritan strain of thought. Taking a mechanical view of social interactions, the Puritans also conceived of life as a series of contracts. A Puritan has a contract ("covenant") with God, a contract with his church, a contract with his nation—leading some to characterize Puritanism as a "spiritual commercialism."[78] This contractual and commercial outlook extended to the workings of the mind as well, where the Puritans saw good and bad impulses, good and bad thoughts, all contending and seeking to work out a tenuous balance.

Michael Walzer explains that the Puritan personality is preoccupied with an "endless struggle with the devil"—whose modern namesake becomes the "irrational." The Puritan feels beset by emotions over which he has only a tenuous control; his life is an "experience of 'unsettledness' " that causes the Puritan to feel "anxious, depressed, unable to work, given to fantasies of demons, morbid introspection, or fearful daydreams." The Puritan faithful were taught that the means of dealing with this life requires "willfulness, calculation, nerve, and perhaps above all an anxious, introspective discipline and self-control—requiring that is, a conscience such as Calvinism supplied to its [Puritan] saints." All this was reflected in the Puritans' desire that they should become "masters of themselves," an effort "accompanied by painstaking introspection." These Puritan efforts and introspection were necessary because that Puritans "saw the self as a divided being, spirit at war with flesh"—over which "they sought control and government."[79]

Thus, Freudianism later embodies a kind of secular Puritanism. The

Puritan world of the flesh becomes the aggressive and unruly sexual instincts of the Freudian id. For both the Puritan and the Freudian, these instincts are ever threatening to get out of rational control. The Puritan response, like that of Freud, is introspective self-mastery. This process for the Puritan requires an understanding that the internal battleground of the mind is part of God's purposeful design. The Freudian sees his internal anxieties as a manifestation of a new divine will: the scientific laws discovered by Freud of the evolution of the psyche.

Life is a great testing ground of will and character to determine whether the Puritan faithful are going to retain their trust in God, resist the temptations of sin and the Devil, and learn to subdue the impulses they find within themselves. Life similarly tests the faith of Freud's followers in the laws of psychic development and their ability to achieve self-mastery. The Puritans and Freud both find that there is much to be said for a life of hard work. It is a means by which dangerous urges can be brought under greater control—the relieving of a sense of "sinfulness" in the Puritan scheme; the "sublimating" of unruly sexual urges in the Freudian understanding. In short, if Marx is the descendent of Luther, and Spencer follows closely after Calvin, Freud is a modern heir of the Puritans.

A revival of the characteristic Puritan outlook in a secular dress is of no small significance for modern economic theology. It will be recalled that the Puritan "revolution of the saints" was a political and economic as much as a theological revolution. The Puritans did not limit their introspection, self-understanding, and intellectual discipline to their inner thoughts. Their attitudes of critical scrutiny were extended to society, as well. When they did so, it resulted among the Puritans in a "fierce antagonism to the traditional world" and "radical social criticism." Repelled by what they saw as the moral decay of the society around them, the Puritans assumed an "activist role . . . in the creation and maintenance of a new moral order."[80]

Puritanism became a decisive force in England in completing the overthrow of a medieval and Roman Catholic heritage that had been altered but not fully discarded by the Anglican church. The radical new social vision of the Puritans provided a critical justification for ideas of individual liberty and of government based on social contract. It "opened the way to . . . impersonal commitments among men"—a system in which the Puritan affinity for formal contracts replaced the old feudal system of less formal social understandings.[81] As translated to a modern language by John Locke, Puritan individualism played a major role in shaping the economic prescriptions of Adam Smith and later of Spencer.

Freud was primarily concerned to probe the workings of the individual psyche. In most cases he accepted the constraints of civilization as a given—the necessary rules of social interaction that were required to prevent what would otherwise be intolerable discord in society. The psychological problem was how best to adapt to a hard social reality. Yet, as was the case for Puritan theology, there were potentially radical implications contained within Freud's outlook. Different civilizations had different rules for managing human interaction, some potentially more successful than others—perhaps capable of achieving a greater overall level of social happiness. If so, why not change the social rules, rather than persist in a more stressful accommodation of individuals to poorly conceived rules?

Freud thus writes in *Civilization and Its Discontents* that "some civilizations, or some epochs of civilization . . . have become 'neurotic.' " It may be possible to develop a "pathology of cultural communities" that will yield prescriptive measures for removing less healthy tendencies in society. Indeed, with respect to our own Western civilization, Freud finds that "it is impossible to overlook the extent to which civilization is built up upon a renunciation of instinct, how much it presupposes precisely the non-satisfaction . . . of powerful instincts." Due to the workings of guilt, conscience, and the super-ego, "the price we pay for our advance in civilization is a loss of happiness."[82]

There is, moreover, still another deeply subversive message contained in the Freudian theory. The internal restraints of religion, morality, and culture are seen by Freud as subjective; they are no more than particular devices by which a civilization seeks to reconcile individual drives for sexual gratification with the hard social reality that not all urges can be satisfied at all times. But if social arrangements and beliefs lack objective validity, they could just as well be changed, depending on the specific advantage to be gained. If Freud himself had no strong inclination to follow this path, the "Freudian revolution" of the twentieth century would show that many of his disciples were much less reluctant. If Marxism was the theology of twentieth-century political revolutions, and the social Darwinism of Spencer the theology of a late nineteenth century industrial revolution, Freudianism would be the theological inspiration for a twentieth-century revolution in cultural practices.

As seen by many of Freud's disciples, a better society is not one with superior instruments for repressing instinctual drives. It is rather a society with fewer constraints on the individual—not only with respect to sexual matters, but in other respects as well. For many followers of Freud, relations among individuals must be governed by consent rather than coercion, a consent that will often take the form of a contract (if perhaps only implicit). The modern sexual revolution has a number of explanations, but its legitimacy is most of all derived from the Freudian message that individual satisfaction need be limited only by a principle of voluntary consent and avoidance of personal harm. In an earlier period, contractual relations characterized Puritan society; the Freudian revolution adapts this goal of the Puritan revolution to modern dress.

The influence of Freud gave a great boost to the many "rights" movements of the twentieth century. Women, minorities, ethnic groups, and all kinds of social groups have come to understand that past attempts to assign them a particular place in society were not based on immutable requirements or otherwise foreordained. Rather, they were changeable elements in a particular social system of repression of basic drives. Once it is recognized that the current roster of social relationships is not a given, each person is free to negotiate an individual contract that sets out the rights of each of the parties involved. This attitude leads, for example, to the understanding that marriage is no longer an indissolvable social bond. Marriage should instead last only as long as it serves the individual interests of either party to continue the contract. Modern divorce practices represent an application of the Freudian message of individual autonomy to the realm of family life.

This extension of an individualistic and contractual outlook has been occurring in other areas of society as well. The military draft was once a shared social obligation, but today military service has become instead a labor market contract. The deregulation movement represented a shift away from the idea that firms in the transportation, communications, and other industries are part of a social arrangement in which they receive government licenses to operate in return for providing important social services. Much as feudal society was one of reciprocal military and other social obligations, the holder of a broadcasting license had originally been expected to provide services in exchange for holding the license. Instead, in a deregulated world, industries operate according to the impersonal rules of contracts and market relationships.

In the relation of the citizenry with government, there is a growing tendency to regard the citizen as having individual "rights" to receive government benefits. One writer labels such individual rights to government actions as "the new property," including rights to receive benefits of welfare, pensions, farm programs, and various other government services.[83] The tendency for the relationship between citizens and government to become contractual stems partly from the declining sense of social community. For the Puritans, and now in the message of Freud as well, society is not an organic entity, but a gathering of independent individuals who join together for their mutual convenience. As the Puritan was free to work out his own relationship with God—to negotiate his own contract—so the Freudian faithful are free to discover their own values, define their own purposes in life, and to negotiate contracts and assert individual rights consistent with their individual needs.

By undermining traditional social relationships and by promoting a strongly individualistic orientation, Freud provides a new legitimacy for two elements critical to sustaining the existence of a market economy. A market is by its nature a set of impersonal relationships based on contractual agreements. The actors in a market behave not out of concern for some social good, but in their own interest as individuals. The Protestant Reformation and especially the Puritans (more so than Adam Smith) were responsible for undermining the feudal system of social bonds based on personal relationships and status. As twentieth-century scholars have noted with growing frequency, it is above all the Puritans who deserve to be known as the inspiration for modern political and economic liberties. Now a modern Puritan—Freud—is again giving legitimacy to the impersonal relationships that characterize a market. If Freud himself had little interest in or concern for market economics, and if the Freudian encouragement of market relationships was mostly inadvertent, much the same can be said of the large Puritan role in the development of the market system.

Today, there are two distinct and often opposed groups of libertarian outlook. One group—composed of cultural libertarians—advocates individual rights in divorce, sexual practices, use of artificial stimulants, and many other personal matters; the second—composed of economic libertarians—advocates individual rights to engage in business and trade, and otherwise to use property as desired. The former group looks to Freud, the latter group to Adam Smith. Yet they both owe a major debt to a Puritan ancestry.

The secular impact of the Puritan vision was enhanced in the eighteenth century by its fortuitous resemblance to the mechanistic

world of Newtonian physics. There is also a Newtonian quality to
Freud's description of the "balance of power"—like the equilibrium
of the solar system—that the psyche is always working out among the
independent claims of the id, the ego, the superego, and the forces of
an external reality.[84] Yet, as one historian of psychoanalysis has noted,
"Darwin was the great hero" for Freud in his youth, and Freud later
saw himself as a follower of Darwin.[85] Some of the basic assumptions
of Freudian thought were derived from requirements of a valid Darwinian science. Indeed, Freud's theory might be described as having a
static element composed of a Newtonian equilibrium of the forces of
the mind, but an equilibrium that follows a Darwinian course of
evolution over time.

Thus, Freud is a member in good standing of the Protestant church
of Darwin—if offering, like the Puritans, an especially individualistic
interpretation of the characteristic Protestant outlook. If the Protestant
tradition is the fomenter of the great revolutions of history, Freud can
lay claim to being such a revolutionary in cultural matters. If the
Protestant tradition sees men alienated from their reason, Freud sees
pervasive human rationalization, displacement, sublimation, transference, and other ways in which the products of rational consciousness
deeply mislead and misrepresent the underlying psychological reality.
If the Protestant tradition has a pessimistic view of a dangerous world
of fallen men, Freud is capable of writing that each man must be on
guard because other men will seek "to satisfy their aggressiveness on
him, to exploit his capacity for work without compensation, to use him
sexually without his consent, to seize his possessions, to humiliate
him, to cause him pain, to torture and to kill him."[86]

Among his fellow members in the church of Darwin, Freud is in
some ways closest to Marx. Indeed, the Freudian portrayal of the
evolution of the individual psyche could well be described as a Marxism of the mind. The Marxist laws of evolution prescribe perpetual
conflict among economic classes in society; the Freudian laws determine that there will be perpetual conflict among separate domains in
the evolution of the mind. The id, the ego, and the superego are
psychic competitors in a fierce struggle beginning in childhood and
continuing to adulthood for survival of the fittest. As noted above, the
relationships among parts of the mind are even characterized by Freud
on a number of occasions as "economic," as though these psychological relationships are really those of property holders defending their
psychic territories against challenges of acquisitive competitors, following economic laws of mental evolution.

The Freudian laws are, moreover, characterized by anal, Oedipal, and other particular psychological phenomena (a mental "superstructure") that correspond closely to each stage of personal development— as Marx found that particular laws, beliefs, government, and other institutions (a social "superstructure") must correspond to each stage of economic history. The task of psychology is to uncover the precise scientific laws of this process of mental evolution, as Marx aimed to discover the full scientific consequences of the evolutionary laws in the economic sphere.

The Freudian struggle between the id and the ego are a psychological version of the Marxist struggle between the healthy and vigorous proletariat and a rationalist and oppressive capitalist class. The internal struggle has much the same consequences for Freud and Marx: the alienation of human beings from their true nature. Freud no less than Marx sees widespread misery in the existing condition of humanity. The coercive demands of society have caused the ego and the superego to repress the basic and healthier sexual instincts of mankind, much as the capitalist class has repressed the healthier qualities of the working class. Freud thus comments at one point that "civilization behaves towards sexuality as a people or a stratum of its population does which has subjected another one to its exploitation."[87]

It is in the very nature of the Darwinist framework that the products of human thought will lack objective reality and that thinking will instead be a mere instrument in the workings of the evolutionary process. Ideas will not be objectively true or false, but will either contribute or fail to contribute to the workings of evolution. Thus, both Freud and Marx regard religion, art, morals, and other elements of culture as means rather than ends in themselves. They are not in themselves valid and permanent, but instead temporary expedients in the evolutionary process—whether this process occurs as the psychological history of an individual or as the economic history of a society. It is this common rejection of the leading beliefs and institutions of society that gives both Marxism and Freudianism their deeply revolutionary qualities. In fact, this was the single most important characteristic of the Protestant church of Darwin—a rejection of the heritage of Western civilization no less complete and no less radical than the rejection by Luther, Calvin, and the Protestant Reformation of the world of medieval Catholicism. Throughout history, the Protestant tradition has been the source of most of the great rebels and revolutionaries of the West.

In the thought of the nineteenth century, scientific laws take the place of divine commands in giving direction to history. Mankind now looks to secular histories to interpret the meaning and give the purpose of life on earth. Moreover, to contribute to history is to achieve a secular salvation. Many Marxist faithful thus faced martyrdom with an unwavering conviction of the righteousness of their cause—as Christian martyrs once did. The followers of Spencer dedicated themselves to the cause of industrial development with the zeal of monks and priests of old.

Now, Freud offers one more version of the laws of history. There is, however, a new and curious twist. The most important evolution for Freud is not in society; it is, rather, an evolution that occurs in the realm of the individual psyche. For the Freudian faithful, therefore, to contribute to history is to advance along the path of the psychological history of an individual. To be saved is to achieve a maximum individual release of sexual energy within the constraints necessarily imposed by a particular society. In a disciple of Freud such as Wilhelm Reich, these social constraints would be minimized, resulting in a theology that sees the road to personal salvation as lying in the maximization of individual orgasmic activity. If this may seem a bizarre theology, it merely carries to an extreme the nineteenth-century deification of history and then the Freudian recasting of the relevant history to the realm of individual sexual evolution. To be saved is for Freudianism to achieve a successful sexual development. If sexual acts were previously regarded as a mere source of pleasure or of reproduction, they now assume a far more exalted status. While the laws of economics take the place of God in Marxism, in the gospel of Freud it is not an economic divinity but a sexual divinity that assumes command over the affairs of men.

The view that the most important form of evolution occurs within the mind of each individual is the decisive factor in giving Freudianism its strongly individualistic character. For Freud, the individual confronts and is ultimately responsible by himself for his own psychic history and thus for his own salvation. In this respect, the theology of Freud returns to the Protestant theologies of Luther, Calvin, and the Puritans. In the Protestantism of old, salvation was by faith alone— not a matter of following rules prescribed by the church or any other body. It required achieving a proper relationship with God within the mind and soul of each individual. If Puritan individualism proved critical in setting the stage for the political and economic freedoms of the modern age, the individualism of Freudian theology has similarly become a powerful libertarian influence in the twentieth century.

Like Marx, the followers of Freud have often sought to recast his views to ameliorate the harshness of his outlook. Indeed, in the United States, Freudianism has often been interpreted as a scientific guide to human happiness. If Americans have seen science as able to solve all problems, Freud was regarded by many as the great scientist of the human mind who showed the path for the future elimination of mental suffering and distress from the world. This American understanding portrayed Freud as a virtual successor to Jeremy Bentham—as the creator of a new and much superior science of individual utility. Without such a recasting, the success of Freudian psychology would have been unlikely in a nation characterized by a great optimism and faith in reason. Once the pessimism and other harsh elements of the Protestant tradition had been removed, however, the individualistic quality of the Freudian message made for a strong appeal in the United States. If Freud carried forth the banner of Puritan individualism into the twentieth century, the United States had long been influenced by the Puritan heritage—indeed, was founded in part on an eighteenth-century understanding of a Puritan set of ideals.

The Enlightenment encouraged the individual expression of economic self-interest partly in hopes of diverting human energies from warfare into more peaceful pursuits. Freudianism with its redirection of attention to matters of sexual activity offers this same attractive hope. In this regard, it is all the more appealing to the late twentieth century, which seeks above all to avoid a recurrence of the disasters of religious warfare experienced in the first half of the century.

Racial Darwinism: Fomenter of Religious Warfare

Although Freud took a major step toward a valid Darwinist science of human evolution by setting his new science of psychology in the social context surrounding the human reproductive act, his theories—at least in their early formulations—were also deficient. It was a huge simplification to assume, as Freud effectively did, that strong sexual urges would yield men most likely to reproduce the largest number of offspring and thus to prevail in the evolutionary struggle. Indeed, a powerful instinct for aggression and for social dominance might be a clearer harbinger of individual reproductive success. Human sexual activity is embedded in a broader social context where the greatest sexual successes might be achieved not by those with the strongest sexual desires, but by those with the highest social skills. If so, then natural selection would work to encourage these social skills, and sensations of happiness would come to be associated with such qualities, as well as with the release of sexual energies.

Freud's analysis was deficient in another critical respect. Darwinian evolution is a competitive struggle not among individuals, but among whole species. Actions by members of a species that maximize the prospects for survival of any one individual might not necessarily enhance the evolutionary prospects for the entire species. For example, a particular species whose members in some circumstances are willing to sacrifice their lives may prove better adapted to survival as a species than another in whose members this trait is lacking. Indeed, in a Darwinist world the species whose sexual and aggressive instincts are both powerful and directed solely to individual satisfactions might soon face extinction. In short, on further examination the highly individualistic character of the Freudian outlook is not intrinsic to and is in some important ways at odds with a Darwinist framework.

Yet, from the perspective of Darwinist science Freud made a great advance in shifting the focus of evolutionary science from the economic to the reproductive and genetic arena. Ultimate evolutionary success must still lie in this domain. However, Freud's subsequent errors would have to be corrected by redirecting attention from the evolution of the individual psyche back to the evolution of social groups. Unlike Marx, however, these groups would not be identified by economic interests or have economic boundaries. They should instead be defined by common genetic interests and represent genetic communities. Indeed, in the realm of human evolution, the correct social group—the analogue to an animal species in nature—must seemingly be the racial group.

Like an animal species, a race is identified by its common genetic inheritance. Much as the process of natural selection improves the genetic qualities of a successful species in the animal world, a similar competitive process may occur among racial groups and might be expected to improve the genetic qualities of mankind. Indeed, since men no longer face effective competition from any other animal species (other than bacteria, viruses, and other causes of disease), in a Darwinist scheme perhaps the future prospects for permanent human improvement will depend on competition among races. In short, the valid Darwinian laws of history are seemingly not the Marxist laws of class conflict, the Spencerian survival of the economic fittest, or the Freudian laws of the individual psyche; apparently they must be the laws of racial evolution.

Correctly understood, the logic of Darwinist thought then further suggests that to contribute to history means to contribute to the triumph of the superior race (or races). The providential agent in human affairs would not be found in the realm of economic forces, as in Marx and Spencer, or sexual forces, as in Freud. Rather, the new God of history apparently must reside in the commands of racial competition. Salvation would not assume an economic or sexual character, but would be achieved by membership in a superior race of history, the collective "elect" of such a new gospel of racial Darwinism. To live the most worthwhile and moral life—to fulfill the divine purpose in history—would in this theology apparently be to dedicate oneself to the evolutionary triumph of the elect races of history.

Pursuing the theological logic still further, it would be contrary to the laws of history to mix the genes of a superior race with an inferior race. Such mixing would undermine the very evolutionary process on which the hopes for lasting human progress rest. Indeed, in this view, evolutionary progress calls for the purification of the superior race, in order that its genes might be isolated. Once a pure racial stock of superior men is attained, the very salvation of humanity depends on rapid breeding of this race. Its mission in history would be to populate the entire world, perhaps along with other superior races, and thereby to move toward a heaven on earth in the only permanent way possible—through a transformation of the genetic characteristics of the human population of the earth.

However repellant today, beliefs of this kind were in fact widely held in Western civilization in the first half of the twentieth century. They were hardly confined to Germany. However, in Germany alone did they become a state religion, establishing a modern theocracy of racial Darwinism.[88] Germany was, moreover, the most advanced scientific nation in the world. If Darwin's theory of evolution carried all the authority of modern science, and if racial Darwinism was the scientifically most advanced understanding of Darwin's theory with respect to the affairs of mankind, then the Germans were prepared to live and die according to the tenets of this gospel. To do so was nothing less than to demonstrate by concrete acts a full faith in the truthfulness of science and a commitment to personal salvation by contributing to human progress according to the most advanced scientific laws of history.

If the results were not only bizarre but horrible to the rest of the world, it might be recalled that in an earlier era Germany had already launched a religious revolution—one that had destroyed the entire medieval order resting on the authority of the Roman Catholic church. Theological arguments—if in the modern age taking a secular form—seemingly carried a unique weight in Germany. If peoples of many other nations could ignore the typically convoluted reasoning, weak logic, inadequate explanations, and other defects of conventional theology, and thereby follow a course of pragmatism and common sense, Martin Luther had already demonstrated a German propensity to follow a line of theological logic to whatever conclusions might be reached.

Germany under the Nazis took racial Darwinism yet another step—a step most people would have considered entirely unthinkable. If racial evolution is the valid scientific law of history, why wait for the slow processes of natural selection to work their ways? Why not step in to weed out with scientific methods the inferior members within the German race? Why wait for superior races to emerge slowly from the mundane economic, sexual, and other struggles ordinarily occurring among men? Why not, instead, directly weed out inferior races altogether as well? Warfare among racial groups would further serve as a test of superiority—another way of advancing still more rapidly along the route of the genetic progress of mankind.

In the aftermath of World War II, there was a strong inclination to regard Hitler and the followers of National Socialism (the Nazi party) as a fringe band of social deviants who had somehow deceived the responsible centers of German intellectual life. More recent scholarship on Nazi Germany, however, has shown the large degree to which leading German scientists and other intellectuals paved the way for and contributed to Nazi beliefs. A recent book by Robert Proctor examines how the field of "racial hygiene" was widely taught in leading German universities in the 1920s and 1930s. One of its central figures was Fritz Lenz, who was a prominent member of the scientific establishment of Germany and also one of the authors of a book that even today is described as "a monument of scholarship and careful argumentation."[89]

Lenz argued that race is "the ultimate principle of value."[90] He held the view that "the decisive motivating force in racial hygiene" is the understanding that the "roots of most evil lie . . . in hereditary defects."[91] As described by Proctor, Lenz advocated that "the 'tragedy' of modern socialism was that its lofty ideals could never be achieved with the racial quality of present-day man. Socialist ideals could be achieved only by racial means—through selection according

to the principles of racial hygiene. . . . the only true path to socialism."[92]

It was thinking along these lines that led to scientific justifications
that there are "lives not worth living"—at first limited to the mentally
ill, the severly handicapped, the old and feeble.[93] When the Nazis
began killing such people, an American journalist wrote in 1941 that
"their death was the ultimate logic of the National Socialist doctrine
of promoting racial superiority and the survival of the physically fit."[94]
The mass extermination of Jews in the concentration camps later
evolved from the racial theories, administrative arrangements, and
facilities applied initially to destroy inferior Germans. Thus, as Proctor
writes, the "final solution" of genocide was a further "step in a
common program of racial purification." Moreover, the biomedical
community and the medical professions of Germany "played an active
role in both the theory and the practice of each phase of the Nazi
program of racial hygiene and racial destruction."[95] Another observer
similarly concluded that "German scholarship provided the ideas and
techniques which led to and justified this unparalleled slaughter."[96]

Hitler's own thinking was significantly shaped by a social Darwinist
understanding of the world. His outlook was in this respect not an
aberration, but—however horrible and unexpected the consequences—
a popularization of ideas accepted by many Western intellectuals of
the time. In reviewing the development of Hitler's thinking, as one
observer summarized matters:

> Although Hitler was concerned primarily about the struggle between
> human beings, he understood this struggle in terms of the so-called animal
> kingdom. Man is in no essential way removed from the animal nature of
> which he is part. . . . Titmouse pairs off with titmouse, finch allies with
> finch; the species are quite distinct and there is no such thing as a fox
> with humane impulses toward geese, or a cat with friendly feelings for
> mice. People should act in accordance with their nature, uninhibited by
> the false distinctions of culture and politics. Tribal instincts are to be
> nurtured, for the tribe (Race) is the only natural community. The man of
> the coming Reich would find his example in the animal world; he would
> be "Tough as leather, swift as a greyhound, hard as Krupp steel."
> Civilization has corrupted man and robbed him of his potential. . . . All
> our ills derive from our disturbance of the natural order: "God created
> peoples but not classes."
> For Hitler, war was the natural human condition.[97]

When the logic of racial Darwinism was pressed to its farthest
extremes, it yielded precepts that are abhorrent to the Judeo-Christian

heritage of the West. Yet the restraining influence of this heritage had
been severely eroded in the modern age. Indeed, aside from Newton
and Darwin, the two most powerful subverters were Marx and Freud.
If inadvertently and indirectly, both contributed significantly to the
disastrous course of events in Germany of the 1930s and 1940s. Beyond
their specific influence, the barbarities of the first half of the twentieth
century were generally exacerbated by the very framework of thought
that Darwinism advanced. Darwinism preached a meaning of human
existence in which survival becomes the only scientifically valid purpose of history. For many modern men, survival therefore became the
only valid measure of moral value. The entire heritage of Western
civilization was subject to a new scientific test; whether or not it
contributed to evolutionary success. Marx and Freud were only the
two most important of many thinkers to conclude that the most basic
beliefs and institutions of Western civilization really amount to an
elaborate superstructure of illusion. Perhaps this superstructure served
men usefully at previous stages of history, but now it was dispensable
and had no absolute authority over the future.

This rejection of the past was then invested with all the power of
religion. In the Judeo-Christian heritage, to give meaning to history is
to give the very purpose of human existence, to specify the character
of the divine intent for mankind. If an evolutionary struggle was now
seen as the true meaning of history, it would assume this authority. It
was thus not the craven self-promoters and self-seekers of the day but
the saints and priests of the new Darwinist faiths who sought liberation
from all past bonds in order to achieve the reconstruction of society,
the transformation of human existence, a future heaven on earth.

If the scientific laws of history have become in the modern age for
vast numbers of people the will of God, to advance the laws of history
is to be saved and to die for history is to be martyred. Some of the
fiercest warfare of the twentieth century was fought out between
Germany and the Soviet Union during World War II. Age-old political,
geographic, and other tensions were present as always, but they were
now inflamed by religious passions. Germany acted in the name of the
elect race of history—the newest claimant for the role of savior of
mankind. The Soviet Union acted in the name of the elect economic
class of history—a somewhat older candidate.

Religious hatred and warfare brought out the worst in mankind
before the modern era, and can hardly be considered new to history.
The new element is the power of modern technology and economic
organization, which create the potential for much greater death and

destruction. There had, for example, been previous inquisitions and mass slaughters of the Jews. None, however—even if they had tried—could have approached the consequences that modern efficiency made possible in twentieth-century Europe.

Prior to this century, the most recent outbreak of religious warfare on a comparable scale occurred in the aftermath of the Protestant Reformation. The social and economic devastation of that era eventually gave way to the Enlightenment and to a world of more rational men who engaged frequently in economic pursuits. Indeed, the development of modern economics owed much to a revulsion against the violence of religious warfare. Now, in the second half of the twentieth century, the unacceptable consequences of religious conflict would again help bring on a more rational world of economic pursuits—the world of the welfare state. Following the enormous loss of lives and property in World War II, Germany and Japan would find in their postwar economic triumphs a much preferable outlet for energies previously directed to expeditions of military conquest. Western Europe began to blur its age-old divisions and move toward a new unity within the European Economic Community. Instead of political disagreements and warfare, world trade has gradually become the leading vehicle for the interactions of men around the globe. These events were themselves a part of a worldwide retreat from the characteristic outlooks of the Protestant tradition and a turn once again to the Roman tradition.

The new world of the welfare state and of economic pursuits would have to be placed within the context of a broader understanding of the meaning and purpose of human existence. Much of the responsibility for this task would now fall to the economic theologians of the twentieth-century welfare state. The United States would for the first time assume a world leadership role—not only in matters of economic and military power, but also in the development of modern economic theology. It would be a fitting role for the United States, a nation that embodies more than any other in the world the characteristic outlooks of the Roman tradition.

Part III

The Roman Theology of the American Welfare State

Chapter 5

The Progressive Gospel of Efficiency

The United States was settled in its early years largely by members of Protestant faiths. Even today, members of the Roman Catholic church represent fewer than 30 percent of the U.S. population. Any great Roman influence in the United States thus will not be a matter of the strength of numbers. It lies instead in the fact that the way of thinking of the Roman tradition is in large degree the American way of thinking. The founding fathers were products of the Enlightenment; in this respect they held views that, although now taking a secular form, were a continuation of outlooks found widely in the theology of the late medieval Catholic church. Although the influence of medieval ideas on the development of American institutions has not been a central theme in most histories, a growing number of writers recognize this debt. The United States represents a continuation of a long tradition in Western civilization—a tradition that can be traced back through the Enlightenment to medieval theology and before then to beliefs widely held in the Rome of the ancient world.

The Roman Tradition in America

In *The Public Philosophy* (1955), Walter Lippmann stated his conviction that American public life rests on "a body of positive principles and precepts which a good citizen cannot deny or ignore." These beliefs provide the underlying public philosophy on which American

171

institutions are grounded. Without this philosophy it would be "impossible to reach intelligible and workable conceptions of popular election, majority rule, representative assemblies, free speech, loyalty, property, corporations, and voluntary associations." The key underlying ideas are to be found in the "public philosophy . . . known as natural law."[1]

This public philosophy of the United States, Lippmann reported, "was first worked out by the Stoics," and further developed by Thomas Aquinas and other medieval thinkers; it was given a new statement by Locke, and then finally was "re-enacted in the first ten amendments of the Constitution of the United States"—with respect to which "the largest part of the public philosophy was never explicitly stated."[2] As Lippmann saw matters, this core set of ideas is still important for the healthy functioning of American society in the twentieth century. The problem is that fewer Americans now believe strongly in them, and leading intellectuals often spurn them outright.

Lippmann's thinking paralleled developments in Roman Catholic theology of about the same time. The Catholic community of the United States in a sense belongs simultaneously to two churches: a secular church adhering to the "civil religion" of the United States, and an institutional Catholic church headed by the pope in Rome. How, Catholic theologians and lay thinkers now asked, can these dual faiths be reconciled? Are the Catholics of the United States perhaps fated to a permanent state of divided spiritual loyalty and inevitable theological confusion?

As developed by a leading American Catholic theologian, John Courtney Murray, the answer fortunately was no. There need be no conflict of Catholic loyalties because, as matters have turned out, the core U.S. beliefs and the core Catholic beliefs are very similar—on a number of key points, almost one and the same. Thus, Murray found (much like Lippmann), that "the American Republic" was "conceived in the tradition of natural law." The philosophy of the Bill of Rights, for example, is "tributary to the tradition of natural law." Democratic government is not a mechanical exercise but requires a "virtuous people," who understand the "ethical nature of political freedom" and that democratic government is "a spiritual and moral enterprise." To accept this outlook would be to accept important elements of "the premise of medieval society," including the conviction that "the legal order of society—that is, the state—is subject to judgment by a law that is . . . inherent in the nature of man; that the eternal reason of God is the ultimate origin of all law." Indeed, as Murray argued, the

American concept of a free people under limited government "would have satisfied the first Whig, St. Thomas Aquinas."[3]

American institutions such as the Bill of Rights are thus "the product of Christian history." Moreover, it is more a Catholic than a Protestant history. The tradition "of natural law as the basis of free and ordered political life . . . found, and still finds, its intellectual home within the Catholic Church." Hence, there is a "paradox in the fact that a nation which has (rightly or wrongly) thought of its own genius in Protestant terms should have owed its origins and the stability of its political structure to a tradition whose genius is alien to . . . certain individual-istic exigencies of Protestant religiosity." Rather than a Protestant foundation, the "American Consensus" embodies ideas and convictions that more closely reflect a "Catholic intelligence and conscience."[4]

Hence, as a commentator on Murray's writings recently observed, Americans might well look to "Catholicism [for] important insights to an effort to reclaim and extend the American proposition."[5] A similar conclusion is found in another prominent Catholic theologian of the mid-twentieth century—Jacques Maritain—who saw the American understanding of "political society" as involving "a work of reason and virtue." In *Reflections on America*, Maritain explained that the idea of the "common good," traceable as far back as Greek and Roman sources, "plays an essential part in the American consciousness."[6] George Weigel finds in Maritain a viewpoint that the civil faith of the United States is "more congruent with the political philosophy of St. Thomas Aquinas than any other."[7] Yet another contemporary Catholic writer finds that Aquinas in the *Summa Theologica* "concluded that the best form of government combined elements of monarchy, aristocracy and democracy in a manner not very different from the American arrangement of executive, judicial and legislative branches."[8]

Such views are not confined to Catholic theologians. Raised as a Lutheran, Paul Tillich was a citizen of Germany until he fled the Nazis in the 1930s. Tillich could appreciate perhaps more than most Americans the degree to which "the Enlightenment feeling that a new beginning has been inaugurated is part of the American experience." Indeed, the basic outlook of the United States has been "an almost unbroken tradition of [the] Enlightenment." By comparison with Europeans, Americans even in the twentieth century are "much more . . . dependent on the eighteenth century," partly reflecting the fact that in the United States in the nineteenth century the "romanticist reaction against the eighteenth century" had less impact. Instead, the "optimis-

tic and progressivistic attitude of the Enlightenment" has almost
always prevailed.[9]

The Enlightenment could itself draw, Tillich explained, on a "rational, empirical point of view" that had already been found in a "line
from Aristotle to Thomas Aquinas." For Aquinas, "intellect" is not
only the feature that "makes man human" but is also the feature that
"is the primary characteristic of God." The world is a "divine ground"
that has "the character of intellect." As a result, when we seek through
science and other investigations to understand the world, it offers the
hope that "we can discover God in our acts of cognition." In short,
for Aquinas "the knowledge of God, like all knowledge, must begin
with sense experience and men must reach God on this basis in terms
of rational conclusions."[10]

By contrast, Tillich regarded the Protestantism of the Reformation
period as having destroyed not only the authority of the medieval
Roman Catholic church, but also "to a certain extent reason." If the
medieval period and then the Enlightenment were ages of reason,
Tillich explains that it was the great protester Martin Luther who
"detested the idea that God has established a law between himself and
his world. . . . He wanted everything as nonrational, nonlegal as
possible, not only in the process of salvation but also in the interpretation of history and nature." If the medieval mind and then the
Enlightenment saw nature as a harmonious order grounded in the laws
of a rationally designed universe, "Luther's relationship to nature has
much more the sense of the presence of the divine, irrationally,
mystically, in everything that is."[11]

Thus, although members of Protestant faiths shaped the building of
the United States, their beliefs frequently were a long way from the
Protestantism of Luther and Calvin. Americans have been more doers
than protesters; they have not typically regarded the world as fundamentally sinful, man's condition as alienated, most men as condemned,
or humanity as subject to impersonal forces leaving men incapable of
shaping their destiny. Indeed, Americans have generally believed in
progress achieved through the application of reason, in the perfectibil-
ity of human institutions, in the rule of law, and in the fellowship and
equality of all mankind—characteristic outlooks of the Roman tradition.

American society has shown a great openness to change. History
for Americans has been the record of genuine progress—not of a fall
and retrogression from an earlier happier and better natural condition.
Partly because the United States has been so new, and its institutions

less encrusted by custom, the United States has adapted without the degree of revolutionary turmoil and social upheaval experienced in Europe. America was subject to many of the same ideas and the same social and economic forces that swept over Europe in the age of Darwin. In the end, American society was probably no less transformed. But this social transformation could be achieved in the United States on the whole within a framework of reason, gradual adjustment, and respect for law. With the exception of the Civil War, the foundations of American society were never severely threatened.

Such a comparatively peaceful transition was due in significant part to the influence of the American "civil religion"—a religion based on the Constitution and that has seen the United States as the vanguard for the progress of humanity. Moreover, progress in the United States has meant in large degree economic progress. Americans have been sure that they were on the road to material abundance and that ever higher levels of goods and services would provide the foundation for a newly harmonious and happy condition of human existence. It has been a faith particularly suited to a wealthy nation that for much of its history could offer free land, abundant natural resources, and broad economic opportunity.

If the Roman tradition exhibits attitudes of common sense, pragmatism, and moderation, these are American attitudes as well. If the good life is for the Roman tradition the proper goal on this earth, Americans again typically agree. If the Roman tradition has seen all mankind as fundamentally equal, it has been America that has opened its borders widest to the immigrants of the world, offering the opportunity to participate in the forward march of progress. Indeed, of all nations the United States in the modern age has illustrated the characteristic outlooks of this tradition better than any other.

In the mid-nineteenth century, the United States still subscribed to an individualism that was derived from the eighteenth century—an atomistic vision in which the forces of nature acting through each individual combined to yield a harmonious social order. This nineteenth-century individualism would be challenged and to a significant degree supplanted in the twentieth century by a new understanding of a proper social order: that of American progressivism. The doctrines of progressivism would provide the guiding faith for the development in the twentieth century of the American welfare state. Constituting yet another modern economic theology, American progressivism once again preached a message of salvation through economic progress. Still another Roman priesthood, the members of the U.S. economics and other social science professions, would emerge in the progressive era to spread the message of the economic redemption of mankind.

In the twentieth century the Roman tradition in the United States has become important not only to Americans, but to the whole world. Since World War II, economic and cultural developments in American life have often paved the way for social change throughout the world. People everywhere have hoped to match U.S. material progress—a hope that in Western Europe, Japan, and a number of other countries has already been substantially realized. Europe at the end of the twentieth century finds itself moving toward a single economic market, comparable in size to the United States. Gradual political steps toward a United States of Europe have taken place with the creation of a European Parliament and the administrative apparatus for the European Economic Community. American democracy served as an important model and inspiration for the democratic revolution that swept across Eastern Europe in 1989. In the second half of the twentieth century, the economic theology of the United States has thus tended to become a gospel with a worldwide significance.

Richard Ely: Preacher of the Social Gospel

The U.S. economist Richard Ely is best known as the founder of the American Economic Association, which met for the first time in 1885. He taught from 1881 to 1892 at Johns Hopkins University and from then until 1925 at the University of Wisconsin. His students included Woodrow Wilson, Frederick Jackson Turner, and John R. Commons, as well as a number of other early leaders of U.S. social science. Ely was one of the founding fathers of the progressive movement in Wisconsin, serving as mentor to a generation of its leadership.[12] In honor of his many contributions to American economics, a feature lecture is still delivered today in Ely's name at each annual meeting of the American Economic Association.

Ely and William Graham Sumner—the latter a professor at Yale University from 1872 to 1909—were the two most influential economists of the late nineteenth century in American life. Both rejected a confinement of their activities to academic pursuits, instead engaging in vigorous public advocacy. Both criticized their many professional colleagues who were wedded to the eighteenth-century vision of an economic world in happy equilibrium decreed by natural law. Instead, reflecting the growing influence of Darwinist ideas, they argued that life in society should be understood in terms of an evolutionary concept of history.

In their interpretations of history, however, Ely and Sumner stood at opposite poles. Sumner was the leading spokesman in the United States for the social Darwinism of Herbert Spencer. His influence rose for a time to such heights that it has been said that much of America's leadership "preached and exemplified 'Billy Sumner.' "[13] Following Spencer, Sumner viewed life in harsh terms. He said, for example, that society could have equality or liberty, but not both. Efforts to achieve social equality would undermine the evolutionary improvement of the human species, leading to "survival of the unfittest" and "not liberty."[14] Sumner opposed almost all government efforts to relieve the hardships of the poor: "The fact that a man is here is no demand upon other people that they shall keep him alive and sustain him." He argued, however, that if men trusted to the workings of evolution, they would soon be rewarded: "Let every man be sober, industrious, prudent, and wise, and bring up his children to be so likewise, and poverty will be abolished in a few generations."[15]

For Sumner, the role of government should be minimal. Government interventions were considered not only wasteful and unwise, but also futile. Government could not change what nature dictates because "a natural fact is, and that is the end of the matter, whether we men give it our sovereign approval or not."[16] One historian characterizes Sumner's outlook as a belief that "in society, then, there is no possibility of social reform, of planning—human intelligence is inadequate to deal positively with social problems. Men must sit back and allow the forces of nature free play."[17]

While social Darwinism became the foremost public philosophy of the United States in the late nineteenth century, it encountered determined resistance from the social gospel movement. Ely was almost as prominent in this movement as Sumner was in spreading the message of social Darwinism. Ely traveled widely throughout the United States, delivering a message of salvation through earthly progress to religious and all manner of groups. Indeed, a leading study of the social gospel movement comments that during the 1880s Ely was "perhaps the most aggressive advocate of the social gospel" in the United States.[18] His public visibility and impact were such that another historian finds Ely exerting "a pervasive influence on [American] social thought and the course of social reform both during the eighties and the nineties and during subsequent periods of reform."[19]

For Ely, economics and theology were inseparable. He states that the fundamental organizing principle of social organization is the biblical commandment "Thou shalt love thy neighbor as thyself." Ely finds this commandment, however, largely ignored in the daily existence of most Americans. The sharp separation that many men make between the affairs of God and the affairs of this world is strongly rejected by Ely. Instead, "every act and thought and purpose, in our laws and in their administration, in all public as well as private affairs" should follow the rule of love of fellowmen. This commandment extends even to "all our daily acts, in our buying, selling, getting gain." Behavior in the marketplace has no exemption from the rule of love. Men cannot hope both to "serve God and mammon; for the ruling motive of the one service—egotism, selfishness—is the opposite of the ruling motive of the other—altruism, devotion to others, consecration of heart, soul and intellect to the service of others." Hence, the man who "oppresses the hireling in his wages is no Christian, but a pagan." Those who seek to hold down unfairly the wages of labor will find that God has in store a future of "miseries that shall come upon them."[20] Ely's views thus are directly at odds with those of Sumner and other advocates of laissez-faire, who argue that the very progress of society depends on men pursuing their own advantage.

Yet, Ely finds that institutional religion has been ineffective in seeking to bring about the just and ethical world that he seeks. Even when the church has accepted its responsibilities, the clergy has been ignorant of the realities of social and economic life. It is impossible to build a just and joyous society without a foundation of detailed knowledge. Lacking such knowledge, the church leaders "appear like blind leaders of the blind; for they manifestly have never received instruction in sociology" (a subject that Ely and most others of the time consider to encompass economics). Hence, there must be a new "social science" that will deal with "the relation of man to his fellows in what we call society." It will have for "its special province human happiness and well-being, and the underlying conditions of a prosperous, righteous, and progressive state of society." The role of the new social science will be, above all, to "absorb the attention of men seeking to obey Christ's new commandment to love one another, and to promote the true welfare of their neighbors in all those infinite ways which love suggests." Ely recommends that theology students should therefore devote 50 percent of their studies to social science and expresses the hope that "theological seminaries should be the chief intellectual centres for sociology."[21]

In contrast to Sumner, Ely believes that "the economic life of man is to some considerable extent the product of the human will." As the leading spokesman for a new "ethical school of economists," Ely and his fellow school members seek "to direct . . . this economic, social growth of mankind." It is an "ethical ideal which animates the new political economy" and seeks an abolition of the existing "contradiction between our actual economic life and the postulates of ethics." The achievement of this goal will require a "departure of economists from the individualistic philosophy . . . which has gained such a stronghold in America." The ethical school of economists "places society above the individual." It will therefore be necessary to have a "new conception of the state." The state will apply economic knowledge in the service of "the greatest good of the greatest number" and thereby "accomplish the end of human society, the ethical ideal."[22]

Ely is deeply impressed by the productive powers of modern technology. He is of the view that "with the inventions and discoveries of modern times, we seem almost to have solved the problem of production." It is the distributional side that "still awaits a satisfactory solution"—this particularly requiring the attention of economists armed with a Christian ethical sensitivity. By joining economic science with Christian ethics, it will be possible to "guide and direct the forces which control the production and distribution of economic goods, that they may in the highest degree subserve the ends of humanity."[23] Ely envisions the resulting economic system in the following terms:

First of all, we must seek a better utilization of productive forces. This implies, negatively, that we should reduce the waste of the competitive system to its lowest possible terms; positively, that we should endeavor to secure a steady production, employing all available capital and labor power; furthermore, the full utilization of inventions and discoveries, by a removal of the friction which often renders improvement so difficult. Positively this implies, also, that production should be carried on under wholesome conditions.

We must so mend our distribution of wealth that we shall avoid present extremes, and bring about widely diffused comfort, making frugal comfort for all an aim. Distribution must be so shaped, if practicable, that all shall have assured incomes, but that no one who is personally qualified to render service shall enjoy an income without personal exertion. In the third place, there must be abundant public provision of opportunities, for the development of our faculties, including educational facilities and the large use of natural resources for purposes of recreation.[24]

For Ely, the goal of a productive and ethical society is not a matter of passing time on earth, awaiting a more glorious salvation in the hereafter. Instead, Ely believes that "Christianity is primarily concerned with this world, and it is the mission of Christianity to bring to pass here a kingdom of righteousness." What we "learn about heaven" in the Bible is in fact meant to apply "for this world." Indeed, salvation is not for Ely to be found in the hereafter, but instead "God has given to his people this world for salvation."[25]

Ely states that the earthly path to salvation requires "a never-ceasing attack on every wrong institution, until the earth becomes a new earth, and all its cities, cities of God." In his view, "it is as truly a religious work to pass good laws, as it is to preach sermons; as holy a work to lead a crusade against filth, vice, and disease in slums of cities, and to seek the abolition of the disgraceful tenement-houses of American cities, as it is to send missionaries to the heathen." Ely argues that social problems such as child labor, working conditions of women, public corruption, public recreation, and an unjust distribution of wealth are at heart "religious subjects." The solutions to all these problems require the application of extensive social and economic knowledge. Hence, the path to earthly righteousness and salvation "in its elaboration, becomes social science."[26]

These basic tenets of Ely's faith were in fact widely shared in the American social gospel movement of the late nineteenth and early twentieth centuries and would exert a large influence in American life. In his history of the movement, Charles Hopkins writes that for its members "the kingdom of heaven was brought down out of the skies to be realized progressively here and now." The "social salvation" of mankind required the "coming to earth of the kingdom of heaven." Moreover, such salvation was meant in a literal, not a metaphorical sense. For the social gospelers "social salvation never became a mere program of reforms"; rather, "its great prophets were men of spiritual, even mystical, genius whose message was characterized by a fundamentally religious and evangelical fervor."[27]

As the key figure in the creation of the American Economic Association, Ely was seeking to carry out these religious convictions. As seen by Ely, the new association of economists was to be a practical instrument for gathering the data and generating the knowledge for a reconstruction of American society along new ethical grounds. Ely sought to exclude from the new association those economists such as Sumner who were in his view opposed irreconcilably to his aims.[28] At the first meeting of the American Economic Association in 1885, twenty of the fifty who joined were former or practicing ministers. A number of leading social gospelers of the time—including Lyman

Abbott, Washington Gladden, and Amory Bradford—were charter members of the American Economic Association. Although Ely was forced to make some compromises, the first statement of principles of the American Economic Association reflected his purposes in a number of ways. One principle read that "we regard the state as an agency whose positive assistance is one of the indispensable conditions of human progress." Another said that "the conflict of labor and capital has brought into prominence a vast number of social problems, whose solution requires the united efforts, each in its own sphere, of the church, of the state, and of science."[29]

Ely was not the only important economist of the time to be closely associated with the social gospel movement.[30] John R. Commons was a well-known student of Ely; he too preached as a social gospeler, and would later become a leading figure in the American institutional school of economics. Commons taught that "people need not only the heart of love, but also the knowledge to guide their love," which could be "derived only from the science of sociology."[31] Other important early social scientists who were connected to the social gospel movement include Edward Bemis, John Bates Clark, Simon Patten, Edward Ross, and Albion Small.[32] Ross, one of the founders of the American profession of sociology, is the author of *Latter Day Saints and Sinners* in which he stated that a modern saint "goes about checkmating evil"—an activity accomplished by social reform.[33] Although Henry George was not an economist by profession, his economic writings were perhaps the most widely read of any author in the late nineteenth century. George also saw his efforts as being in the service of a deeply religious cause.

Ely and others of the "ethical school" of economists were frequently accused of being socialists—a potentially dangerous label in that era. Some social gospelers in fact expressed strong sympathies or directly embraced socialism. There were, as Ely acknowledged, many similarities. Socialists and the social gospelers were both deeply concerned to improve the conditions of labor. Their specific reform agendas overlapped on many points. Both looked to the state to improve society. Socialists and social gospelers shared a vision of a unified community of mankind, brought together by love and a dedication to the common good. Moreover, as Ely wrote, despite the outwardly secular appearance, there was a common religious underpinning: "Socialism has become . . . a religion to many, and the devotion which it has awakened is something which nothing short of a religious force is able to arouse."[34]

Writing in 1894, Ely approved of much that socialism sought, yet found that it aimed to move too rapidly, had too much the flavor of a "panacea." Men were not yet ready for the abolition of private property, owing to the still "backward state of development of man's social nature" and the fact that "men are still too individualistic in their nature." It would therefore be a "long time to come" before they would be able to meet the "requirements of a socialist state." Ely also saw a threat to liberty in that "those in whose hands were centred political and economic control would have tremendous power."[35]

Despite these reservations, the social gospel that Ely delivered in the 1880s was in its essence a Christian democratic socialism. Ely's message also bore many resemblances to the social vision of Saint-Simon. In his later years, Saint-Simon had prophesied the emergence of a new religion that would join Christian love of fellowmen with the deeper truths and expert knowledge that modern sciences could offer. Society would be organized for the achievement of maximum productive efficiency, each person performing tasks determined by the objective requirements of economic and other scientific knowledge. If Saint-Simon had called for a priesthood of social scientists to lead this new world, Ely was now prepared to take the practical steps to make this vision a reality. The American Economic Association emerged from Ely's commitment to supply the expert knowledge and skills needed to carry out the message of Saint-Simon.

The modern era has frequently seen the secularization of older Judaic and Christian beliefs. With Ely, matters are now reversed; institutional religion absorbs and incorporates a secular gospel. Indeed, as preached through the social gospel of Ely, a branch of Christian theology now becomes in large part an economic theology. The true message delivered by Christ to his disciples is interpreted by Ely to contain fundamentally a message of economic progress on earth. The priesthood responsible for showing the path to salvation will be the professional economists of the world. In short, Ely's social gospel is an example of a common practice in the modern age that might be called "inverse secularization"—the reversion of economic and other originally secular themes of salvation back to a Christian dress.

The Christianity of Ely would have been anathema to central figures of the Protestant tradition such as Augustine, Luther, and Calvin. Typical of the general optimism of the progressive era, Ely's theology lacked almost any sense of human existence as tragic, of humanity fated for sin and suffering, of men alienated from and betrayed by their reason since the fall of man. Ely instead held human capacities, motives, and reasoning in the highest regard. Men by their own knowledge were capable of bringing about their own salvation. As Ely wrote, "the message of Christ" and "the grand distinctive feature of Christianity" were the "exaltation of humanity. I will not say the worship of humanity, but surely it is safe to say all but the worship of humanity."[36]

It was an outlook encouraged by the times. As the nineteenth century drew to a close, scientific invention was rapidly turning out new products that would transform the existence of the average person: the telephone, electric light, and phonograph in the 1870s; the automobile and electric trolley car in the 1880s; the movie camera and wireless radio-wave transmission in the 1890s; the airplane and electric washing machine in the first decade of the twentieth century. New manufacturing techniques were making possible sharp increases in the scale and efficiency of production. Improvements in transportation were drastically reducing the costs and time of moving goods and people among different parts of the United States. Much faster and cheaper means of communication were linking the entire nation together.

If the sense of change was pervasive, most of it seemed for the better. A later student of the progressive era would write that "the change in the externals of living was so amazing, the vistas of the future presented in the Sunday supplements so astounding that anything seemed possible; a Golden Age of peace and plenty for all seemed just a short distance across the years."[37] In this era, Americans were filled with a confidence that, as Woodrow Wilson expressed it, man "by using his intellect can remake society, that he can become the creator of a world organized for man's advantage."[38] A leading Protestant preacher of the day, the social gospeler Walter Rauschenbusch, would echo Ely's views and proclaim that "progress . . . is divine," the mechanism by which God exerted his will to bring about a new heaven on earth.[39]

The God found historically in Christianity had in truth a limited role to play in the theology of Ely. Indeed, it was an unnecessary role—one that could easily be dispensed with. Partly for this reason, it would be primarily to science—not to Christian theology—that many Americans of the progressive era would look for their basic understanding of the world. Science had also fought long and hard to escape the restrictions and roadblocks that institutional Christianity often placed in its way. Science proclaimed a neutral search for knowledge and a freedom from social values and conventions that had often been at odds with Christian teachings. If science and Christian theology were joined together, science risked becoming enmeshed in the bitter history of conflicts within Christianity. Americans had long sought to avoid these conflicts by separating institutional religion from the practical functioning of government.

There was thus little to gain and much to lose in locating the new science of economics within the subject matter of Christian theology, as Ely proposed to do. Indeed, there was opposition among many economists to Ely's aims from the beginning—an opposition that gradually increased, and fairly soon prevailed. By 1892 Ely was forced to resign his position as secretary (chief administrative officer) of the American Economic Association.[40] By the mid-1890s, Ely himself was beginning to acknowledge the need for a professional association of economists that would demand a neutral allegiance to the methods of science, welcoming contributions from all social viewpoints, remaining officially well removed from the doctrines or the organizational framework of any institutional religion. Ely would gradually redirect his own studies to a life of more scholarly and technical tasks. Although playing a less visible role in U.S. public life, he became a leading researcher in the field of land and natural-resource economics, and served for many years as a well-respected figure in the American economics profession.[41]

Secularizing influences were in fact pervasive in the United States in the late nineteenth and early twentieth centuries. The progressive movement was by and large a secular movement. Yet the specific reform agenda of progressivism was largely made up of reforms that had already been proposed by the social gospelers. The progressives often exhibited no less zeal and fervor for the cause. Progressivism, like socialism around the world, had all the qualities and the feel of a religion. Indeed, progressivism was a secularization of the social gospel movement—or as one later historian would write, "the social gospel . . . was, in a sense, the religion of the progressive movement."[42] In carrying the banner of the progressive gospel, however, it would not be Ely but another American economist, Thorstein Veblen, who would achieve great visibility and influence early in the twentieth century.

Thorstein Veblen: Caller to a New Priesthood

Thorstein Veblen has been described by a leading American historian of the progressive era as "the most brilliant mind of his time."[43]

Holder of a Ph.D. from Yale, he taught economics at the University of Chicago from 1892 to 1906 and served for a time as the managing editor of its *Journal of Political Economy*. In the first two decades of this century his writings reached a large audience, causing H. L. Mencken to observe that for a while "Veblenism was shining in full brilliance. There were Veblenists, Veblen Clubs, Veblen remedies for all the sorrows of the world."[44] Professionally, Veblen's writings were a leading inspiration for the institutional school of American economists. One of his pupils, Wesley Clair Mitchell, would state that "no other such emancipator of the mind from the subtle tyranny of circumstance has been known in social science, and no other such enlarger of the realm of inquiry."[45]

Veblen was possessed of a breadth of knowledge and depth of historical scholarship rare among economists. He viewed economics as embedded in culture, studying American business and governing practices from a distance and with the detachment of an anthropologist surveying some new and unfamiliar world. His distinctive perspective was developed in his first book, *The Theory of the Leisure Class*, published in 1899—a work that soon made him famous. Veblen had already applied a similar outlook to the realm of economic ideas in four articles published in the *Quarterly Journal of Economics* from 1898 to 1900. In Veblen's view, economics had yet to escape fully the status of a "primitive animism." Among primitive men, the natural world is seen as "guided by discretion, willpower, or propensity looking to an end." These animistic beliefs typically found expression in religion. Modern economics, to be sure, asserted a scientific status. Yet, Veblen found that the "methods of economic science" were still dominated by an "archaic habit of thought."[46] The origins of this habit were "traceable through medieval channels to the teachings of the ancients."[47] In the most influential modern formulation, the "spiritual" approach of economics is seen in the theories of natural law. A continuity runs from "over-ruling providence" to the "order of nature, natural rights and natural law" of the eighteenth century. All represent efforts "to formulate knowledge in terms of absolute truth; and this absolute truth is a spiritual fact."[48]

The services of modern economists have often been devoted to the maintenance of "ceremonial adequacy." Economists have taken "what the instructed common sense of the time accepts as the adequate or worthy end of human effort" and transformed this common sense into a "canon of truth." At its most successful, Veblen finds that economics yields a "body of logically consistent propositions concerning the normal relations of things.'' This task involves an exercise in the classification of events in the world according to economic categories—investment, demand, labor, profit, and so forth. Like the nineteenth-century science of biology, but unlike the scientific method of Newton, the result is a ''system of economic taxonomy.''[49]

Adam Smith, as Veblen sees him, achieved a major advance in that he offers ''a larger and more painstaking scrutiny of facts, and a more consistent tracing out of casual continuity in the facts handled.'' Smith also offers ''a different, more modern ground of normality.'' Yet, these elements should not obscure the animistic qualities also found in Smith's writings. Veblen finds that ''with Adam Smith the ultimate ground of economic reality is the design of God.'' In making this design, ''the Creator has established the natural order to serve the ends of human welfare; and he has very nicely adjusted the efficient causes comprised in the natural order, including human aims and motives, to this work that they are to accomplish.'' Nature has provided a guiding mechanism that surely and inevitably works autonomously ''to enforce the divine purpose in the resulting natural course of things.''[50] Thus, the hidden hand of Adam Smith is not an accident of nature or a product of human purpose, but is in fact the hand of God—guiding events benevolently and purposefully, if beyond the view and understanding of most men in the course of their affairs.

Veblen sees Smith's successors among the economists of the nineteenth century as still reflecting a strong theological influence, but in ways less visible and less central to their conclusions. The utilitarians, who rejected the natural-law framework, were—by comparison with Smith—''undevout.'' In Malthus, there was still a ''divinely sanctioned order,'' but its role was ''somewhat sparing and temperate.'' The classical followers of Smith showed a ''different distribution of emphasis,'' but not a ''new and antagonistic departure.'' In relation to the actual workings of the economy, classical economics still had a ''ceremonial'' role that continued to serve a purpose of ''legitimation.''[51]

Veblen believes, however, that trends in the modern age are moving rapidly beyond the animistic conceptions of the past. The development of industrial processes is forcing modern men to think with ever greater logic and rational precision. Their thought processes must now match the rationality of the machines and the complex systems with which they work. As Veblen writes, the workings of industry ''are not safely to be construed in terms of propensity, predilection or passion. Life in an advanced industrial community does not tolerate a neglect of mechanical fact.'' The result will be that the need for clear thinking in industry eventually "shapes their habits of thought"—an influence that will inevitably extend beyond work activities to other areas of life.[52] Although he makes his assertions less dogmatically and prophetically, Veblen follows Marx in finding that the underlying economic and material realities determine mankind's ways of thinking.

A further implication of Veblen's viewpoint is that men attuned to the mechanical realities of industry—who think rationally and are free of animistic and ceremonial atavisms—are the most suitable to lead their fellowmen. Such rational men in modern society are to be found especially among the engineers of the industrial system. In 1921 in *The Engineers and the Price System,* Veblen summed up his grand design for a future industrial society led by its engineering and other scientific elites.

The early twentieth century had inherited not only a body of economic writings, but economic institutions out of touch with the realities of industry. The requirements of technology thus had "outgrown the eighteenth century system of vested rights" defended by Adam Smith. Under the economic realities of the early twentieth century, "the technicians are indispensable to productive industry of this mechanical sort; the Vested Interests and their absentee owners are not." Indeed, the vested interests are not only unnecessary, but positively harmful. Veblen explains that their continued role in the managing of industry has yielded "an incredibly and increasingly uneconomical use of material resources, and an incredibly wasteful organization of equipment and manpower in those great industries where the technological advance has been most marked."[53] At one point Veblen suggests that a properly expert management of American society might even increase total industrial output by three to twelve times.

Under the existing institutional arrangements of the economy, both "statesmen" and "captains of finance" have the power to "touch its mechanism," which yields "dissension, misdirection, and unemployment of material resources." It is a system where "industrial experts are . . . required to take orders and submit to sabotage at the hands of the statesmen and the vested interests." Instead of by technological competence, the power to decide the fate of the industrial system is allocated according to the twin evils of "politics" and financial "investment." The situation must be corrected by "a revolutionary overturn as will close out the Old Order of absentee ownership and capitalized income." With the abolition of absentee ownership, "industrially useful articles will presently cease to be used for purposes of ownership, that is to say for purposes of private gain" that subvert the goals of the larger community.[54]

Power to control the industrial system therefore should shift from politicians and absentee property owners to the most knowledgeable personnel. A "Soviet of Technicians" should be created to include prominently "Production Engineers" and "Production Economists." These "economists and engineers . . . will have to be drawn together by self-selection on the basis of a common interest in productive efficiency, economical use of resources, and an equitable distribution of the consumable output." This is not only a technical undertaking, but "provision must also be made for the growth of such a spirit of teamwork as will be ready to undertake and undergo this critical adventure." The production engineers and economists will understand that "they are . . . the keepers of the community's material welfare," who are not to be moved by "commercial interest" but by a "common purpose."[55]

There must also be an "extensive campaign of inquiry and publicity" in order to enlighten the public as to the technological realities that demand the control of qualified experts. Finally, as a practical matter, it will probably be impossible to wrest power from its current holders without "the working-out of a common understanding and a solidarity of sentiment between the technicians and the working force." When superior knowledge is finally matched with instruments of social control, the result will be a system that is "impersonal and dispassionate," whose workings are "a painstaking and intelligent coordination of the processes at work," driven by "technological knowledge" of an "altogether unbusiness-like nature," and which is "exactingly specialized, endlessly detailed, reaching out into all domains of empirical fact."[56] As Veblen sums up his new economic message,

> The technology—the state of the industrial arts—which takes effect in this mechanical industry is in an eminent sense a joint stock of knowledge and experience held in common by the civilized peoples. It requires the use of trained and instructed workmen—born, bred, trained and instructed at the cost of the people at large. So also it requires, with a continually more exacting insistence, a corps of highly trained and specially gifted experts, of diverse and various kinds. These, too, are born, bred, and trained at the cost of the community at large, and they draw their requisite special knowledge from the community's joint stock of accumulated experience. These expert men, technologists, engineers,

or whatever name may best suit them, make up the indispensable General Staff of the industrial system; and without their immediate and unremitting guidance and correction the industrial system will not work. It is a mechanically organized structure of technical processes designed, installed, and conducted by these production engineers. Without them and their constant attention the industrial equipment, the mechanical appliances of industry, will foot up to just so much junk. The material welfare of the community is unreservedly bound up with the due working of this industrial system, and therefore with its unreserved control by the enginers, who alone are competent to manage it. To do their work as it should be done these men of the industrial general staff must have a free hand, unhampered by commercial considerations and reservations; for the production of the goods and services needed by the community they neither need nor are they in any degree benefited by any supervision or interference from the side of the owners.[57]

Like so many social gospelers and progressives, Veblen in such passages unmistakably reflects the influence of Saint-Simon. Veblen is another disciple—the message of Veblen another adaptation—of the religion of humanity. If God made a rational world, it will now be scientific experts—the priesthood of Veblen's new church of science— who reveal its rational structure. The moral authority of the Catholic priest is now bequeathed to the professional expert. In the message of Veblen, it will be these experts who decide the legitimacy of social and economic practices, who preside over the priestly ceremonies of modern society.

Like a number of other leading thinkers of the modern age, Veblen is acute when it comes to recognizing a theological inspiration in his predecessors. Yet when it comes Veblen's turn to lead the way into the future, he offers yet another prophecy of heaven on earth, yet another economic road to salvation, yet another modern economic theology.

Veblen's differences with Adam Smith are, therefore, not a question of Smith's theological economics versus Veblen's scientific economics. Rather, Veblen is the spokesman for a different theological viewpoint. Veblen speaks for a Roman tradition that has largely eliminated the vestiges of Protestant individualism. Smith is also of the Roman tradition, but the influence of Calvin is nearer and stronger. For Smith, as for the Protestant Reformation, the autonomy of the individual best serves God's purposes. For the Reformation, this autonomy is found in matters of personal faith, which are decisive for salvation. As found later in Adam Smith, this autonomy is to be maintained in economic matters, which have become the modern road to salvation.

In the Roman Catholic church, however, it is the pope, the priesthood, and the institutional church that reveal the divine intent for
mankind. The word of God arrives from on high; the individual must
not claim a higher authority for his own individual conscience. It is the
institutions of the Roman Catholic church that are the repository of
divine wisdom—not a hidden hand that works through the independent
beliefs and actions of many autonomous individuals. So it is with the
progressive gospel of Veblen as well. There is only one truth for
Veblen's church of science, which is the scientific truth discovered and
verified by the institutional practices of science. The deliverers of this
truth represent a new priesthood—the professional experts who can
uncover the laws of the universe through the application of the scientific method.

Veblen explains that, like the Roman priesthoods of old, the new
class of technical experts will act with regard to the "benefit to the
community at large." The ethic of expert professionalism is "teamwork"—not individual advantage.[58] Men of science will not abuse the
immense power that Veblen seeks for them because—again, like earlier
priesthoods—they will be of high character and deep commitment to
the service of their fellowmen. The experts of the future must, as
Veblen acknowledges, assume responsibility for the distribution of
outputs, along with the production of these outputs. But Veblen is not
concerned that there will be an unfair distribution, because his ruling
body of expert technicians will have the welfare of all society at heart.
To be sure, Veblen has no scientific demonstration, no proof, no causal
explanation for all these meritorious qualities of the professional. For
Veblen, it is self-evident that the call to a priesthood of selfless
engineers and economic experts will be answered. Partly by a process
of self-selection, the modern priesthoods of expertise will attract
individuals willing to devote their lives to the higher purposes of men
on earth.

Veblen's message in this and in other respects was the message of
the American progressive movement of the first two decades of this
century. As a thinker, Veblen was not fundamentally opposed to or
divorced from his time. Rather, he developed the core ideas of progressivism in a particularly colorful, graphic, and dramatic way. Historians
would later observe for example, how the new expert professionals of
the progressive era did in fact find that "the shared mysteries of a
specialty allowed initimate communion" such as had also been found
in the priesthoods of the Roman Catholic church. The professions
offered a sense of "prestige through exclusiveness," a brotherhood of

men brought together by their common "desire to remake the world," and a "deep satisfaction" that accompanied a "revolution in identity" that followed initiation into a select class. The rites of professional life in the progressive era were designed to ensure that "the process of becoming an expert, of immersing oneself in the scientific method, eradicated petty passions and narrow ambitions."[59]

The goal of the progressives was an ever more productive organization of society, the means by which an ever greater abundance of goods and services would be obtained. The progressive movement pursued this goal with such commitment and fervor that progressivism would later be characterized by the historian Samuel Hays as the "gospel of efficiency."[60] Dwight Waldo would similarly write that "it is yet amazing what a position of dominance 'efficiency' assumed, how it waxed until it had assimilated or over-shadowed other values, how men and events came to be degraded or exalted according to what was assumed to be its dictate." Tracing in essence the evolution of the Roman tradition, Waldo found that "every era has a few words that epitomize its world-view and that are fixed points by which all else can be measured. In the Middle Ages they were such words as faith, grace and God; in the eighteenth century they were such words as reason, nature, and rights; during the past 50 years in America they have been such words as cause, reaction, scientific, expert, progress—and efficient."[61] Another historian, Samuel Haber, described a United States that in the progressive era seemed to be possessed by "an efficiency craze" that represented "a secular Great Awakening."[62] Still another spoke of "the efficiency movement," which was presented "as a panacea for the ills of mankind" and sparked "a moral fervor that had all the earmarks of a religious revival."[63]

In order to maximize social efficiency, as Veblen said, it would be necessary to assign each man to the task and location best suited to his individual talents. Americans in the past had often exalted decentralization and individuality, but in the progressive era a new sense of the nation as a single community emerged, scientifically and centrally managed by an expert elite. William Schambra comments that progressivism emphasized a vision of "a genuine national community which could evoke from the American people a self-denying devotion to the public good, a community in which citizens would be linked tightly by bonds of compassion and neighborliness. Americans would be asked to transcend their traditional laissez faire individualism (which had been aggravated by the forces of modern industrialism) in order to bond themselves as one to the 'national idea.' "[64]

If less sophisticated and less colorful in his language than Veblen, an even more influential proselytizer for the scientific management of industry was Frederick Taylor. Even in the Soviet Union, Lenin enthusiastically recommended the widespread application of Taylor's scientific methods to problems of industrial production. The scientific management movement found existing American businesses lacking in the attitudes and skills necessary to achieve the full productive efficiency of industry. Believing—like Veblen—that those who have the scientific knowledge should also have the authority, Taylor and his disciples advocated a controlling role for the class of engineers. In a newly complex and technological age, large numbers of progressives believed that it would be necessary to place "control of the huge and delicate apparatus of industry into the hands of those who understood its operation." Engineers were widely seen in the progressive era as "a new industrial intelligentsia, standing between capital and labor, and peculiarly fitted to resolve the nation's social conflicts."[65]

Educated in engineering at Stanford University, Herbert Hoover acquired his international reputation in part by skillfully administering European food assistance and other humanitarian concerns. Hoover's public reputation was as an "engineer-economist-organizer."[66] Yet another enthusiast for scientific management and leadership by engineers, he stated that "the one-hundred thousand professional engineers in the United States, men trained in exact thinking and in administrative responsibility, who were drafted into civilian and military service during [World War I], vindicated the scientific attitude in dealing with problems of social organization."[67] Selected by Hoover, the authors of the "Hoover Report" in 1921 stated that "engineers come in contact with and influence every activity in industry and as a body possess an intimate and peculiar understanding of intricate industrial problems. . . . It is peculiarly the duty of engineers to use their influence individually and collectively to eliminate waste in industry."[68]

Influenced by such ideas, scientific management did in fact spread rapidly throughout the U.S. business world. In the 1920s Alfred Sloan introduced modern management to the automobile industry, building up a new giant—General Motors—managed by a corporate headquarters filled with experts in many fields.[69] A new breed of trained professional was assuming a leading role in the operation of U.S. business, applying cost accounting, quality control, budgeting, investment analysis, demand research, and other technical methods.[70] The American system of professional business education was expanding rapidly to supply the demand for expert personnel equipped with specialized knowledge and skills.

The progressives sought also to apply scientific management to government. The operation of the U.S. Congress in the late nineteenth century appeared to many progressives as "a forum in which private groups served themselves as best they could."[71] In order to introduce expert methods, it would be necessary to separate much of government from the influence of politics—especially the harmful influence of special interests. In a famous 1887 essay, Woodrow Wilson observed that formerly "the functions of government were simple, because life itself was simple." Now, however, "the functions of government are every day becoming more complex and difficult." Hence, there was no choice but to assign the administration of such tasks to professionals. Ordinary democratic processes should guide the overall policy directions, but "in the oversight of the daily details and in the choice of the daily means of government, public criticism is of course a clumsy nuisance."[72]

A few years later Frank Goodnow laid out a similar prescription in greater detail: "There is a large part of administration which is unconnected with politics, which should therefore be relieved very largely, if not altogether, from the control of political bodies. It is unconnected with politics because it embraces fields of semi-scientific, quasi-judicial and quasi-business or commercial activity."[73] The institution of the independent regulatory commission would emerge from the progressive conviction that the administration of government should be separated from democratic politics. The leadership and staff of independent commissions such as the Federal Reserve Bank were to be well-recognized experts with specialized skills appropriate to management in a disinterested fashion.[74] New professional schools to teach scientific methods of public administration were created, matching the new professional schools of business. Waldo captures well the guiding faith of the progressive reformers of American government:

> Students and reformers of all kinds fell to making human relations and governmental practices scientific . . . This faith in science and the efficacy of scientific method thoroughly permeates our literature on public administration. Science had its experts: so we must have "experts in government." Science relies upon exact measurement: so let the data of administration be measured. Science is concerned only with facts: so let the "facts" be sovereign. Science makes use of experiment: so let the mode of administrative advance be experimental.[75]

There were, of course, some dissenters. Woodrow Wilson in his later years shifted away from the scientific management of society to preach the "new freedom"—a political philosophy involving a greater role for individual pursuit of self-interest as long as there is no excess of market power. Others argued that the scientific management of society was a formula for suppressing democratic freedoms and for installing an oppressive elite with dictatorial powers. There was an important populist strain within progressivism that looked to popular democracy and sought answers more in the voice of the people than in any group of scientific experts.

Yet, much of the political and economic history of the United States in the twentieth-century has been a history of the success of the progressive message of scientific management of American society.[76] If somewhat modified, progressivism in fact remains today the guiding faith of the American welfare state. It still provides social legitimacy for contemporary American government. Whatever the realities, government actions must still be said to be in the public interest as determined by objective methods based on the expert skills of professionals.

The economic theology of nineteenth-century America was derived from the Enlightenment vision of a harmony of the forces of individual self-interest, from Adam Smith, and from John Locke. With progressivism, the theological lineage shifted to Comte and Saint-Simon. A contemporary would say of a leading theorist of American progressivism—Herbert Croly—that he was "the first child christened in Comte's 'religion of humanity.' "[77] Among U.S. economists, Veblen was the leading preacher of this faith. His promised land was, as a later scholar would describe it, "a self-operating utopia where dispassionate, expert engineers would oversee a society of individuals comprehending and loving their work."[78] The message of Veblen was—like Ely and other social gospelers—the arrival of mankind at a future heaven on earth through the application of economic (and other expert) knowledge. It was a message especially well suited to an age enthralled by the impacts of science. As Walter Lippmann wrote in the 1920s, "the miracles of science seem to be inexhaustible. It is not surprising, then, that men of science should have acquired much of the intellectual authority which churchmen once exercised. Scientists do not, of course, speak of their discoveries as miracles. But to the common man they have much the same character."[79]

Given legitimacy by the progressive gospel, the federal government in Washington would in the twentieth century assume for the American public the aura and the administrative authority earlier found in the medieval period in Rome. The progressive prescription for a separation of science and politics in U.S. government assigned to science a domain that addressed matters of truth and salvation—the former domain of the medieval Roman church. Politics in the progressive scheme dealt with petty conflicts in the affairs of men, as the Roman church had looked to kings and lords to supervise such mundane matters in medieval times. The modern research university took the place of the medieval monastery. The expert professions assumed the mantle of the Roman priesthoods of old. As in the medieval Roman church, ordinary persons now as well could not challenge the teachings of the progressive experts. In neither period could ordinary persons even speak the special languages of the priesthoods: Latin in medieval times; mathematics and other scientific languages in the modern era. The progressive church and the medieval Roman church were, in short, sources of ultimate truth—a truth delivered by church authorities, providing common standards and rules for the community of the faithful. The resulting unified and harmonious community should, in principle, encompass all the world in a theocratic embrace. In the twentieth century the United States would seek—and in many aspects achieve—the fulfillment of yet another theology of the Roman tradition.

Thurman Arnold: New Deal Prophet of Corporate Socialism

If the progressive era set the stage for the American welfare state, it would not be until the New Deal that much of it was actually realized. New regulatory agencies such as the Federal Communications Commission and the Securities and Exchange Commission were created in the 1930s, while the powers of older agencies such as the Interstate Commerce Commission were expanded. Social Security, welfare, and public housing programs established the foundation for a national system of income redistribution. The Wagner Act greatly strengthened labor unions. The federal government in the New Deal years assumed responsibility for maintaining the incomes of farmers. The Bureau of the Budget was significantly strengthened and shifted from the Department of the Treasury to the White House, contributing to the development of an administrative presidency with powers and personnel for a more professional management of the executive branch.

The New Deal was more notable for practical accomplishments than for intellectual creativity. Indeed, much the same might be said for U.S. economics during this period. Many economists came to Washington to help write and administer the new laws. Professional economists began to assume what would eventually become an important role in the administration of the American welfare state. Yet no American economist of a stature comparable to Ely or Veblen emerged to put the New Deal in a broad perspective that would defend its efforts. Indeed, many prominent figures in American economics were opposed to its programs. The president of the Brookings Institution, Harold Moulton, was a leading critic of New Deal initiatives.[80] Many other economists argued that government intervention would only aggravate the economic problems of the day; self-correcting mechanisms within the economic system would work, if only given enough time and allowed to operate freely.

The brain trust of the New Deal was populated above all by lawyers. In this respect it is appropriate that it would fall to a lawyer—Thurman Arnold—to develop the leading New Deal statement of the economic theology of Ely and Veblen. Arnold accomplished this task in *The Folklore of Capitalism*, published in 1937. It was a brilliant polemic in defense of the reforms of the New Deal, also offering an insightful dissection of American economic and legal culture.

Arnold's writings are not today as well known or as much read as Veblen (and to a lesser extent Ely). Indeed, Arnold is better known as a founding partner of Arnold, Fortas, and Porter, which in the years after World War II became one of the leading law firms in Washington, D.C. Arnold's was the classic story of the New Deal intellectual. After early successes in an academic career, he left the faculty of the Yale Law School in 1938 to come to Washington. He served as the head of the antitrust division of the Justice Department from 1938 to 1943, establishing a reputation as one of its most aggressive and effective leaders. Like many New Dealers, on leaving government Arnold stayed on to become a longtime member of the informal governing establishment.

In his early writings Arnold followed a trail that Veblen had already blazed. The economic opponents of the New Deal were the preachers—Arnold said—of an "economic theology" that was derived from the eighteenth and nineteenth centuries and that was largely irrelevant to the real world of twentieth-century American business and government. The "folklore of 1937," Arnold wrote, consisted of the "sound principles of law or economics," which were widely regarded "as inescapable truths, as natural laws, as principles of justice, and as the only method of an ordered society." These beliefs were in fact a particularly important and influential new "religion" of the day. For the faithful, they showed "the way of economic and legal salvation." This faith was led by its "priests [who] are lawyers and economists." There was also a "Devil," who was to be found as the political "demagogue" who ignores sound economics and law and is "constantly misleading the people by making the worse appear the better reason."[81]

Economists might develop the doctrines but it is the institution of the law that enforces them. Arnold wrote that the God of the current day "was not always the God of the Church. Lawyers found one in the Constitution." The members of the Supreme Court even wear much the same garments as the priests of old—part of their effort to surround themselves with an aura of religious mystery. The objective is to ensure that "the judicial institution is worshiped" and to foster popular acceptance that "within its priestly portals, the language of the law is used with truth, with logical finality, and with authority." The best antecedents for the U.S. legal system are to be found in the Middle Ages, where scholars then as well "spent their lives studying those fundamental principles, the violation of which brings ruin. Their logic was as unassailable as the economic and legal logic of today." Like the Middle Ages, Arnold's own day was found to be "an age where Reason is still king"—however out-of-touch the actual results of the elaborate legal reasoning purused in late medieval times and now again in twentieth-century America. In the current age, "the Supreme Court, above all institutions, [stands] for the finality of rational principles."[82]

Arnold's assessment of the economics of his day was similar. Contending schools of economic thought were engaged in "theological dispute," he wrote. The role of economists was in large part ceremonial, being called on to dispense "priestly incense." Economists "regretted man's tendency to follow false economic reasoning, just as the preachers regretted man's tendency to sin." The only answer was "constant preaching, which had the weakness of all preaching throughout the centuries, in that sin and heresy were always rising against it." For economists, the greatest source of sin and of evil influences was the iniquitous domain of "politics."[83]

Economists believed that, if mankind would only heed their message, men would find the path to the "laissez faire heaven." Economic progress to a heavenly future had replaced the "Heaven in the Middle Ages," leaving all else to be regarded "as temporary, shifting and ephemeral." Like all priesthoods, economists were more concerned with future salvation than with the conditions of the moment. Thus, as Arnold wrote, "the quaint moral conceptions of legal and economic learning by which the needs of the moment could be argued out of existence were expressed by 'long run' arguments."[84] The meaning of the long run, in short, was the path along which the way to heaven was to be found.

When it came to the practical problems of managing society in the New Deal years, however, Arnold considered that the teachings of economists were virtually "useless." Modern U.S. industry had become so large and concentrated that it found its true antecedents in the Middle Ages, now compromising a system of "industrial feudalism." Society was in genuine need of "a set of observations about the techniques of human organization." By the 1930s, Arnold found that "men are beginning to realize their complete interdependence." What was needed was "a science of the diagnosis of maladjusted organizations in an age where organizations have replaced individuals as units." Instead, what economists were offering was a set of writings that were "no more descriptive of social organization today than the theology of the monarchy was descriptive before the French Revolution."[85]

Yet while competition was not the real driving force, the modern business corporation was an "extraordinary, efficient machine" that had vastly increased the standard of living of the American people. American business with its "natural organizing ability" had developed a "productive plant which was the marvel of the modern world." As Veblen had argued that real control had passed to those who possessed the critical knowledge, Arnold now similarly found that the successes of U.S. industry were attributable to "the rise of a class of engineers, salesmen, minor executives. . . . Current mythology puts them in the role of servants, not rulers." But the truth is that "it is this great class of employees, working for salaries, which distributes the goods of the world." American industry was large because "specialized techniques made bigness essential to producing goods in large enough quantities and at a price low enough." American business thrived in "the most highly organized and specialized society the world has ever known" by mastering the techniques of organization, based on expert knowledge.[86]

Arnold also followed Veblen in arguing that in twentieth-century America the distinctions between government and business had become artificial. Large business and large government required the same organizational methods, the same fields of expertise, and the same skilled personnel. Society was a large and complex system that required scientific planning throughout its parts. Moreover, the use of social resources by a business consumed the resources just as completely as the equivalent amount of use by a government agency. Pressing the logic of this view to its ultimate conclusion, Arnold argued that business use of the resources of society amounted to another form of "taxation"—on a par with government taxation.[87] Arnold's was in essence a socialist vision, regarding all the basic instruments of production as part of the common property of society.

To be sure, in American business "any expenditures, however fantastic," and however profligate in the use of limited social resources available to meet national needs, were not commonly regarded by Americans as a drain on society. But who could deny that "the great industrial organizations collected the money which they spent from the same public from which the government collected"? In point of fact, Arnold now argued, the different public attitudes with respect to government spending and industrial spending were merely an "emotional reaction" that could not be justified "by any rational process of argument." It was another artifact of the "folklore of capitalism"— not a matter for economic analysis, but suitable for an anthropological form of inquiry.[88]

Yet there was a great irony because the "pure fiction" maintained in the United States that large business was private was in fact essential to the success of the little recognized and de facto form of socialism that was practiced in the United States. The fiction of privateness gave business the great advantage that it was free to make full use of expert skills and thus to pursue its goals efficiently. By contrast, interest-group pressures, ideological demands, and other irrational elements of American political culture frequently immobilized American government, holding it far short of its productive potential. Arnold thus wrote that the United States had "developed two coordinate governing classes: the one, called 'business,' building cities, manufacturing and distributing goods, and holding complete and autocratic power over the livelihood of millions; the other, called 'government,' concerned with the preaching and exemplification of spiritual ideals, so caught in a mass of theory that when it wished to move in a practical world it had to do so by means of a sub rosa political machine." Government was confronted by "a desperate spiritual need to impose impossible standards." On the other hand, American mythology gave business— in truth a public enterprise, even though regarded as private—a freedom from such burdens, allowing it to achieve with great success the productive aims of the nation.[89]

The members of the American economics profession, as Arnold contended, performed a vital practical role in maintaining this unique system of corporate socialism American style. It was their role to prevent the American public from achieving a correct understanding of the actual workings of the American economic system. Economists instead were assigned the task to dispense priestly blessings that would allow business to operate independent of damaging political manipulation. They accomplished this task by means of their message of "laissez faire religion, based on a conception of a society composed of competing individuals." However false as a description of the actual U.S. economy, this vision in the mind of the American public was in practice "transferred automatically to industrial organizations with nation-wide power and dictatorial forms of government." Even though the arguments of economists were misleading and largely fictional, the practical—and beneficial—result of their deception was to throw a "mantle of protection . . . over corporate government" from various forms of outside interference. Admittedly, as the economic "symbolism got farther and farther from reality, it required more and more ceremony to keep it up." But as long as this arrangement worked and there could be maintained "the little pictures in the back of the head of the ordinary man," the effect was salutary—"the great [corporate] organization was secure in its freedom and independence."[90] It was this very freedom and independence of business professionals to pursue the correct scientific answer—the efficient answer—on which the economic progress of the United States depended.

The progressives had earlier made the famous argument that there should be a strict dichotomy in government between politics and administration. Arnold was now arguing, in effect, that this progressive scheme had already been substantially realized in American society. However, it had been realized under false pretenses and in a deeply misleading way. Contrary to public belief, American business was in truth part of government. It was here that the scientific, expert, and efficient side of American government—the part of government divorced from politics—was actually to be found. If the United States had already adopted socialism without saying so, the business world was the vanguard of the de facto American system of corporate socialism.

If American socialism was in fact corporate socialism, it was in the world of U.S. business that the religion of humanity of Saint-Simon, the social gospel of Ely, and the Soviet of Technicians of Veblen were being realized. If the salvation of mankind was to be achieved on earth, following along a path of expanding productivity and growth of economic output, it was the managers and professional experts of the American corporate world who were leading the way to heaven on earth. Arnold's mission was to enable the formal and thus far ineffective institutions of American government to make their proper contribution to economic progress as well. The official agencies of government should be allowed to operate like businesses, thereby further expanding the realm of scientific management in American life.

Arnold's biting and sarcastic probe raised some difficult problems that he did not fully address. Since business freedom and independence from political interference—the very source of American economic efficiency—depended on antiquated and ever less convincing priestly incantations of economists, the prognosis might seem bleak. As the falsity of economic pronouncements was more widely recognized and the existing theological protections of business wore thin, the misleading distinction between "public" and "private" organizations might gradually disappear. If government then extended its direct influence to control the affairs of business as well, the efficiency of American business could be undermined. Rather than the current condition of efficient business and inefficient government, the future outcome might be inefficient business and inefficient government alike.

However, while this conclusion might easily be drawn from his analysis, it was not the conclusion of Arnold. Indeed, he sought with his argument to support the case for the New Deal expansion of the role of government. *The Folklore of Capitalism*, written in the 1930s in the heat of public controversy, was an attempt to provide intellectual support for the greater "exercise of national power to solve national problems in America."[91] His sarcastic portrayal of economic and legal theology was in fact designed to discredit this theology. By so doing, Arnold hoped to undermine the obstacles that were being raised in the courts and by economists to the adoption of New Deal programs. Like other progressives, Arnold had a deep faith in the ultimate triumph of scientific reason. He believed that, if the truth of the matter were laid bare for public scrutiny, the rational course would be for American government to become as expert, as professional, as skilled, as efficient as American business already was. If this required major changes in American government, and in American political culture, rational men should be able to find the way.

If Arnold acknowledged that American government was not yet

fulfilling the progressive expectation, it was an observation that would be made with growing frequency in the years to come. As Arnold had hoped, government responsibilities increased rapidly. Yet, contrary to Arnold's intention, government administrators seldom obtained the independence and freedom of their business peers. Arnold had assumed that a better understanding of American economic folklore would allow for a more rational and efficient exercise of government responsibilities. The actual results in the succeeding years would suggest that American society might not yet be prepared to confront the deep tensions that exist between popular democratic government and expert scientific government. Perhaps some myths and fictions were still socially necessary even to protect business efficiency. Perhaps the economic folklore of Arnold's day would be needed for a considerable time to come, continuing to help to smooth over these tensions.

One more important attempt would be made to reformulate the progressive gospel. In the years after World War II, it was John Kenneth Galbraith who undertook this task.

John Kenneth Galbraith: Announcer of the Arrival of Heaven on Earth

While the New Deal moved the specific reform agenda of the progressive movement decisively forward, it also advanced a spirit that was in some ways at odds with the progressive gospel. Indeed, the political practices of the New Deal raised questions that would challenge the feasibility of the progressive governing scheme.[92] This scheme depended on the existence of a unified national community able to act in concert and to which the professional administrators of the government would loyally devote their efforts. The creation of major new government power, if wielded by administrators for parochial or personal purposes, could well be more a social menace than a social benefit. The progressive vision demanded, in short, that a spirit of communal sacrifice and teamwork should infuse government and society—an outlook that the progressives in fact sought actively to instill in engineering, economic, and other professional groups.

Yet the progressive reforms of the New Deal were accomplished in significant part through the formation of interest-group coalitions. Woodrow Wilson had been the progressive idealist who believed that even the whole world might become a community of free men. Franklin

Roosevelt was the hardheaded realist who knew what was required to achieve practical results in politics.[93] Roosevelt did not depend on high-minded appeals, but sought to bring together constituencies to their mutual benefit. He sought to show them not how to sacrifice for the greater good, but how to use American democratic politics to their advantage. Indeed, to many of Roosevelt's critics—including old progressives such as Walter Lippmann—his attitudes often appeared jaded and cynical.

During World War II, a state of emergency gave the American national community a great common cause. After the war, however, some fundamental questions would have to be faced. To what extent was the United States a single community—or instead made up of coalitions of interests that pursued their own goals, sometimes finding it convenient to join together in American politics? To what extent did the specific institutional arrangements of American government, which prescribes a division of powers almost unique in the world, encourage a fragmented politics of interest-group interaction? Was there, on the other hand, any common interest identifiable in advance that could guide government administrators? Such questions were at the heart of the basic issue of reconciling democratic politics and the professional management of government. How could government be administered by expert elites with professional skills and training, while still adhering to American democratic principles of government not only "for" but also "by" the people?

To be sure, such issues were of ancient lineage. Theologians over the centuries had wrestled with the question: How could individual freedom of religious conscience coexist with the authority of the church? The Roman Catholic church had answered the question one way, emphasizing central church authority and limiting the role of individual understandings of faith. Protestantism had answered another way, emphasizing individual responsibilities for belief and a decentralized church structure.

In addressing such questions once again, another economist—John Kenneth Galbraith—would step forward to become a leading spokesman for the progressive gospel. Galbraith's vision was in many respects a redevelopment of the themes of Ely, Veblen, and Arnold. For example, Galbraith argued that it was important to recognize "capitalism" as resting in significant part on a "system of theology." The theology was obscuring the fact that capitalism is also a "practical matter" requiring pragmatic answers.[94] Many economists, however, were engaged in a "religious rite." Like others who preach the "conventional wisdom," their efforts were an "act of affirmation like reading aloud from the Scriptures or going to church." It was a necessary ceremony in order to "placate the gods" of the modern era.[95]

Economists devoted elaborate efforts to the analysis of the hypothetical world of perfectly competitive markets, while ignoring the realities of the American business world. As Arnold had argued, Galbraith also found that U.S. industry tended to have a feudal structure: "In the business peerage the ducal honors belong to the heads of General Motors, Standard Oil of New Jersey, Du Pont and the United States Steel Corporation."[96] Like the lords of feudal manors, the heads of large U.S. corporations exercised large discretionary power over their employees and other members of society. In the orthodox competitive model, no such discretionary power could exist, because the forces of market competition effectively circumscribe the actions of any individual business. If a business should raise prices above the competitive level, no one would buy the product. If a business should cut the wages of labor arbitrarily, it would lose its work force. Hence, prices, wages, and other economic results were objectively determined by impersonal mechanical forces—in a perfect market, that is.

However, Galbraith now found that in the U.S. industrial system "privately exercised economic power is less the exception than the rule." Indeed, it was necessary in the years after World War II to come to the "realization that economic power belonging to the genus monopoly was commonplace in the economy."[97] Galbraith would seek in the 1950s and 1960s to work out an answer to this question: Is this new power of American business—a political power over the lives of millions of people—compatible with American values and ideals?

Over the years, Galbraith developed two replies—both, in fact, reassuring and affirming of the legitimacy of existing economic arrangements. The first was the concept of "countervailing power," presented in *American Capitalism* in 1952. If big business should threaten to become too powerful, then big labor would emerge to check the power of business and to protect the wages of labor. Galbraith found that there was a general tendency for "power to be organized in response to a given position of power." Moreover, the existence of the one would prevent abuse by the other. Hence, "as a common rule, we can rely on countervailing power to appear as a curb on economic power."[98]

Galbraith also saw the role of government largely in these terms:

"The support of countervailing power has become in modern times perhaps the major peacetime function of the federal government."[99] If one party grew too powerful, then government could step in to reestablish the balance. Government could act to encourage the growth of countervailing private power—as it had done in the New Deal years, for example, in supporting the growth of labor unions. Alternatively, the powers of government might be wielded directly to assist weaker parties, as in the enactment of minimum wage legislation. The government should generally try to assume a role not of direct producer, but of the fair broker in a system of competition among alternative power centers.

Galbraith would later give a second and considerably different answer to the problem created for the American industrial system by concentrated power in private hands. Indeed, it was an answer closer to the tradition of Veblen, Arnold, and other progressive thinkers. Power in the large corporation did not actually constitute a problem, because it did not really belong to any one or a few individuals. Rather, as Galbraith would explain in 1967 in *The New Industrial State*, "power . . . has passed to the technostructure." It might appear that individuals were important but, in truth, "because individuals have more standing in the culture than organizations, they regularly get credit for achievement that belongs, in fact, to organizations." The transfer of power to the technostructure was not intended, but could not be avoided. The structure of U.S. industry entailed "complex tasks of planning and control" that demanded the services of experts. Moreover, sophisticated technology demanded still further "specialized talent" and "more comprehensive planning." American industry had thus today reached a stage that "only a group of men sharing specialized information could ultimately operate [it]."[100]

In the business world, as Galbraith explained, "the mature corporation . . . is not compelled to maximize its profits and does not do so." In large corporations, "the stockholders are without power" and the board of directors become the "passive instrument" of the corporate management. Within the corporation, beyond some minimum "the offer of more money to an engineer, scientist or executive may bring in little or no more effort." Instead, individuals were motivated to serve the corporation for the achievement of "some significant social goal." Moreover, since the corporation functioned in the "economic society" of the United States, "economic growth" and thus the growth of corporate production would "surely be a central goal." Another closely related corporate goal would be "rapid technical advance," which was in fact a key ingredient in the continued economic progress of society.[101] Further, the setting of goals was a circular process, as the goals of the corporation would tend to become the goals of society, and vice versa.

The corporation maintained its independence from government control on grounds of the existence of free-market competition that were "palpably bogus"—the same priestly incantations that Arnold had found were critical to keeping American "industrial government" free of political interference. Instead, the corporation was largely able to pursue the goals of the "members of the technostructure." The dominance of specialized knowledge existed not only within the firm, but extended across all society—involving similar outlooks, attitudes, and goals wherever the technostructure was found. Thus, although government did not control industry, the two existed in "intimate association," linked together as part of an informal but nevertheless effective "planning system." Because of the general "agreement on economic growth as a social goal," it was possible for members of the technostructure everywhere to have a "strong social purpose." Members of the technostructure could find motivation and satisfaction in their lives "in the secure knowledge that they are serving a larger purpose than their own."[102]

Veblen in the progressive era had called for a Soviet of Technicians, the displacement of absentee ownership, and the management of society by an elite core of production engineers and production economists. Arnold in the 1930s announced the arrival of corporate socialism, which made American industrial productivity the envy of the world, although government was still falling well short of its proper role. Galbraith in the 1960s confirmed Arnold's finding that the corporate world was in fact a world of American socialism and further stated that government as well had now come substantially into the hands of a technocratic and professional elite. The successes of the New Deal, Keynesian economics, and the general spread of public administrative skills had not only increased greatly the scope but also the capacity of U.S. government.

The social gospeler Ely had preached that a kingdom of heaven on earth could be reached through economic progress—a vision that was secularized by the progressives and that the New Deal sought to put into practice. Galbraith now pronounced this vision largely fulfilled, although some throwbacks to the old order still remained. The pursuit of economic growth gave meaning to the lives of the engineers, administrators, and other expert professionals who actually ran American society. They were not motivated by personal financial gain—at least as long as a basic standard of living was provided—but, like many of their priestly predecessors, by the needs of their fellowmen. The achievement of economic progress was the real meaning of history, the objective by which events could be interpreted and judged, the true road to modern salvation. Many professionals committed their lives to scientific discovery and technological advance, recognizing that in these areas lay the decisive instruments of economic progress. This progressive faith held the large and diverse elements of the American welfare state together; it was the critical glue that made it possible to forge a unified American community.

In 1957 Galbraith asserted in *The Affluent Society* that, at least in the United States, economic growth had already yielded a world of "great and quite unprecedented affluence."[103] In truth, the happy responsibility had fallen to Galbraith to announce that the arrival of heaven on earth was now finally at hand. The millennium was virtually an accomplished fact, though its arrival had been less sudden than many expected. It was therefore no longer appropriate to think in the old and outmoded terms of the problems of the road to affluence and salvation. The United States had already been blessed with a new and unprecedented event in all of history, and now faced only the problem of learning how to enjoy the bounties of a heavenly existence right here on earth.

The United States was the fulfillment not only of the hopes and prophecies of Ely, Veblen, and Arnold, but before them of Saint-Simon and Comte.[104] Galbraith would now preach the religion of humanity not as a hope for the future, but—to a remarkable degree—as something already realized. If Saint-Simon had called for a national council of Newton, and for many local temples of Newton, the American technostructure used other labels but had already substantially realized the prophecy. The American priesthoods of experts were found throughout the United States, managing its affairs competently and efficiently. The businesses of corporate America were among the leading temples of expertise. Americans lived in happy and affluent harmony, as Saint-Simon had foreseen—guided by the impersonal and scientific dictates of the progressive gospel of efficiency, as carried out by the industrial and government technostructure.

While the consequences may have been less redemptive than expected, Galbraith was essentially correct in his finding that the United States had attained many of the characteristics of a socialist country. Even though its economic folklore and the teachings of its economic priesthoods said otherwise, the reality of American socialism was sometimes so compelling that even the economic priesthood could no longer deny it. Eventually, Milton Friedman would be forced to admit that "almost every economic plank of the 1928 Socialist platform has been enacted by the U.S. in the period since."[105] The welfare state was indeed an American theocracy of science, based on the progressive gospel of efficiency. It was also a theocracy of the Roman tradition, a new Roman church of broad scope, encompassing many millions of people in a diverse community, a successor to the medieval Roman Catholic church that once covered most of Europe. The United States—most wedded of all nations to the Roman tradition—was the place of realization of the faith in reason, progress, law, equality, and the good life that has characterized this tradition over many centuries.

Yet neither ancient Rome nor the medieval Roman church had offered a permanent solution to the problems of the human condition. Indeed, despite Galbraith's picture of the peaceful and prosperous existence that had been realized in the United States, there were a few discordant notes even in his analysis. Partly reflecting his recognition of the realities of New Deal politics, Galbraith made surprisingly frequent reference to the concept of "power." Yet, power is an alien presence in a heaven where all people should be living in happy harmony. Power presupposes conflict and the desire of one person or group of persons to impose their will on others. True, Galbraith emphasized the workings of power more in 1952 in *American Capitalism* than in 1967 in *The New Industrial State*. In the latter book, the vision was further removed from human selfishness, irrationality, and sin. Yet, the problem suggested by Galbraith in 1952 could not be so easily banished. Many would not be able to agree with Galbraith's descriptions of a current society of corporate socialism in which all was well and good in American life—in essence, a fundamentally conservative vision, despite Galbraith's reputation to the contrary. Indeed, although Galbraith held high hopes, the more common finding of social analysts in the years after World War II was that the progressive vision of Ely, Veblen, and Arnold had been gravely flawed. If the United States had in effect already adopted its own form of socialism without saying so, American socialism was not altogether what had been advertised.

Ever since formulated in the early nineteenth century by Saint-Simon, the gospel of efficiency had depended on the existence of an objective and impersonal answer—the one scientific answer. Lacking such, the determinations of expert elites could easily come to represent the assertion of discretionary and arbitrary power by one person or class over another. Yet, those who examined closely the contents of American social science in the 1940s and 1950s exhibited a growing unease. In the key field of administrative science, Herbert Simon (later to win the Nobel prize in economics in 1978) announced in 1946 that all the efforts up until then had yielded meager results—consisting not of a set of valid scientific laws, but mostly of loosely formulated "proverbs" and in some cases even mutually contradictory proverbs at that.[106] In the years to follow, the questioning of the scientific qualities of a great deal of social science knowledge would not diminish, but intensify.

Another important element of the progressive design was the conviction that the decision-making role for democratic politics should be limited to nontechnical matters. Moreover—according to the famous progressive dichotomy—as scientific knowledge of government advances, the domain of expertise should expand while the domain of politics should shrink. But in the years after World War II, a number of leading American political scientists made their reputations by showing the deficiencies and (to a considerable degree) the failure in practice of the progressive prescription. There was in fact little evidence that experts were being granted independent authority over the administration of government. Even in areas that seemed to involve matters suitable for the professional exercise of technical skills, politics intruded regularly. Indeed, members of Congress and other politicians seemed to feel little hesitation in becoming actively involved in almost any kind of detail in almost any area of government, sometimes interfering in minor technical elements of administration.

In many cases, such political involvement was not intended to serve the interests of the national community. Rather, the motive was frequently to benefit one or another special interest group. Political scientists in the years after World War II generalized this observation to develop a new understanding of American politics. Rather than the progressive ideal of objective decision making by professional experts, most of American government was actually a domain of interest-group politics. Within this domain, decisions were reached by negotiation and compromise among the contending private parties. As explained in 1952 by political scientist David Truman in *The Governmental Process*,

Many . . . assume explicitly or implicitly that there is an interest of the nation as a whole, universally and invariably held and standing apart from and superior to those of the various groups included within it. This assumption is close to the popular dogmas of democratic government based on the familiar notion that if only people are free and have access to "the facts," they will all want the same thing in any political situation. . . . Such an assertion flies in the face of all that we know of the behavior of men in a complex society. Were it in fact true, not only the interest group but even the political party should property be viewed as an abnormality. The differing experiences and perceptions of men not only encourage individuality but also . . . inevitably result in differing attitudes and conflicting group affiliations.

Assertion of an inclusive "national" or "public interest" is an effective device in many . . . situations. . . . In themselves, these claims are part of the data of politics. However, they do not describe any actual or possible political situation within a complex modern nation.[107]

The progressive vision was still further undermined by the observation that American government could seldom establish any clear values or policy directions in advance. Rather, as Charles Lindblom wrote in 1959, government actually operated through a process best described as "the science of 'muddling through.' "[108] It was a process in which social values and policy directions typically emerged after the fact, inextricably mixed with the making of administrative and other expert decisions. Rather than clear goals served by comprehensive rational planning, government typically muddled forward incrementally. This observation raised a crucial issue: If values were to a significant degree embedded in technical decisions, then decisions made by the experts alone might also mainly reflect the social values of the experts themselves—an outcome much at odds with American democratic expectations.

By the mid-1960s, some observers were suggesting that a major crisis in American political thought existed, perhaps even grave enough to pronounce "the end of liberalism." Theodore Lowi thus found that in the years after World War II a new interpretation of American liberalism had become the conventional wisdom, which he labeled "interest-group liberalism." Galbraith's theory of countervailing power was only one among many theories in this genre. Lowi found, however, that interest-group politics was undermining the very legitimacy of American government. It was putting the powers of government at the service of private purposes. It often resulted in government actions that not only were poorly designed, but were also at cross-purposes with broader social needs and goals. As Lowi explained, "liberal governments cannot plan. Planning requires the authoritative use of authority. Planning requires law, choice, priorities, moralities. Liberalism replaces planning with bargaining. Yet at bottom power is unacceptable without planning."[109]

In summary, the progressive gospel encountered a crisis of faith in the years after World War II.[110] Despite Galbraith's reassuring messages of the 1950s and 1960s, his announcement of the arrival of heaven on earth was apparently premature (and Galbraith himself would later confess some doubts). There were a number of responses, but the most important was an attempt to reinterpret the progressive gospel—preserving its central tenets, yet redesigning the instruments of planning and administration. Rather than relying on direct administration by government, there would be a new emphasis on using the market mechanism to achieve socially determined goals. The planning role for government would be to design market incentives in a manner suitable to the realization of these goals. This reinterpretation of progressivism was carried out in large part by members of the economics profession, and its message may well be labeled "economic progressivism."

Chapter 6

The Message of Economic Progressivism

Professionally trained economists did not arrive in large numbers in most governments around the world until the second half of the twentieth century.[1] In the United States the number of economists began to rise significantly in the federal government during the Depression years of the 1930s, followed by larger waves during World War II.[2] After the war, the number of government economists then grew steadily until the 1970s, when it leveled off. By and large, these U.S. government economists—like most of their university peers—were disciples in the gospel of American progressivism. The progressive outlook had been modified, however, to respond to new currents of thought arising in the first half of the twentieth century. The result in many cases was an economic reinterpretation of the progressive gospel, the message of economic progressivism.

The Age of the Economist

Bertrand Russell believed until World War I that, "if rational men cooperated and used their scientific knowledge to the full, they could now secure the economic welfare of all." The discoveries of modern science for the first time in history had made possible the "conquest of nature," which would lead to a situation where not everyone would be "as rich as Croesus, but everybody could have as much of this world's goods as is necessary for the happiness of sensible people."

Mankind thus would find "the problem of poverty and destitution eliminated," which would yield a "more friendly and cooperative attitude between human beings" and allow for "the liberation of the impulses that make for joy."[3]

After World War I, however, Russell experienced major doubts concerning this happy faith of his youth. The war had shown that economic progress and the associated "thrift, industry and public spirit" could also be "used to swell the magnitude of the disaster by producing a greater energy in the work of mutual extermination." Contrary to Russell's early optimism, the satisfaction of the economic needs of mankind evidently did not serve to eliminate distrust, hatred, maliciousness, and other destructive forces of history. Men were evidently influenced in their behavior by factors beyond economic well being. Russell observed that "most of the people who were enthusiastically in favor of the war were going to lose money by it." Some observers still sought to explain the war in economic terms, but this was "in the nature of a rationalization." However regrettable, the truth was that "people wish to fight," even though they sometimes mask their violent urges by claiming "that it is to their interest to do so."[4]

World War I is generally considered to mark the end of the progressive era in the United States. The conclusions Russell drew were those of a whole generation of impressionable minds. The very heart of the progressive gospel was called into question. Economic progress might not be the path to heaven on earth, economic efficiency perhaps not the instrument of salvation. The progressive gospel would continue to guide the development of the American welfare state through the rest of the twentieth century and would still inspire influential spokesmen such as Thurman Arnold and John Kenneth Galbraith, but it would never again offer the certainties that had been so widely felt in the years prior to World War I.

In the 1930s and then World War II, even more dismal events caused faith in the transforming powers of economic abundance to be profoundly shaken. Indeed, it was readily apparent to a number of observers that the world was witnessing a revival of the horrors of religious warfare. Soon after the carnage of World War II, widely read interpretations would explain that "the hammer and sickle and the swastika are in a class with the cross. The ceremonial of their parades is the ceremonial of a religious procession. They have articles of faith, saints, martyrs, and holy sepulchers." Both the Bolsheviks and the Nazis offered a sense of "dedication, devotion, loyalty and self-surrender" in which the unmistakable character of a religion—if now assuming a secular form—could readily be seen.[5]

The preachers of a Darwinian struggle for survival of the fittest had brought mankind not toward a heaven on earth, but toward a new hell. The fiercest religious passions and most extreme hatreds had been stirred among followers of Darwinist convictions. The effect was not only to spur a reassessment of the benefits of economic progress, but also to challenge the position of Darwin's theory of evolution as the preeminent model for social thought. A more tolerant view of self-interested pursuits was encouraged. Perhaps the seeking of one's own advantage or satisfaction might prove after all a superior outlet for human energies, as compared with the military activities that had yielded such baneful consequences. If the religious crusaders of the first half of the twentieth century had tended to regard self-interest as "something tainted and evil," then the pursuit of individual economic gains might now have to be regarded in a newly favorable light.[6]

Even before World War I and World War II, it had been possible to look back on a nineteenth century filled with "grandiose philosophies of history and irrefutable laws of historical development." One theory of history had succeeded another—each severely critical of and exposing the deficiencies of its predecessors, and yet each in turn grossly overstating its own scientific merits. It was hard to avoid the conclusion that the high hopes of the nineteenth century for a grand theory of human existence had not materialized and that "the sciences of man were obliged to revert to less spectacular techniques, more similar to those employed in the physical sciences."[7] Rather than employing the historical method of Darwin, it would perhaps be necessary to return to the more rigorous method of Newton, which had so dominated the eighteenth century. The twentieth century would in fact be characterized as the "age of analysis"—more in tune with the Enlightenment and its "age of reason," while representing a reaction against the nineteenth century and its "age of ideology."[8]

In 1873, James Clerk Maxwell published his *Treatise on Electricity and Magnetism*. Maxwell's work was a milestone in the process by which physics in the twentieth century would reassert its preeminence in the popular understanding of valid scientific method. Electricity was the first fundamental discovery of physics with direct technological application, yielding products that deeply affected the life of the average person. Einstein then followed in the steps of and overshadowed Maxwell, much as Newton had succeeded Galileo. In 1905 Einstein published the special theory of relativity, as well as a second paper laying important foundations for twentieth-century quantum mechanics.

Einstein's efforts were guided by a faith that "nature is the realization of the simplest conceivable mathematical ideas." In developing scientific knowledge, the mathematics was central, because "experience may suggest the appropriate mathematical concepts, but they most certainly cannot be deduced from it." Instead, "the creative principle resides in mathematics," after which empirical studies then are undertaken to assess the "physical utility of a mathematical construction."[9] It was a reaffirmation of the scientific method of Newton. As applied by Einstein, this method had once again yielded startling and momentous results.

Seeking to find fundamental building blocks and hoping to develop knowledge as rigorously grounded as that of physics, the philosophy and social science of the twentieth century would also turn to mathematics and to other abstract methods. Even twentieth-century art departed from the literal imagery of previous centuries and adopted abstract forms that sought a reduction to fundamental entities beyond common sense and ordinary observation. Twentieth-century architecture rejected ornate design for sparse lines that should reveal deeper essences. Literature abandoned the linear, historical plots of the nineteenth-century novel—a literary version of the Darwinian story of evolution. Instead, twentieth-century writers have frequently explored the character of language or, like modern physicists, devised and dissected what were by conventional standards artificial worlds. These writers put the emphasis on the local context and on the individual detail, retreating from past efforts to give a grand statement of meaning and purpose (or perhaps indirectly saying that no such meaning and purpose were to be found).

The American progressives were out of touch with these trends of the twentieth century. They had not formulated their ideas with a mathematical or other similarly precise logic. Although preaching scientific management, they had failed to follow the scientific method in their own efforts. Indeed, progressive economists such as Ely and Veblen were often at odds with fellow members of the economics profession who relied heavily on mathematical methods. The latter usually used these methods to analyze a static world of social equilibrium that lacked the historical and evolutionary orientation of nineteenth-century thought. The efforts of mathematical economists reflected an outlook characteristic not of the nineteenth century, but of the eighteenth century.

The progressives saw society as a unified community, guided from on high by the skills of scientific experts. But twentieth-century physics began with electrons, protons, and other elementary particles and then built upward. Newton had similarly started with the motion of individual planets and moons to understand the workings of the solar system. A return to the framework of thought of physics would begin with the individual members of society and then seek to analyze the cumulative consequences—a mode of thought in fact characteristic of the Enlightenment.

As experience accumulated in the first half of the twentieth century with the actual practice of national economic management, disquieting developments raised further doubts about the progressive vision. In the twentieth century, many Marxist, socialist, and progressive parties came to power around the world. They were gaining opportunities to administer governments scientifically, to direct economies expertly, and generally to put designs for the scientific management of society into practice. In the Soviet Union under Lenin, the attempt at scientific management of the economic system—concerning which Marx had so little to say—soon yielded disarray. It would be an experience repeated by many newly socialist nations in different parts of the world.

The early view of orthodox Marxist-Leninist parties had been that, once social conflicts relating to the class struggle were abolished, the task of "planning and administration is extremely simple." It could simply be assumed that "the technical specialists (e.g., engineers, agronomists) will carry on as before and social rationality" will be readily forthcoming. The possibility that "the establishment of social rationality might be a complex matter, involving social and technical difficulties, is completely ignored." No difficulties in motivating managers and workers had been expected, for example, because the new social solidarity would mean that "everyone will have internalised the need to work in accordance with the national plan." Indeed, "implementation of the plan was assumed, by Marxists, to be a non-problem."[10] Experience, however, soon proved otherwise.

In democratic societies, the social scientists who arrived to bring rational and expert methods to government also often received a rude awakening. In the United States in the 1920s, the first economist to direct the new Bureau of Agricultural Economics in the U.S. Department of Agriculture soon departed, undermined by political enemies. Describing the encounter of professional experts with the world of politics, an historian of the New Deal writes that "some of those who had considered their mission to Washington a new step forward in the

relation between government and the academic community left with
the feeling that they had, in part at least, been subjected to a political
trick."[11] Indeed, the experiences of the New Deal years often suggested that "political elites only used social science for ends that still
fit into the jungle politics science was supposed to be eliminating."[12] It
also seemed that, when given a degree of actual power, some social
scientists were inclined "to act more like politicians than scientists, to
use scientific methodology loosely, conveniently, even irresponsi-
bly."[13]

Marxism, socialism, and progressivism were all—in one form or
another—theologies of the millennium, foreseeing the arrival of a
heaven on earth in the not-so-distant future. Many Judaic and Christian
messiahs in earlier centuries had similarly announced the expected
arrival of the millennium; occasionally they had even specified the day,
only to disappoint the hopes of followers. Two thousand years ago,
Christ was understood by his followers to have foretold the coming of
the kingdom of heaven on earth within a generation or two. When this
prophesy failed to materialize, early Christian theology needed to
rethink the future prospects for earthly existence. Christian theologians had little choice but to study practical problems such as church
organization and discipline, relations between church and state, and
other detailed concerns of the present world.

Many early Christians believed that private property and coercive
government—both products of human sinfulness since the fall of
man—were incompatible with Christian ideals. Some of them further
believed that the Christian faithful should join together to live communally without the coercive and thus evil influences that the institutions
of property and government inevitably introduced. Early Christian
theologians were compelled to address these issues as well in considering what Christianity might mean in a world where hatred, strife,
power seeking, cruelty, and other corruptions of human nature evidently were not about to disappear as rapidly as had been expected.
Now, in the first half of the twentieth century, the evident failure of
scientific and economic progress to fulfill the prophecies of heaven on
earth had created a similar set of concerns. Indeed, there were a whole
host of practical matters that called for new answers. Should the
control of industry be held in the hands of government, of managers,
or of workers—or should the goal of socialized ownership and control
perhaps be abandoned as unrealistic, and individual private ownership
encouraged? The progressive design had originally suggested that
business and government would blend together into one grand admin-

istrative apparatus under the dominance of engineers, economists, and professional experts of all kinds. Did this mean, for example, that there would be no significant distinctions maintained between government activities and business activities?

Many of the leading economists of the modern era—Marx, Spencer, Saint-Simon, Bentham, for instance—had not been formally trained in the field of economics (in many cases no such formal discipline had yet existed). However, the growing conviction that the scientific management of society was possible led in the late nineteenth century to the widespread creation of economics and other specialized departments within American universities. It would be the task of these departments to supply the detailed technical knowledge to administer governments, manage businesses, and generally support the efforts of all manner of social organizations. When the experiences of early socialist and progressive government suggested that the scientific management of society might be a much more difficult undertaking than previously suspected, the task of developing new answers would now be assumed in many cases by men professionally trained as economists.

Members of the economics profession were well placed in several respects for this responsibility. First, the scientific management of society necessarily involves as a central element the production of goods and services. Second, economists were mostly comfortable with—indeed, many had long based their analyses on—the assumption that human behavior would be motivated to a significant degree by self-interest. As compared with the characteristic assumptions of social solidarity and other altruistic motives of early progressivism, this typical outlook of economists now seemed in closer touch with the real world of human behavior that the history of the early twentieth century was revealing. And third, in the late nineteenth century a number of economists had begun to develop their knowledge in a mathematical framework. Of the branches of social science, the subject matter of economics was most suited to a mathematical formulation. Economists were therefore prepared to conduct their analyses and to develop their conclusions in the same language that twentieth-century physics was employing with such startling success.

The course followed by economists was not to abandon the progressive design, but to reinterpret it. The core progressive faith in human progress achieved by the application of rational analysis would remain. Salvation was still to be achieved by following a path of economic progress, directed by men possessed of expert knowledge—if now supplied by economic professionals. Indeed, the new gospel, "economic progressivism," moved the progressive gospel closer to Aristotle, Aquinas, Adam Smith, and other central figures of the Roman tradition. They too had assumed that self-interest would characterize the behavior of ordinary men on this earth. For them as well, the pursuit of happiness and of the good life was considered a proper cause for most men—until perhaps they meet another fate in the hereafter.

John Maynard Keynes: Architect of Economic Progressivism

The importance of John Maynard Keynes in the twentieth century has been compared with that of Adam Smith and Karl Marx to earlier centuries. Keynes is in fact the only economist of the twentieth century with whom a "revolution" is associated. The Keynesian revolution sought not the violent overthrow of the government, but the establishment of the welfare state with which we are so familiar in the second half of the twentieth century. Keynes was the leading spokesman for the new economic interpretation that would supplant the orthodoxies of American progressivism and of European socialism in guiding the welfare state.

Keynes, an Englishman, had absorbed well the message of World War I and other disturbing events of the early twentieth century. As he would write in 1936 in *The General Theory*, there were "dangerous human proclivities" at large in the world, which threatened to yield "cruelty, the reckless pursuit of personal power and authority, and other forms of self-aggrandisement." Moreover, the prospects did not appear to Keynes to be good for "the task of transmuting human nature." More promising was "the task of managing it." Fortunately, it was possible to direct existing impulses into "comparatively harmless channels by the existence of opportunities for money-making and private wealth." Although someday there might be an "ideal commonwealth" where men would "take no interest in the stakes," at present "prudent statesmanship" required a recognition that "a significant section of the community is in fact strongly addicted to the money-making passion." Exhibiting again his gift for the apt phrase, Keynes explained that "it is better that a man should tyrannise over his bank balance than over his fellow citizens." This strategy could further be turned to public benefit because "there are valuable human activities which require the motive of money-making and the environment of private wealth-ownership for their full fruition."[14]

The Keynesian design thus offered a "wide field for the exercise of private initiative and response" within which "the traditional advantages of individualism will still hold good." In this arena, "private self-interest will determine what in particular is produced." Indeed, Keynes finds that such a system is a superior way of organizing the production of goods and services. There is "no reason" to believe that the private sector "seriously misemploys the factors of production which are in use." There is further a great "advantage to efficiency of the decentralization of decisions and of individual responsibility."[15]

Besides its efficiency, the second great advantage of a system of private ownership is that it is "the best safeguard of personal liberty." It gives leeway for a "variety of life" that "preserves the traditions which embody the most secure and successful choices of former generations." The lack of such opportunity is the great defect of the "homogeneous or totalitarian state" that has proven so attractive to many twentieth-century thinkers. One major advantage of "authoritarian state systems" is that they solve the critical problem of unemployment, but this advantage is obtained "at the expense of efficiency and freedom." Hence, Keynes is strongly of the opinion that a private economy "is the most powerful instrument to better the future."[16]

There remains, however, the grave problem of unemployment—particularly pressing in the midst of the Depression of the 1930s. What is needed, Keynes reasons, is "a right analysis of the problem to cure the disease whilst preserving efficiency and freedom." Indeed, *The General Theory* is the answer. According to its prescription, the state will be required to undertake a "somewhat comprehensive socialisation of investment." By manipulating properly the aggregate levels of investment, in order to keep aggregate investment in balance with aggregate savings in society, it will be possible to ensure that social resources are kept fully employed. Because only investments need be manipulated, it will be possible to avoid the creation of "a system of State Socialism which would embrace most of the economic life of the community."[17]

Investment can be substantially influenced by government policies with respect to interest rates and by other influences on "the basic rate of reward" to owners of productive resources. Direct government investment through public expenditures may also be required, but only in sufficient magnitudes to make up for any shortfalls of private investment below desired levels. The overall approach is thus to adopt those government policies that are necessary in order to direct investment, as well as in order to direct private behavior in some other limited areas "in which the free play of economic forces may need to be curbed or guided." The result will admittedly involve "a large extension of the traditional functions of government," but in most areas "there is no more reason to socialise economic life than there was before."[18]

Thus, as developed in *The General Theory*, the Keynesian system is—like the orthodox progressive gospel that preceded it—directed to the achievement of efficiency. But it is a new gospel of efficiency, now to be realized in large part through the marketplace. If the progressives had looked to skilled technical experts to guide society, the Keynesian system still relies on experts, but they will now be economic experts whose science is the economic workings of the market. If the progressives had sought to achieve aims through government, Keynesians will still look to government, but now government will accomplish social goals through the manipulation of the market. Instead of government planning for the specific organization of industry, government experts will develop a design for what might be called a "planned market." If progressives had sought a separation of government administration from politics, it will still be necessary in the new Keynesian scheme to achieve a separation of economic experts from politics. In short, it is still a progressive gospel, but as now interpreted by Keynes it becomes a new economic version: the gospel of economic progressivism.

In the United States, the creation of the Council of Economic Advisors in 1946 was a key step toward the realization of this vision. American disciples of Keynes such as Lawrence Klein were spreading the word in the 1940s that "the Keynesian economic system is essentially a machine which grinds out results according to where the several dials controlling the system are set. The functional relations are the building blocks of the machine, and the dials are the parameters (levels and shapes) of these functions."[19] The 1930s were preoccupied with the problems of unemployment, but the dials could be set to serve other social purposes as well. Solving pollution and other problems of the environment, for example, might require government to step in to alter private incentives through the use of taxes or through other manipulations of the market outcome.

Having achieved a maximum total output, it would be appropriate to redistribute the social benefits among the various segments of society. In the years after World War II, some groups in the United States contributed as much as 90 percent of their income on the margin to federal tax payments. Therefore, not only could the Keynesian system solve the problem of unemployment, but also the high level of goods and services that it produced became in significant degree the collective property of all society. With comprehensive instruments of redistribution available, the final allocation of income became a matter of social choice as well—potentially far different from the market outcome.

Outside the United States, the doctrines of economic progressivism were more likely to bear a democratic socialist label. In Western Europe, a new pragmatic socialism was emerging, learning from the false hopes and the economic mistakes of earlier years. It would apparently be necessary to permit a much wider pursuit of self-interest, to encourage private industry, and to make other compromises with socialist orthodoxies of earlier years. These ideas, which sought important roles both for government and for the market, became the guiding faiths of the welfare states of Western Europe.[20] Following the political upheavals of 1989, Eastern Europe has begun to move in this direction as well. The Soviet Union, China, and other communist nations have been more tentative, but have also given the use of markets a greater role in their recent planning.

The Keynesian message was innovative not only in matters of economic substance, but also in the manner of its presentation. In this respect, Keynes again showed a sensitivity to the trends of his time. Although *The General Theory* dealt with broad questions of social organization, Keynes directed his book to his fellow economic professionals. He announced on the first page that the book dealt with "difficult questions of theory," thus acknowledging the influence that expert professional elites were now wielding in government centers of power. Keynes further filled *The General Theory* with an algebra of "supply functions," "marginal propensities to consume," "investment demand schedules," and "multipliers." By using such mathematics, he was able to draw on some of the immense social authority of physics in the twentieth century.

In fact, in *The General Theory*, Keynes went out of his way to create parallels between his efforts and those of Einstein. Einstein had discovered a "general theory" of time and space; Keynes had now discovered a "general theory" of economic interactions. Einstein's theory of relativity had shown that dynamic factors could fundamentally alter the conclusions of Newtonian physics; Keynesian economics now showed that dynamic factors could yield new and unexpected laws fundamentally altering the behavior of the economy. Indeed, as Einstein had shown for physics, the old and comfortable Newtonian equilibrium might well prove similarly incorrect and misleading in a dynamic economic context. Newtonian mechanics had been reassigned as a special case of Einsteinian physics; now classical economics became a special case of Keynesian economics. Keynes's intent was apparent to some of his contemporaries, one of whom remarked critically that "Einstein has actually done for Physics what Mr. Keynes believes himself to have done for Economics."[21] The eighteenth century had wrapped its social ideas in the mantle of Newton, the late nineteenth and early twentieth centuries in the theories of Darwin; now social thinkers later in the twentieth century would seek to cloth themselves in the dress of Einstein.

Besides efficiency and freedom, Keynes saw one further key advantage to his design: that private ownership and a market system "might be more favorable to peace." One of the main causes of war has been "the competitive struggle for markets." If the problem of unemployment of resources could be solved through the application of economic knowledge, there need be "no important economic forces calculated to set the interest of one country against that of its neighbours."[22] In short, the efficiency of a modern industrial economy—if properly harnessed—could bring about the abolition of one of the prime causes of warfare throughout history. It would be a critical step along a path by which economic progress could be expected to yield a future world of peace and prosperity on earth.

Indeed, economic progressivism is—like the older orthodox progressivism—yet another modern economic theology, yet another gospel of the salvation of mankind through economic progress. As material abundance renders past sources of conflict irrelevant, human existence will be fundamentally changed—although perhaps not so rapidly or so easily as earlier progressives had assumed. Keynes himself once stated his conviction that "the economic problems may be solved, or be at least within sight of solution, within a hundred years. This means that the economic problem is not—if we look into the future—the permanent problem of the human race." In the long run, and it is not so very long at that, there is every reason to believe that the conditions of earthly existence will be radically new. We can look toward a heavenly future, which Keynes on one occasion portrayed in the following terms:

There are changes . . . which we must expect to come. When the accumulation of wealth is no longer of high social importance, there will be great changes in the code of morals. We shall be able to rid ourselves of many of the pseudo-moral principles which have hag-ridden us for two hundred years, by which we have exalted some of the most distasteful of human qualities into the position of the highest virtues. We shall be able to afford to dare to assess the money-motive at its true value. The love of money as a possession—as distinguished from the love of money as a means to the enjoyments and realities of life—will be recognized for what it is, a somewhat disgusting morbidity, one of those semi-criminal, semi-pathological propensities which one hands over with a shudder to the specialists in mental disease. All kinds of social customs and economic practices, affecting the distribution of wealth and of economic rewards and penalties, which we now maintain at all costs, however distasteful and unjust they may be in themselves, because they are tremendously useful in promoting the accumulation of capital, we shall then be free, at last, to discard.

I look forward, therefore, in days not so very remote, to the greatest change which has ever occurred in the material environment of life for human beings in the aggregate. But, of course, it will all happen gradually, not as a catastrophe. Indeed, it has already begun.[23]

Like other prophets of the millennium, Keynes had his loyal disciples. They formed what Albert Hirschman finds to have been "a group of extraordinarily devoted followers" who functioned as "a band of sect-like initiates and devotees." These followers of Keynes were bound together by "the exhilarating feeling of possessing the key to truth while being beleaguered by a coalition of ignoramuses and sinister interests." It was their mission to show the world that there was "an attractive 'third way' that could compete with the various fascist and Marxist creeds of the time." It was in fact the way of the welfare state. Keynes's disciples undertook with great energy and commitment to "spread the message" and "to preach their gospel to a variety of as yet unconverted natives"—not only in the United States, but throughout the world.[24]

The Keynesian message of economic progressivism proved, of course, to be a great triumph. Its answer to the problem of the division of responsibility between the government and the market would be embodied in the American welfare state of the second half of the twentieth century—and in many other nations as well. Yet, as has often turned out to be the case in the modern age, the Keynesian gospel soon ignited new controversies. Much as in the age of Newton, and then in the age of Darwin, now again in the age of Einstein disciples soon fell to quarreling among themselves. The proper scientific understanding of Keynesian economics seemed more elusive with the passage of time. Reviewing the spate of economic controversies, one economist recently commented that, "again and again, violent polemical claims are made, which are subsequently withdrawn." There was a "continuing quarrel about what Keynes really meant," which in some cases could be blamed on Keynes himself because "*The General Theory* contains at least three, and perhaps more, versions of Keynesian theory." All in all, it was "one of the most frustrating and irritating controversies in the history of economic thought"; and as with other economic controversies, it often bore a distinct resemblance to "medieval disputations at their worst."[25]

Besides the scholastic qualities of the economic debate, and despite vast changes in economic circumstances, the American welfare state of the late twentieth century resembles in other ways as well the Roman Catholic church of the late medieval era. The medieval encouragement of individual pursuit of the good life was conditioned on compatibility with the basic goals of the church. Today, the private sector is similarly subordinate to higher goals of the welfare state, which seeks to "use" the market for its own purposes. The medieval grounds for necessary intervention in private markets closely resemble the grounds asserted in the welfare state. The medieval scholastics condemned monopoly, finding that a market price was "just" only when sufficient market competition existed. Antitrust and other policies of the welfare state have reflected a similar sense of economic justice and a need for social regulation of monopolistic practices. The scholastics of the medieval church argued that price discrimination and other discriminatory trading practices were unjust. The activities of the Interstate Commerce Commission and the Federal Trade Commission have been based in part on a similar interpretation of economic ethics, originally spurred by popular resentment of the discriminatory pricing rules of the railroads.

The citizens of the welfare state have regarded with disfavor any large accumulation of speculative profits and other financial rewards unrelated to production—another characteristic attitude of the medieval Roman church. Efforts to improve the condition of workers and the poor represent a welfare-state acceptance of the special obligations to the poor long recognized by the Roman Catholic church, which built an elaborate system of medieval charitable institutions to serve this purpose. High rates of income taxation in the welfare state have required each individual to share at least in part the product of his or her labor with other members of the community—yet another element of the welfare state embodying a medieval concept of economic justice.

The gospel of economic progressivism is, in short, the most recent theology to develop the characteristic outlook of the Roman tradition.

Paul Samuelson: Author of the Bible of Economic Progressivism

During the second half of the twentieth century, Paul Samuelson has been probably the best-known living economist in the world. In 1969, he became the third economist to receive the Nobel prize. Two of his books—both published in the late 1940s—had a major impact on the economics profession of the following decades. The *Foundations of Economic Analysis* was directed to Samuelson's professional peers, and it helped to shape the content and set the tone for the research efforts of the next generation of economists. Samuelson's second book was directed to a popular audience—especially university students. Among economists, the authorship of a successful textbook is not typically regarded as deserving of the highest professional prestige. Yet, the publication in 1948 of Samuelson's new textbook, *Economics,* was a significant event in itself for the history of modern economic theology.

The book would go through many editions and be read by millions of readers not only in the United States, but in other nations around the world. For the first time, the gospel of economic progressivism was being taught in a systematic and accessible way. If Keynes had put forth the key concepts, Samuelson produced the new bible. Samuelson's *Economics* was the first comprehensive and widely available statement of the economic gospel of the late-twentieth-century welfare state—a set of beliefs on which the social legitimacy of American governing institutions today still depends.

Samuelson filled the textbook with numerous illustrations and examples, seeking to present many details of a twentieth-century economy. *Economics* also contains the basic principles on which the economic system is said to rest. The first task is to ensure that society will make full use of its resources. Achieving the maximum productive efficiency of the economy does not allow for idle workers or factories. While some unemployment is part of the normal course of changing jobs and reordering a dynamic economy, beyond that there should be no unemployed resources. Fortunately, as Samuelson explained to a generation of readers, Keynes had provided the solution to this problem. If political leaders and public opinion could be sufficiently enlightened, economists now had the technical understanding to keep the economy in full employment.

In 1961 in the fifth edition of *Economics*, Samuelson thus stated that there was a broad agreement among American economists on what might be called "the neo-classical economics." It was "accepted in its broad outlines by all but a few extreme left-wing and right-wing writers." Guided by the economic knowledge now available to prescribe appropriate "monetary and fiscal policies," it would be possible to "avoid the excesses of boom and slump and [we] can look forward to healthy progressive growth." Fiscal measures would be critical contributors to the "maintenance of a growing, high-employment economy free from excessive inflation or deflation." In short, by means of "the modern analysis of income determination, . . . the economist is now justified in saying that the broad cleavage between microeconomics and macroeconomics has been closed."[26] The deep worries aroused by the Depression of the 1930s—the fear that Marxist and other previous critics might be correct with respect to inevitable large instabilities of a free-market economy—need no longer be a serious concern.

Keynes's remarkable new message is especially to be welcomed because Samuelson agrees with Keynes that the workings of the market offer the most efficient way of organizing consumption and production in society. Indeed, Samuelson's manner of explaining the efficiency of the market represented an especially important contribution of *Economics*. The economy for Samuelson is a single mechanical "system." The economic engineers of this system must devise a technical solution to the following complex problem: "What" will be the levels and types of production; "how" will this production be obtained; and "for whom" will the production be intended?[27] As society's scientific experts on the workings of the economic system, economists recognize that it presents an immense burden of calculation. Every part of the economy is in at least some small way linked to every other part. A change in a factor of production here, or some other economic factor there, could affect aspects of production and consumption in innumerable ways.

Hence, in order to solve the economic problem, it is necessary to break the economic system up into constituent and more manageable parts. If each of these parts performs efficiently, then perhaps the parts can be linked together in a way that will maximize the efficiency of the overall system. In the same way, a computer programmer might currently seek to avoid a brute-force solution to a complex problem, and instead seek to devise an efficient algorithm by which the solution to a number of smaller problems can be reached and then combined to yield a grand solution. The competitive market is—as described by Samuelson in *Economics*—just such an algorithm, solving the immensely complicated technical problem that is presented by an economic system serving a large twentieth-century nation.

The market becomes in Samuelson's explanation a computational instrument that is the most effective of all available systems for calculating the economic solutions needed in a large modern economy. The market is an "elaborate mechanism for unconscious coordination through a system of prices and markets." This "market mechanism" provides a "communication device for pooling the knowledge and actions of millions of diverse individuals." Through the workings of the market mechanism, society achieves a solution to "one of the most complex problems imaginable, involving thousands of unknown variables and relations." Although "nobody designed it" originally for this purpose, the market—as it has informally developed—functions like a "central intelligence." The price system of the market "is society's signaling device. Like a master who gives his donkey carrots and kicks to coax him forward, the price system deals out profits and losses to get the What, How, and For Whom questions answered."[28]

Just as a computer system requires oversight and repairs, government economic managers may in some cases have to intervene to correct defects in the market mechanism. It thus may be necessary to regulate monopoly as well as to "use taxes or subsidies to offset distorting external diseconomies and economies."[29] Where market incentives do not yield a socially optimal result, the government should not step in directly but should instead manipulate the market mechanism indirectly through altering the incentives that determine the behavior of private parties. In this way, social goals can still be achieved by government design, but without sacrificing the allocational efficiency of the market mechanism.

Once government has assured the achievement of the full productive potential of society, there remains the further concern that the distribution yielded by the operation of the market mechanism may be objectionable. In the welfare state, Samuelson finds that this problem is remedied by both taxes and "transfer expenditures." By means of the latter, "the more fortunate citizens are paying for the consumption of the less fortunate," and in the welfare state "most people will feel that this is not improper"—at least within reasonable bounds. Moreover, "one must include in the activities of the modern welfare state any redistribution of income it brings about by the way it differentiates in its tax system"—a tax system that is in fact highly progressive in at least its formal structure.[30] For Samuelson, the American welfare state thus consists of an organic community—a "society"—that manages its affairs in the following way: Society maintains full employment by means of government macroeconomic policies; coordinates production and consumption (its "microeconomic" tasks) through use of the market mechanism, thus ensuring productive efficiency; and achieves the socially desired distribution of income by taxing away goods and services from some people and transferring them to other people.

Allowing for the desired distribution of income, Samuelson describes the economic problem as being reduced finally to a selection from "society's menu of choices." This menu is given by the "production-possibility curve"—a set of alternative goods and services available to society that depends only on "fixed totals of resources" and "given technological knowledge."[31] The achievement of the full productive potential of society thus is a matter of combining inputs into production and distributing outputs in an efficient way. It is this technical problem that the informational efficiency of the market solves better than any comparable instrument of human design.

Samuelson assures his many readers that, if these tenets of the American welfare state are accepted and properly implemented, society will enter onto a path leading "to rapid economic progress and security, to efficient pricing and economical use of all our resources." The U.S. "mixed-economy"—that is, based on direct government assumption of some responsibilities such as national defense, but largely on government planning of the market mechanism—has already demonstrated "the most rapid advance of productivity and living standards ever achieved anywhere. If our people really want faster growth, it is capable of giving this to them." The American welfare state thus has a "great future [lying] before it."[32] If this vision was not original to Samuelson—Friedrich Hayek, for example, had emphasized the information advantages and coordinating efficiencies of a market mechanism in a famous 1945 article—it would be Samuelson's *Economics* that spread the new gospel farthest and widest.[33]

The enthusiastic American reception for *Economics* reflected in part Samuelson's status as the leading young economist of his generation. Samuelson did not achieve this status by *Economics,* but from his many writings directed to other members of the economics profession—especially his *Foundations of Economic Analysis* (1947). Until the 1930s, arguments by economists were still typically developed in the written word. When quantitative research was undertaken, it usually consisted of the manipulation of geometrical diagrams, the assembly of simple facts and figures, and the preparation of charts and tables. Yet, it was a time when the age of Darwin was losing out to the age of Einstein, when social authority would increasingly be derived from mathematics. If economic laws were not mathematical in character, then they would not pass the new and more demanding tests for validity of the twentieth century. The conclusions of economists might well be lumped with other ideological and metaphysical baggage of past eras that was now rapidly being discarded.

The Nobel prize that Samuelson received and his general prominence in the economics profession rest on his having accepted this challenge. Samuelson has been to twentieth-century economics what Bertrand Russell was to twentieth-century philosophy and mathematics—both men hoping to ground their subject in pure principles of logic, and removing the imprecisions inherited from earlier efforts. Samuelson stated at the very beginning of *Foundations* that "I have come to feel that Marshall's dictum that 'it seems doubtful whether any one spends his time well in reading lengthy translations of economic doctrines into mathematics' . . . should be exactly reversed. The laborious literary working over of essentially simple mathematical concepts such as is characteristic of much of modern economic theory is not only unrewarding from the standpoint of advancing the science, but involves as well mental gymnastics of a peculiarly depraved type."[34]

In fact, as seen by many of his professional peers, Samuelson achieved a great success in reworking economics to justify its status as a valid science. In 1948, one prominent economist announced in a professional review that in *Foundations* "all the various branches of economic analysis are unified by a small number of basic principles"— much like the discoveries of Newton and Einstein had accomplished for physics.[35] Samuelson succeeded in bringing the scientific rigor of physics to economics, or so it would seem to a whole generation of American economists.

In their enthusiasm,. however, economists often fail to notice that, unlike Newton or Einstein, Samuelson's use of mathematics has not yielded any remarkable new conclusions concerning the workings of economic systems. Indeed, Samuelson's mathematics in many cases showed that conclusions similar to those already reached by previous economists could still be reached, if now using more precise reasoning. Along with many other economists, Samuelson spelled out more exactly the initial necessary assumptions. He often added refinements and modifications. Yet, when all was said and done, the results of previous economics were more altered in form—transformed to a newly mathematical appearance—than altered in substance. In one of his most famous articles, for example, Samuelson showed how government should cumulate the demands of individual members of the public in determining how much to produce of a public good or service.[36] The conclusion was not much of a surprise, but Samuelson now developed it in a new mathematical way that spawned a large new literature.

With respect to the conduct of the affairs of the world, Samuelson had much more to say, and his influence was much greater through the message of *Economics*. Keynes had paved the way for the final abandonment of classical faith in the Newtonian market, operating according to natural laws based on the fundamental force in society: the force of self-interest. With *Economics*, Samuelson completed the task of reinterpreting faith in the market. The market of *Economics* is not a Newtonian solar system in natural equilibrium among its parts; it is instead a mechanical instrument engineered by economic experts in the service of whatever purposes society may deem appropriate. Samuelson's vision owes as much to the inspiration of Saint-Simon and his plans for the scientific management of society as it does to the writings of Adam Smith.

In Samuelson's new telling, the hidden hand of Adam Smith has become a scientific intelligence for planning and coordinating all the activities of society. Admittedly, the market was not originally created and designed by men; it was in fact an unintended and unforeseen gift. But now that the market exists, mankind must do more than humbly submit to the dictates of the forces of self-interest. Men must actively seek to understand the workings of the market, to discover its laws, that the market may be better used for human purposes. To understand and to make available the secrets of the market is to provide the basis for social progress. It is to reveal the ways of the instrument that has given modern men a power on their own to achieve a heavenly future of peace and prosperity—to gain their own earthly salvation.

To use the market is, therefore, to employ an instrument that in the modern age has assumed powers that in earlier eras could be assumed only by God. In the market mechanism, mankind has been blessed with yet another unseen and unplanned "central intelligence"—a secular divinity now found in the mid-twentieth century that can show humanity the way to a heavenly future. As the medieval God of Aquinas expected that men should help themselves through the exercise of their reason, so the unseen central intelligence of Samuelson also requires rational understanding as a condition for reaping the full divine reward.

In the years following World War II, the American economics profession would in fact devote the largest part of its research efforts to a systematic and painstaking inquiry into the laws of the market mechanism. Economics journals were filled with analyses of market outcomes under assumptions of almost every imaginable kind. It was all part of the effort to lay the basis of rational knowledge for the economic salvation that the American welfare state held in store.

If *Economics* delivered this important message, the role played by *Foundations* was in large part symbolic and ceremonial. The formalism of *Foundations* assured the world that economic discoveries had in truth achieved the status of scientific knowledge. The market mechanism thus could be counted on to deliver as prescribed; any market failings could be correctly diagnosed and remedied by the economic priesthood. After Samuelson, the economics profession would increasingly be split into two camps: one of applied economists fulfilling the practical message of *Economics,* and a second group of theoretical economists performing the ceremonial duties of *Foundations*. The first group said what to do; the second bestowed theological blessings and asserted moral authority. There were, to be sure, some economists such as Samuelson who moved back and forth between the two functions.

Indeed, portrayals of future heavenly qualities have frequently been prominent in religious symbolism. Paintings of angels and of paradise were celebrated in the Middle Ages. Scholastic theologians sought through finely developed webs of reasoning to deduce qualities of a heavenly existence in the hereafter. These efforts served to affirm and to strengthen the convictions of the medieval faithful. Now in the twentieth century the heavenly future would be on earth, reached through a new central intelligence guiding the affairs of men—that of the market mechanism. The economic priesthood of the twentieth-century welfare state would therefore explore the full details of a different heavenly future. An enormous body of economic analysis would be produced to describe in every aspect the characteristics of this future world of the market mechanism, whose perfect efficiency must fairly soon mean also the abolition of economic scarcity.

Such economic portrayals in the great majority of instances took as their starting point the assumption that market participants were perfectly informed in every respect relevant to their market role, that final market equilibriums were reached in a perfectly costless fashion, and that the level of competition in all markets was perfect as well. In truth, under these assumptions any economic system—market or otherwise—will achieve perfect efficiency. Indeed, in a world of perfect information, only a political dispute can prevent the achievement of perfect efficiency, because any decision that results in inefficiency must by definition be made knowingly. Yet, economists treated issues of politics as outside their proper scope. As a result, their analyses shed little light on practical questions, while instead serving an artistic and symbolic purpose—portraying for and thus assuring the faithful of the prospect of a future heavenly existence.

This happy world pictured in economic analysis was also a world always in perfect equilibrium, never in transition from one economic circumstance to another. As a result, there were no unemployed workers, bankrupt businesses, or industrial ghost towns to be found. As one economist has recently noted, "the concept 'equilibrium' . . . evokes the image of a world in harmony."[37] If the market in practice functions as a trial-and-error learning process—potentially involving high costs and much discomfort to many participants—the imagery offered by most economists ignored these elements. Perhaps they were not worthy of attention; they could be regarded as mere blemishes marring a picture that was meant above all to inspire faith.

Symbolically, economists were in effect saying that the losers in the competitive system are making a proper contribution to the forward march of progress on earth. Compared with the salvation of mankind, the temporary sufferings of particular individuals have always had limited theological interest. In medieval theology as well, the affairs of this world—the medieval "short run"—ultimately were regarded as a minor concern, as compared with reaching the medieval "long run" in the next world. The economists of the welfare state thus follow a well-established trail in focusing on the long run and relegating the adjustments and discomforts of the short run to the status of inconsequential.

Admittedly, some economists have sought to portray the actual qualities of the market as it is experienced by many participants. Joseph Schumpeter, for example, portrayed a business world of big winners, big losers, short-lived monopolies, and a steady succession of firms.[38] In the past few years, economists have begun increasingly to examine economic worlds in which ignorance is widespread and in which mistakes and errors are permitted to occur. They propose to introduce decision-making costs, information costs, and error costs into their analyses. Two such economists not long ago acknowledged that "the organization of decision making (and the corresponding errors, costs, and consequences) has played little or no role in some of the most important previous work" with respect to the character of alternative economic systems.[39]

In truth, the market mechanism has never been analytically demonstrated to be the most efficient means of producing and distributing the resources of society, when all costs—including information costs, search costs, costs of wasted resources due to failures, and other trail-and-error costs—are taken into account. Neither, however, has any other economic system ever been shown to be superior to the market. At the level of economic theory, the issue remains almost entirely unresolved. Indeed, it is more obscured than illuminated by most existing economic theory.

It is only at the level of practical economic experience that a verdict in favor of the market seems to stand on firm ground. The evidence of practical experience all over the world has been that market economies exhibit greater economic efficiency and more rapid growth. Indeed, the market economies of the world have set the pace in achieving the enormous improvements that have occurred in the material standard of living during the modern age. Contemporary economists can observe this fact and can give many commonsense explanations. But the most highly developed theoretical apparatus thus far produced by the economics profession is almost powerless to explain it.

All this calls to mind Veblen's observation almost 100 years ago that the economic writings previous to his own time served mainly the purposes of "ceremonial adequacy." Earlier economists had taken "what the instructed common sense of the time accepts as the adequate or worthy end of human effort" and by means of their theories had projected this common sense into an "accepted ideal of conduct" and a "canon of truth."[40] Taking the common sense of observed higher efficiency and economic superiority of market economies, the professional economists of the welfare state have elevated this empirical reality into a heavenly vision of the perfect efficiency of the market mechanism. The result is a new interpretation of the "religion of humanity" of Saint-Simon and Comte and of the old progressive "gospel of efficiency" of Veblen, Arnold, and Galbraith. The guiding scientific knowledge of society of the older socialist and progressive visions has now become the guiding scientific understanding of the market.

In Samuelson's preaching, the gospel of economic progressivism was not a plea for change; Samuelson's version instead offered in large part a conservative blessing of the status quo. Like Keynes, Samuelson was seeking above all to curb the misguided aims of the older progressive gospel. Directing his message to the progressive faithful, Samuelson maintained that the market system should be preserved; that it could be put powerfully to use in serving progressive purposes; and that the market role in society therefore should not shrink further, as many old-style progressives still sought. If progressivism was a U.S. version of European socialism, the practical effect of Samuelson's message was to affirm a conclusion of Thurman Arnold. The most important instrument of the American version of socialism was the business corporation, misleadingly labeled as "private." With high rates of business taxation and appropriate policies to influence the market, the United States already had in place—in many respects at least—a well-functioning system of market socialism.

However, a comparison of the institutional arrangements of American society with the guiding tenets of economic progressivism could also yield a more controversial conclusion. Perhaps American government was already involved directly in too many tasks. Many existing responsibilities of American government were in fact outgrowths of the old progressive orthodoxies; they would be hard to justify by the new tenets of economic progressivism. Private provision of current government functions might well yield more efficient results. With a few exceptions (such as a recommendation in *Economics* for less government supervision of agriculture), Samuelson was inclined to skip over such potentially divisive issues in American society. It would fall instead to another leading American economist, Milton Friedman, to issue the call for a restructuring of American political and economic institutions in accordance with the doctrines of economic progressivism.

Milton Friedman: Chief Planner of the Market Mechanism

Milton Friedman follows only Samuelson in prominence and prestige within the U.S. economics profession in the years since World War II. Friedman received the Nobel prize in economics in 1976. Like Samuelson, he is the author of highly successful writings both for popular and professional audiences. For many years Friedman was the foremost spokesman for the school of economics led by the department at the University of Chicago.

In *Economics,* Samuelson regards government as benevolent, if perhaps prone to zealous excesses of well-intentioned interference in markets. The possibility that American government would pose a genuine threat to American freedoms is—by implication at least— difficult for Samuelson to imagine. By contrast, Friedman regards the distinctive feature of government to be its power of coercion. Viewing the history of the twentieth century—seeing, for example, the "massive tyranny and despotism that hold sway in Russia"—Friedman feels much less secure than his distinguished contemporary.[41] All too many governments around the world have not only confiscated the wealth but slaughtered the lives of their citizens. Such behavior, although perhaps diminishing, seems hardly to have been eliminated in the second half of the twentieth century. The United States is no doubt less susceptible than most nations around the world. But even in the United States, Friedman believes that a constant vigil against government oppression is imperative.

In his most influential book, *Capitalism and Freedom*, Friedman argued in 1962 that the conditions for political liberty are fragile and require careful cultivation. Indeed, history shows that "capitalism is . . . necessary . . . for political freedom." Competitive capitalism achieves a necessary separation of "economic power from political power and in this way enables the one to offset the other." Imagine, for example, a strong critic of the government seeking to publish his views in a society where government owns all the resources of production. As Friedman observes, the obstacles would include having to "persuade a government factory making paper to sell to him, the government printing press to print his pamphlets, a government post office to distribute them among the people, the government agency to rent him a hall in which to talk, and so on." Hence, for Friedman a compelling advantage of the market is that it is based on the "voluntary co-operation of individuals." In this way, and in contrast to government direction of the economy, "co-operation is . . . achieved without coercion." Since "political freedom means the absence of coercion of a man by his fellow men," the market is the one economic system that can be said to rest squarely on the principle of individual liberty.[42]

There is, moreover, no conflict for Friedman between personal freedom and economic well-being. Here agreeing with Samuelson, Friedman sees "the market technique" as an effective mechanism for coordinating economic functions. Friedman also finds the freedom of each individual to pursue his or her own goals to be a powerful force in advancing economic progress. The market releases an "extraordinary fecundity" that is based on "one of strongest and most creative

forces known to man—the attempt by millions of individuals to promote their own interests, to live their lives by their own values."[43] If
individuals are given the opportunity to develop their own talents and
ideas in ways that they see fit, based on voluntary cooperation with
other people doing the same, society can expect an outpouring of
productive effort.

But the great stumbling block is government. Friedman finds that "a
revolution in politics, in science, and in technology" have created the
expectation that with "modern tools and modern science" it will be
possible for government to achieve great things for Americans. An
examination of the actual results, however, shows that "the record is
dismal. The greater part of the new ventures undertaken by government in the past few decades have failed to achieve their objectives."
In one of the worst instances, government monetary mismanagement
must be assigned "primary responsibility" for the Great Depression
of the 1930s. Furthermore, although the consequences were much less
severe, government housing programs begun in the New Deal years
have "worsened the housing conditions of the poor, contributed to
juvenile delinquency, and spread urban blight"—a result that Friedman
finds all too typical of previous government efforts, however well
intentioned.[44]

The fundamental cause of this failure of government has been the
mistaken idea that new government programs will be "run by able,
disinterested men, free from the pressure of special interest groups."
The creation of a new government program merely creates a new arena
in which the natural and irrepressible creative energies for the pursuit
of individual self-interest will be released. However, in government—
unlike the market—these energies are not channeled to the benefit of
society as a whole. Instead, government programs have "the opposite
of the effects intended" because the machinery of government ends
up serving private purposes, leaving government often captive to the
interests of particular clienteles. The high hopes for regulation of the
railroads, for example, had been undermined by the turning of the
regulatory machinery into an "instrument whereby the railroads could
protect themselves from the competition of newly emerging rivals—at
the expense, of course, of the consumer."[45]

Friedman's analysis leads him to the conclusion that "governmental
measures constitute the major impediments to economic growth in the
United States." The urgent need in the United States "for both
economic stability and growth" depends on a "reduction of government intervention" in the economy.[46] Such a reduction will both curtail

the wasteful diversion of resources into ineffective public programs and also free the productive powers of Americans to pursue more constructive undertakings privately. In *Capitalism and Freedom*, Friedman calls for the abolition of a whole host of government programs and government interventions in the market, including agricultural price supports, import tariffs, rent controls, and minimum wages. Friedman further suggests the elimination of existing government roles in areas such as Social Security, public housing, national parks, and the operation of major intercity highways. Other Friedman proposals include a recommendation for abolishing the military draft and a suggestion to revoke the monopoly status of the Post Office.

These proposals are compatible with a laissez-faire philosophy that a social Darwinist of the nineteenth century might have advanced. Friedman makes another set of proposals, however, that show a different outlook. He acknowledges that, although currently extended well beyond its proper scope, there are still a number of legitimate activities for government. Some of these, such as national defense and maintenance of the justice system, are familiar enough to laissez-faire economics. But Friedman also accepts some basic aims of the welfare state. Unlike many nineteenth-century advocates of laissez-faire, Friedman raises no basic objection to the redistribution of income in the welfare state. Although finding that the task has been poorly managed, he also does not reject in principle the necessity of government operation of the monetary system.

Friedman seeks, however, to accomplish such social goals with as little government exercise of discretion and as little interference with market mechanisms as possible. This strategy yields, for example, his famous proposal for a "negative income tax" according to which the poor would receive rather than make income-related payments. By this approach Friedman aims to integrate the welfare system with the labor market in a manner that minimizes the financial penalties from moving off welfare and into a paying job. Rather than an abrupt cutoff, welfare payments should decline only gradually as income earned in a job increases. The philosophy should be, as Friedman explains, "so far as possible, . . . while operating through the market, not [to] distort the market or impede its functioning."[47]

Another well-known proposal of Friedman is for a system of education "vouchers." Earlier in the history of the United States, the public schools perhaps served the nation well, when the purpose was to integrate a large and steady stream of immigrants into American society. But Friedman argues that "our problem today is not to enforce

conformity; it is rather . . . to foster diversity" and thus to meet widely
varying needs of current teachers and students.[48] Replacing the govern-
ment-financed schools with a system of vouchers given by government
directly to parents would maintain strong government financial support
for education, but also allow the competitive pressures of the market
to stimulate improvements in the quality of schooling.

Friedman acknowledges the need for substantial tax revenues to
finance government operations, but calls for a much simplified tax
structure based on a "flat-rate tax on income above an exemption,
with income defined very broadly" to eliminate loopholes.[49] Administration of government monetary policy should be similarly simplified,
leading Friedman to suggest a nondiscretionary rule of steady growth
of the money supply. With respect to foreign exchange rates, Friedman
sees no need for government control and recommends a shift to a
system of floating rates.

Indeed, seen almost 30 years later, *Capitalism and Freedom* is a
remarkable book, one of the most influential in the history of American
social thought. The list of its successful policy proposals—many of
them radical and seemingly having slight political prospects at the time
Friedman made them—is long. Two of the most important political
developments in American government over the past 15 years have
been the deregulation movement and the movement for tax reduction
and simplification. Both reforms were vigorously advocated by Friedman in 1962. Other far-reaching proposals that would later be adopted
by government include floating exchange rates and the abolition of the
military draft. Measures already suggested by Friedman in 1962 that
have been partially adopted or for which government experiments have
been conducted include the following: fixed monetary growth rates;
the negative income tax (now labeled the earned income tax credit);
education vouchers (helping also to inspire current "choice" programs
within public schools); greater competition for the Post Office; reduc-
tions in occupation licensing restrictions; and abolition of limits on
bank interest rates. If Friedman was not necessarily the first or the
only one to suggest these policy changes, he gave them wide visibility
as part of the comprehensive package.

Thus, Friedman has far outstripped Samuelson or any other of his
contemporaries among economists when it comes to the prolific generation and dissemination of major policy innovations. *Capitalism and
Freedom* helped to set the stage for a new era in the American welfare
state. Attention would turn from the expansion of government to the
fine tuning of its scope. Borrowing ideas from Friedman and other

writers, the economic planners of government would now start to tinker with the instrument of the market mechanism, relying on the market more heavily in some areas, manipulating it more skillfully in others, removing government from still further areas altogether. The general task would be to rethink and readjust the boundaries between government and the market. As the leading source of ideas in these areas, Friedman has been a leading American architect of the market mechanism of the American welfare state, a major contributor in the United States to the gospel of economic progressivism.

It is in some ways a paradoxical role. The general language and philosophical argument of *Capitalism and Freedom* at times seem to echo, most of all, Herbert Spencer. It is Spencer whose writings included essays entitled "The Sins of Legislators," "Over-legislation," "From Freedom to Bondage," and "The Coming Slavery."[50] Spencer, like Friedman, finds that the threat to freedom compels a reduction in the size of government. In 1891 Spencer issued a warning that, "when a general socialistic organization has been esablished, the vast, ramified, and consolidated body of those who direct its activities, using without check whatever coercion seems to them needful in the interests of the system (which will practically become their own interests) will have no hesitation in imposing their rigorous rule over the entire lives of the actual workers." If freedom and liberty were not protected more diligently, the future would hold in store—Spencer predicted—"an official oligarchy, with its various grades, exercising a tyranny more gigantic and more terrible than any which the world has seen."[51] Spencer was a fierce antagonist of the trends that could be seen even in his day leading toward the twentieth-century welfare state.

Although Friedman often employs a similar rhetoric, his economic proposals would not have had much impact if they had been perceived as an attempt to revive a social Darwinism or to undermine the welfare state. They were successful in the United States not in the spirit of Spencer, but in the spirit of Samuelson. Few readers shared Friedman's forebodings with respect to the future loss of freedom in the United States; they could, however, be enthusiastic about any new means suggested to improve the workings of the market mechanism. Proposals of this sort offered the promise of a more efficient allocation of resources and a higher economic productivity for the American system—goals on which there could be wide agreement.

Even the staunchest defenders of the American welfare state had to acknowledge the inefficiency of some government programs. Political scientists, moreover, were increasingly describing American politics as a system of interest-group negotiation and compromise. As democratic politics became more and more a matter of the trading of goods and services, it represented in effect an increasingly important system of exchange in American life. However, political "prices" were never known precisely, nor was political "currency"—the total political clout and chips a politician had to work with—well defined. Political exchange was in essence barter exchange. Yet a barter system of trading on the scale of a nation as large as the United States must be extremely cumbersome.

By contrast, the market is an organized system for exchange in which each private interest knows reasonably well its exchange options, because a system of prices regularly gives the going rates of trade. The use of money as a medium of exchange greatly simplifies the task of mental calculation necessary to trading. In short, by an efficiency standard, the system of barter exchange that American politics was increasingly coming to represent would necessarily fall far short of a market level of performance. Although economists typically spun webs of elaborate technical reasoning to make the case for the social use of the market, in many ways this case was no more complicated than that a money system will generally far outperform a barter system. It was a message that Friedman delivered in stark terms; and in the process, he offended many powerful beneficiaries of the existing U.S. political system based on barter exchange.

The message that the efficiency of the market mechanism could be put to use for progressive purposes may have been initially that of Keynes, and this message may have then been spread widely by Samuelson, but the task of developing the specific plans for using the market mechanism would be undertaken above all by Friedman. If American progressivism in the early twentieth century was a close cousin of European socialism, and if economic progressivism later was closely related to European market socialism, the "conservative" Friedman becomes in effect one of the leading planners of a new market socialism, American style. Friedman has been the leading innovator in proposing new ways to use the market mechanism for the goals of the American welfare state. That Friedman would be widely regarded as an antagonist of progressive purposes merely illustrates the widespread misconceptions that exist with respect to the true workings of the U.S. economic system.

Like Samuelson, Friedman's high prestige among his fellow economists has been mainly based not on his popular writings, but on his technical and professional publications. In this arena, Friedman and Samuelson were allies in the campaign to convert economics to a newly rigorous and mathematical science. Friedman's many professional articles and books often won high praise from fellow economists for technical proficiency. Early in his career, Friedman stated his objective: a system of "positive economics [that] is, or can be, an 'objective' science, in precisely the same sense of any of the physical sciences." All economic propositions must be formulated with scientific precision and then accepted into the body of economic knowledge after passing "the only relevant test of the validity of a hypothesis": a "comparison of its predictions with experience."[52]

If carried out to the letter, very little in Samuelson's *Economics* would have passed the test—and essentially none of Friedman's *Capitalism and Freedom*. Friedman's arguments concerning the proper economic method served more a symbolic role than a practical purpose. The symbolic message was that economics is a science whose verdicts are entitled to the same social authority accorded to the conclusions of the physical sciences. Moreover, because economics is a science, it is capable of producing a body of scientific knowledge that will provide the basis for the scientific management of society. The "positive" science of economics to which Friedman dedicated his efforts could be traced back to Comte's "positive" physics of society (the origins of sociology)—one of the founding visions of early socialism in the nineteenth century.

Thus, it was not only Friedman's practical proposals for government use of the market mechanism that place him in a paradoxical role. Friedman also contributed significantly to a scientific symbolism offered by economists in support of their expert role as chief engineers of society. If economists such as Friedman were devoting their efforts to discovery of the specific laws of an economic system, should not their discoveries be used for social benefit? Did not a comprehensive scientific understanding of society make possible the comprehensive scientific management of society? In his arguments concerning economic method, Friedman offered strong support for even the old orthodox understanding of the progressive gospel. A strong advocate of individual freedom in some of his writings, Friedman on other occasions offered influential support for a social engineering outlook that in the twentieth century has sought to subordinate the individual to the welfare of the community.

Occupying a prominent position in American political debate, Friedman has not been a revolutionary. Rather, he once acknowledged that, while improvements were no doubt needed, the American welfare state was serving its citizens well enough: "The United States has continued to progress; its citizens have become better fed, better clothed, better housed, and better transported; class and social distinctions have narrowed; minority groups have become less disadvantaged; popular culture has advanced by leaps and bounds."[53] Substantial progress had in fact been already made toward a future abolition of economic scarcity. This was the outlook not of the Protestant tradition—which some of Friedman's rhetoric might suggest—but of the Roman tradition as embodied in the American welfare state.

In few U.S. economists has the manner of the preacher been more evident. One biographer registered a common reaction in describing Friedman as a "prophet" for his economic views. Friedman himself has written of the "miracle of the market" that offers the prospect of "peace and widely shared prosperity" as the "ultimate prizes."[54] Friedman has preached his own interpretation of the gospel of economic progressivism, blending together elements—if often with little philosophical depth or consistency—from sources as diverse as Comte and Spencer. When first presented, Friedman's message fell on the fringes of American public debate. Almost 30 years later, it is now close to the mainstream, having contributed significantly to a number of important changes in the policies and practices of American government.

Charles Schultze: Preacher of Economic Efficiency

Charles Schultze was director of the Bureau of the Budget (now the Office of Management and Budget) from 1965 to 1967 and chairman of the Council of Economic Advisors from 1977 to 1981. After leaving government, Schultze in each case remained in Washington, D.C., to study economic policy issues at the Brookings Institution. President of the American Economic Association in 1984, Schultze in his books and other writings offers the most recent of the leading interpretations of economic progressivism.

Schultze finds that, despite the best efforts of professional economists, the old progressive orthodoxies have not entirely lost their influence. Admittedly, no significant movement to nationalize industry exists in the United States. But he observes in 1977 that there nevertheless has been a "rash of new regulatory mechanisms established in recent years—for pollution control, energy conservation, industrial

health and safety, consumer-product quality and safety, and the like."
Despite the best efforts of the economic progressives, many political
leaders have tended to see "only one way of intervening" to accomplish social objectives. This is the old-style progressive way of removing responsibilities from the market and instead "transferring them to
the command-and-control techniques of government bureaucracy."[55]

However well intentioned these programs may have been, the results
often worked poorly. They were reminiscent of the experiences of
progressive and socialist reformers earlier in the twentieth century
who pursued idealistic objectives but were often undermined by their
own economic naiveté. Once again, poorly designed progressive measures were generating a new "backlash of resentment against excessive
red tape and bureaucratic control." Public faith in the welfare state
might even be placed at risk, as citizens became "disenchanted with
the ability of government, especially the federal government, to function effectively."[56]

Such erosion of public confidence in government was all the more
unfortunate, because there was a "growing need for collective influence over individual and business behavior that was once the domain
of purely private decisions." Government had a major role to play in
accomplishing social goals that the market, left to itself, was not
serving. However, unless more enlightened policies could be developed, government was likely to fail in many of its efforts. At present,
American government was "going about the job in a systematically
bad way that will not be mended simply by electing and appointing
more competent public officials or doing better analysis of public
programs."[57]

Schultze develops these themes in *The Public Use of Private Interest*. American government should look to "techniques for collective
intervention" that are based on "modifying the incentives of the
private market." What is needed is a basic new approach to policy
making that relies on "creating incentives so that public goals become
private interests." Instead, American government is leaving "private
interests . . . unchanged," while seeking a coercive imposition of social
goals—an approach in which "obedience to the public goals is commanded."[58]

Schultze finds a number of advantages to the use, instead, of
markets. A market relies on private incentives to lead each individual
and each business to do what is socially desired. Since outright
coercion is generally difficult and can easily stir resentment and
attempts at subversion, command-and-control strategies will work only

if there is substantial voluntary compliance. Such compliance relies on a large element of "compassion, patriotism, brotherly love and cultural solidarity." But the moral capital of society is in "short supply" and is easily depleted. If society seeks to increase the supply, the effort all too easily degenerates into "preaching, indignation and identification of villains," thereby getting "in the way of results." For example, if society seeks to "cut down on pollution, indignant tirades about social responsibility can't hold a candle to schemes that reduce the profits of firms who pollute."[59]

The market also provides effective "feedback mechanisms that do not depend on explicit knowledge of the unknowable." As Keynes, Samuelson, and Friedman had said before him, Schultze also finds that these mechanisms contribute to making the market "an efficient information processor." For example, in order to implement an efficient nationwide command-and-control system for regulating pollution, the government would need to know the "production function, the range of technologies for pollution control, and the demand curves for every major polluter," potentially covering a universe of hundreds of thousands of individual actors. However, if a price were instead charged by the government in each appropriate basin for each unit of pollution emitted, the burden "to grope toward a least-cost approach to pollution control" is shifted to the polluters, leaving a "sharply lessened" burden of government information.[60]

The information efficiency of the market is much more important in a dynamic environment. Indeed, in a world of purely static technology, population, resources, and other factors of production, knowledge would eventually accrue and be disseminated to all parties needing it. In a static world, all economic systems would in the longest run achieve similar results because at some point even the least adept and least informed members of society will have learned what they need to know. Schultze thus acknowledges that, "while the formal economic theory of the market emphasizes its static-efficiency characteristics, . . . what is far more important is its apparent capacity to stimulate and take advantage of advancing technology." Indeed, it is to the dynamic, not the static, properties of the market that mankind can attribute the increase "by orders of magnitude" in its living standard that has occurred within the modern era. Yet, in seeking by government fiat to impose a technological solution for problems of environmental pollution, the wonderful dynamic assets of the market were being lost. When firms are given the proper private incentives, modern history shows a consistent "stimulation and harnessing of new technologies and resources."[61]

Why, then—given these seemingly compelling advantages—has society failed to make proper use of the market, not only in environmental but in many other areas of social concern. For Schultze, the answer lies to a large degree in the American political culture. Once a social problem is determined to be a matter for political resolution—as environmental protection has come to be seen by many Americans—the responsibility for "explicit decisions about the fate of particular groups and communities" falls into the hands of government. Yet, American political culture shows great attachment to (and closely observes) a rule of "do no direct harm." Because market approaches "rely on decentralized reactions to prices, they seem to deprive government of control of case-by-case results," thus failing to provide necessary assurances against the imposition by government of any harm.[62] Moreover, some parties already perceive themselves as the potential losers in a market regime, and in American politics they often have an effective veto on any movement toward greater use of the market mechanism.

The political rule of do-no-direct-harm not only prevents adoption of market solutions, but also significantly limits the ability of government to implement in a direct fashion the most efficient command-and-control solutions. Most government actions that would "generate gains for society in the form of higher living standards" also result in the deprivation of at least "some firms and individuals of income." Unless a form of monetary or other compensation for the losers can be devised, American political practices frequently require the design of collective actions to ensure the "prevention of loss."[63] Yet, such a requirement is often difficult to meet, thereby placing major constraints on what government can actually accomplish and seriously hindering the pursuit by government of the most efficient methods and plans.

Indeed, as Schultze bluntly puts the matter, another major "advantage of the market as a means of social organization is its 'devil take the hindmost' approach to questions of individual equity." In contrast to American political culture, the American social conventions relating to behavior in the private market adopt the rule that "those who may suffer losses are not usually able to stand in the way of change." Owing to the different rules within these two domains of American life, "efficiency-creating changes are not seriously impeded" in the market, while the very same steps in many cases would not be acceptable in the political arena.[64]

Schultze in this respect departs from Samuelson and many other current economists. He is suggesting that the decisive efficiency advantage of the market is perhaps not a mechanical or technical feature—the computational proficiency of an unseen central intelligence—but a matter of American cultural beliefs. The market succeeds because American economic theology allows firms in the market the freedom to pursue efficiency, while government agencies are denied the same freedom. If government is typically inefficient, it may not be because government administration is inherently incapable of efficiency. It may be because American political culture creates formidable and often insuperable obstacles.

Although Schultze does not acknowledge a direct influence, his analysis in this respect is strikingly similar to that of Thurman Arnold in the 1930s. As Arnold saw it, American culture created a burden of priestly and ceremonial expectations that were undermining attempts to achieve efficiency in government. As a result, Arnold considered the progressive vision to have been thus far realized only in the arena of corporate socialism, although this arena was misleadingly labeled a part of the "private" sector. While a similarly effective utilization of scientific skills and expert methods had been denied to government, Arnold was optimistic that the American political and economic culture would soon become more enlightened and rational. He therefore called not only for improved practices of government administration, but also for bigger and stronger government. Writing forty years later, and observing the results of the expanded federal role since the New Deal, Schultze is less optimistic. He calls instead for a greater reliance on the incentives of the corporate world with its proven record of efficiency and effectiveness.

Yet, Schultze does agree with Arnold that the popular distinctions between public and private are artificial. In truth, as Schultze explains, "the free enterprise system . . . carries the label 'made by government.' " The market is a public instrument for accomplishing public purposes no less than other instruments that serve to fulfill government responsibilities. The design of the market mechanism is as much a planning task for government as the design of an administrative system. Rejecting the views of the classical economists of old, Schultze argues that there is no such thing "as a 'natural' laissez faire system"—an eighteenth-century idea that in the late twentieth century is readily seen to be a myth. The market is "an efficient instrument for society" in light of which government has the affirmative responsibility to take "corrective action to create efficient markets."[65]

Although Schultze does not himself acknowledge or confront the issue (in this respect like most other economists), his views contain an almost irresolvable tension. On the one hand, Schultze is proposing a more accurate public understanding with respect to the socially constructed role of the market mechanism. On the other hand, he is proposing a greater use of the market mechanism that may depend for its very advantage on continued public acceptance of popular fictions concerning the market. It is only because most Americans believe that the market is "private" that the workings of the market mechanism remain outside the cultural rules of U.S. politics. Schultze, however, would undermine with one argument what he proposes with another, relying on the market but exposing it to political influence and manipulations.

The great efficiency advantage of the market mechanism may be that it achieves in practice the separation from politics that progressives have long believed necessary for efficient administration. If this separation depends on continued public acceptance of popular myths, a more accurate public understanding might well act to destroy the separation of the market from politics, thus destroying the efficiency of the market. The fundamental theological problem of economic progressivism lies in just this dilemma: how to assert that the market is a social creation yet should be left free of direct social control, as its efficiency seemingly requires.

If market freedoms are to be maintained, their defense may therefore in the end have to be found elsewhere than in the promotion of efficiency. Friedman in his writings emphasizes the defense of individual liberty. Schultze also finds a major advantage of the market to be its voluntary and noncoercive character. But the attention Schultze gives to this market feature is much less.

In *The Public Use of Private Interest* and other writings, Schultze develops the themes of economic progressivism with subtlety and sophistication. Yet it is a message whose success depends, in the end, on faith. As Schultze states, "I believe—I have no choice but to believe—that the American people can deal intelligently with issues" when they are presented with a "high level of political argument."[66] It is still the message of the Enlightenment: that rational intelligence will ultimately guide the affairs of men. Indeed, it is the message of the Roman tradition from Aristotle to Aquinas to the Enlightenment to the economic theology of the late-twentieth-century welfare state. In the United States, this message originated in the Enlightenment beliefs of the founding fathers and has been revised and reinterpreted once again in the various progressive doctrines of the twentieth century.

What is rational for Schultze as well as his progressive predecessors is not merely to follow a particular method of reasoning. For the orthodox progressives of old and more recently the economic progressives, rationality means fundamentally to pursue efficiency. But why should efficiency stand in such high stead, above other goals of mankind? The answer is that efficiency is not an ordinary goal; it is in fact the operational means by which the long-run production of goods and services will be maximized and great material abundance eventually achieved. With modern technology, mankind now has the power at some point not so far off to abolish economic scarcity. If limited resources have in the past led men to fight, quarrel, and otherwise behave in evil ways, it will now be possible to abolish the competition for scarce resources and material possessions that has so often served as grounds for misbehavior. If men have faith, and behave rationally and cooperatively to maximize efficiency, they will continue along a path that leads to a future heaven on earth.

In the progressive gospel, to behave rationally (and thus efficiently) is therefore to find the path of salvation. For Thomas Aquinas and other theologians of the medieval Roman Catholic church, right reason would correctly reveal the divine intent for mankind. To perfect reason in the medieval era as well was to enter onto a path leading toward a future harmony and happiness on earth—and one could hope eventually culminating in a still greater perfection with God in heaven. Indeed, the saving influence and moral basis for reason holds not only for Aquinas and twentieth-century American progressives, but for the whole long history of the Roman tradition—now well over 2,000 years old.

The gospel of economic progressivism falls in other respects as well within the Roman tradition. Like its predecessors, economic progressivism encourages a utilitarian outlook and favors the good life; supports the pursuit of individual self-interest; favors the rule of law; finds all men to be created equal; and seeks a process of incremental progress—achieved through the gradual perfection of society—rather than a sudden transformation of the human condition imposed by some outside and revolutionary force.

In pursuit of this vision, Schultze was led to recommend the introduction in government of "a new set of participants . . . which for want of a better term, I have labeled partisan efficiency advocates. At each level of the [government] decision process these participants become particular champions of efficiency and effectiveness as criteria in decision making."[67] Since the 1960s, American economists have sought to introduce concepts of discounting, opportunity cost, marginal instead of average benefit, internal rate of return, and other such economic tools in government. The practitioners of "systems analysis," "policy analysis," and "program planning" are all engaged in undertakings of this kind. New schools of public-policy analysis have been created in a number of leading universities, in large part to provide professionally trained personnel to serve as effective advocates for efficiency in government.[68]

If Saint-Simon had called for a priesthood of scientists to manage society efficiently, public-policy schools now seek to do their best in answering the call. They also draw on the ideas and methods of Jeremy Bentham. The goal to maximize social benefits minus social costs seeks to put into practice the utilitarian principle of Bentham, now in a twentieth-century form. Like Bentham, contemporary policy analysts also argue that utility ("benefits") can be measured in precise quantitative terms, thus allowing in principle an exact numerical determination of the relative desirability of government actions. In the ideal, the policy analyst should frame all the reasonable alternatives available to the government, and then calculate the dollar value of the net social benefits minus costs for each, enabling society to choose precisely the action offering the highest gain.

If the message of economic progressivism belongs to the Roman tradition, the role sought for professional economists is once again that of the Roman priest. In proposing the placement of "partisan advocates for efficiency" throughout government, Schultze was in effect expressing a hope that the new priesthood of economists and policy analysts would be able to win converts—at a minimum, have their message heard—among the practitioners of politics. Politics emphasizes the comforts of the moment over the hard decisions necessary to efficient government. Politicians are all too often soft—unable to refuse any popular demand, unable to impose any real pain, even when necessary to make economic progress. Politicians lack true convictions, often have no real principles on which to stand. By appealing to higher values, however, the priesthood of economists and policy analysts might be able to enlist at least some politicians to support a greater and more worthy cause. These politicians might come to see that their final judge would be history—not the popular clamor of the moment. In the verdict of history, the place of a political leader will be judged by his or her contribution to economic progress and thereby to the elimination of economic scarcity and all the evils that result from competition for scarce resources. To make a commitment to efficiency would therefore be to serve the cause of salvation—the one valid basis by which theologies through the ages, and now modern economic theology, render final judgment.

Admittedly, as in the past, many politicians would still prefer sin to righteousness. Mankind has not yet eliminated scarcity. Heaven has not yet arrived on earth. Until economic progress yields a heavenly condition of human existence, sinful behavior will persist. As many kings and lords previously ignored their papal and priestly advisors, there will no doubt now be many politicians of the welfare state who place narrow and parochial concerns—in many cases, short-run advantages—above the long-run economic progress of mankind.

Samuelson, Friedman, Schultze, and other preachers of the gospel of economic progressivism have seen it become the guiding faith of the American welfare state. Yet, today as the end of the twentieth century draws near, a new set of questions is arising. There is now a greater skepticism with regard to the redeeming consequences of economic growth. What if the guiding economic faith of the welfare state should be rejected in the future by a large number of people? What if many people should conclude that economic progress does not in fact bring mankind closer to heaven on earth? What if "rational" then appears more an artifact of a particular culture than a single objective and universal truth? What if the path of economic efficiency is not in fact the path of human salvation? By what right would economists and policy analysts then claim to interpret the verdict of history? On what basis would economists and policy analysts assert a claim to priestly authority—an authority to establish moral legitimacy in the current American society? Why should "partisan advocates for efficiency" be assigned a priestly role as advisors at the highest levels of American government, when the proponents of many other beliefs are not offered a similar opportunity?

Yet, despite growing doubts, the majority of Americans may well continue to subscribe to the economic faith of the American welfare state. They may still hold to the tenets of economic progressivism, or some closely related gospel of modern economic theology. In fact, President George Bush still found it politically advantageous in 1990 to state that his administration was "committed to an agenda for growth" and that "achieving solid and sustainable growth is my most fundamental domestic priority."[69] If this is still the majority view that drives public policy, how shall minority positions be accommodated? In the past, in order to avoid theological issues, Americans have sought a strict separation of government from institutional religion. But what if modern economic theologies should be acknowledged outright to have a religious character as well—not just in a metaphorical but in a literal sense? Would not the principle of separation of church and state become an impossibility?

Such questions have only begun to be explored. For most of the modern age—beginning in the late seventeenth century—faith in science, economic growth, and the progress of mankind spread further and further throughout society. Although there have been many critics of modern economic theologies, they have been fighting a losing cause—at least until recently. However, the Holocaust, the atom bomb, and other events of the twentieth century have raised large doubts even within the camp of progressivism. Thus, it may be appropriate to inquire further into such questions—to inquire what a "postmodern" economic world might look like.

Part IV

Entering a World of Postmodern Economics

Chapter 7

Toward a Theology of Economic Pluralism

The Judeo-Christian tradition teaches that there can be only one truth, only one valid message for mankind. The religious pluralism that emerged in the Christian world after the Protestant Reformation was disorienting, tending to subvert the Christian faith. In the modern age, the prophets of economic and other secular theologies have similarly argued that there can be only one valid understanding of history. If many Christian theologians earlier could not conceive that God would have multiple answers for mankind, secular theorists in the modern age have found it almost as difficult to believe that science would yield multiple correct understandings of the human condition. Yet the modern profusion of secular theologies in the name of science has been no less than the earlier multiplicity of Christian faiths. As Christianity earlier had to come to terms with a seeming permanent pluralism within institutional religion, modern secular thought is today being compelled—and not without great stresses and strains—to consider the prospect of a long-term social and economic pluralism. Indeed, such a pluralism could well be a defining feature of the "postmodern" world—the emergence of which many social thinkers are now predicting.

A Crisis of Progressive Faith

In his *History of the Idea of Progress,* Robert Nisbet explains that the roots of the idea of progress are religious, derived from "the vision

257

of all humanity in necessary advancement, stage-by-stage, from a remote and primitive past to a distant and glorious future, the whole process unfolding of initial Providential design." In the Enlightenment this faith was secularized, a process by which many men shifted from a belief in "Providence-as-progress" to a new belief in "progress-as-Providence." It was accompanied by the rise of a "lay clerisy" and lay "intelligentsia" whose role was "to succeed the clergy as the dominant class so far as citizen's beliefs are concerned."[1]

However, just as the authority of institutional Judaic and Christian faiths had earlier been eroded, Nisbet saw in the twentieth century a great weakening in "the fabrics of secular faiths" as well. Even outside a traditional religious context, "the aura of the sacred remained with the arts and sciences until well into the twentieth century." But this sense of sacredness "is absent now," even with respect to science; and whether it can ever "be recovered, we cannot know." The late twentieth century is characterized by a "revolt against reason" with a consequent loss of respect for the "kind of knowledge that proceeds from reason and its intrinsic disciplines." The present age is in fact "bedeviled" by a widespread "irrationalism," resulting in an "erosion of status . . . in the ranks of scholars and scientists."[2]

Belief in human progress, Nisbet finds, has long had a "close relationship" to a faith "in the necessity of economic growth and development." Yet, there is today "within steadily enlarging sectors of Western and particularly American society . . . an outright hostility toward economic growth," thereby contributing to a growing sense of "the futility of hopes for human progress." Past economic development has yielded a circumstance of "more leisure than any population in history has ever had." This leisure, however, has often yielded a "boredom" that has helped to spur an "increasingly widespread and chronic indifference to ordinary values, pursuits, freedoms and obligations." Considering all the trends of the late twentieth century, Nisbet finds it difficult to avoid the conclusion that, "when the identity of our century is eventually fixed by historians, not faith but abandonment of faith in the idea of progress will be one of the major attributes."[3]

Among the events of the twentieth century that seriously challenged progressive faith, none had more impact than those in Germany in the 1930s and 1940s. Until World War II, Germany had been the leading scientific nation of the world—a country that prided itself on commitment to a life of the mind. The Germans had produced a good part of the mathematics, physics, philosophy, and music of Western civilization. Germany had also given birth to the Protestant Reformation and a 30-year war in Europe, but that had been three centuries earlier. It seemed unimaginable to many that a repetition of the same religious strife on the same vast scale of hatred, brutality, and destruction could occur in the world of reason, science, and economic progress of the twentieth century. Nevertheless, events would suggest that in some unexplainable way a new kind of modern devil had been set loose, operating on a national scale, casting a malevolent spell over all Germany. The Holocaust would become the leading symbol for the late twentieth century of the potential for irrationality that still apparently lurks even in many modern men and women who possess education, scientific knowledge, material assets, and the finer things of life.

If whole nations, then, can spin out of control and behave irrationally, the powers of modern economic productivity could be as much a menace as a benefit. The foremost symbol of the destructive potential lying in economic and technological progress has been the atom bomb. Two enormous shocks to the Western mind—the discovery of the full dimensions of the Holocaust, and the dropping of atom bombs on Hiroshima and Nagasaki—occurred within a few months of each other in 1945. Even as the end of the twentieth century approaches, the rethinking that must be done to adjust to these and other shocks of this century is still incomplete. As Nisbet emphasizes, however, one consequence has been a widespread crisis of faith in the progressive gospels of the modern age.

Whatever the ultimate explanation, an immediate cause of the Nazi horrors is to be found in the racial Darwinism that had become a state religion for Germany.[4] The explosion of the atom bomb further gave a new and unacceptable meaning to any Darwinian laws that prescribe warfare as the predestined path of a new economic class or other elect group in history. One clear lesson drawn in the second half of the twentieth century was that the Darwinist messages of the survival of the fittest are too dangerous to tolerate. In an age largely indifferent to attacks directed at institutional religion, any significant use of racial attributes in public discourse were now treated much more harshly; bigotry may be regarded as a true form of blasphemy for this era, subject to strong social sanctions.

As a nation in which Marxism was the official state religion, the Soviet Union had to develop a state response to these developments. Would it still insist on worldwide revolution as the necessary route to the triumph of the proletariat? In 1961, official state theoreticians

decreed a new doctrine of "peaceful coexistence." This official abandonment of Marxist orthodoxy was only a particularly visible example
of a pervasive turn away from Darwinist beliefs. The followers of
Freud set about creating a new psychology—one in which the aggressive role of the id and of sexual and other instinctual drives would
receive much less emphasis. Instead, "ego-psychology" addressed
emotional growth and maturity; appropriate psychological goals became "self-actualization" and "personality integration." In the writings of psychologist Erich Fromm, the Freudian world of sexual
striving and fierce competition became instead a world of "love,"
which was the "answer to the problem of human existence."[5]

Instead of the historic message of violent class struggle, some
Marxists now discovered an "early Marx" of more peaceful and
humanitarian spirit, whose views had mistakenly been given short
shrift by later followers. But Michael Harrington thought that "the
unknown Marx" was really the later Marx, who was "a moderate"
and whose efforts were partly responsible for "the rise of democratic
socialism."[6] A new amalgam of Freud and Marx also yielded what
some now called "Freudo-Marxism." Among the leading prophets of
this new gospel, they found "no intrinsic reason why the libido cannot
enjoy free expression, once mankind has been emancipated from the
economic and sexual repressions that may have been necessary for
culture-building in lower states of civilization." Once repressive forces
have been lifted from mankind, there will be a "new order of free labor
in companionship and love." The choice is between a "competitive,
power-dominated society" and "love and security in true democratic
socialism."[7]

The message of the third of the great followers of Darwin—Herbert
Spencer—was also reinterpreted after World War II. Although Marx
and Freud remained respectably at the center of intellectual life,
Spencer was too directly associated with the spread of social Darwinism. Hence, Spencer was banished from polite conversation. Nevertheless, the thinking of Spencer—like that of Marx and Freud—contained
elements that appeared newly attractive in the wake of the events of
World War II. For all three, these elements lay in a concern for human
freedom and individual self-expression. Neo-Marxists emphasized the
necessity for individual freedom from large, impersonal, and alienating
economic institutions. Neo-Freudians emphasized the necessity for
freedom from sexual and other cultural restrictions. For neo-Spencer-
ians, the emphasis was on the necessity for individual freedom from
another source of social repression: government itself. Neo-Marxist,

neo-Freudian, and neo-Spencerian influences have all contributed to a powerful libertarian trend in the thought of the late twentieth century—a recognition that grave dangers lie in excesses of coercive authority.

Darwinist thought in this respect met a fate similar to the Protestant Reformation of Luther and Calvin. Earlier in the seventeenth century and now in the twentieth century as well, the disasters of religiously inspired warfare, combined with a revolt against the inherent austerity and harshness of the Protestant outlook, brought about a strong counterreaction. If only as an accidental by-product, Protestantism in the sixteenth and seventeenth centuries and then the Darwinist messages of the late nineteenth and early twentieth centuries both ended up spurring a powerful individualism in Western civilization.[8]

A related powerful trend of thought of the late twentieth century is better characterized not as libertarian, but as pluralist. Freedom perhaps does not mean that each person should live as an isolated individual. Rather, it might instead mean that each person has the right to join with others to pursue a common vision, which may include even the rejection within the group of an individualistic outlook. If the twentieth-century erosion of faith in reason and progress signals the end of the modern era—as Nisbet and a number of other contemporary observers believe may be the case—the postmodern era may well be defined by a new acceptance of pluralism in the characteristic outlooks found around the world.

The New Pluralism

In *Mathematics: The Loss of Certainty*, a former professor of mathematics and leading student of the history of mathematics—Morris Kline—describes the twentieth-century discovery that "mathematics is a human activity . . . subject to all the foibles and frailties of humans." Despite heroic efforts, mathematicians have proved unable to establish a firm rational foundation for their subject. Indeed, in 1931 Kurt Godel startled the mathematical world by proving that the full consistency of key mathematical systems could never be fully demonstrated within the bounds of widely accepted principles of logic. As Kline remarks, mathematics at present has reached a circumstance where "any formal, logical account is a pseudo-mathematics, a fiction, even a legend, despite the element of reason." The very nature of mathematics "has never been less clear. The subtle analysis of the obvious has produced a spiral of never ending complications."[9]

Kline understands full well that this state of affairs may have consequences going well beyond mathematics. Mathematics has been the decisive instrument in the modern age for discovering the divine intent for the world. If there now exists a state of "confusion about what valid mathematics is," this confusion could have profound theological repercussions. Uncertainty could extend to the very understanding of reason and what it means to live in a rational world. Kline writes that "mathematics is man's most extensive and most profound effort to achieve precise and effective thinking and what it accomplishes measures the capacity of the human mind."[10] If mathematics itself cannot be fully grounded in a rational development, it may not be possible to argue convincingly from first principles that the world is rational through and through. Perhaps it can no longer be said that the world follows a mathematical logic that itself can be grounded in reason alone. Perhaps the truths of mathematics—and of the broader world as well—must at the deepest level be taken in some degree as a matter of experience and faith.

For many men who have held to the rational faiths of the modern age, as Kline observes, "this turn of events is not far short of an intellectual disaster."[11] One of the leading mathematicians of the twentieth century, Hermann Weyl, thus commented in 1946:

> We are less certain than ever about the ultimate foundations of mathematics and logic. Like everybody and everything in the world today, we have our "crisis." We have had it for nearly fifty years. Outwardly it does not seem to hamper our daily work, and yet I for one confess that it has had a considerable practical influence on my mathematical life; it directed my interests to fields I considered relatively "safe," and has been a constant drain on the enthusiasm and determination with which I pursued my research work. This experience is probably shared by other mathematicians who are not indifferent to what their scientific endeavors mean in the context of man's whole caring and knowing, suffering and creative existence in the world.[12]

As Weyl indicated, the crisis in mathematics was hardly unique. Einstein refused to accept the full results of quantum mechanics because they violated his sense of the necessary rational qualities of nature. The laws of physics no longer precisely determine every event in the universe; rather, these laws can in some cases express only a set of probabilities. Although a full comprehension of quantum mechanics requires the use of mathematics, several of the best-known physicists of the twentieth century have sought to alert the public at large to the radical consequences that follow from its understanding of the universe. Robert Oppenheimer, for example, would comment in 1953 in *Science and the Common Understanding* that, in quantum mechanics,

> To what appeared to be the simplest questions, we will tend to give either no answer or an answer which will at first sight be reminiscent more of a strange catechism than of the straightforward affirmatives of physical science. If we ask, for instance, whether the position of the electron remains the same, we must say "no"; if we ask whether the electron's position changes with time, we must say "no"; if we ask whether the electron is at rest, we must say "no"; if we ask whether it is in motion, we must say "no." . . . They are not familiar answers for the tradition of seventeenth- and eighteenth-century science.[13]

The new world of quantum mechanics was, as Oppenheimer called it, a world of "uncommon sense"—a world where what had appeared to be fixed and immutable rules of the rational workings of nature now would have to be suspended. It gave "a sharp reminder that ways of thinking about things, which seem natural and inevitable and almost appear not to rest on experience so much as on the inherent qualities of thought and nature, do in fact rest on experience; and that there are parts of experience rendered accessible by exploration and experimental refinement where these ways of thought no longer apply." For example, ordinary common sense says that one event causes another event. This table moves only when I push on it, or when some other force is applied to it. Yet, seemingly fundamental mechanical principles do not necessarily hold in the world discovered by quantum mechanics, which offers "a very different view of reality from Newton's giant machine. It is not causal; there is no complete causal determination of the future on the basis of available knowledge of the present. The application of the laws of quantum theory restricts, but does not in general define, the outcome of an experiment."[14]

Another twentieth-century physicist, Niels Bohr, would similarly feel the need to communicate to lay audiences that "the special situation in quantum physics is above all . . . that the information gained about atomic objects cannot be comprehended along the lines of approach typical of the mechanical conception of nature. Already the fact that under one and the same experimental arrangement there may in general appear observations pertaining to different individual quantum prophecies entails a limitation in principle of the deterministic mode of description.''[15] Writing in 1930, the Nobel prizewinning U.S. physicist Robert Millikan would comment that ''an atom is now an amazingly complicated organism, possessing many interrelated parts and exhibiting many functions and properties—energy properties, radiating properties, wave properties and other properties quite as mysterious as any that used to masquerade under the name of 'mind.' Hence the phrases—'All is matter,' and 'All is mind'—have now become mere shibboleths completely devoid of meaning.''[16]

Earlier in the century, Einstein had already demonstrated that the conclusions of Newtonian physics are a special case, depending on the relative speed and direction of objects. Einstein's discovery that matter and energy can be interchangeable—also depending on relative motion—further defied the mechanistic understanding of the world that Newton had seemingly revealed. The physics of relativity and quantum mechanics exposed a world in which ''scarcely anything [was] left by way of support from physics'' for the ''scientific foundation on which the nineteenth century form of materialism was based.'' The result was that questions of ''determinism and naturalism'' were reopened ''within a far wider framework than that of the nineteenth century.''[17]

If a mathematical truth could be defined no more precisely than what all mathematicians—or at least all mathematicians who counted—accepted as a truth, then the real foundation for mathematics must lie in the culture of mathematics. Similarly, twentieth-century physics was now yielding conclusions with respect to the behavior of nature that were ''irrational'' by the standards of past science. Reason by itself, it appeared, was not capable of verifying the truths of this world. As in mathematics, the truths of physics would have to be judged by a pragmatic standard: whether they predicted accurately and otherwise ''worked'' in practice. Since it was now recognized that the verification of any law of physics is accomplished in a community of scientists who operate under the behavioral rules of ordinary men and women, the truths of physics could no longer be established within a scientific framework alone. Rather, they must, in the end, emanate from a scientific culture that maintains its social authority by its ability at some point to deliver in practice what it has promised.

Leading physicists of the twentieth century have thus seen their own work pointing in the direction of greater legitimacy for nonscientific modes of expression and for a less formally structured approach to understanding human existence. One of the founders of modern quantum mechanics, Werner Heisenberg, commented in the 1950s that

The general trend of human thinking in the nineteenth century had been toward an increasing confidence in the scientific method and in precise rational terms, and had led to a general skepticism with regard to those concepts of natural language which do not fit into the closed frame of scientific thought—for instance, those of religion. Modern physics has in many ways increased this skepticism; but it has at the same time turned against the overestimation of precise scientific concepts, against a too-optimistic view on progress in general, and finally against skepticism itself. Whenever we proceed from the known into the unknown we may hope to understand, but we may have to learn at the same time a new meaning of the word "understanding." We know that any understanding must be based finally upon the natural language because it is only there that we can be certain to touch reality, and hence we must be skeptical about any skepticism with regard to this natural language and its essential concepts. In this way modern physics has perhaps opened the door to a wider outlook on the relation between the human mind and reality.[18]

Outside the domain of science, some philosophers argued that "the very conception of an ideal universal objective science which involves the mathematization of nature appears to depend on something more fundamental." It depends on an "everyday life-world [that] is pre-scientific not only in that it existed prior to the development of modern science, but also that it is presupposed in all our scientific endeavor." Because of this, there is an "underlying transcendental subjectivity" with its "a priori structures" for both the scientific and commonsense worlds.[19] The philosopher P. F. Strawson stated that

There is a massive central core of human thinking which has no history— or none recorded in the histories of thought; there are categories and concepts which, in their most fundamental character, change not at all. . . . They are commonplaces of the least refined thinking; and are yet the indispensable core of the conceptual equipment of the most sophisticated human beings. It is with these, their interconnections, and the structure that they form, that a descriptive metaphysics will be primarily concerned.[20]

If science is now to be regarded as a special type of language and culture, the sociology of this culture assumes a much greater significance. Indeed, leading social thinkers have turned in recent years to the study of the history of the scientific endeavor. A pioneer in this effort, Thomas Kuhn, found that scientific discovery proceeded less incrementally, and more in sharp departures, whenever a new fundamental "paradigm" came along to replace another old way of thinking.[21] The timing of the shift from one paradigm to another was not a matter solely of the moment when some scientific truth was first demonstrated; rather, these shifts depended on complex behavioral patterns within the scientific culture itself.

A still more radical critique was offered by Paul Feyerabend, who reported that "I found that important physical principles rested on methodological assumptions that are violated whenever physics advances; physics gets authority from ideas it propagates but never obeys in actual research."[22] David Oldroyd, a contemporary student of the philosophy of science, describes such views as holding that "science has no special method of its own that makes it a privileged form of activity, worthy of esteem because it can produce true knowledge. Indeed, . . . science cannot be regarded as a strictly rational enterprise; for when an important theoretical advance is made the new ideas are often 'irrational,' judged by the canons of thought of the previous theoretical position."[23]

Wherever all this may eventually lead, for the moment at least it seems that the foundations of even the physical sciences are very much in doubt. As Oldroyd sums up the current state of affairs,

> There is no certain and secure method which, if carefully followed, will enable one to acquire certain and secure scientific knowledge. Ideas, hunches, hypotheses, can be drawn from any manner of sources, in no rigorously characterizable way, and yet science can progress all the better because of this "anarchistic" component within its structure. But it does not follow, thereby, that certain carefully controlled procedures . . . are irrelevant to science. There is, I suggest, a constant fruitful union in science between "disciplined" and "undisciplined" elements. Positivists such as Comte tended to emphasize the ordered, disciplined aspect. Methodological anarchists such as Feyerabend would have it all the other way. . . . We are, at the moment, I believe, passing through a period where the anarchistic element is in the ascendancy. . . . This metascientific view of the world may indeed be a reflection of the social circumstances of our time: knowledge . . . is shaped by social imagery. . . . I must agree with Feyerabend that there can be different forms of rationality within different societies, and that what is regarded as rational in one time and place is not necessarily seen in the same light in another.[24]

If science is now unsure of and questions its rational foundations, then the great hope of the modern era for a single valid and internally consistent understanding of the human condition is itself placed in doubt. Truth not only in physical science but in other areas of life may become a matter of social practice. The feasibility of prescribing one correct and objectively grounded society or cultural system becomes questionable. There may be no one philosophy of life or interpretation of history, no one theology that can claim a certain superiority over all others.

A number of philosophers in recent years have in fact developed these themes. Richard Rorty writes of philosophy that it is, properly speaking, the practice of a discussion among informed participants. It has no given structure or ground rules; rather, an appropriate view of philosophy "sees the relations between various discourses as those of strands in a possible conversation, a conversation which presupposes no disciplinary matrix which unites the speakers, but where the hope of agreement is never lost as long as the conversation lasts." In such a philosophy the best hope emerges from the engagement of a wide range of viewpoints. There should be few restrictions on participation because, as Rorty states, "to be rational is to be willing to refrain . . . from thinking that there is a special set of terms in which all contributions to the conversation should be put."[25]

Rorty, like other contemporary advocates of an incremental and evolutionary pluralism, is especially critical of assertions to superior knowledge based on claims of using scientific methods. Even physical science is today much more cautious in this regard. For Rorty an appropriate philosophical "justification" is defined by "social practice."[26] What is true is what emerges as accepted truth from philosophical debate, in whatever informal fashion that this emergence may take place. Philosophy in this respect reaches an outcome similar to mathematics and the physical sciences, which earlier failed in attempts to ground their efforts in reason alone.

Another leading contemporary philosopher who has been reaching conclusions of this kind is Harvard professor Robert Nozick. He writes of philosphy as an "art"—one that can no more yield absolute truth than can other forms of art. In the past, "many philosophers have dreamed of setting philosophy upon the sure path of a science [but] this dream is not mine. . . . Surely we long ago reached the point when philosophy should cease striving for so much more while accomplishing so much less."[27] Rather than producing certain conclusions, the philosophy to which Nozick is attracted often yields paradox and seeming contradiction. Instead of finding this a cause for dismay, Nozick suggests that the ironies and paradoxes of rational argument should be regarded as part of a playful game that can be enjoyed as such—similar to Rorty's description of philosophy as "conversation."

Nozick characterizes his own thinking as a "philosophical pluralism" that is a reaction against the old claims of "coercive philosophy,"[28] which asserted that there can be only one philosophic truth
and one final answer that can be said to be "rational." Nozick is far
from arguing that all philosophies and beliefs are valid. Many ideas,
thoughts, religions, and so forth can be shown to be objectionable for
sound and defensible reasons. Nevertheless, even after weeding out all
the many concepts and philosophical systems that can be rejected on
one or another ground, a plurality of acceptable philosophies is likely
to remain. As Nozick explains,

> I see the situation as follows. There are various philosophical views,
> mutually incompatible, which cannot be dismissed or simply rejected.
> Philosophy's output is the basketful of these admissible views, all to-
> gether. One delimiting strategy would be to modify and shave these
> views, capturing what is true in each, to make them compatible parts of
> one view. While I know of no reason in principle why this cannot be
> done, neither has anyone yet done it satisfactorily. Perhaps, as knowing
> a subject (such as logic or physics) involves seeing the different ways it
> can be organized and viewed, the different ways around it, so too (only
> this time the views are incompatible so the analogy is imperfect) knowing
> the world involves seeing the different ways it can be viewed.[29]

Contemporary students of religion have also, in some instances,
been caught up in the pluralism of the times. A prominent writer on
the sociology of religion, Peter Berger, finds that some set of religious
beliefs is a human necessity: "Every society provides for its members
an objectively available body of 'knowledge.' To participate in the
society is to share its 'knowledge.' " Indeed, "the anthropological
presupposition for this is a human craving for meaning that appears to
have the force of instinct. Men are congenitally compelled to impose a
meaningful order upon reality." To be deprived of all ordering belief is
to face the "ultimate danger . . . of meaninglessness. This danger is
the nightmare par excellence, in which the individual is submerged in
a world of disorder, senselessness, and madness. Reality and identity
are malignantly transformed into meaningless figures of horror."[30]
Berger does not think, however, there is any one religion that can
claim the allegiance of all men or that is inherent to human existence.
Drawing parallels to Einstein's theory of relativity, he describes a
world of theological pluralism in which each society is responsible for
creating its own religious frame of reference. Thus, for each society,

"its patterns, always relative in time and space, are not given in nature, nor can they be deduced in any specific manner from the 'nature of man.' If one wants to use such a term, . . . one can only say that it is the 'nature of man' to produce a world. What appears at any particular historical moment as 'human nature' is itself a product of man's world-building activity."[31]

Berger recognizes full well that the acceptance of such a pluralism might drain particular religions, and religion in general, of the energy and conviction that go with a claim to uniqueness and absoluteness. It creates a "market situation" in which it might even be said that "the religious institutions become marketing agencies and the religious traditions become consumer commodities." Religious institutions in the late twentieth century are therefore confronted with an admittedly painful choice: "They can either accommodate themselves to the situation, play the pluralist game of religious free enterprise, and come to terms as best they can with the plausibility problem by modifying their product in accordance with consumer demands. Or they can refuse to accommodate themselves, entrench themselves behind whatever socio-religious structures they can maintain or construct, and continue to profess the old objectives as much as possible as if nothing had happened."[32] Although Berger formally adopts an agnostic posture, his view seems clear enough that, barring some new religious revelation, there is no real choice for men and women of integrity and sophistication. Each society must have its religion, and for the foreseeable future it seems that the religions of different societies will themselves at least sometimes be different.

The libertarian and pluralist influences of the late twentieth century can be found not only in mathematics, physics, philosophy, and theology, but also in economics. The spokespersons for these latter influences include several prominent economists. Their writings, however, have often fallen outside the mainstream of professional economics. Moreover, their full impact has yet to be felt in the political and economic arrangements by which people live. Their ideas may well be more fully realized not in this century, but in the twenty-first century. Nevertheless, important clues to the political and economic design of the postmodern world can already be found within the writings of these contemporary economists.

Charles Lindblom: Apostle of Administrative Pluralism

Trained as an economist and a self-described member of the economics profession, Charles Lindblom is better known to the field of public administration and political science. His 1959 article in the *Public Administration Review*, "The Science of 'Muddling Through,'" proved to be one of the most influential writings of U.S. social science in the years since World War II.[33] A longtime professor at Yale University, Lindblom's numerous books and articles have crossed over the conventional disciplinary boundaries. For Lindblom, economics often involves bargaining, and thus is a form of politics. Yet, politics often determines the allocation of resources, and in this respect is central to economics.[34]

It is to Lindblom—perhaps more than any other critic—that the demise of the "rational" model of public administration can be attributed. As in mathematics, physics, philosophy, and other fields of study, a crisis of rational faith also beset public administration. Since the rational administrative model was also a cornerstone of the progressive theory of government, Lindblom's criticisms in the 1960s proved to be among the most influential challenges to the political vision of the American progressive gospel.

In the progressive orthodoxy, government decision making was seen as proceeding in a logical and rational sequence. As Lindblom characterized the process, the decision maker first "identifies, scrutinizes and puts into consistent order those objectives and other values that he believes should govern the choice of a solution to the problem." The next step is to survey comprehensively "all possible means of achieving those values." Then the decision maker "exhaustively examines the probable consequences of employing each of the possible means." And last, the decision maker "chooses a means—that is, a particular policy or combination of policies—that will probably achieve a maximum of the values or reach some acceptable level of achievement."[35]

In the field of public planning and administration, this scheme of decision making was the conventional understanding for many years; often it was offered as a model under the label of "comprehensive planning." In economics, a similar vision has been expressed in a mathematical framework. Social policies and values are contained in an "objective function," while alternative means of accomplishing the objective are embodied in the "constraints." The rational decision maker then calculates mathematically the one solution that maximizes the objective function, subject to the satisfaction of all the constraints. Such rational models are, as Lindblom notes, a "method of decision making" that is "consistent with scientific canons" (as developed in the mode of Newtonian science). By putting the policy and value considerations into a separate phase, a distinct domain is preserved in which the goal of a "purely scientific analysis" is pursued free of any "contamination by ethical components."[36]

Yet—Lindblom concluded—despite continuous preaching by public administration professionals over many years, in the majority of instances this rational process bears little relationship to the actual workings of government. It is not merely that politicians have often refused to make way in government for the proper exercise of technical expertise. Rather, the rational ideal has failed in other critical respects as well. First, in a heterogeneous society with many conflicting beliefs, it is often impossible to achieve any clear agreement in advance on values. Second, the idealized rational process ignores the severe problems of assembling and digesting the large amounts of information required. As a result, "for complex public policy problems no one can approximate the [rational] ideal."[37]

Information is costly to gather. It may be difficult to know even what information will be needed. As a result, "inadequate information is inescapable," but the rational ideal "is simply not adapted to this fact." Even when information can be obtained in a raw form, it must be processed and related to the decision at issue—a task that places "increasingly severe strains on man's cognitive faculties." In order to simplify the computational burdens, decision makers typically seek to focus on narrowly defined problems. But this effort will be defeated by the fact that "public policy problems . . . each encompass a host of disparate but interlocked problems of individuals and groups." In a political process that must often accomplish the "reconciliation of interests," the result is "a more continuous process than it is ordinarily conceived to be."[38]

In fact, given the impossibility of following the rational model, government functions through a process that Lindblom labels as "disjointed and incremental problem solving." Because it would normally be impossible to undertake a "comprehensive survey and evaluation," decision makers focus their attention only on "feasible political change," which has the character that it "changes social states only by relatively small steps." In practice, "the total number of alternative policies considered . . . is greatly restricted." Even among the alternatives entertained, "important consequences of policies under analysis are simply disregarded, often deliberately," reflecting the fact that the decision maker belives he "cannot master his decision making problem without simplifying it" and thereby reduce "demands on the intellect and demands for information."[39]

The potential damages of working with inadequate information are limited by the small steps and incremental character of the process. Government administration and policy making consist of "problem solving as successive approximation"—the old-fashioned method of trial and error. A decision maker can assume that if "his move was a failure or was marked by unanticipated consequences, someone's (perhaps even his) next move will attend to the resulting problem." Lindblom emphasizes that even the concept of a "solution," as found in the rational model, is inappropriate. There is no solution because "taste and means change and . . . information about them is growing or at least changing." Hence, government administration "does not successively approximate to any solution," but is merely an indefinite series of adjustments and reactions by the participants in the governing process.[40]

The breakdown of the rational model thus had much the same consequence for public administration that it would have in philosophy and other fields: a shift in emphasis from the end sought to the workings of the process. If administrators no longer saw the prospect of agreement, because there no longer appeared to be any one rational solution, they would have to learn to live indefinitely with a plurality of ends sought and means followed. In philosophy, Rorty had employed the metaphor of a continuing philosophical "dialogue" or "conversation," while Nozick spoke of living in and accepting a world of "philosophical pluralism." More than a decade in advance of their writings, Lindblom had already examined the workings of a world of administrative "pluralism." If an indefinite conversation was now an appropriate method of practicing philosophy, Lindblom had already prescribed an indefinite process of "partisan mutual adjustment" for the conduct of American public administration.

Both in philosophy and public administration, the loyal adherents to the rational model feared that its breakdown and abandonment must yield chaos and confusion. If irrational is the opposite of rational, then government that lacks a rational foundation would necessarily be irrational. However, the advocates of both administrative and philosophical pluralism sought to provide reassurances. Few could deny that pluralism was an accurate description of existing events. To recognize formally and to bless a pluralist world was thus to do no more than to accept the legitimacy of the existing world. Moreover— as experience plainly showed—while existing practices might fall far short of perfection, neither were they outright disorder. In some practical if poorly understood way, the philosophical, administrative, and other pluralistic processes seemed to work adequately most of the time.

In government, the process of partisan mutual adjustment did operate under some informal rules that helped to ensure its adequate functioning. In politics, strong opponents often had the power to block government actions (the "do-no-direct-harm" rule observed by Charles Schultze). Hence, compared with the market, effective political action required a substantially greater degree of consensus. Yet, this consensus building would not necessarily work to block needed government actions. But it did mean that, wherever an action was proposed by someone who expected to benefit, the proposer must also find ways of adequately compensating potential losers—a compensation that could in principle be accomplished through legislative logrolling and other political tactics of long standing.

Indeed, in a perfectly informed and frictionless world (the same world examined by economic theory), all actions beneficial to at least one party, and not harming any other party, would be attainable. There would be no transactions cost or other obstacles to working out political arrangements to provide compensation. The political trading mechanisms of Lindblom's partisan mutual adjustment would therefore be capable, at least in theory, of achieving a level of efficiency just as great as the efficiency resulting from the trading mechanisms of the market. In a perfectly frictionless world, the only differences could be distributional—the requirement in politics that losers must actually receive compensation, while in a market system there would be no requirement for compensation. Thus (and contrary to the beliefs of most economists), in the abstract world in which most economists conduct their analyses, the market has no special efficiency advantage to offer—and many would probably judge it inferior on equity grounds.

Lindblom argued that in a pluralist political system there were in fact powerful forces of self-interest at work to achieve an efficient use of society's resources and to take other socially beneficial actions. If Samuelson had been impressed by the unplanned and unseen "central intelligence" of the market mechanism, Lindblom now described another unplanned and unseen instrument of social coordination. Lindblom called this new political hidden hand the "intelligence of democracy." Even though it was nowhere to be directly seen or touched, this powerful central intelligence of democratic government enabled people to "coordinate with each other without anyone's coordinating them, without a dominant common purpose, and without rules that fully prescribe their relations to each other." Although the system had developed without any clear intent or design, the pluralistic processes of American government were capable of achieving results that Lindblom regarded as representing "calculated, reasonable, rational, intelligent, wise—the exact term does not matter—policy making."[41]

Lindblom's hidden hand guiding American democratic processes was still another image of an intervening force that is outside human control or clear human understanding but assures a meaningful and purposeful direction to events. It was yet another secularization of a divine function, another unseen central intelligence directing the world in ways that the frail powers of human reason cannot fully comprehend or reduce to rational terms. But now that the presence of such a hidden purpose—previously obscure—was coming to be recognized, the pluralist workings of American politics could be accepted with much greater peace of mind. Lindblom offered reassurances that pluralism was not sinful, as so many believers in the necessity of a comprehensive rational plan for government had believed. Rather, it was part of a more subtle grand design. If the progressive gospel was firmly within the Roman tradition, Lindblom now shifted at least somewhat toward the Protestant tradition, where the divine plan is often further hidden from human understanding, where reason by itself is inadequate to discover the divine intent, where pluralism has been the usual outcome.

While not much recognized at the time, Lindblom's concept of government by partisan mutual adjustment raised some difficult questions for American governing concepts. In a pluralistic society, it was difficult if not impossible, as Lindblom had said, to achieve any agreements on social values in advance. Yet, the actions of government would in the end reflect some values. In a system that moved by small increments, the social values of government would emerge after the fact, discovered as outcomes of the process of mutual adjustment. By contrast, in the orthodox progressive gospel of old, theorists such as Woodrow Wilson (especially in his early years) and Frank Goodnow had prescribed a clear separation of value decisions from the routine administration of government. The social values should be argued out first, and the agreed-on values then incorporated into administration by value-neutral experts.

Now, however, Lindblom was saying that "in the actual process of policy making fact and value elements are in fact closely intertwined."[42] Hence, if administration were to be left to professional experts, then seemingly the conduct of administration either would lack values or else would reflect closely the personal values of the administrative experts themselves. How, then, might the strong advocates for a particular set of social values—say, a church or other religious group—react to the new process of political pluralism described by Lindblom? If this group believed that the direction of government policy should reflect its own values (as a religious group of strong convictions very well might), the group would have no choice but to become directly involved in the detailed administrative decisions of government. There would be no other way to ensure that—as social values were realized incrementally, proceeding through many small decisions involving many minor steps and administrative details—the values of the religious group would in fact be reflected in the outcome.

It was just such a consideration that had motivated Charles Schultze to argue for the placement of economists as "partisan advocates for efficiency" throughout the policy-making apparatus of government. In an incremental process of partisan mutual adjustment, the spokespersons for efficiency would need to be placed strategically to exert a continuing influence on the routine course of government decision making. The members of an institutional religion could easily come to a similar conclusion—that if genuine church input into partisan mutual adjustment was to occur, then partisan spokespersons for church beliefs would have to be placed throughout all areas and aspects of government, including administration. To exclude these church members, while welcoming participation of an economic priesthood, would be to engage in a form of religious discrimination.

Lindblom's message of incremental pluralism thus raised a troublesome question: How could incremental pluralism be reconciled with the American constitutional principle of separation of church and state? If institutional religion were excluded from the routine administration of government, it would be excluded from a key process by which society's values were continuously being worked out and decided. If government were small, such exclusion might not be a grave concern. But in the welfare state of the late twentieth century, the values of society are in significant part expressed through the administrative decisions and actions of government.

If Lindblom's new vision thus raised the prospect of active religious participation throughout the activities of government, the history of strong past disagreements among religious groups did not auger well for the results. When questions of basic religious conviction have been at issue, compromises have often been difficult to find, as illustrated in recent years by the policy debate with respect to abortion. All too often in the past, partisans of competing religious values have turned to violence when the results of political negotiation seemed too slow or otherwise unsatisfactory.

Indeed, it seems quite possible that Lindblom's happy expectation of a guiding hidden hand of democracy rested on an implicit belief that the real issues and conflicts in American society were economic. The challenge in dividing an economic pie is much less than in splitting a religious belief. As an economist by training, economic issues may well have been foremost in Lindblom's mind. Economic disagreements are further defused if economic progress is yielding an ever greater abundance of goods and services. If the end of economic scarcity is not far off (perhaps less than 100 years, as Keynes once suggested), the grounds for mutual cooperation are strong. If salvation and the attainment of a heavenly future are at stake, coreligionists bound together on the path of salvation ought to be able to reach agreement. In short, Lindblom would seem to have preached yet another modern economic theology. Lindblom's new gospel was a product of the 1950s and early 1960s, when postwar prosperity was riding high and a common set of American goals and values seemed secure.

Yet, events in the second half of the twentieth century were yielding a pluralism deeper than mere disputes over the economic distribution of goods and services. As Peter Berger suggested, the future might find many differing religions that would coexist among one another, sometimes seeing much different worlds. If it could no longer be assumed that there was one rational structure for the world—as thinkers in many fields were now suggesting—there would also be no certainty that the understanding of human existence would gradually converge everywhere. Indeed, in the 1970s and 1980s, the actual trends in American society seemed less toward theological convergence and more toward divergence. Environmental and other leading issues in U.S. politics often raised issues of basic values, yielding strong disagreements and placing greater strains on the American system. Partisan mutual adjustment could well add up to sharp conflict in a world of theological pluralism. If so, Lindblom had uncovered a grave problem, because his descriptions and explanations of the workings of American government were, on the whole, accurate.

So long as the United States had a core faith—in the twentieth century a civil religion of economic progress—the issue of separating church and state did not arise. The state was in effect the most vital church in American life; the government was the embodiment of and the instrument for realizing the progressive gospel and its vision of American society in the welfare state. But what if American life in the future were to be characterized by a growing pluralism of basic beliefs—in truth, religious beliefs, including some of a secular kind? What if a separation of church and state could not be reasonably defended in a world of incremental movement by partisan mutual adjustment, where society's religious values were significantly determined through the details of public administration? Would admission into the same government of partisans for diverse faiths yield religious conflict and the severe stresses that had typically been associated with religious disagreement in the past? Or would another approach be found? One possibility might be a decentralization of governmental responsibilities and a clustering of coreligionists in common geographic regions, achieving in each region a greater theological homogeneity and thereby defusing questions of the relationship of church and state.

Lindblom's description of American governing processes also raised more immediate questions concerning the ability of government to deliver on the economic front. Even assuming agreement on the benefits of economic progress, were the delivery mechanisms of pluralist American politics capable of yielding a rapid rate of economic growth? The effort to answer this question would direct attention to the makeup and behavior of the interest groups that were leading participants in American pluralism. It was still another economist, Mancur Olson, who would provide some of the most influential answers.

Mancur Olson: The Religious Logic of Collective Action

Like Lindblom, Mancur Olson is another economist whose writings have had more impact outside the mainstream of the economics profession. Anthony Downs, James Buchanan, and Gordon Tulloch preceded Olson in developing many of the main themes of the "public choice" school of economists—contributions for which Buchanan would receive the Nobel prize in economics in 1986. But Olson then took public choice ideas and showed with unusual lucidity and persuasiveness how they could be applied to a number of important political and economic issues. His 1965 book, *The Logic of Collective Action*, has been one of the significant contributions made to American social thought in the era after World War II.

Olson was attracted to the study of collective behavior partly because he recognized the existence of an "intellectual climate" that had proven increasingly "favorable to the growth of this view . . . known as 'pluralism.' " Writers such as Galbraith among economists, and David Truman and V. O. Key among political scientists, were more and more portraying the workings of U.S. government and politics in pluralist terms, emphasizing the interactions of interest groups as the driving force. Yet, as Olson found matters, the conventional understanding of interest-group behavior was gravely flawed: "The customary view that groups of individuals with common interests tend to further these common interests appears to have little if any merit."[43]

Writers in all fields assumed that individual behavior in organizations is "rational" and that in practice this rationality usually means that "organizations . . . perform a function . . . to advance the common interests of groups of individuals." Individuals thus were believed to join an organization to advance their own self-interest, and the organization in turn should act to advance the collective interest of its members. The shocking revelation that Olson drove home in *The Logic of Collective Action* was that organizational behavior could not be explained in these rational terms. If people behaved rationally, many organizations would not be able to exist. In many cases, an individual who was acting rationally would decide not to join an organization, because of what has come to be known widely as the "free rider" problem. As Olson wrote, "the loss of one dues payer will not noticeably increase the burden for any other one dues payer, and so a rational person would not believe that if he were to withdraw from an organization he would drive others to do so." Nor is the individual action of any one member of a large organization able to affect significantly the direction of the organization or its ability to accomplish its mission. As a consequence, "it would not be rational for him to sacrifice his time and money to support a lobbying organization" or any other organization with a collective purpose.[44]

How then do organizations survive? Olson answered that some collectives—such as the government itself—solve the problem by the use of coercion. Similarly, by obtaining laws for closed shops, labor unions have been able to use government powers to compel union membership. Most organizations, however, had to solve the problem by providing services and other assistance for the benefit of their members. Such assistance must be worth enough to the members individually to offset the dues and any other personal costs of membership. Professional associations, for example, often provide inexpensive insurance, journals, magazines, and other information services in return for the dues of their members.

Nevertheless, the conditions that make it possible for an organization to survive in this way have been limited. Thus, many a group of people with shared common interests would nevertheless remain "the unorganized group—the group that has no lobby and takes no action." The most favorable circumstance for organizing was to be found when only a few members were needed to finance and sustain an organization, thus minimizing the free-rider problem. Olson argued that in American politics the logic of collective action therefore strongly favored the business world, where it is common for an industry to have an oligopolistic structure with a few large firms. It was the "fairly small number of firms" in the typical U.S. industry that explained "the high degree of organization of business interests, and the power of these business interests" in American government.[45]

At the other end of the spectrum, large but thinly spread groups such as "taxpayers" and "consumers" collectively have a very large stake in government decisions. Yet the impact of a government decision on each individual member would normally be small. The resulting difficulty of sustaining an organization for such groups tends to leave them either feebly represented or not represented at all. If the American political system has tended to yield an equilibrium of interest-group power, Olson concluded that—contrary to the prevailing pluralist view of the time—this system must yield a serious distortion of the public interest. For example, "the consumers are at least as numerous as any other group in society, but they have no organization to countervail the power of organized or monopolistic producers."[46] More generally, a politics of interest-group pressures must strongly favor concentrated interests over diffuse interests and must in other ways act to undermine broader social purposes.

This conclusion would be the central contribution of the public choice school of economics to American political understanding. It is an argument that in fact seems to find repeated confirmation in American political experience, and has today become part of the conventional wisdom of public debate. Complemented by similar themes found in the writings of Theodore Lowi and other critics of "interest-group liberalism," public choice arguments would significantly influence the development of American progressive thought.[47] If the scientific management of society was incompatible with U.S. democratic institutions, and if political pluralism now had to be rejected as well, many American progressives would turn to yet another progressive gospel: that of economic progressivism. The market mechanism was considered by them to be the best instrument to achieve progressive purposes in society. The market offered an institutional arrangement in which self-interested behavior was presumed, but here this behavior could be channeled much more constructively than in the interest-group interactions of pluralist politics in the United States.

If Olson's contributions in these respects have come to be well recognized, there are other important elements of his analysis that have not been so widely appreciated. Olson's analysis of the dynamics of organizations was directed not only to organizations serving the private interests of their members, but also to those organizations that serve altruistic purposes. As Olson noted, even in these cases an individual "would not rationally contribute toward the provision of any collective or public good, since his own contribution would not be perceptible." In a large organization, such an act of individual "sacrifice would not bring a noticeable benefit to anyone," because the actions by any one individual can have no meaningful impact on the overall success of the organization in achieving the collective purpose.[48] As a result, Olson suggested, it would be rational for those who want to serve collective purposes to direct their efforts to areas and causes where they can have some real effect by themselves.

As has by now been widely remarked, Olson's and other similar analyses of collective action lead directly to the conclusion that the act of voting in a democratic election is irrational. In a national or other large voting body, the probability that any individual voter will have any influence on the election outcome is, for all practical purposes, zero. Yet there is a cost in time and effort required for an individual to vote. Hence, by the standard of economic rationality, no rational citizen would bother to vote. Indeed, it is not only voting but many other acts of political citizenship—letter writing, working in campaigns, sending donations, and so forth—that are irrational in this same sense. Effective political citizenship requires the gathering of the necessary information to make an informed contribution to politics. Time spent reading newspapers, watching television, or in other acts intended to acquire information for individual participation in democratic life is irrational, in economic terms. Such acts are futile gestures and, by a standard of economic self-interest, a misallocation of individual time and effort.

The range of irrational actions in society also extends well beyond politics. To volunteer in wartime for the armed services—assuming it is not to avoid what would otherwise be a draft call—defies a conventional economic understanding of rationality. The individual may seriously risk life and limb, yet his or her individual contribution will make no perceptible difference to the overall military success or failure. In domestic life, the act of serving voluntarily as a witness in a court case involving other parties who are strangers is similarly irrational. The purpose of the court system is to maintain general law and order, which will not be affected by the results of any one trial.

In the same way, many elements of person-to-person interaction among strangers in a large society are irrational. Individual efforts to reward the proper behavior of a stranger or to punish improper behavior serve vital social purposes—enforcing and maintaining cultural standards of proper conduct, making it possible to have some idea in advance what to expect of strangers, and deterring antisocial actions. But the establishment of these social rules is a collective undertaking in which no individual can make a perceptible individual difference. Since dealing with strangers can be risky and involves a potential cost—they may react violently, for instance—no economically rational individual will undertake such an effort. Similarly, many small donations to national charities, many voluntary contributions of time and effort to national causes, many individual complaints against national wrongs and injustices, all these and many other commonplace actions of individual citizens are not explainable by the conventional logic of rational economic behavior.

Since the widespread existence of such actions can hardly be denied, Olson's analysis yields an unintended and unexpected conclusion. It would seem that large numbers of people must be behaving irrationally in many areas of their life—at least by the standard of economics and its logic of self-interest. Moreover, the continuation of such irrational behavior is essential to the basic workings of American social and political institutions. This is yet another of the blows dealt in the late twentieth century to a rationalist understanding of the world.

Indeed, the conclusion seems inescapable that a viable national political community must be regarded in somewhat the same manner as a church. It cannot thrive and serve its members well unless there is a large dose of behavior that historically it has been the province of religion to inspire. Throughout the centuries many religions have called successfully for acts of individual altruism and self-sacrifice. An organization as large as the Roman Catholic church has for centuries commanded the dedication, commitment, and loyalty of many millions of faithful followers, who have often received no direct economic or other reward for actions taken in support of and at the direction of the church.

In U.S. democracy, the act of voting must apparently be understood in a similar manner. It is a symbolic statement—an act of affirming membership and participation in the American national community. A key ritual of American democracy is the collective march to the altar of the ballot box at appointed intervals. The most vital church of the United States is today the welfare state. Despite all the challenges of the twentieth century, the faith of this church remains progressivism, as reinterpreted most recently for many in the message of economic progressivism. In short, following in the path of the medieval Roman Catholic church, the United States has its own version of a Roman theocracy, built on a shared national faith that belongs to the Roman tradition.

Olson's analysis in *The Logic of Collective Action* can itself be read not only for the analysis provided, but as itself a symptom of changes in American life and thought. The very assumption made by Olson that collective behavior should be explained in terms of individual economic rationality reflects a declining sense of the power of community. When faith is strong, few even think to ask why the faithful follow the dictates of the church. It is when beliefs are under challenge and eroding that the question arises. When Olson asked in the mid-1960s why members join and contribute to organizations, the very raising of the issue suggested that the sense of community purpose in the United States was eroding.

In the Protestant tradition, it was the Puritans who conceived all relationships—even between man and God—as properly contractual in nature. In saying that a voluntary contribution to an organization is irrational, Olson is in effect saying once again that a relationship without a contract (implicit if not explicit) lacks full legitimacy. There can be no valid contract because the individual receives nothing—no further benefit is conveyed—in relation to the magnitude of his or her own efforts. In modern economic theology, rational and moral become synonymous; while there is much disagreement among economists concerning the substantive content of rational behavior, there is agreement that to be rational is to obey the proper standard of behavior. Olson's analysis offered a secularization of the moral outlook of the Puritans—a theological individualism that played a decisive role in the development of modern political and economic freedoms. The underlying message of Olson's analysis is further evidence of powerful individualist and libertarian trends at work today in the late twentieth century.

These trends are corrosive of the sense of national community that has sustained the American welfare state. Indeed, if such an individualism were to become the state religion of the United States, powerful pressures would arise for the decentralization of American community and of its political life. As Olson's analysis of collective action makes clear, the smaller the group, the less important is the free-rider problem and other obstacles to successful collective action. Maintenance of common cultural standards, for example, is much easier for a neighborhood than for a whole nation. A next-door neighbor will have opportunities to punish directly a transgressor against neighborhood standards, while the members of a nation will almost always be strangers to one another.

At the local level, there is less need for the unifying influence of a shared faith, less demand for "moral capital" to sustain the community, and less threat of its depletion. In a society in which all is based on contractual relationships among individuals, as soon as the community expands beyond a modest size, the number of contracts (some formal but many informal) becomes hopelessly large. In a small group, each person can know the others personally, and each person can form a contract—if typically unwritten—with other individuals in the community. If to be rational is to behave according to the requirement that all behavior must be based on a contract, then it is only in the small community that life can be lived by such a rational standard.

In the long run, the most important message of Olson may be the same message that Lindblom and so many others of the second half of the twentieth century have offered—not to affirm the power of reason, but to call into question what had seemed to be solid rational foundations. If rationality was limited to the rational concept of economists, then much of the political and economic life of the welfare state exhibited—indeed, relied heavily on—irrational behavior. Alternatively, the meaning of rationality might not be restricted to the economists' concept, raising the possibility of multiple rationalities. The implication (if unintended) of Olson's analysis was that once again a priesthood of the Roman tradition—now the economists and other rationalist defenders of the American welfare state—had overestimated the power of its own rational understanding. If the characteristic outlooks of the Roman tradition are suited for governing large empires while the Protestant tradition fosters pluralism and localism, Olson's analysis further suggested that in a period of uncertain rationality a turn toward this latter tradition might result.

Donald McCloskey: Economic Heretic

Donald McCloskey taught for a number of years at the University of Chicago and is currently a professor of economics at the University of

Iowa. Although his field of specialization is economic history, McCloskey has also written on the methods of inquiry currently employed by the economics profession. Compared with Lindblom and Olson, McCloskey's efforts are more recent and have not had a similarly large influence. Nevertheless, his thinking has begun to receive growing attention within the American economics profession.

Unlike most economists, McCloskey has read Rorty, Feyerabend, and other mathematical, scientific, and philosophical pluralists of the day. He seeks, therefore, to bring an analysis of "the rhetoric of economics"—its form of "conversation"—to bear on the methods employed by members of the contemporary economics profession.[49] His mode of inquiry, like Thorstein Veblen, Thurman Arnold, and a number of other predecessors, is that of a sociological or anthropological investigator into the culture of economics.

Also like many of these predecessors, McCloskey finds in economics the qualities of a religion. The economics profession is today one of the important branches of the "church of science." Economics is part of a general social trend whereby "as religious faith retreated among the intelligentsia in the nineteenth and twentieth centuries, a modernist faith flowed in." The "economic and other sciences" have their own "Ten Commandments and Golden Rule." There is "modernist chanting, supported by hooded choruses" that can be "good for the soul." A "trinity of fact, definition, and holy value" lies at the core of modern economic belief. Since the 1930s, economic modernism has gone through successive stages: a young and vigorous "crusading faith" that with time "hardened into ceremony" and now has reached the stage of an institutional religion with a full fledged church and its "nuns, bishops and cathedrals."[50] For McCloskey, in short, contemporary economics looks like, acts like, and feels like a religion.

The "modernist faith" that dominates contemporary economics did not emerge victorious until after World War II.[51] It marched behind the conviction that past economics had failed to live up to its scientific aspirations and that a rededication to scientific rigor and a more strictly enforced use of the scientific method would be necessary. It was a reflection of the ascendancy of physics in the 20th century as again the preeminent model of scientific thought, also part of the reaction against the emotional and rhetorical excesses of late-nineteenth- and early-twentieth-century thinkers.

However, McCloskey finds that, in turning back to physics, economic modernism looked not to Einstein or to quantum mechanics but to "the early twentieth century's understanding of certain pieces of nineteenth century and especially seventeenth century physics." Much as the men of the Enlightenment had once believed, the highest forms of knowledge were again to be obtained through the use of mathematics. Economic modernists would create a "mathematics-saturated environment" in which professional discipline required almost all economists to adopt a "mathematical way of talking." Following a proper scientific approach, economists would strictly separate themselves from any subjective or ideological elements; they "ought not to have anything to say as scientists about the oughts of value, whether of morality or art." Within the now rigorous science of economics, "only the observable implications (or predictions) of a theory matter to its truth."[52]

McCloskey is prepared to acknowledge that there is much that is "noble" in the efforts of economic modernism. Yet, in the final analysis it joins a long list—longer in fact than McCloskey examines in his writings—of attempts to return to the true science of Newton, a theme that recurs throughout the modern age from the late seventeenth century onward. Despite its good intentions, McCloskey finds that modernism has yielded "many crippled economists" who are "bored by history, disdainful of other social scientists, ignorant of their civilization, thoughtless in ethics, and unreflective in method." All this might not make much difference, if economists were proving to be good scientists by the modernist prescription, able to follow scientific rules to discover the laws of the market mechanism and of other fields of economic activity. But many key concerns in economics do not lend themselves to the use of mathematical and other modernist methods. Hence, if all economists were to follow strictly modernist prescriptions—McCloskey finds—"they would have nothing to say."[53]

Instead, economists have managed to carry on age-old debates and controversies, still suffused with ideology, value judgments, and other subjective elements. But these discussions are now dressed in a scientific language of modernist rhetoric. As McCloskey explains, "modernism promises knowledge free from doubt, free from metaphysics, morals and personal conviction. What it is able to deliver renames as scientific methodology the . . . economic scientist's metaphysics, morals and personal convictions."[54] But because economists refuse to acknowledge the actual character of their efforts, they carry on their philosophical and ethical debates in an uninformed and crude fashion. Many economists are, for example, ignorant of the history of philosophy and of the many lessons previously learned.

Even in well-defined areas, the modernist application of scientific methods has failed to live up to its own expectations. It is true, for example, "that no proposition about economic behavior has yet been overturned by econometrics," which would hardly suggest that the procedure constitutes a rigorous testing. The pretense to scientific conclusiveness, compared with the actual record, makes the practice of much econometrics an "intellectual scandal." Referring to one of the most influential articles of contemporary economics—developed in a technical language—McCloskey writes that "its obscurity . . . became a rhetorical advantage once it had been made the holy writ of a faith. It is composed in a foreign language, but the language is a sacred one, like an Old Church Slavonic. Its style is the key to its rhetorical appeal, because it is the style of scientism."[55]

McCloskey argues that economics must give up the view that there is "one path to Justified True Belief," the demand that there can be only one economic "church." Instead, as Rorty prescribed for philosophy, economists also must come to understand that they are engaged in a "conversation"—an exercise not in modernist science, but in the art of "rhetoric."[56] There is no one method for judging success; as in other artistic endeavors, the verdict is rendered by a whole culture and society. The real concern is not to follow a particular form of argument, but to achieve a more fundamental goal: to genuinely persuade, however the persuasion may be accomplished.

Once the fact of its "literary" quality is accepted, McCloskey finds that, despite its "neurosis of an artificial methodology of science," the field of economics at present is actually "moderately well off." Economists have succeeded in telling "quite brilliant stories about the past, stories on which they often agree." If their successes in this regard are often hidden behind a misleading scientific facade, McCloskey suggests that they would do well simply to drop the facade. Economists should abandon scientistic posturings and acknowledge the practice of the literary art form that economics actually represents. Economists would then be saved the considerable time and effort now given to a false scientific dress and instead would be released to improve their writing skills, their use of appropriate metaphors, and in other ways to develop a greater "rhetorical sophistication."[57]

McCloskey is saying for contemporary economic method what Lindblom was already arguing in the 1960s with respect to the field of public administration. If the world in practice regularly violates the canons of the rational model, Lindblom and McCloskey both find that there is no great cause for concern. Existing practices still work well enough. The most important task is to eliminate intellectual confusion by acknowledging actual practice for what it is: "partisan mutual adjustment" in public administration, and a "rhetorical" exercise in the art of "conversation" in economics. Having provided a better understanding of the actual behavior in their respective fields, Lindblom and McCloskey also suggest that the way may thereby be opened to modest improvements. But no fundamental changes are necessary because partisan mutual adjustment and current economic rhetoric do work in practice much better than they are formally understood.

Thus, McCloskey effectively dismisses the importance of the outward symbolism and ceremony of economics. Symbolism—he seems to be saying—has little practical significance, especially in the rational world of government and business that is the domain of economics. It is thus possible, in the course of waging a revolution in economic method against the trappings of the "church of science," to concede the scientific status and symbols of economics and yet find that there would be few practical consequences for economists or for the acceptance of their advice.[58]

As Mancur Olson's analysis had strongly suggested, however, symbol and ritual play a central role in the workings of the American welfare state. Indeed, going all the way back to Aristotle, many men have found their guide to human conduct in the exercise of human reason. Whole empires have grounded their laws on a faith in the power of reason to reveal one correct answer. Through the ages, this faith has then frequently been affirmed by the symbols and ceremonies of the church. In the modern age, it has been faith in the scientific method that has assured mankind of a common future outcome to the reasoning of human beings all over the world. But what if economic and other expert professionals are not actually engaged in "science," but instead in a loosely structured "conversation." If the "scientific method" does not apply to economics and other social sciences (and its supposed canons may be typically violated by the physical sciences as well), what is to assure the convergence of rational thought to one future outcome? To abandon the scientific method, in short, may be to undermine a basic faith of the American welfare state—a faith as deeply embedded in Western civilization as the Roman tradition of thought.

Theologically, McCloskey is moving in the direction of a shift potentially as momentous as the shift from the medieval Roman Catholic church, possessed of the one truth and the one priesthood, to the conversations within and among the denominations of the Protestant Reformation, each of the Protestant faithful now possessing freedom of individual religious conscience. If each Protestant still believed in principle that there was a single divine message, in actuality there was a pluralism of faiths, often disagreeing sharply in the answers given to basic questions of the divine purpose and the rules for living on earth. The consequences were hardly limited to debates among theologians. In the modern era, it has been economic theology that has served for many men as the guide to salvation, the valid revealer of the path to a heaven on earth. The conflicts among communist, fascist, socialist, and other gospels of economic theology have yielded consequences for the world no less momentous than those experienced in the Reformation era.

McCloskey and others are now calling for a recognition of the legitimacy of pluralism and a consequent cessation of hostilities. The expectation that reason, properly applied, will yield one correct outcome is to be abandoned. As Europe following the Reformation eventually had to come to terms with a world of Christian pluralism, McCloskey now counsels a similar course with respect to the practices of modern economic thought. In the seventeenth century the acceptance of pluralism fostered a growing religious tolerance that played a major role in the spread of modern political and economic freedoms. McCloskey's new economic pluralism is yet another contribution to the forces of individualism, decentralization, and local autonomy in contemporary American life—yet another influence acting to weaken the characteristic preeminence of central authority in the Roman tradition.

In short, if McCloskey is a heretic in the church of economic modernism, his heresy is of a kind that may be capable of undermining empires and inspiring revolutionary changes in political and economic affairs. The American welfare state rests on a foundation of rational faith grounded in the authority of the scientific method and of its social science practitioners. If this progressive faith should come to be questioned widely—as there are many signs is happening today—the result could transcend issues of proper method. Indeed, it could even at some point place in jeopardy the legitimacy of the American welfare state. If this should prove to be the outcome, James Buchanan might well come to be recognized as one of its significant prophets—a modern protestor who, like Martin Luther, once again finds wanting the ways of the Roman tradition.

James Buchanan: Caller for a New Reformation

James Buchanan is, as noted earlier, one of the founders of the "public choice" school of economics, making contributions for which he received the Nobel prize. Although his work fell outside the mainstream of the U.S. economics profession for many years, his Nobel prize reflected the growing influence of Buchanan and other public choice writers. Indeed, by the late 1980s, public choice explanations for the failure of American government to achieve greater efficiency and effectiveness were part of the standard discourse of American political discussion.[59] Government as interest-group compromise—supervised by self-interested administrators—has failed to achieve public purposes because the structure of private incentives created in government almost assures a failure in this respect.

Buchanan's detailed criticisms of government have been infused by a broader set of convictions. He criticizes the American welfare state not primarily to improve it (although there is no objection to the use of his analysis for constructive purposes), but to dismantle it. Specific criticisms today help to lay the groundwork for what, it may be hoped, will someday be more radical changes. The American welfare state should be abandoned because it is morally bankrupt, internally corrupt, and not worth saving. In the final analysis, it rests on false theological premises.

If the American welfare state originates in the gospel of American progressivism, as widely reinterpreted by economic progressivism, Buchanan finds that these progressive doctrines have imbued the welfare state with a pervasive "social engineering" mentality. In pursuing a vision of the scientific management of society, government and other welfare-state institutions have come to play the role of a "potentially benevolent despot." It is the role of scientists to "counsel this despot on, first, the definition of [the] general interest and, second, the means of furthering it." Scientists seek to "advance solutions to all of society's economic ills, solutions that government, as *deus ex machina,* is, of course, expected to implement. . . . Politics . . . should be allowed to interfere as little as is possible with the proper business of government." In practice, this progressive ideal of independent scientific management proves wholly unattainable.[60]

In the welfare state—according to the progressive prescription—the community is paramount. Speaking with the voice of authority for the community, the church of science is the deliverer of ultimate truths. The commands of the scientific church (directed by professional priesthoods who speak languages and have knowledge inaccessible to the average person) must in the end be obeyed. Buchanan's great mission, however, is to make a modern protest against this oppressive collectivism. Men must shift their fundamental allegiances "from the

organizational entity as the unit to the individual-in-the-organization.''
It is imperative that "man must cling to that uniquely important
discovery, . . . the discovery of man, the individual human being.'' If
men will not stand up to the false claims of scientific collectivism, then
they will "be drawn along any one of the many roads to serfdom by
false gods.'' Indeed, if men are so craven as to fail to assert their
individual freedom and dignity, to assert their individual conscience
against the imperial claims of science, then "we do not deserve to
survive."[61]

Contemporary economics is, for Buchanan, one of the chief corrupting forces in the welfare state. Economics asserts that men should
behave rationally—a standard that economic science is said to reveal
through its scientific investigations. The perfect man, living perfectly
by the highest standard of the welfare state, would be governed by the
rational ideal as decreed by economic science. Yet, as Buchanan
laments, life for such a man "could not be concerned with choice at
all.'' In order that there be choice, there must be a multiplicity of
"imagined 'possibles.' '' It is "internally contradictory" to speak of
individual "choice making under [scientific] certainty."[62] As a result,
the economic faith of the American welfare state reduces the individual
to an automaton who should follow with unfailing loyalty the decrees
of economic science. If Martin Luther once argued that the Roman
Catholic church had undermined the role of individual faith, Buchanan
now calls for a new Reformation directed against the theocracy of
science as found today in the American welfare state.

Like the Roman priesthoods of old, the economic priesthood of the
welfare state both preaches a false doctrine and has itself fallen into
evil ways. Buchanan believes that economics once had its better days
but that in the twentieth century, especially under the influence of the
same modernism that McCloskey decries, a great mistake has been
made, attempting to mold economics to the same methods as physical
science. This mistake is closely associated with the adoption of the
formal utility-maximizing framework of contemporary economics, according to which every economic question is reduced to a mathematical problem of maximizing a utility or other objective function. The
result has been not science, but instead "scientism"—a false pretense
of science. Economics has been led into the "escapist puzzles of
modern mathematics.'' Instead of progress, there has been retrogression—"a continuing erosion of the intellectual (and social) capital that
was accumulated by 'political economy' in its finest hours."[63] The
economics profession today is merely another of the grand priesthoods

of history that have fallen into a condition of cynicism, internal decay, and loss of purpose.

While their complaints are similar, Buchanan does not take the benign view of McCloskey—that is, merely adjust the rhetoric and lower the expectations to fit a satisfactory reality. The economic theology and the fate of the American welfare state are for Buchanan closely interwoven. Abandon one, and the other is no longer tenable. If few of his colleagues are willing to venture into such uncharted waters, Buchanan does not shrink from exploring the full consequences.

A unified community on the scale of the American welfare state is simply not, in Buchanan's view, sustainable over the long run. Inspired by the tenets of American progressivism, a large state with a large administrative apparatus has been erected in the twentieth century, centrally headquartered in Washington, D.C. Yet, the federal government is filled with "elected and appointed politicians and bureaucrats [who] are not different from other men. They are motivated at least in part by their own interest, not by some higher vision of the 'social good.' " When such people find themselves in control of the coercive instruments of a large government, the predictable result is that "the realizable surplus made available to society only through the workings of markets may be dissipated, and the grosser . . . inequalities of political power increased."[64] These kinds of problems can be found in government at any level, but they are exaggerated in a nation-state as large as the United States.

Buchanan thus finds that, as "markets are replaced or subverted by government interventions, the dependence of order on some extended range of moral responsibility increases." The sustenance of a " 'social order' requires general acceptance of a minimal set of moral standards."[65] Although such a common set of values may be obtainable at a local level, it is improbable in a large nation with its typical diversity of beliefs, values, and backgrounds. It is because community values and common identity are so difficult to achieve at a national level that national politics so easily degenerates into the beggar-thy-neighbor practices that have become widespread in the United States today.

What can a person be predicted to do when the external institutions force upon him a role in a community that extends beyond his moral-ethical limits? The tension shifts toward the self-interest pole of behavior; moral-ethical principles are necessarily sublimated. The shift is exaggerated when a person realizes that others in the extended community of arbitrary and basically amoral size will find themselves in positions comparable to his own. How can a person act politically in other than his own narrowly defined self-interest in an arbitrarily sized nation of more than 200 million?[66]

It is only in periods of emergency such as the United States experienced in World War II that a national community really exists. The persistence of the Cold War and the legacies of wartime attitudes further maintained an unusual degree of national unity through the 1950s. But the Vietnam War and other events of the 1960s brought this anomalous period in American history to an end. At that point, a real danger lay in the possibility that a president or other leader might be tempted to stir false fears of military threats in hopes of shoring up the fragile national bonds of community and identity.

Despite the flags and the tall ships of 1976, there is relatively little moral-ethical cement in the United States which might bring the internal moral-ethical limits more closely in accord with the external community defined inclusively by the national government. There is no "moral equivalent to war," and since Vietnam, we must question whether war itself can serve such a function. Nonetheless, experience suggests that war and the threat thereof may be the only moral force that might sustain the governmental Leviathan. Viewed in this light, it is ominous that each president, soon after entering office, shifts his attention away from the divisive issues of domestic politics toward those of foreign affairs. We must beware the shades of Orwell's 1984, when external enemies are created, real or imaginary, for the purpose of sustaining domestic moral support for the national government.[67]

Buchanan calls for a radical decentralization of responsibility in the American welfare state, the abolition of the institutional products of American progressivism. It is worth at least raising the possibility of the "secession" of some regions from the United States. Even if a movement for secession were not successful, at least "such a threat [might] itself force some devolution of central government power."[68] As a contemporary protester against the American church of science, Buchanan is seemingly prepared to accept the potential disorders that would accompany a major schism in the church.

As a leading spokesman for libertarian trends in American thought, Buchanan also finds that it is the large nation-state that represents the greatest threat to market freedoms. In a state of this size, government interventions almost always turn out to serve one interest group to the detriment of another interest group—as Olson suggested, often a small concentrated group benefiting at the expense of a large diffuse group. However, in a state of small size, any group seeking government favors would soon be forced to tax its own members. It is the ability to spread tax collections over a large nation—extending far beyond the immediate beneficiary group, thereby tapping millions of small contributors— that makes the "pork-barrel" strategy so attractive in American government today. A radical decentralization of power would thus represent a major step in asserting a greater influence for the market. Economic transactions across nation-states are transactions accomplished voluntarily among independent parties who are motivated by self-interest. A turn toward smaller sovereign communities would therefore represent a turn away from the internal political transfers that mark the welfare state and a large step toward a world driven by contractual relationships.

Buchanan finds few allies in these regards within the mainstream of the current economics profession. Surprisingly, his strongest potential alliance—if one thus far marked by mutual suspicion—may well be with the contemporary environmental movement. Environmentalists do not typically share Buchanan's vision of a world marketplace that maximizes the worldwide production of goods and services. However, they do, or at least many of them do, share his deep antagonism toward the progressive gospel of efficiency. No less than Buchanan, many environmentalists see their values endangered by a powerful central government that acts in the name of science, giving license to government administrators to implement the scientific management of society in the name of economic progress. Like Buchanan, many environmentalists seek to undermine the progressive gospel and to advance the cause of a sharp decentralization of political authority in American society.

Also like Buchanan, many environmentalists today challenge the basic assumptions and the very method of thought characteristic of science—at least as applied to human affairs. The features that give scientific thought its distinctive qualities include its skeptical and analytical spirit, its use of abstractions (especially mathematical), and its tendency to reduce human existence to these abstractions. Science in this respect is the opposite of art. An artist portrays a broad picture—"a whole"—while the scientist generally breaks down experience into numbers and formulas, manipulating abstract categories through mathematical methods. Many critics of science today find that in the process the essence of what is human is lost. This scientific mentality not only is unable to justify human values, but often leads to a general outlook that erodes such values.

This view was expressed by a number of prominent philosophers in the past (including Alfred North Whitehead), and in recent years has significantly influenced the thinking of the environmental movement.[69] Two current advocates of "deep ecology" thus contend that

> Technological society not only alienates humans from the rest of Nature but also alienates humans from themselves and from each other. It necessarily promotes destructive values and goals which often destroy the basis for stable viable human communities interacting with the natural world. The technological world view has as its ultimate vision the total conquest and domination of Nature and spontaneous natural processes. . . . The ultimate value judgment upon which technological society rests— progress conceived as the further development and expansion of the artificial environment necessarily at the expense of the natural world— must be looked upon from the ecological perspective as unequivocal regress.[70]

Such views are intended to be a direct challenge to "not only the growth addict and the chronic developer, but science itself."[71] Admittedly, it is only the more venturesome and rebellious in the environmental movement who state views of this kind explicitly. Yet, in mostly implicit ways, their impact has extended far into mainstream American thought today. In a leading recent study of the conservation movement in the United States, Stephen Fox states that

> To the recurrent question of whether conservationists are against progress, the answer would seem to be yes—at least to progress as it has normally been defined in the West. . . . In the striking connection between its religiosity and its skepticism toward the onward march of secular events, conservation implies a vision radically different from the American norm. . . . Dissenting from both the capitalists and the communists, they declare that history is not a line but a circle; that meaning resides less in matter than in spirit, less in striving than in stasis, less in humans than in Nature, less indoors than outdoors.[72]

One of the most important political trends of recent years has been a strong new strain of localism and regionalism in American life. Fierce local resistance has often blocked both market forces and central government plans. Local groups are no longer persuaded by the claims of progress, the argument that economic growth serves the cause of the whole nation (or all mankind)—a cause that properly commands deference and sacrifice among local citizens of good will. Rejecting accusations of selfishness, parochialism, and infidelity to the cause of progress, many local environmentalists have spearheaded the opposition to high-density housing, shopping centers, dams, mines, highways, and all manner of development. The not-in-my-backyard syndrome today makes it a severe challenge to locate many necessary but obtrusive facilities. Until recently, the problem had been less severe because some citizens could usually be found who felt that it was their civic duty to accept these same facilities in the name of progress.

As a result of all the growing resistance, however, the location of such facilities may well prove in the future to be possible only with the provision of compensation, perhaps by direct monetary payment. Given frequent environmentalist skepticism concerning the use of market methods, it is paradoxical that environmentalism is in effect creating strong pressures for a society organized by contract, a society in which the progressive gospel and the church of science will be too weak to accomplish many necessary social tasks by moral authority alone. In lieu of moral authority, these tasks may have to be accomplished through the mechanism of voluntary exchanges of a market character. When the power of faith and of the community prove insufficient, society may have to look to the power of the dollar to achieve its aims. In this respect, the current protest is again reminiscent of an earlier period when the Protestantism of Luther regarded the market skeptically but, in its practical effects, tended to advance a society based on contractual relationships. As Ernst Troeltsch once observed, the greatest social consequences of the Protestant Reformation were in large part unintended consequences.

There are also environmentalists who share with Buchanan an interest in secession as a remedy to excessive federal power. Secession might be a practical means to achieve a new world based on local community and autonomy—a social arrangement in fact envisioned as long ago as Plato's *Republic*. In a modern work called *Ecotopia*, an environmentalist visionary portrays a utopian existence as consisting of a pastoral life in the Pacific Northwest. This region has seceded, suspending both market and political relationships with the United States and the rest of the world. It has done so in order to avoid any disruptions from the outside, whether market or government originated. The fundamental problem, and the reason for seceding, is seen as the deep offensiveness to the social values of Ecotopia of the "underlying national philosophy of America: ever-continuing progress, the fruits of industrialization for all, a rising Gross National Product."[73]

This is not the first time in history that a call has been made for a break with a Roman church. If human reason is not universal, if the exercise of rational thought does not yield one correct answer, if instead a number of answers have equal claims to authority, then the centralizing influence in the Roman tradition will not hold. If pluralism is the new order of the day, it also will not be the first time that the world has had to address the consequences of multiple theologies, multiple churches, a sharp decentralization of authority, and other developments characteristically associated with the Protestant tradition.

Kenneth Boulding: Seeker of a Universal Church of the World

Kenneth Boulding is yet another important contemporary economist whose writings are more influential outside the mainstream of professional economics. Yet, he has been well respected within the profession, serving in 1968 as president of the American Economic Association. An active Quaker since his student days, Boulding's economic writings are suffused with a strong sense of the Quaker outlook. His distinctive contribution to contemporary social thought has been a lifelong effort to bring an economic perspective to bear on the problem of preserving peace in the nuclear age. Boulding's beliefs have recently been examined in *Three Scientists and their Gods*, a book that takes for granted that science in our day provides many of the answers that would have been given by institutional Judaic and Christian religion in an earlier era.[74]

For Boulding, the whole world has now become a single scientific system, linking the fate of all human beings together as coinhabitants of "spaceship earth." Unlike Buchanan, however, Boulding regards this development in favorable terms. One of Boulding's favorite sayings is the "interconnectedness" of all things. Due to the marvels of twentieth-century communications, transportation, and other technology, "today the world has become a neighborhood."[75] Drawing on ecological analogies, Boulding sometimes compares the world to a pond in which every creature has its own special niche.

Boulding is in many ways an heir to Saint-Simon but now at a global level, offering a vision of the scientific management of the whole world. The world is a single organic system; humanity makes progress through discovery of the scientific truths of this worldwide system; and it is through the spread of science that men and women achieve the capacity to live in ever greater harmony. Thus, for Boulding "the most significant thing that has happened, perhaps in the whole history of mankind, is the formalization and systemization of the learning process itself in what we know as science." This scientific learning process is "the key to the dynamic process in social evolution." It is the worldwide "increase of knowledge" that represents "the essence of political development as well as of all other development."[76]

Like Saint-Simon, Boulding is deeply disturbed by the frequent refusal of his fellow human beings to recognize their good fortune. Science has for the first time in history opened the way to the perfection of human existence, but this perfection requires of each individual the coordination with and mutual support of other fellow individuals. Instead, as the history of the twentieth century so frightfully shows, human beings persist in fighting with one another, indeed sometimes slaughtering one another. Boulding thus is eventually forced to conclude—as Saint-Simon did—that the spread of a new world harmony through the creation of a scientific society must also be accompanied by the spiritual regeneration of mankind. Science therefore must educate people not only in the expert methods to build better machines and to operate more complex systems, but in the proper values of a scientific society. Science must train its professional priesthoods to serve as missionaries not only in the expert methods of science, but also in the ethics of science. These ethics should extend all around the world.

Boulding laments—however—that, even though "the international system" is one of "enormous complexities," thus far "the role of science is extremely limited, indeed, almost nonexistent."[77] The exclusion of science is to blame for the fact that the worst pathologies of human behavior are to be found in international affairs. Indeed, the current hopes for future peace lie in the worldwide spread of science. As Boulding writes, the moral values of science must replace the pervasive sinfulness that characterizes international relationships at present.

> Almost every principle we have learned about scientific information gathering, processing, and reality-testing is violated by the processes of the international system. Indeed, the conflict of values between the subculture of science and the subculture of the international system may well turn out to be one of the most fundamental conflicts of our age. In

science secrecy is abhorrent and veracity is the highest virtue. In science there is only one mortal sin: telling a deliberate lie. In the international system, on the other hand, secrecy is paramount and veracity is subordinated to the national interest. The national interest can indeed be said to legitimate almost every conceivable form of evil: there is not one of the seven deadly sins that is not made into a virtue by the international system. Another fundamental characteristic of the scientific community is that it is basically a community of equals for the very good reason that hierarchy always corrupts communication. A dialogue can only exist between equals.

Finally, in the scientific community power is supposed to have a low value and truth the highest value, whereas in the international system the reverse is the case. It is not surprising that under these circumstances the international system is so spectacularly pathological in an organizational sense. . . . It is the organization, not the individuals, which is pathological, by reason of the corruption of both the information and the values that have produced it.[78]

Boulding is a progressive who, like most economists of the generation following World War II, turned to the economic interpretation of progressivism. Boulding finds the same two great advantages in a market system that Keynes saw: its efficiency, and its freedom. The proper science of society in matters of ordinary production and distribution thus is for Boulding the science of the market mechanism. It is only through the unseen central intelligence of the market that the world can ever hope to achieve effective economic coordination.

Long before the terms came into wide use, Boulding in 1952 was writing that society must strive for a "positive sum" enlargement of the total economic pie, rather than creating "zero sum" conflicts over the division of a fixed pie. The essence of politics is distributional conflict, while the mechanism of the market promotes the efficient use of resources and increases the total production of goods and services. The market also involves actions taken by mutual consent and for a mutual benefit. The market is an "exchange system" that in the modern world has increasingly and desirably substituted for the "threat system" of politics. Politics is an inferior system not only because it involves coercion—in starkest form becoming "slavery"—but because politics encourages the division of men into factions that then threaten war.[79]

Indeed, the importance of relying on the market mechanism is all the greater in the nuclear age when the threat relationships of politics—currently the characteristic mode of international relations—promote a tendency toward conflict and instability that is so grave as to endanger future human existence. Admittedly, the workings of the market sometimes yield a distribution of income that is not ideal. Boulding believes, like most progressives, in equality as the goal. But this goal today must be balanced against the urgency of avoiding nuclear war. Thus, if necessary—as Boulding believes—"it would be worthwhile paying a good deal of injustice for the establishment of a stable peace."[80]

The desirable move from a world of political relationships to a world of market relationships is at present frustrated by the artificial boundaries of nation-states. Because their interactions are political and thus based on coercive threats, nations feel obliged to arm themselves—if not for offensive purposes, then to assure their own defense. In this international climate, Boulding finds that the arms race results from a pathology known in economics as the "prisoners dilemma." Each nation commits more and more national resources to soldiers and weapons yet achieves no greater security as a result, when others match the commitment. Further buildup of arms then follows. Making matters even more dangerous, "the armed forces of the world have become a social system almost completely divorced from the states which they ostensibly defend." The answer, Boulding concludes, must lie in some form of "world social contract" or world "constitution" that is "the highest-priority task of our time." It should include a means for "the separation of the armed forces from the state."[81]

The very future survival of mankind may in fact depend on the abolition of the system of nation-states. Nations exist today, as Boulding sees it, to satisfy the strong human need for a sense of community. But the fanning of nationalist sentiments is a poor way to serve this need. Here sounding much like Buchanan, Boulding writes of "the present bankruptcy of the national state, which can provide us with neither security, justice, peace, nor honor," but instead reflects "the adolescent disease of nationalism." For the future protection of mankind, "the nation-state can no longer be treated as a sacred institution; there must be a deflation of the emotions and values that attach to it." Indeed, in light of the unacceptably high prospect of nuclear annihilation, Boulding is prepared to abolish the existing system of nation-states altogether, arguing that "if the continuance of the system of the sovereign national states implies that we shall all live on algae in caverns, then I say 'To hell with it.' "[82]

Boulding recognizes, however, that any monolithic world government is out of the question. Not only would that be a practical impossibility, but it would be undesirable in principle as well, because the world contains too great a diversity of local values and cultures. Moreover, world government creates the risk of world tyranny. While rejecting the nation-state as a basis for community, Boulding is less certain about the future sources of communal identity. He seems to believe that, while it is necessary to have a new sense of world community based on the worldwide spread of science, there may be other identifications as well as that are directed to regions smaller than the nation-state. Boulding therefore finds that, once the limits of scientific knowledge have been reached, "the harder it becomes to resolve the arguments." As a result, "the solution which seems to be working itself out is one in which we have a number of different cultures, each embodying a different ethical principle. . . . Within a complex society there is room for many such subcultures and many ethical systems, ranging from the Amish to the Zoroastrians." In another discussion, Boulding contends that the need is to "invent a 'mosaic society,' composed of many small subcultures, each of which gives to its participants a sense of community and identity which is so desperately needed in a mass world, and which can at the same time remain at peace with its neighbors and not threaten to pull the society apart."[83]

The responsibility for building this world of the future will fall in significant part on economists. Economists are, Boulding suggests, responsible for a "silent revolution" that may yet have consequences for humanity as important as the past efforts of engineers and physicists. There has been a "Great Change in economics" that is "associated above all with the name of the late Lord Keynes" and that has brought us to the edge of a "New Era." This new era will advance still further that "fabulous increase in human skill which constitutes the scientific and technological revolution" of the twentieth century. If we will but follow the guidance of its message, we can be assured that "economics . . . looks toward a free-trading world society, claims that the business of living even in a complex society can be accomplished with a small minimum of police coercion, urges that plenty is the source of power and war the greatest enemy of plenty."[84]

Yet, as full of optimism as he is, Boulding has also seen in the history of the twentieth century that this prospect is not guaranteed. Economics creates the prospect of a "kingdom of heaven on earth" where "war, poverty, and disease are abolished," but also of a "hell on earth" where there would be "an indestructible and universal tyranny, securely based on the power of both physical and social science." Sounding once again much like Saint-Simon, Boulding suggests that mankind therefore needs not only the achievement of modern economic efficiency, but also appropriate "love systems," which are marked by the feature that "the individual comes to identify his own desires with those of another."[85] Family ties have a critical role to play in sustaining such love relationships, but in a wider arena much depends on religion.

Indeed, Boulding comments that, while economics has given us the ability "to get what we want," it is "religion" that stresses "the question of whether we want the right things." Men and women now hold in their own hands the "power and knowledge" to build a "permanent and universal civilization" of peace and prosperity. Whether they in fact do so will depend on the "all-important" character of their "religious experience," which may very well "tip the great scales toward either heaven or hell on earth."[86] In short, if modern economics holds the keys to human salvation, this salvation for Boulding is not assured by economic science alone. Mankind today requires a theology that fully incorporates but does not stop at the message of the economic knowledge of the modern age.

Therefore, the pressing need is for a great new religious synthesis of scientific and economic truths with the wisdom found in the past in Christian and other religions. Christianity once faced the task of reconciling Greek reason—wonderful in its powers, yet dangerous as well—with its own church teachings. The man who stepped forth then to accomplish this heroic task was Thomas Aquinas. As Boulding writes of the state of mankind in the late twentieth century, "we long for a new and greater Aquinas, to bring together once again Grace and Truth, Wisdom and Power, Faith and Knowledge in blessed union."[87] The Roman empire must for Boulding now be the whole world. The world must be guided by a tolerant faith, grounded in scientific reason. This faith should respect property, assure individual freedom, allow for the expression of individual interests, and encourage people to pursue the good life in their diverse ways. The worldwide church of science should, above all, mediate any serious divisions within mankind, assuring that such divisions are never again permitted to escalate into the violence of warfare among nations.

As with the visions of Saint-Simon, there is much that seems utopian and unlikely in the writings of Boulding. The thought is sometimes disorganized, the logic unclear, the means to the end uncertain, the flavor of the whole enterprise too obviously that of old-style religion rather than of the science in whose name Boulding himself claims to speak. Yet, in an earlier era Saint-Simon's rambling thoughts proved a remarkably acute—and in many respects superior—guide to the future, as compared with the carefully reasoned arguments of many contemporaries. The development of the worldwide culture that Boulding envisions has in fact already made remarkable strides in the twentieth century and seems to be moving forward today at an accelerating pace. The political revolutions of 1989 in Eastern Europe might well prove to have been a large step toward the fulfillment of Boulding's hopes. As Boulding has prophesized, the foundations for world unity today include the ever wider acceptance of the merits of market exchange among the peoples of the world.

While some groups in the West have been experiencing a crisis with respect to the "values" of science, the rest of the world has been more concerned to obtain greater scientific knowledge and to achieve the material comforts that science has made possible. The less developed nations have been making great efforts to increase the educational levels of their populations. By "education" has been meant a change from non-Western and premodern beliefs to the adoption of at least significant elements of the new, vastly more powerful method of reasoning of the West and the conclusions it yields, based significantly on science. Indeed, in the past two centuries the spread of scientific and economic thought around the world has represented the greatest mass religious movement in the recorded history of mankind. The world now faces the real possibility that, sometime in the twenty-first century, almost all of its people will for the first time share much the same beliefs about the origins of the universe, the character of subsequent history, and the proper organization of worldwide relationships. All this is envisioned in Boulding's writings to a degree shared by few of his economist peers.

No contemporary nation has renounced modern technology, said that it does not want economic growth, and sought to preserve instead a prescientific existence. Whether the guiding faith is Marxist, socialist, free market, or some other, virtually every nation looks to modern economic theologies for guidance along the path to a future destiny of material abundance. As communist and other nations around the world today turn to ideas of planned markets, and a similar economic progressivism holds sway in the United States, the prospect of a common economic theology for the entire world also seems less distant than ever before.

Events in any case are running ahead of ideas. The speed at which the transformation to a single world marketplace is occurring can be startling at times. Most Americans, for example, realized their high dependence on world oil markets only when they experienced sudden OPEC price shocks and petroleum shortages. Evidence of the spread of worldwide markets for automobiles, electronics, and other consumer goods is encountered in daily purchases. In the not-too-distant future, a single worldwide stock exchange will no doubt be operating 24 hours a day. A still more radical development—a single world banking and financial market—is likely to follow. Interest rates and other terms of financial transactions will tend toward an equalization on a worldwide basis. Proposed new industries in any one nation will be competing to show that they can earn a rate of return competitive with rates of return in other nations. The closely linked worldwide banking system creates the prospect—hardly imaginable as recently as a century ago—of economic decisions effectively coordinated on a worldwide basis.

A worldwide culture is developing as well. Scientific elites in all nations share a common language and set of interests. The vastly improved technology of communications now makes it possible for all the world to watch together the same televised theatrical, sporting, and other events. Basketball, gymnastics, and a number of other sports previously confined to a few nations now attract large audiences and wide participation in many countries. The same books and movies are distributed to worldwide audiences.

The twentieth-century discoveries of astrophysics show the earth to be a tiny speck in an enormous universe, far larger and more diverse than imagined until recently. Men are the coinhabitants of a common ground—a sense also driven home by pictures of the earth transmitted from outer space. Modern technology has created forms of pollution that affect and conceivably could threaten the earthwide ecosystem. The release of chlorofluorocarbons into the atmosphere is believed to pose a threat to the ozone layer that shields the earth from ultraviolet radiation—creating the risk of a higher incidence of cancer, crop damage, and climatic changes. Other pollutants such as acid rain may carry well beyond the boundaries of individual nations.

There are, in short, not only powerful forces of decentralization and pluralism at work in the world today, but also powerful forces of worldwide centralization and unification. While critics charge that science is a less rational exercise than has been depicted, the practical products of science are rapidly changing the world. The grounds for assuming that Western culture will converge to a common standard of the progressive, rational, and enlightened human being are today being

contested. Yet—in practice—a common culture of scientific, economic, sporting, literary, and other interactions is rapidly enveloping
the globe. Within nations, there are regional and other demands for
significant decentralization of authority. Yet, the development of a
worldwide economy and the sharing of a worldwide environment call
for the creation of new supranational institutions of economic and
environmental coordination.

The future resolution of these tensions cannot be predicted with any
confidence. They are, moreover, far from new—the world having
previously seen empires rise as well as break up. The nation-state is a
fairly new development in world history; it could recede in importance
as rapidly as it rose. The tide of human reason has previously flowed,
tending to unite mankind, and then ebbed, spawning challenges to a
common rational order. It is a battle as old as the tensions between the
members of the Roman and the Protestant traditions. What is new
today is that the stakes for humanity have been drastically raised by
the efficiency of modern technology. The central concern of Boulding's
economic writings—the substitution of peaceful for past violent means
of settling disagreement within humanity—stands as the one absolute
imperative of our time. Unless nuclear war can be prevented, other
issues relating to the possible character of a future world of postmodern economics may be irrelevant.

Chapter 8

The Right of Free Secession

The welfare state of the twentieth century has been grounded in the American progressive gospel and similar ideas of democratic socialism in Western Europe. Yet, the Holocaust, the atom bomb, and other events of the twentieth century have undermined the core progressive conviction that economic progress will abolish evil and bring about the arrival of heaven on earth. Economic progress may still be a necessary condition of salvation, but for many today it is no longer a sufficient condition. The character of the postmodern era may well be defined by the theological answer given to the loss of faith in modern progressivism and its various offshoots.

While new faiths may emerge, it is well to keep in mind that Western civilization seems as wedded as ever to the Judeo-Christian outlook, with its expectation that history is the record of progress to a heavenly future—on earth, or in the hereafter. Thus, the central theological problem of the current age would seem to be to find the new route of progress in history, whether this involves a return to older religious convictions or a turning to new theological understandings. Whatever the answer, the implications will be far reaching. As the previous chapters of this book have examined, ideas do have consequences, and theological ideas frequently the greatest consequences. If postmodern theologies emerge to take the place of the progressive gospel, changes in social institutions are likely to occur of a similar magnitude. If the theological foundations of the welfare state are undermined, its institutional forms might not survive either.

The possibility cannot be ruled out that, if we could somehow know the political and economic structures of the world in future centuries,

they would seem as strange and unfamiliar to us as modern arrangements would appear to feudal and other premodern sensitivities. Economists and other social scientists, like the priesthoods of old, are often
conservative in their outlook and slow to recognize powerful forces at
work to change the world. Social arrangements of long standing often
seem more permanent than they really are. This lack of vision was
recently illustrated by the general failure of the experts to foresee the
radical pace of change in the Soviet Union and Eastern Europe from
the mid-1980s onward.

In fact, the current era seems in many ways to be a period of
fundamental transition. In Western Europe, significant elements of
national sovereignty have been conceded to the European Community,
creating a degree of European unity without precedent since perhaps
the thirteenth-century era of papal authority over all Europe. If the
welfare state is a modern theocracy of economic progressivism, Brus-
sels in the late twentieth century has replaced Rome as the headquarters of the Western Europe branch of the world church. In the Third
World, a number of nations are moving rapidly to create modern
economies with major improvements in the health and overall standard
of living of their populations. In economic matters, the world is moving
toward a global community, closely linked by modern transportation
and telecommunications capacities. The twentieth century has witnessed the first religious revolution ever to encompass the entire world:
the spread of modern economic theology in one or another of its creeds
to almost every place on earth.

My purpose in this chapter will be to offer some speculations on
where all this change may be headed. Such an undertaking inevitably
involves major risks and uncertainties. More questions will be raised
than will be answered. My hope is merely to offer a brief suggestive
sketch of world political and economic arrangements that could well
emerge from current trends in modern (or perhaps now it is postmodern) economic theology.

The Roman and Protestant Traditions Today

We live in the late twentieth century in a new Roman era. Spencer
was the first of the secular Protestants to meet general condemnation;
Marxism by the 1990s has seemingly reached a similar state. If Freud
continues to exert influence, it is the individualistic and libertarian
elements of his theology that prove most attractive. The world has

turned away from warfare to economic pursuits as a superior outlet for competitive strivings, led in many cases by the very nations that previously had instigated global conflict. It is an age where in many ways the characteristic outlooks of the Roman tradition are ascendant—utilitarianism, worldliness, the pursuit of self-interest, pragmatism, and a sense of the world as one community bound together by common interests.

Indeed, to a degree unique in the history of mankind, the twentieth century in key respects has seemed to confirm the characteristic outlooks of the Roman tradition. Human reason, as developed and perfected in the scientific method, has succeeded in transforming the human condition. Although much poverty remains, the level of material well-being and the good life now widely achieved would have seemed for many men in earlier centuries a literal heaven on earth. Seemingly, mankind by the power of its reason alone has already proven its capacity to attain its own salvation.

Yet, from another perspective the evidence of twentieth-century history could as well be read as attesting to the greater wisdom of the characteristic outlooks of the Protestant tradition. Perhaps science and other ideas of the modern age are the greatest and the most dangerous in a long series of snares and delusions in the minds of men, the most devious trick yet played by the Devil. Due to science, mankind for the first time has acquired the power literally to destroy the human presence on earth—indeed, possibly the very presence of life on earth. Influenced by various modern ideas, the powers of technology in the first half of the twentieth century were used for barbarous purposes, visiting immense death and destruction on humanity.

Today, the authority of social science, legal, and other priesthoods is under challenge. The law is said to lack a rational grounding, and to advance only the interests of the powerful. Economic professionals are portrayed in a similar vein, out of touch with the real world and engaged in activities reminiscent of the sterilities of late-medieval scholasticism. The spreading use of drugs, growing rates of suicide, ever more crowded prisons, Wall Street fraud, failures of the educational system, and a whole host of contemporary problems are seen by many as the signs of a Roman civilization in decline.

These characteristic outlooks of the Protestant tradition are found not only in the teachings of fundamentalist Christian preachers, but in new secular versions of much the same message. Indeed, the characteristic Protestant themes often seem newer and fresher as revealed by secular prophets, and their message thus becomes all the more powerful. Current environmentalism encompasses a wide range of beliefs, some environmentalists seeing the proper goal as merely a more valid application of science and rational methods to environmental problems. There is a deep strain within the contemporary environmental movement, however, that is skeptical of twentieth-century civilization, judging its consequences harshly. Economic progress in this view has not yielded spiritual advance. Rather, the record of economic progress in this century is better understood as the story of the Protestant tradition—a record of human retrogression and moral decline.

In the United States, such messages are at the heart of "radical environmentalism," which offers a theology similar to the Green parties in Europe. One of the best-known radical environmental groups has been Earth First, which has encouraged "tree spiking," destruction of logging equipment and other acts of "ecotage" designed to protect nature from human "rape" and "assault." The founder of Earth First, Dave Foreman, delivers a sermon of fire and brimstone— a secular message that also owes a large debt to another member of the Protestant tradition: Karl Marx. If Marx once believed that the class struggle for surplus production had yielded the alienation of mankind from its true nature, Foreman now contends that "human destruction of the wild" is the central event of history, the "keystone to understanding our alienation from Nature, which is the central problem of Civilization." Foreman follows Marx in locating the fall of man in history; it is at the arrival of agriculture and an organized society. If advancing technological capacity for Marx first made surplus production possible and thereby yielded class struggle, Foreman now finds that it was the "nascency of agriculture" about 10,000 years ago that first left human beings "apart from the natural world" and yielded the evils of "city, bureaucracy, patriarchy, war and empire."[1]

Marx saw history as revealing a deepening corruption and degradation, and Foreman now finds history to be the story of "an ever widening rift" that opens "between the wilderness that created us and the civilization created by us."[2] In the gospel of Foreman, it was the wilderness that created man, but man has rebelled against his primitive naturalness and fallen into sin. Not only does the message revisit Marx, but one can hardly fail to note the environmental retelling in secular form of the Genesis story—the creation in the Garden of Eden and the original sin of Adam and Eve (the pursuit of knowledge) causing mankind to be cast out into sin and iniquity.

The current age is, in short, a Roman era that is being challenged by a new band of protesters against its theological foundations. The current circumstances are at least in this respect reminiscent of ancient Rome, which in its later years faced the strong protests of Augustine. The medieval Catholic church eventually encountered the fiery attacks of yet another protester against Rome: Martin Luther. In the modern age, the Enlightenment and its followers of the scientific revelations of Newton—members of yet another Roman church—eventually encountered the fierce protests of Marx, Spencer, and Freud. If the world is today again in a Roman era, the possibility remains that the future could hold yet another full-scale revival of the Protestant tradition—an outcome already sought by U.S. radical environmentalists, European Greens, and other groups.

To be sure, any such prospect must be regarded with deep apprehension. In the history of the West—and whatever the actual intent—it is the Protestant tradition that has inspired the greatest disorder. If true belief is a matter not of reason but of the strength of inner conviction and faith, the authority of law and other existing institutions comes under challenge. If human reason is not the correct guide to human affairs, social visions of all kinds are set loose in the affairs of men. Lacking objective criteria and without the authority of Roman legal and other priesthoods, the most righteous are easily convinced of their own special merit. In the service of a divine cause revealed only to the few elect of history, violence and conceivably warfare may come to seem acceptable.

Yet, if it is in some ways impossible to live with the Protestant tradition, it is in other ways impossible to live without this tradition. The Roman priesthood has often failed by its own rational tests. It is not enough to say that Roman authority is necessary for the peace and prosperity of the world. The Roman priesthood must command authority by the power of its rational persuasion. If priestly powers fail, the authority of Rome will lack legitimacy, becoming the mere exercise of coercion by the state. Power without valid rational purpose invites the misuse and corruption that are also a central part of the history of the Roman tradition.

Thus, it is Roman abuse and decline that has usually paved the way for Protestant chaos and disorder. If a tendency to disorder and warfare is the great historic failing of the Protestant tradition, the great historic failing of the Roman tradition is the tendency to bureaucratic and legal decay. The laws of nature—the basis for a rational world—all too easily become the laws of the powerful and the rich.

Speaking at cross-purposes and operating from fundamentally different premises, the members of the Roman tradition and of the Protestant tradition have all too often found warfare to be their only meaningful form of dialogue. In a nuclear age, however, the common interest of mankind in survival requires that these traditions discover a new way of both serving their historic purposes and resolving their historic tensions. The world may have to devise an organizational arrangement that provides ample scope for Protestant pluralism, but fits this pluralism within a Roman framework capable of maintaining worldwide order and prosperity. To sustain any such arrangement, a theological foundation will be necessary, as a theological grounding has been necessary for all previous social arrangements. It can therefore be hoped that the postmodern age will find a theology that allows ample scope for pluralism in some matters of personal faith where people seemingly find universal agreement impossible, but also a structure of order and reason in areas where demonstrable truth can be established to the satisfaction of the entire world.

Environmental and Libertarian Prophets of a New Order

Possible arrangements of this kind are today already being probed in some of the writings of spokespersons for the two current groups that have been most vocal in rejecting the progressive gospel: the contemporary environmental movement, and the contemporary libertarian movement. Along with a renewed vigor also found within some branches of institutional Christian and Judaic religion, the environmental and libertarian movements both represent a search for answers to the decisive question of our time: If the progressive gospel has been fatally undermined by the historical record of the twentieth century, and if it will be unable to survive in the twentieth-first century as the civic religion of the United States and other national states, what theology might take its place?

The existing nation-state is seen by many contemporary environmentalists as poorly constituted to solve the most pressing problems of the age. Barbara Ward and Rene Dubos explain in *Only One Earth* that

All these concerns with global air pollution lie beyond the effective protection of individual governments. It is no use one nation checking its energy use to keep the ice caps in place if no other government joins in. It is no use the developed nations suggesting lower energy use just at the moment when the developing nations see increased use as their only exit from the trap of poverty. The global interdependence of man's airs and climates is such that local decisions are simply inadequate. Even the sum of all local separate decisions, wisely made, may not be a sufficient safeguard and it would take a bold optimist to assume such general wisdom. Man's global interdependence begins to require, in these fields, a new capacity for global decision-making and global care. It requires coordinating powers for monitoring and research. It means new conventions to draw up ground rules to control emissions from aircraft and to assess supersonic experiments. It requires a new commitment to global responsibilities. Equally, it needs effective action among the nations to make responsibility a fact.[3]

An effective response to worldwide environmental problems is seen as demanding a new sense of worldwide community. Ward and Dubos thus suggest that "it is not wholly irrational to hope that the full realization of planetary interdependence—in biosphere and technosphere alike—may begin to affect man in the depths of his capacity for psychic commitment." If this happens, then new worldwide arrangements for political authority become a real possibility: "In such a world, the practices and institutions with which we are familiar inside our domestic societies would become, suitably modified, the basis of [a new] planetary order." This would not require a wholesale departure from our familiar ways, however, because there are already trends at work whereby "in many of our present international institutions the sketch of [a new worldwide] system already exists."[4]

Yet, at least up to now, contemporary environmentalism has in practice served more as a force for decentralization. Environmental groups seek to establish local autonomy from national political and economic pressures by blocking government and private projects of all kinds. Ward and Dubos see a healthy trend in this strong localism, as well; there is a great "importance of developing the distinctive genius of each place, each social group, and each person—in other words of cultivating individuality." Local allegiances also protect mankind from a centralization that in the past has sometimes yielded efforts to "dragoon other groups into subjection. That kind of 'unity' is rejected in our day with unequalled vehemence by all nations, great and small." Ward and Dubos further state that "as a decentralized way of satisfying a million different tastes and needs, the market system could hardly be matched." In short, "the world is [today] committed to pluralism and decentralized decision-making." At the same time, people must learn to balance their strong sense of local identity with a strong world community, so that "the emotional attachment to our prized diversity [also] need not interfere with our attempts to develop the global state of mind which will generate a rational loyalty to the planet as a whole."[5]

The ultimate and most menacing form of pollution of the earth's atmosphere is, to be sure, nuclear radiation. In *The Fate of the Earth*, Jonathan Schell argues that fear of nuclear war could be the decisive bond that will yield a new sense of worldwide community: "For nothing underscores our common humanity as strongly as the peril of extinction." Creating a new worldwide community demands fundamental institutional rearrangements; hence, a desperate search must be undertaken to identify "the practical steps by which mankind, acting for the first time in history as a single entity, can reorganize its political life." Schell in fact is convinced that the abolition of the sovereignty of nations must be a starting point for a new worldwide system. Historically, the nation-state came into existence as an instrument of war. Thus, sounding much like Kenneth Boulding, Schell asserts that "the connection between sovereignty and war is almost a definitional one—a sovereign state being a state that enjoys the right and the power to go to war in defense or pursuit of its interests." If nation-states were created for war, the abolition of war suggests to Schell the abolition of the nation-state. At present, "the peril of extinction is the price that the world pays not for 'safety' or 'survival' but for its insistence on continuing to divide itself up into sovereign nations."[6]

Contemporary libertarian thought offers writings that are equally skeptical of the merits of the large nation-state. The boundaries of the nation-state pose the greatest obstacle to the establishment of a world marketplace that would enshrine a worldwide principle: that relationships among people must remain noncoercive. Norman Macrae is an economic journalist of libertarian inclination who has served for many years as a writer and editor for the *Economist* magazine. Macrae agrees it is the threat of nuclear war that is most likely to force a "retreat from governments" and the undermining of the independent nation-state.[7] Current powers of nuclear destruction are simply far too dangerous for the fragile and unpredictable political systems by which the nations of today are governed.

As Macrae observes, it is frightening to realize that "in earlier decades of the twentieth century enormous decisions had been taken by democratically elected men now known to have been incapacitated by illness at the time. Woodrow Wilson in 1920; Roosevelt at Yalta;

Churchill in the middle of his last 1951–55 premiership; Eden, who had a terrible tummy-ache when he invaded Suez in 1956." Decisions affecting human survival have today become too momentous to leave to the light-headed and often ignorant and unreliable heads of state who lead many nations around the world: "The nuclear bomb on Hiroshima in 1945 should have seared the message into reasoning men that this toleration of megalomania had to stop." As a first step, the world superpowers are seen by Macrae as coming together at some future point to sponsor "some sort of international token force to depose megalomaniac tyrants in undemocratic countries" who seriously threaten world peace.[8]

Although Macrae sees the nation-state as too small for worldwide purposes, it is often too large for other purposes. The members of the large nation-state are too heterogeneous to offer the strong sense of community for which the need is widely felt today. Macrae suggests instead a world of "genuine pluralism." It would have a few worldwide institutions that perform key global tasks, but otherwise would encourage "the free dispersal into small communities" where everyone could "set up their own forms of very local government—communes, monasteries, profit-making local governments run by private-enterprise performance contractors, beach clubs on desert isles."[9]

Macrae thus offers a sort of modern feudalism. Each person finds his or her own fiefdom and is there free to join with others in creating a community of like-minded people. However, unlike the feudalism of the medieval era, trade would blossom in the postmodern age. Indeed, the spread of technology and the growth of economic interrelationships would bind the world together more closely than it ever has been before. Ever-improving telecommunications technology would play an especially important role, transforming not only the ease of personal communication but also job markets, which could become highly decentralized: "By the early years of the 21st century brain workers— which in rich countries already meant most workers—no longer needed to live near their work. They could live on the beach of Tahiti if they wanted to, and telecommute daily to computers and other colleagues in the New York or London or Hamburg or Timbuctoo-tax-haven office through which they worked."[10] Macrae sees market relationship largely displacing the political allocation of resources in the future. Because cheap transportation and new technology would result in markets of worldwide scope, consumers would benefit from intense global competition and would have very broad options in their purchases of goods and services at low prices.

This consumer choice would be extended into the political realm as well: "Human beings began to see that they would not be free until they were allowed, in the smallest possible groups, to answer the question: how much government do you want, having been told that this is what you will have to pay if you are going to choose government of such and such a quantity and quality (with the quality preferably defined in terms of performance contracts—that is, tax payments are reduced if, by objective tests, performance in the so-called public services does not reach a certain standard)." Much of existing government thus would be regarded as merely the provision of a market service; the contract would be cancelable at the option of the recipients of these services. The residents of Los Angeles, for instance—rather than looking to municipal administration—could instead choose to have their public services "administered by a Japanese multinational corporation, which offered a particularly daring performance contract" for their delivery.[11]

The role of "government" could be reduced to the selection of the best contractors. Carried to the ultimate conclusion, democratic elections would no longer have the purpose of choosing public officials; rather, the vote would serve to select the best private contractor to manage local administrative chores for the next few years. The existing role of political parties might be taken over in the global society of the future by administrative service corporations of a multinational character.

Macrae is optimistic that this future world substitution of economic for existing political relationships will yield unprecedented material abundance. Science and technological advance are moving faster than the growth of world population and demand—which will result in declining real prices for most goods. Macrae's faith in the benefits of new technology is illustrated in his vision of a single computer "Centrobank" that consolidates all of the world's economy into one information system and then makes the necessary calculations to control world money flows and credit policies.[12] It would be an impersonal mechanism, based on objective tools independent of the foibles of democratic politics. The result would be a rational set of computer-driven policies serving to support maximum growth of the world economy.

While Macrae is offering a vision of a still distant future, one can find elements of his vision already realized in the European Economic Community (EEC) over the past 40 years. After centuries of division, Europe is now making through the EEC the most serious effort at unification since the breakup caused by the Protestant Reformation. The guiding faith of the new European community, like the new political and economic institutions, is still evolving. It is possible to speculate, however, that the future of Europe may hold a diversity of cultures, lifestyles, languages, and ethical outlooks, corresponding roughly to the boundaries of existing European nations. These diverse cultural and language communities may all be linked closely together through the workings of a common economic marketplace, monitored and guided by central rule-making institutions for all of Europe.

It could be Europe, and not the United States, that offers the model for the global organization of the future. In the U.S. model, authoritative decrees of the American civil religion are imposed over a vast area—larger in size than all Europe—with substantial uniformity and central control. The individual states of the United States are bound together not only by the common economic rules of a single marketplace, but by many common requirements extending into cultural details of family life, sexual practice, housing arrangements, and personal lifestyle. In recent years, even matters such as maximum driving speeds on superhighways and minimum ages for drinking alcoholic beverages have been decreed by central authorities in Washington.

To be sure, there are some signs in the United States, as well, of a move toward pluralism. The U.S. Supreme Court has ruled that a single standard of obscenity should not hold everywhere, leaving local groups considerable latitude to determine their own standards.[13] The approval in 1988 of an economic union between Canada and the United States suggests the possibility—if still distant—of a North American political and economic union that might evolve toward the European model. In 1981, a reporter for the *Washington Post*—Joel Garreau—published *The Nine Nations of North America*. The North American "nations" include "Quebec," "New England," "The Foundry," "Ecotopia" (in the Pacific Northwest), "Mexamerica," "Dixie," and the "Breadbasket." As compared with the existing states and provinces, Garreau found the "Nine Nations" to characterize the real communities of North America, which at some point in the future could provide a closer alignment of community values with political boundaries.

Garreau argued that "each [of the Nine Nations] has its capital and distinctive web of power and influence. . . . Each has a peculiar economy; each commands a certain emotional allegiance from its citizens. These nations look different, feel different, and sound different from each other, and few of their boundaries match the political lines drawn on current maps." Garreau suggested that "the more self-assured each of these Nine Nations becomes, the less willing it is to be dictated to by outsiders who show no interest in sharing—or even understanding—local values." It was his view that "as resources and opportunities are dispersed, each nation, at least theoretically, be-comes increasingly capable of solving its own problems at its own level, although habit and institutions often do not cooperate." Despite the modern assumption that increasing education leads to shared beliefs and values, Garreau found that "increased sophistication" was instead yielding a diversity that "emphasizes the real, enduring, and basic economic and social differences of each region, manifested in attitudes towards everything from nuclear power to unions to abor-tion."[14]

To these suggestive trends of the time, one might add the messages examined in the previous chapter that are contained in the writings of economists such as Charles Lindblom, Mancur Olson, Donald McClos-key, James Buchanan, and Kenneth Boulding. Whether or not they intended such a result, radical conclusions can be drawn from their arguments. Many of the fundamental values of modern society are not worked out in advance through debate and then implemented by value-neutral government administrators. Rather, these values emerge through the incremental processes of ordinary government decision making—what Lindblom labeled "partisan mutual adjustment." Be-cause any attempt to separate value formation from government ad-ministration is artificial, and if a society has a religion (as all must in one way or another), then the full range of government activities must represent an important way of realizing that society's religious beliefs. It follows that effective government is not likely to extend beyond the boundaries of commonly shared values—however wide or narrow these boundaries may turn out to be.

Olson pointed in this direction when his analysis had the unintended effect of showing that a considerable portion of the civic life of the United States is best understood as an act of religious affirmation, ritual, and ceremony. Americans exhibit the motivating power of religious conviction in certain political actions (such as voting) that conventional economic rationality is powerless to explain. For Ameri-cans, to vote in a national election is to declare once again membership in an American church whose founding bible is the Constitution. In this regard, U.S. voter participation rates provide a direct measure of the breadth and strength of the American national faith. How many

among the populace will still come forward to affirm their commitment? The steady decline in voting levels in recent decades is further
evidence of a weakening sense of American national community. If
effective government is not likely to extend beyond the boundaries of
a shared theology, then the demands for decentralization are likely to
grow in American political life.

McCloskey's assertion that modern economics offers a pluralism of
economic truths then becomes all the more important. It carries the
implication that there may have to be a pluralism of political and
economic arrangements, possibly grounded in different understandings
of economic truth. Within a nation as large as the United States, a
diversity of economic truths would imply a diversity of economic
systems. Buchanan and Boulding both point in such a direction, as
well; they find the large nation-state to be outmoded, and look to
communities smaller than existing large nations as the focal point for
individual loyalties.

Buchanan and Boulding—so different in personality, in outlook, and
in other respects—each find the nation-state today serving above all a
military purpose, a dangerous purpose that makes the dissolution of
the international system of nation-states all the more urgent. For both,
the instrument for achieving coordination on a worldwide scale should
not be world government—which would require a single worldwide
theology extending into all areas of life—but the mechanism of the
market. If worldwide willingness to participate in the global marketplace may itself admittedly require acceptance of a worldwide theology
of sorts, it is a less rigid and demanding theology—a theology of
pluralism and noncoercion—that may win a general acceptance never
previously found within all of humanity.

Assuming that economic and other prophets are correct in their
sense of a new world order emerging, what might be desirable organizing principles of such an order? What might be the main tenets of an
acceptable worldwide theology? The remainder of this chapter will
offer some speculations on these matters and a brief assessment of
possible world consequences in several important respects.

Free Secession in a Postmodern World

Although freedom of religion is said to be an accepted principle of
the current age, this position becomes problematic if religion is understood broadly—as this book has argued it should be. Indeed, under a

broad understanding that encompasses economic theology and other secular religions, much of politics consists of the expression of a theology (to the extent that politics is not mere interest-group trading). In this light, full freedom of religion can be attained only by granting each individual a right to join with other coreligionists to form a sovereign state. This state could then be administered in accordance with the common theology. To put such a principle into practice, any group of coreligionists desiring to form their own state would have to be free to withdraw from the existing nation. In short, in a postmodern world, full freedom of religion would seem to require a worldwide guarantee of the right of free secession.

For a nation shaped by an economic theology, secession becomes the means of accomplishing the historic act of withdrawing from one church to form a new church. Over the course of history, such a right has been denied more often than granted. In the Middle Ages, the Roman Catholic church branded withdrawal as heresy and showed little mercy, sometimes burning at the stake those who pressed the demand too vigorously. Although the professed intent to withdraw from the nation-state may not be branded as "heresy" but as "treason," the modern age frequently has not been much more tolerant. Despite the acceptance of diverse institutional religions shown in the United States, when a grave challenge to the founding religion of the U.S. nation-state occurred, little willingness to meet Southern demands was shown, resulting in a bloody civil war to block Southern secession. In many nations of the twentieth century, the members of irredentist movements have been executed, imprisoned, and tortured—shown little better treatment than medieval heretics received from the church of that era.

Freedom of religion has spread in the modern age in approximate proportion to the loss of authority of institutional religion. It is easy enough to recognize a freedom of religion, when the religion no longer has a critical impact on people's lives or on the activities of government. Men and women of diverse faiths can live together easily enough when these faiths have few practical consequences. The difficulty arises when those of passionate conviction seek to impose their own design on the state and society, yet disagree profoundly on what this state should be. Indeed, there is no way that two very divergent economic theologies can both be fully realized within the same state. Full religious freedom under these circumstances will therefore be attainable only if members of each group are free to join with coreligionists to form their own state.

To be sure, this understanding of freedom of religion also implies the power to impose a state theology on all those who choose to reside within a given state. If every state is necessarily grounded in one or another set of theological convictions, the authority of government will be put at the service of theology within each state. In the postmodern world the principle of separating church and state will seemingly have to be abandoned. It may be seen as a discriminatory vehicle of the modern age, whereby men wedded to particular secular theologies sought to avoid sharing their governing responsibilities with churches based on Judaic, Christian, and other institutional religions of a more traditional character. Some modern priesthoods have thus been given legitimacy to pursue the realization of a theocratic vision, while the priesthoods of an older vintage were denied a similar opportunity.

The Western outlook is that there can be only one true religion. The medieval Roman Catholic church taught that it had the one and only valid faith. Even within the great diversity of Protestantism, each Protestant sect believed itself to have discovered the one and only correct understanding of the divine intent. Similary, every great economist—Adam Smith, Marx, Keynes, and others—has believed that economic truths are universally valid, that the correct economic answer can and should be applied to all kinds of circumstances and societies. Classical liberals of the nineteenth century conceived a future world in which there would be a universal free market. The prophecies of socialist thinkers have foreseen a world of the same socialism everywhere. Economic liberals and socialists alike have believed that tendencies toward pluralism would create divisions within mankind, the threat of one nation exploiting another, the erection of barriers to free movement of people and commerce, and other disruptions to the long-run goal of a world communal solidarity and harmony. Contemporary advocates of democratic capitalism and of democratic socialism maintain much the same attitude.

A world of economic pluralism thus is as offensive to the thinking of modern secular faiths as to the traditional views of institutional religion. If there is one God, then there is one truth of human existence. To admit of multiple correct interpretations may be to suggest a great heresy: that there are multiple gods exercising authority in the universe. However offensive such a thought is to the Western religious heritage, and however grave the theological offense, institutional religion has been compelled in the modern age to accept the reality of an indefinite pluralism of Judaic and Christian truths. Religious pluralism in a postmodern age may require a similar tolerance with respect to diverse economic theologies and corresponding real-world economic organizations found throughout the world.

A key area in which a pluralism of economic theologies may yield diverse answers is likely to be the proper scope of contracts and of individual rights within a sovereign state. If noncoercion should govern relations among sovereign states, this rule need not apply within every state. It is possible to imagine an economic faith based on noncoercive relationships and a complete individualism with respect to values, the meaning of life, and all other issues. Life in such a society would seek to recreate the atomistic relationships of a perfectly competitive market, basing social ties in every area on contractual and thus noncoercive bonds. Most people, however, are likely to want to join with others in a social arrangement that involves at least some collectively imposed restraints on individual contracting. No society today fully respects individual rights to engage in the buying and selling of heroin, cocaine, and other drugs. No society allows a person to sell himself or herself into permanent servitude or slavery. Individual rights to engage in the buying and selling of sexual favors are curtailed in most societies. Various forms of contracting with public officials are prohibited as "bribery"—for example, a private payment for a government policy action.

Indeed, some societies might prefer to eliminate most contracting and to govern social relationships according to the prescriptive tenets of a single guiding plan. A religion might rule out contracted relationships because the presence of a contract is taken to signify the absence of a sufficient communal purpose and to undermine a spirit of group loyalty. While it is difficult or impossible to imagine a large nation-state successfully organized on this basis, such a theology may be feasible on a small scale. The vision of a society of persons living and working joyfully for the simple pleasures of helping one another— where the compulsions of formal contracts are absent—has been found throughout the history of religion. In Christianity, it has been located both in the past in the Garden of Eden and in the future when the kingdom of heaven is attained. In modern secular forms, this age-old vision becomes a state of nature found in a tribal golden age of the past, and a future earthly utopia in which material and other needs will be fully satisfied. While the prospects for this communal existence seems to many observers unlikely, full religious freedom in a postmodern age would mean that there should at least be the opportunity to try.

Although a society might regard contracts as socially divisive and theologically offensive, it might show different attitudes with respect to insiders and outsiders. Both Judaism and Christianity, for example, have in the past sometimes prohibited usury in dealing with fellow religionists, but approved the charging of interest outside the faith. In the modern age as well, the signing of contracts and market relationships could be encouraged outside a given society, but disallowed within the citizenry of a sovereign state.

Since the late nineteenth century, the most important community for many people—aside from family—has been based not on local geography, but on work and professional loyalties. That is where the closest personal ties have been maintained and where many people find a personal identity and status. One of the most powerful cultural influences in the modern age—often a decisive shaper of social values—has been the private corporation and its standards of justice, ethics, and behavior. Many multinational corporations have shifted their employees back and forth all over the world, keeping them tied to the corporation for a sense of permanent association. Many professionals similarly have moved from university to university, or job to job, all the while feeling their strongest sense of membership within the priesthood of the professional community.

If the importance of economic tasks and of professional identities were to decline, and if theological diversity were to increase, local geography might come to play a greater role in personal identity. In the years to come, the corporate culture may lose some of its significance to the regional or local community. The idea of moving from one geographic area to another, as job and professional considerations dictate, might lose its ready acceptability; some U.S. corporations have in fact already encountered a new reluctance in recent years. If people looked more to regional and local geography to find common values and goals—a regional and local theology—this would offer yet another reason for granting the right of free secession. In this way local and regional communities would acquire the rights and powers that private corporate communities have long possessed. The corporation is in most cases free to enter or depart from (to "secede" from) a particular state and to enforce well-defined and sometimes narrow standards of behavior on those who want to live within the corporate community.

The existence of a right of free secession would say little about the potential frequency with which such a right might be exercised. Recent events in the Soviet Union suggest that a number of its republics may want to secede right away. Similarly, Tibet probably would want to secede from China, the Kurds from Iran, and Biafra from Nigeria. It is doubtful that any region of the United States would be ready to secede today. In recent years Alaska would probably have been the leading candidate, especially when oil prices were rising rapidly and resentments were running high with respect to the pervasive federal control of Alaska lands. In Canada, Quebec came close to secession, then backed away, and has recently shown renewed interest.

World government in a postmodern age could assume greater responsibility but might consist of a series of special purpose organizations. There might, for example, be a world organization specializing in ecology, another organization for scientific research, and a third for space travel. A set of institutions would no doubt be required to monitor, set ground rules for, and otherwise to oversee worldwide trade. The International Monetary Fund, the World Bank, the General Agreement on Tariffs and Trade (GATT), and other current international economic organizations might prove to be parent bodies for future generations of worldwide economic and trading organizations.

Keeping the peace and avoiding nuclear war would, of course, be essential to the success of any future world order. If the world decentralized to a larger number of smaller sovereign states, there might be some sort of international arms control agency, responsible for monitoring the behavior of individual states and taking actions to prevent any one state from seriously endangering the peace of the world. Unless there were wholesale violations of international peace-keeping norms, the functions of a worldwide organization would presumably have to be undertaken peacefully. It could rely on a combination of the forces of world opinion and direct economic sanctions. Worldwide enforcement might be based on a "pariah" strategy—such as has been employed in recent years in the international attempts to induce South Africa to change its racial policies. In place of warfare and other destructive conflicts of the past, the nuclear age would seem to make imperative a less coercive means of settling even bitter disagreements.

Economic Ethics in a World of Free Secession

In a world of free secession, where a significant number of regions might eventually secede from existing large nations to form new states, there would be a number of important consequences for acceptable economic practices within and among the states of the world. Free secession would probably result in more and more of world economic interaction coming within the sphere of world trade. Sovereign states of smaller size would necessarily look to a worldwide economy to supply demands for most goods and services. The tariffs, quotas, and other devices that currently impede world trade are to some extent products of the internal politics of the large nation-state. Domestic manufacturers and the associated labor unions are often geographically concentrated, giving them political clout to win protective measures even when the total costs imposed on national consumers may greatly exceed the local benefits realized. This form of internal politics would be undermined, however, in a world of many smaller sovereign states. Consumers would much more often be found residing in a different sovereign state from manufacturers. Consumers in Florida would be immune, for example, from pressures for automobile quotas now imposed at the request of car manufacturers and unions in Michigan and other Midwestern states.

However, some features of a world of free secession might work against free trade. Many current advocates of free trade in effect seek to achieve a single economic theology over the whole world. To demand that a sovereign state must abandon state subsidies and otherwise open up its own internal markets is effectively to dictate some elements of the theology for that state. High tariff barriers, for example, may be based on a conviction that existing businesses uphold the culture and the living arrangements required by the theology of a particular state. Outside insistence that existing businesses must instead be subject to worldwide market competition—and perhaps be pushed aside by more efficient international competitors—will in effect also be seeking to dictate elements of the religious beliefs of that state. This is a modern reflection of the crusading spirit of Western religion, which has always believed in one message for all the world. Christian missionaries thus had no doubt that all the world must eventually accept the one and only true faith: the Christian faith. In a postmodern age, however, each nation might be left to decide its trade policies according to the precepts of its own internal theology, economic or otherwise. The market verdict would rule in relations between separate and sovereign states, but the same would not necessarily be true within the same state.

In the international area, the equivalent of the interest-group bargaining of U.S. domestic politics is found in the *realpolitik* of relationships among nation-states. If interest-group bargaining is a wasteful way of allocating resources domestically, political allocation of resources is equally wasteful at the international level. Hence, an improvement in international economic efficiency would be achievable if market relationships were allowed to develop directly among states. If any one nation-state wanted another state to take a specific action, the first state might be allowed to make a monetary payment directly to the second state, rather than bringing international political pressures to bear. The international arena is currently among the last places where political relationships are expected to prevail in all matters. Indeed, to the degree that in a postmodern age there would be large numbers of small sovereign states in the world, market exchange directly among such states might well become a necessity for effective worldwide economic coordination.

At present, sovereign states in fact often do bargain over matters that concern their mutual self-interest. However, because overt monetary payments are prohibited (considered as "bribes") in the current international system, exchanges among states almost always take the form of barter. As in other contexts, commercial dealings based on barter among states are an ineffective way of organizing transactions and of reaching exchange agreements. It is partly the routine allowance of direct monetary payments that facilitates the commercial dealings between private business corporations (which can be larger than sovereign states). It would equalize matters if sovereign states were allowed to have the same opportunities for market trading now possessed by corporate communities.

If sovereign states did have such rights, negotiation of a worldwide treaty to reduce carbon dioxide emissions into the atmosphere might, for example, involve the direct purchase by rich nations of an extensive set of regulatory controls in poor nations. There have been proposals made recently to compensate Brazil for protecting the Amazon rainforests by forgiving portions of its foreign bank debt. This illustrates a possible broader pattern of future international relations. Rich nations might similarly purchase protective measures from poor African countries in an attempt to ensure the long-run survival of rare and endangered wildlife in these countries. Market trading among states could extend into nonenvironmental areas as well.

In a postmodern world, the multinational corporation will probably continue to have a central place. Since the multinational corporation would be subordinate to the sovereignty of many small individual states, worldwide corporations might have to adapt to more widely varying economic rules, reflecting a greater diversity of local economic theologies. It is possible that the multinational corporation would come increasingly to resemble a worldwide franchise operation that would work in each sovereign state in close conformance with the particular economic beliefs and standard operating practices of the state.

The opposite of secession would be the right to form a new union, based on whatever degree of economic and political integration was desired. Like the right to secede, a world with full freedom of religion would also have to treat the forming of a union as a matter of right. The overall world system might come therefore to consist of an ebb and flow of secession and union, as the corporate world today sees a continuing flow of mergers and divestitures. It would be a world that would facilitate frequent political realignments, and might indeed see many of them. State jurisdictions would come about as a trial-and-error process; people would use the greater freedom available to work out the political boundaries and governing arrangements that best met their needs. A worldwide competitive process—rather than any world-wide political theory or prescriptive theology—would be the means of determining for different peoples the best sizes and configurations of their governing institutions.

If the right of free secession were to be assured, any use of violence by an existing union against a state wishing to secede would be precluded. However, this ban need not preclude the existing union from offering economic incentives to keep a disgruntled constituent state from leaving. It also need not preclude imposition of economic penalties. Negotiations between unions and their states could involve a wide range of bargaining chips and forms of agreement—the only absolute constraint being that the agreement must in the end be reached without the use (or threat) of force of arms.

Historically, two great concerns with respect to a market economy have been that it yields too much inequality and that it is subject to large cyclical fluctuations. If a worldwide system of economic plural-ism were to be established and grounded in a globally accepted right of free secession, such concerns would once again be raised. It would be difficult to require large-scale redistribution from wealthier to poorer regions of the same sovereign state, because any such redistribution might cause the wealthier regions to exercise their right to secede. Currently, efforts of sovereign states to tax especially high-earning individuals are sometimes similarly frustrated, if attempts at taxation merely cause these individuals to move elsewhere.

Therefore, large-scale redistribution from one group to another probably would be feasible only where such redistribution was voluntary. For example, the redistribution might be part of a worldwide insurance plan against economic risk—a plan that enjoys the support of current rich and poor nations alike, and into which nations make regular payments. Moreover, if they accepted the ethical merits of transfers to poorer groups, wealthier members of society might not secede or emigrate in an effort to avoid redistributive burdens. Indeed, Roman Catholicism has traditionally instilled a strong concern for the poor; in the Middle Ages the church itself provided much of the care for the indigent. The welfare state today similarly accomplishes substantial internal redistribution with the approval of many of the wealthier contributing members of the community.

A world of free secession would also create powerful new forces for worldwide equality. The poorest parts of the world have one great economic asset: their low labor costs. But their ability to take advantage of this asset is much restricted by the internal politics of large nation-states. For example, in the United States, textile shipments from poor undeveloped countries to the huge market in California may be blocked by U.S. textile manufacturers in the South. Yet, if California had the sovereign right to set its own trade policies, protectionist pressures would have little or no impact on future California textile trade. If all the Californias of the world were set free to establish their own tariffs on textiles and other products, it could offer a large boost to the economic prospects of the Bangladeshes of the world.

Economic pluralism could also promote greater worldwide equality through impacts within less developed nations themselves. It is a long and slow process to change the economic practices and supporting institutional framework—to spread a new message of economic theology—in a nation-state as large as India or China, involving hundreds of millions of people. A small region within such a large nation might be able to undertake much more rapidly the cultural and institutional transformations necessary for rapid economic development.

However, the ability to undertake these transformations is at present much constrained by the internal politics of the large nation-state. If a particular region becomes unusually productive and economically successful, the rest of the nation may tax away many of the benefits for redistribution to poorer areas. For example, there may be potential South Koreas, Taiwans, Hong Kongs, or Singapores within the current nation of India. Yet, the emergence of any such "growth spot" within India would be difficult as an isolated event. If this region had the right to secede from India, its opportunity to exploit its development potential would be greater. The Soviet Union is another large nation where the right of free secession could well significantly boost the economic prospects of some republics within its existing boundaries. Indeed, as some Soviet analysts are today suggesting, a drastic decentralization of political authority may be the only effective long-run solution to the economic woes of this nation.

Worldwide equality might in fact be enhanced by a spurt of new growth in individual regions that will have seceded from larger nation-states. Under current arrangements, the perception is the opposite, because equality is measured by reference to the boundaries of the existing nation-states. Thus, rapid new growth in a successful region in India today might well be perceived as creating greater world inequality, because it would heighten economic disparities within India itself. From a worldwide perspective, however, one poor region of the world would be better off; no other region would be poorer off; and overall world equality therefore would have to be regarded as improved.

A world of free secession would also raise concerns with respect to the future stability of the worldwide economy. If large nation-states were to break up into smaller states, it would undermine the macroeconomic management of the large nation-state. Yet, the degree to which economic pluralism or economic union would actually offer more or less stability is difficult to say. A large economic union would offer broader coordination, more resources to develop specialized data and knowledge, and perhaps greater skills in stabilization; but a failure in one part of the union might also drag down the rest.

Indeed, a decentralized world of many small states would offer the protection of the law of large numbers. Ecologies that contain many species all interacting with one another may be more stable than ecologies containing only one or a few dominant species. According to some prominent interpretations, the severe Depression of the 1930s was caused by policy mistakes in the United States and a few other countries. Then, the appropriate remedial steps were blocked by the dominant policy outlook in these nations. Yet, a smaller nation such as Sweden was able to embark in the 1930s on Keynesian types of policies well in advance of other nations. If Sweden had been part of some larger and coordinated system of European stabilization, its innovative efforts might have been blocked.

In Defense of Free Secession

The right of free secession might thus supersede economic principles of free markets, free trade, and other past freedoms in providing a founding principle for a postmodern economic order. Market ties would govern relationships among sovereign states. Internal to a given state, free markets would be seen as one among many legitimate economic arrangements in a world pluralism of Judeo-Christian, economic and other theologies. Free secession would open the way to a pluralism of state economies to match the scientific, philosophical, administrative, and other pluralisms of our time—as found in Chapter 7 in the writings of Lindblom, Rorty, Nozick, and other contemporary social thinkers.

The long-run trend in the size of economic unions, the size of constituent states, and other such matters could then emerge from a wide range of experimentation around the world. If on a much larger stage, this would resemble Lindblom's "partisan mutual adjustment" in public administration, or McCloskey's "conversations" in economics. Each group of people would be free to enter into or to secede from an economic union, according to their perception of the merits of union. The states of the world might differ sharply in their internal arrangements—a matter to be determined by their own state theologies, whether based on modern economic theologies or other theological convictions.

A world order of free secession would serve five fundamental purposes. First, the morality of one person's imposing a religion on another person may be as doubtful in the case of a modern economic theology as when it involves institutional Judaism or Christianity. For many modern people, economic pursuits have held the same significance as the following of a path to salvation in the hereafter held for people in earlier eras. Freedom of religion in matters of economic theology can be achieved only by guaranteeing dissenting coreligionists the right to secede from the state to form a new state grounded in their own economic beliefs. It also requires, of course, a guaranteed right of minorities to emigrate from a state where the majority theology is unacceptable to them.

Religious conflict in the past has all too often resulted in warfare. In a nuclear age, there is a special urgency to establishing a worldwide freedom of religion, based to the greatest degree possible on an ethic of religious noninterference and tolerance. Including all kinds of religion within this principle, the right to form a separate society according to one's economic beliefs would have to be assured. A main purpose in a world of free secession would be to reduce the likelihood of religious tensions escalating to the point where nuclear warfare might result. In the United States, for example, it would probably have been necessary in the nineteenth century to allow the South to secede, if the South had been armed at that time with nuclear weapons.

Second, the political process in a large nation that includes a great diversity of people and preferences has many weaknesses. In a homogeneous society, government may well function effectively. But where there is too great a range of values, government easily deteriorates into beggar-thy-neighbor conflicts among interest groups. It is difficult to devise a way to reconcile very divergent and strongly held beliefs within the same governing process. Political disagreements among groups in a diverse nation erode the moral capital and sense of community needed to make government work well. Some observers currently propose to hold the large nation together by offering ever greater concessions to interest groups—in effect, purchasing their allegiance. A world of free secession would provide the alternative of dividing into smaller and more homogeneous sovereign entities where there is much greater internal agreement on social goals.

Third, as modern life has seemed impersonal—and the nation-state too large and distant to create a deep sense of community—many commentators have begun to look to smaller geographic areas for this community. If most social thinkers have not envisioned creating new sovereign states at regional and local levels, a few have been willing to go this far.[15] Fourth, a related benefit in a world of free secession might be a strengthening of social values and communal bonds at the regional and local level—if not necessarily the same values and bonds for everyone in all places.

Fifth and finally, although this may seem in some respects paradoxical, a world of free secession could also be a world with a stronger sense of global identification. The large nation-state in many respects promotes a separation into "us" and "them." Why, for example, are American welfare programs directed to U.S. citizens alone and not directed to aid poor mothers with dependent children in impoverished sections of Africa? If a small portion of U.S. poverty funding were devoted to Africa, it would do much more to relieve the totality of worldwide deprivation. Similarly, if the principles of the free market were followed to the extent of accepting a free right of immigration into the United States from African states, the total well-being of the world would undoubtedly rise sharply. However, the principles of social justice and the principles of free economic interaction are today interpreted to stop at national borders. Implicitly, U.S. nationalism sharply devalues other lives as compared with the life of any American. If nations came to mean less in the world, there might be a stronger immediate community surrounding each individual, but also greater attention and charity in recognition of a worldwide common humanity.

A world order grounded in a right of free secession would offer a synthesis of characteristic outlooks of the Roman tradition and the Protestant tradition. Worldwide economic, scientific, and environmental integration would be supported by worldwide organizations to serve these purposes, grounded in characteristic outlooks of reason, progress, and the search for the good life of the Roman tradition. Economic, scientific, and environmental matters raise issues and involve concerns on which worldwide agreement seems within reach. The right of free secession and the resulting theological diversity within individual states would provide a vehicle allowing for local divisions within mankind: local asceticism, zeal for sacrifice, pluralism, and other characteristic outlooks that have been found throughout the history of the Protestant tradition. In many matters of local culture, there is little assurance of future worldwide convergence; indeed, many commentators see signs of possible future divergence, even among people exposed fully to scientific, rational, and "enlightened" thought.

However one regards the prospect, current trends suggest a significant possibility that the world of free secession will become a postmodern reality in the twenty-first century. To be sure, this is far from suggesting that all theologies or all political and economic arrangements within states are equally meritorious or defensible. The history of the political and economic arrangements adopted in the twentieth century in the name of Marxism, for example, has amply demonstrated the contrary. It is to suggest, however, that the world may not converge to any one economic or other theology or to any one corresponding set of political and economic arrangements. At a minimum, it would be very hazardous to try to shape a future world order on the basis of an assumed single worldwide theology that encompassed matters of moral and other beliefs.

Conclusion

On February 21, 1990, the recently installed president of Czechoslovakia—Vaclav Havel—addressed the U.S. Congress. It was a poignant moment, as Havel paid his respects to a nation that he saw as having contributed in two world wars and in other actions "to the salvation of us Europeans, of the world, and thus of yourselves." U.S. assistance for many years had been critical to the efforts that only in recent months had succeeded in freeing Eastern Europe from a system that imposed "a legacy of countless dead, an infinite spectrum of human suffering, profound economic decline and, above all, enormous human humiliation." There was no turning back now because the world had entered a period of "revolutionary changes" that was part of an "historically irreversible process." Havel perceived that "the human face of the world is changing so rapidly that none of the familiar political speedometers are adequate."[16]

The changes that were occurring and the future that lay ahead were being influenced by many economic and technological developments. But Havel believed that "the hope of the world lies in human consciousness." People can help to shape their own fate because "consciousness precedes being, and not the other way around, as the Marxists claim." The world that Havel would now be working to achieve would be a world where change occurs through "nonviolent evolution." There would be a "multinational body politic," part of "a new pan-European structure" in which "the borders of the European states . . . should gradually become less important." Politics in the new Europe would be characterized by a "genuine political pluralism" that would guarantee "the rights of the nations to their own integrity." It would be characterized by "a working—that is, a market—economy."

Yet, the market should not reign supreme because "the salvation of this human world lies nowhere else than in the human heart." It is always necessary "to put morality ahead of politics, science, and economics." The affairs of the world must remain subordinate to an "order of being where all our actions are indelibly recorded and where and only where they will be properly judged." Mankind is still significantly in the sway of "interests of all kinds—personal, selfish, state, nation, group, and . . . company." The current indulging of these parochial and divisive interests would have to give way to a deeper recognition of our common interests as members of the global "family of man."

Havel's was a vision of markets, local political pluralism, and democratic freedoms—all this to be worked out noncoercively, while still recognizing a deep loyalty to fellow human beings in the global community. It was a vision of a twenty-first century in which free secession seemingly would have to be a core right. Indeed, Havel's 1990 appearance in Washington, D.C., reflected a secession of a sort that had already occurred: the secession of Czechoslovakia from the postwar Soviet empire. Havel's brief speech perhaps better illuminated the likely character of a postmodern world than the contents of all the vast outpourings of the legal, social science, and other priesthoods of the day. As Havel observed, "political scientists who spend their whole life studying the realm of the probable . . . have less experience with the realm of the improbable than us, the playwrights." It might therefore be wise to look to such a playwright to learn what the world of the future will be.

Notes

Preface

1. See Robert H. Nelson, *Zoning and Property Rights: An Analysis of the American System of Land Use Regulation* (Cambridge, Mass.: MIT Press, 1977); Christopher K. Leman and Robert H. Nelson, "Ten Commandments for Policy Economists,"*Journal of Policy Analysis and Management* (Fall 1981); Robert H. Nelson, *The Making of Federal Coal Policy* (Durham, N.C.: Duke University Press, 1983); Robert H. Nelson, "The Economics Profession and the Making of Public Policy," *Journal of Economic Literature* (March 1987); Robert H. Nelson, "The Office of Policy Analysis in the Department of the Interior," *Journal of Policy Analysis and Management* (Summer 1989); and Robert H. Nelson, "Introduction and Summary," in Joseph A. Pechman, ed., *The Role of the Economist in Government: An International Perspective* (New York: New York University Press, 1989).

2. Carl Kaysen has written, for example, that in many areas "the role of the economist in policy formation . . . is almost diametrically opposite to that envisaged in the formal theory of policy-making." In fact, this role "is essentially ideological." See Carl Kaysen, "Model-makers and Decision-makers: Economists and the Policy Process," *The Public Interest* (Summer 1968), pp. 82–83.

3. Charles Schultze has stated that "political values permeate every aspect of the decision-making process in the majority of federal domestic programs. There is no simple division of labor in which the 'politicians' achieve consensus on the agreed-on set of objectives while the 'analysts' design and evaluate—from efficiency and effectiveness criteria—alternative means of achieving those objectives." See Charles L. Schultze, *The Politics and Eco-*

333

nomics of Public Spending (Washington, D.C.: Brookings Institution, 1968), pp. 2–3.

4. Alec Cairncross remarks that it is the "way of thinking" of economists that represents their key contribution to policy making. See Alec Cairncross, "Economics in Theory and Practice," *American Economic Review* (May 1985), p. 4. See also Steven E. Rhoads, *The Economist's View of the World: Government, Markets, and Public Policy* (New York: Cambridge University Press, 1985) and Paul Heyne, *The Economic Way of Thinking* (New York: Macmillan, 1991; first ed. 1973).

5. Laurence H. Tribe, "Policy Science: Analysis or Ideology?" *Philosophy and Public Affairs* (Fall 1972).

6. Charles Schultze writes that an economist in government should be a "partisan advocate for efficiency." See Charles L. Schultze, "The Role and Responsibilities of the Economist in Government," *American Economic Review* (May 1982), p. 62.

7. See Arnold J. Meltsner, *Policy Analysts in the Bureaucracy* (Berkeley: University of California Press, 1976); Aaron Wildavsky, *Speaking Truth to Power: The Art and Craft of Policy Analysis* (Boston: Little, Brown, 1979); and Robert H. Nelson, "Economists as Policy Analysts: Historical Overview," in David L. Weimer, ed., *Policy Analysis and Economics: Developments, Tensions, Prospects* (Kluwer-Nijhoff, forthcoming).

8. Such opposition to the economic way of thinking is graphically portrayed in John McPhee, *Encounters with the Archdruid: Narratives about a Conservationist and Three of His Natural Enemies* (New York: Farrar, Straus, and Giroux: 1971).

9. Michael Pertschuk writes of his experiences in leading the "consumer movement" that "we recoiled from economic models that reduced pain and suffering to numbers, milking 'market failures' of their humanity. . . . Out of mingled distrust and frustration, consumer advocates denounced the economists and their misbegotten offspring, cost–benefit analysis." See Michael Pertschuk, *Revolt against Regulation: The Rise and Pause of the Consumer Movement* (Berkeley: University of California Press, 1982), p. 139.

10. See Donald N. McCloskey, "The Rhetoric of Economics," *Journal of Economic Literature* (June 1983); and Arjo Klamer, *Conversations with Economists: New Classical Economists and Their Opponents Speak Out on the Current Controversy in Macroeconomics* (Totowa, N.J.: Rowman and Allanheld, 1984).

11. The necessity of introducing ethical considerations into economics is argued in Amartya Sen, *On Ethics and Economics* (New York: Basil Blackwell, 1987). See also Amitai Etzioni, *The Moral Dimension: Toward a New Economics* (New York: Free Press, 1988); and Allen Buchanan, *Ethics, Efficiency, and the Market* (Totowa, N.J.: Rowman and Littlefield, 1988).

12. Among many examples that could be cited, one writer recently commented that the "hard core of economic principles is a little like the Ten

Commandments"; that these principles tend to be treated "as axioms or almost as self-evident truths"; and that in a number of respects "economics . . . is closer to religion than to science." See Craufurd D. Goodwin, "Doing Good and Spreading the Gospel (Economic)," in David Colander and A. W. Coats, eds., *The Spread of Economic Ideas* (New York: Cambridge University Press, 1989), p. 172.

13. Chester E. Finn, Jr., "Comment: An Executive Branch Perspective," *Journal of Policy Analysis and Management* (Fall 1989), p. 634.

14. One exception is a current economist and former theology student, Paul Heyne, who writes that "I believe that any economics which purports to be relevant to policy-making contains a hidden (sometimes not even well hidden) theology." Michael Novak comes close to this view when he argues the need for a new "theology of economics," stating that "a huge systematic task awaits the theologians of the coming generation as they apply sustained theological reflection to economic realities." See Paul Heyne, "Clerical Laissez-Faire: A Study in Theological Economics" and "Reply," in Walter Block and Irving Hexham, eds., *Religion, Economics, and Social Thought: Proceedings of an International Symposium* (Vancouver, B.C., Canada: Fraser Institute, 1986), p. 161; and Michael Novak, *The Spirit of Democratic Capitalism* (New York: Simon and Schuster, 1982), p. 239. See also Walter Block, Geoffrey Brennan, and Kenneth Elzinga, eds., *The Morality of the Market, Religious and Economic Perspectives: Proceedings of an International Symposium* (Vancouver, B.C., Canada: Fraser Institute, 1985).

15. See Frank E. Manuel and Fritzie P. Manuel, *Utopian Thought in the Western World* (Cambridge, Mass.: Harvard University Press, 1979); see also Robert Nisbet, *History of the Idea of Progress* (New York: Basic Books, 1980).

16. Robert H. Nelson, "Unoriginal Sin: The Judeo-Christian Roots of Ecotheology," *Policy Review* (Summer 1990).

17. See Richard Neuhaus, *In Defense of People: Ecology and the Seduction of Radicalism* (New York: Macmillan, 1971).

18. "The Power of Wilderness," editorial, *Los Angeles Times*, April 18, 1989. See also William C. Dennis, "Wilderness Cathedrals and the Public Good," *The Freeman* (May 1987).

19. Bill McKibben, *The End of Nature* (New York: Random House, 1989), p. 71.

20. Curt Suplee, "Apocalypse Now: The Coming Doom Boom," *Washington Post*, December 17, 1989, p. B2.

21. Willis B. Glover, *Biblical Origins of Modern Secular Culture: An Essay in the Interpretation of Western History* (Macon, Ga.: Mercer University Press, 1984), p. 150.

22. Ernst Cassirer, *The Philosophy of the Enlightenment* (Princeton, N.J.: Princeton University Press, 1979; first ed. 1932); and John Herman Randall, Jr., *The Making of the Modern Mind: A Survey of the Intellectual Background*

of the Present Age (New York: Columbia University Press, 1976; first ed. 1926).

23. Carl L. Becker, *The Heavenly City of the Eighteenth-Century Philosophers* (New Haven, Conn.: Yale University Press, 1932).

24. See Paul Johnson, *Modern Times: The World from the Twenties to the Eighties* (New York: Harper and Row, 1983).

25. There have been a number of efforts by theologians in recent years to link economics and theology. See Robert Benne, *The Ethic of Democratic Capitalism: A Moral Reassessment* (Philadelphia: Fortress Press, 1981); J. Philip Wogaman, *The Great Economic Debate: An Ethical Analysis* (Philadelphia: Westminster Press, 1977); M. Douglas Meeks, *God the Economist: The Doctrine of God and Political Economy* (Minneapolis, Minn.: Fortress Press, 1989); Max L. Stackhouse, *Public Theology and Political Economy: Christian Stewardship in Modern Society* (Grand Rapids, Mich.: W. B. Eerdmans, 1987); and Prentiss L. Pemberton and Daniel Rush Finn, *Toward a Christian Economic Ethic: Stewardship and Social Power* (Minneapolis, Minn.: Winston Press, 1985).

26. Existing studies by economists of theological issues include Frank H. Knight and Thornton W. Merriam, *The Economic Order and Religion* (Westport, Conn.: Greenwood Press, 1979; first ed. 1945); Kenneth E. Boulding, *Beyond Economics: Essays on Society, Religion, and Ethics* (Ann Arbor: University of Michigan Press, 1970); and Meir Tamari, *With All Your Possessions: Jewish Ethics and Economic Life* (New York: Free Press, 1987). A recent book seeks to ground a libertarian political and economic philosophy in a theological context; see Doug Bandow, *Beyond Good Intentions: A Biblical View of Politics* (Westchester, Ill.: Crossway Books, 1988).

27. The growing interest in the connections between economics and theology is illustrated by the decision of the Roman Catholic bishops to make pronouncements on this issue. See National Conference of Catholic Bishops, "Economic Justice for All: Catholic Social Teaching and the U.S. Economy— Third Draft" pastoral letter, Washington, D.C., June 4, 1986. See also Thomas M. Gannon, ed., *The Catholic Challenge to the American Economy: Reflections on the U.S. Bishops' Pastoral Letter on Catholic Social Teaching and the U.S. Economy (New York: Macmillan, 1987).*

Introduction

1. Ronald H. Coase, "The Problem of Social Cost," *Journal of Law and Economics* (October 1960). While Coase has not yet received a Nobel prize in economics, he is often mentioned as a leading candidate, based in significant part on this article.

2. Meir Tamari, *With All Your Possessions: Jewish Ethics and Economic Life* (New York: Free Press, 1987), p. 290. See also Jacob Neusner, *The Economics of the Mishnah* (Chicago: University of Chicago Press, 1990); and Ephraim Kleiman, " 'Just Price' in Talmudic Literature," *History of Political Economy* (Spring 1987).

3. Tamari, *With All Your Possessions,* p. 291.

4. Charles Schultze advocates that the proper role for economists in government is to be "particular champions of efficiency and effectiveness as criteria in decision making." See Charles L. Schultze, *The Politics and Economics of Public Spending* (Washington, D.C.: Brookings, 1968), p. 101.

5. John Maynard Keynes, *The General Theory of Employment, Interest, and Money* (New York: Harcourt, Brace, and World, 1965; first ed. 1936), p. 376.

6. John Maynard Keynes, "Economic Possibilities for our Grandchildren" (1930), in Keynes, *Essays in Persuasion* (New York: Norton, 1963), pp. 371–72.

7. Victor F. Weisskopf, *The Privilege of Being a Physicist* (New York: W. H. Freeman, 1989), p. 195.

8. *Report of the Study for the Ford Foundation on Policy and Program* (Detroit, Mich.: Ford Foundation, 1949), quoted in Craufurd D. Goodwin, "Doing Good and Spreading the Gospel (Economic)," in David Colander and A. W. Coats, eds., *The Spread of Economic Ideas* (New York: Cambridge University Press, 1989), p. 163.

9. Goodwin, "Doing Good and Spreading the Gospel (Economic)" p. 164.

10. Walter W. Heller, *New Dimensions of Political Economy* (New York: Norton, 1967), pp. 13, 11.

11. Richard Mauer, "Oil, a Foundation of Alaska, Works to Rebuild Its Image," *New York Times,* November 29, 1989, p. 1.

12. "Home Is Where the Heart Is: Companies Try Harder to Meet the Personal Needs of Workers," *Time* (October 3, 1988), p. 53.

13. Marcelo Dascal, "Reflections on the 'Crisis of Modernity,' " in Avner Cohen and Marcelo Dascal, eds., *The Institution of Philosophy: A Discipline in Crisis* (Lasalle, Ill.: Open Court, 1989), p. 226.

14. A leading contemporary economist, Amartya Sen, thus observes that in modern economics "human beings are assumed to behave rationally and . . . characterizing rational behavior is not . . . ultimately different from describing actual behavior." It is, however, true that, as still other observers explain, "economic agents, like ordinary people, are subject to errors and inconsistencies in decisionmaking. However, the fallibilities of economic agents are assumed [by economists] to be of a random rather than a systematic character." See Amartya Sen, *On Ethics and Economics* (New York: Basil Blackwell, 1987), p. 11; and Robin M. Hogarth and Melvin W. Reder, "Introduction: Perspectives from Economics and Psychology," in Hogarth and

Reder, eds., *Rational Choice: The Contrast between Economics and Pyschology* (Chicago: University of Chicago Press, 1987), p. 6.

15. Steven E. Rhoads, *The Economist's View of the World: Government, Markets, and Public Policy* (New York: Cambridge University Press, 1985), p. 8.

16. Sen, *On Ethics and Economics,* p. 12.

17. Herbert A. Simon, *Models of Bounded Rationality,* vol. 2, *Behavioral Economics and Business Organization* (Cambridge, Mass.: MIT Press, 1982), p. 477.

18. George J. Stigler, "Competition," in the *International Encyclopedia of Social Science,* vol. 3 (New York: Macmillan, 1968), p. 181, quoted in Amitai Etzioni, *The Moral Dimension: Toward a New Economics* (New York: Free Press, 1988), p. 218. See also George J. Stigler, *The Economist as Preacher and Other Essays* (Chicago: University of Chicago Press, 1982).

19. Gunnar Myrdal, *Beyond the Welfare State: Economic Planning and Its International Implications* (New Haven, Conn.: Yale University Press, 1960), pp. 33, 35, 36, 193.

20. Etzioni, *Moral Dimension,* p. 137.

21. At the highest levels, over a twenty-year period from the Eisenhower to Carter administrations, 8 percent of all Cabinet secretaries and under secretaries had Ph.D.s in economics. See Steven E. Rhoads, "Economists and Policy Analysis," *Public Administration Review* (March/April 1978).

22. Robert Nisbet has written of "the present crisis of the idea of progress [which] lies in the inability of a constantly growing number of people to accept" the premises on which this idea has rested. See Nisbet, *History of the Idea of Progress* (New York: Basic Books, 1980), p. 317–18.

23. For the concerns of one economist who now questions the gains from further economic growth, see Ezra J. Mishan, "Religion, Culture, and Technology," in Walter Block, Geoffrey Brennan, and Kenneth Elzinga, eds., *The Morality of the Market, Religious and Economic Perspectives: Proceedings of an International Symposium* (Vancouver, B.C., Canada: Fraser Institute, 1985).

24. Arthur Okun, while cautious by comparison with earlier generations of economists, still could observe in 1975 that industrial capitalism had the ability to eliminate "economic misery and deprivation" for all and to bring about "the eradication of poverty"—achievements of immense magnitude by comparison with all previous human history. See Arthur M. Okun, *Equality and Efficiency: The Big Tradeoff* (Washington, D.C.: Brookings, 1975), pp. 117–18.

25. Robert G. Clouse, "Introduction," to Clouse, ed., *The Meaning of the Millennium: Four Views* (Downers Grove, Ill.: InterVarsity Press, 1977), p. 8.

26. Ibid., pp. 8, 9.

27. Anthony A. Hoekema, "Amillennialism," in Clouse, *Meaning of the Millennium,* p. 181.

28. Ibid., p. 187.

29. Ernest B. Koenker, *Secular Salvations: The Rites and Symbols of Political Religions* (Philadelphia: Fortress Press, 1965).

30. Richard Neuhaus, *In Defense of People: Ecology and the Seduction of Radicalism* (New York: Macmillan, 1971), p. 38.

31. Jean Starobinski, *Jean-Jacques Rousseau: Transparency and Obstruction* (Chicago: University of Chicago Press, 1988; first ed. 1971), p. 112.

32. Arend T. van Leeuwen, *Christianity in World History: The Meeting of the Faiths of East and West* (New York: Charles Scribner's, 1964), p. 23, 333.

33. Ibid., pp. 268, 107, 16.

34. Ibid., pp. 436–37.

35. Willis B. Glover, *Biblical Origins of Modern Secular Culture: An Essay in the Interpretation of Western History* (Macon, Ga.: Mercer University Press, 1984), pp. 107, 220, 196, 200, 149.

36. Ibid., p. 228.

37. John Courtney Murray, *We Hold These Truths: Catholic Reflections on the American Proposition* (New York: Sheed and Ward, 1960), pp. 201, 317, 113, 112.

38. Ibid., pp. 191, 190.

39. Will Herberg, *Protestant–Catholic–Jew: An Essay in American Religious Sociology* (Garden City, N.Y.: Doubleday, 1956), pp. 287–88.

40. "Menti Nostrae," apostolic adhortation, September 23, 1950, quoted in ibid., p. 163.

41. Michael Novak, ed., *Liberation South, Liberation North* (Washington, D.C.: American Enterprise Institute, 1981).

42. Charles E. Lindblom, "The Science of 'Muddling Through,' " *Public Administration Review* (Spring 1959).

43. Paul Buck, ed., *Social Sciences at Harvard, 1860–1920: From Inculcation to the Open Mind* (Cambridge, Mass.: Harvard University Press, 1965); and Burton J. Bledstein, *The Culture of Professionalism: The Middle Class and the Development of Higher Education in America* (New York: Norton, 1976).

44. See Michael Novak, *The Spirit of Democratic Capitalism* (New York: Simon and Schuster, 1982); and Novak, *Free Persons and the Common Good* (Lanham, Md.: Madison Books, 1989).

45. Paul Tillich, *A History of Christian Thought: From Its Judaic and Hellenistic Origins to Existentialism* (New York: Simon and Schuster, 1967), p. 476.

46. Ibid., pp. 488, 491.

47. Murray, *We Hold These Truths*, pp. 184, 187, 185.

48. Ibid., pp. 189, 191, 192, 193.

49. Morris Kline, *Mathematics in Western Culture* (New York: Oxford University Press, 1964), p. 97.

50. See Robert Green McCloskey, *American Conservatism in the Age of Enterprise* (Cambridge, Mass.: Harvard University Press, 1951), pp. 27–28;

and Richard Hofstadter, *Social Darwinism in American Thought* (Boston: Beacon Press, 1955; first ed. 1944), p. 51.

51. See Isaiah Berlin, *Karl Marx: His Life and Environment* (New York: Time Books, 1963; first ed. 1939), p. 113.

52. John Herman Randall, *Hellenistic Ways of Deliverance and the Making of the Christian Synthesis* (New York: Columbia University Press, 1970), p. 220.

53. Ibid., p. 231.

54. Myrdal, *Beyond the Welfare State;* and C. A. R. Crosland, *The Future of Socialism* (New York: Schocken Books, 1963).

55. Several other efforts have been made recently to characterize Western thought as a long-standing clash of enduring "traditions" or "visions." See Thomas Sowell, *A Conflict of Visions: Ideological Origins of Political Struggles* (New York: William Morrow, 1987); and Alasdair MacIntyre, *Whose Justice? Which Rationality?* (Notre Dame, Ind.: University of Notre Dame Press, 1988), pp. 8–9. See also Alasdair MacIntyre, *After Virtue: A Study in Moral Theory* (Notre Dame, Ind.: University of Notre Dame Press, 1984; first ed. 1981).

56. See Etienne Gilson, *The Spirit of Medieval Philosophy* (New York: Charles Scribner's, 1936); Jaroslav Pelikan, *Jesus through the Centuries: His Place in the History of Culture* (New Haven, Conn.: Yale University Press, 1985); Kenneth Scott Latourette, *A History of Christianity* (New York: Harper and Row, 1975); and William C. Placher, *A History of Christian Theology: An Introduction* (Philadelphia: Westminster Press, 1983).

57. See Ernst Troeltsch, *Protestantism and Progress: A Historical Study of the Relation of Protestantism to the Modern World* (Boston: Beacon Press, 1958; first ed. 1912).

58. Joseph Cardinal Ratzinger with Vittorio Messori, *The Ratzinger Report: An Exclusive Interview on the State of the Church* (San Francisco: Ignatius Press, 1985); see also Richard John Neuhaus, *The Catholic Moment: The Paradox of the Church in the Postmodern World* (San Francisco: Harper and Row, 1987).

Chapter 1

1. Paul A. Carter, *Revolt against Destiny: An Intellectual History of the United States* (New York: Columbia University Press, 1989), pp. 22, 20.

2. Guglielmo Ferrero, *The Greatness and Decline of Rome* (New York: Putnam, 1909), quoted in ibid., p. 213.

3. Clark Clifford, quoted in David S. Broder, "Nation's Capital in Eclipse as Pride and Power Slip Away," *Washington Post*, February 18, 1990, p. A1.

4. Carter, *Revolt against Destiny*, p. 269.

5. Overton H. Taylor, *The Classical Liberalism, Marxism, and the Twentieth Century* (Cambridge, Mass.: Harvard University Press 1960), p. 13.

6. David G. Ritchie, *Natural Rights: A Criticism of Some Political and Ethical Conceptions* (New York: Macmillan, 1924), p. 35.

7. Ibid., p. 34.

8. Quoted in Louis I. Bredvold, *The Brave New World of the Enlightenment* (Ann Arbor: University of Michigan Press, 1961), p. 10.

9. Ritchie, *Natural Rights*, p. 36.

10. See Ernest Barker, *Traditions of Civility: Eight Essays* (Hamden, Conn.: Archon Books, 1967; first ed. 1948), pp. 10–11.

11. A historian writes that "one of Rome's most characteristic contributions to the Western world was its understanding of private property" and that in Rome "the notion of property developed a sacred quality that it had lacked in ancient Greece." See Justo L. Gonzalez, *Faith and Wealth: A History of Early Christian Ideas on the Origin, Significance, and Use of Money* (San Francisco: Harper and Row, 1990), p. 15.

12. R. W. Southern, *Western Society and the Church in the Middle Ages*, Pelican History of the Church no. 2, (New York: Penguin Books, 1970).

13. G. K. Chesterton, *Saint Thomas Aquinas: "The Dumb Ox"* (Garden City, N.Y.: Doubleday, 1956; first ed. 1933).

14. Frederick Copleston, *A History of Philosophy*, vol. 1, *Greece and Rome* (Garden City, N.Y.: Doubleday, 1985; first ed. 1946).

15. Herbert A. Simon, "The Failure of Armchair Economics," *Challenge* (November/December 1986), p. 19.

16. Ibid., pp. 22–23.

17. Ibid., p. 22.

18. Richard Zeckhauser, "Behavioral vs. Rational Economics: What You See Is What You Conquer," in Robin M. Hogarth and Melvin W. Reder, eds., *Rational Choice: The Contrast between Economics and Psychology* (Chicago: University of Chicago Press, 1987), p. 252.

19. Ibid., p. 251.

20. See William C. Placher, *A History of Christian Theology: An Introduction* (Philadelphia: Westminster Press, 1983), chs. 12, 13.

21. See D. J. Allen, *The Philosophy of Aristotle* (New York: Oxford University Press, 1970); and Frederick J. E. Woodbridge, *Aristotle's Vision of Nature* (New York: Columbia University Press, 1965).

22. Henry B. Veatch, *Aristotle: A Contemporary Appreciation* (Bloomington: Indiana University Press, 1974), p. 127.

23. Barker, *Traditions of Civility*, p. 10.

24. Aristotle, *Nichomachean Ethics*, T. Irwin, trans. (Indianapolis, Ind.: Hackett Publishing, 1985), p. 166 (1143b, 4–5).

25. Jonathan Barnes, *Aristotle* (New York: Oxford University Press, 1982), p. 9.

26. Aristotle, *Nichomachean Ethics*, p. 16 (1098a, 1–5).

27. Ibid., p. 15 (1097b, 21–22).

28. Ibid., p. 150 (1139a, 30–31).

29. Emil Kauder, "Genesis of The Marginal Utility Theory: From Aristotle to the End of the Eighteenth Century," *Economic Journal* (September 1953), pp. 638–41.

30. Stephen T. Worland, "Aristotle and the Neoclassical Tradition: The Shifting Ground of Complementarity," *History of Political Economy* (Spring 1984), p. 112.

31. Aristotle, *Nichomachean Ethics* III, 3, quoted in ibid., p. 112.

32. Worland, "Aristotle and the Neoclassical Tradition," p. 134.

33. Herbert A. Simon, *Models of Bounded Rationality*, vol. 2, *Behavioral Economics and Business Organization* (Cambridge, Mass.: MIT Press, 1982), p. 406.

34. Aristotle, *The Politics*, B. Jowett, trans. (London: Oxford University Press, 1885), p. 43 (1266a).

35. Ibid., p. 34 (1263a).

36. Ibid., p. 34 (1263b).

37. Ibid., p. 35 (1263b).

38. Ibid., pp. 33–34 (1263a).

39. Joseph A. Schumpeter, *History of Economic Analysis* (New York: Oxford University Press, 1954), p. 59.

40. William Ebenstein, *Great Political Thinkers: Plato to the Present* (New York: Holt, Rinehart, and Winston, 1962; first ed. 1951), p. 73.

41. Exodus 22:25; quoted in Sidney Homer, *A History of Interest Rates* (New Brunswick, N.J.: Rutgers University Press, 1963), p. 69.

42. Aristotle, *Politics*, pp. 101–02 (1287a,b), 162 (1307b).

43. Aristotle, *Nichomachean Ethics*, p. 21 (1099a, 30–35).

44. Martha C. Nussbaum, *The Fragility of Goodness: Luck and Ethics in Greek Tragedy and Philosophy* (New York: Cambridge University Press, 1986), p. 347.

45. Martha Nussbaum, "Recoiling from Reason," *New York Review of Books*, December 7, 1989, p. 41.

46. Worland, "Aristotle and the Neoclassical Tradition," p. 133.

47. Paul Johnson, *A History of Christianity* (New York: Atheneum, 1987; first ed. 1976), pp. 130–31.

48. Arend T. Van Leeuwen, *Christianity in World History: The Meeting of the Faiths of East and West* (New York: Charles Scribner's, 1964), p. 286.

49. Jaroslav Pelikan, *Jesus through the Centuries: His Place in the History of Culture* (New Haven, Conn.: Yale University Press, 1985), p. 144.

50. J. Gilchrist, *The Church and Economic Activity in the Middle Ages* (New York: St. Martin's Press, 1969), p. 7.

51. Paul Tillich, *A History of Christian Thought: From Its Judaic and Hellenistic Origins to Existentialism* (New York: Simon and Schuster, 1967), p. 210.

52. B. Tierney, *Medieval Poor Law: A Sketch of Canonical Theory and Its Application in England* (Berkeley: University of California Press, 1959), p. 109.

53. Robert Nisbet writes that "the period running from the tenth to the start of the fourteenth century is 'one of the great inventive eras of mankind.' Moreover, industrial dynamism was accompanied by 'psychological dynamism,' . . . something that not only extended itself into many areas of thought and work but is the real beginning of those forces which, after a period of relative decline in the fourteenth and fifteenth centuries, flowered in the seventeenth and eighteenth centuries, the period commonly categorized as the beginning of the modern work ethic and also of the industrial or mechanical revolution." See Nisbet, *History of the Idea of Progress* (New York: Basic Books, 1980), p. 79.

54. James Westfall Thompson, *An Economic and Social History of the Middle Ages* (New York: Century, 1928), p. 794.

55. Tina Stiefel, *The Intellectual Revolution in Twelfth-century Europe* (New York: St. Martin's Press, 1985).

56. Etienne Gilson, *The Philosophy of St. Thomas Aquinas* (New York: Dorset Press, undated; first ed. 1924), p. 53.

57. Etienne Gilson, *The Spirit of Medieval Philosophy* (New York: Charles Scribner's, 1936), p. 336.

58. Thomas Aquinas, *The Summa Theologica*, translated by the Fathers of the English Dominican Province (London: Burns, Oates, and Washbourne, 1927), vol. 8, pp. 2, 56–57 (II-I: q. 90, art. 1; q. 95, art. 2).

59. Gilson, *Philosophy of St. Thomas Aquinas*, p. 41.

60. Gilson, *Spirit of Medieval Philosophy*, p. 101.

61. John Courtney Murray, *We Hold These Truths: Catholic Reflections on the American Proposition* (New York: Sheed and Ward, 1960), pp. 113, 117, 119.

62. Taylor, *The Classical Liberalism, Marxism, and the Twentieth Century*, p. 15.

63. Aquinas, *Summa Theologica*, vol. 8, p. 4 (II-I: q. 90, art. 2).

64. Schumpeter, *History of Economic Analysis*, p. 92.

65. Thomas Aquinas, *Commentary on the Nichomachean Ethics of Aristotle* 8, lecture 12, quoted in Placher, *A History of Christian Theology*, p. 155.

66. Thomas Aquinas, *De Regimine Principum*, quoted in John C. Cort, *Christian Socialism: An Informal History* (Maryknoll, N.Y.: Orbis Books, 1988), p. 56.

67. George O'Brien, *An Essay on Medieval Economic Teaching* (New York: Augustus M. Kelley, 1967; first ed. 1920), p. 69.

68. Thomas Aquinas, *Summa Theologica*, vol. 10, p. 224 (II-II: q. 66, art. 2).

69. Mark Blaug, *Economic Theory in Retrospect*, 4th ed. (New York: Cambridge University Press, 1985), p. 29. Blaug comments that the "just

price" was "identified . . . with the market price, the price given to an individual which he cannot himself affect."

70. Jacob Viner, *Religious Thought and Economic Society: Four Chapters of an Unfinished Work*, Jacques Melitz and Donald Winch, eds. (Durham, N.C.: Duke University Press, 1978), pp. 84–85.

71. Ephraim Kleiman, " 'Just Price' in Talmudic Literature," *History of Political Economy* (Spring 1987), pp. 26, 35.

72. See Gilchrist, *The Church and Economic Activity in the Middle Ages*; Alejandro A. Chafuen, *Christians for Freedom: Late-scholastic Economics* (San Francisco: Ignatius Press, 1986); and Karl Pribram, *A History of Economic Reasoning* (Baltimore: Johns Hopkins University Press, 1983) pp. 14–15. Some qualifications are indicated in Stephen T. Worland, "Justum Pretium: One More Round in the 'Endless Series,' " *History of Political Economy* (Winter 1977).

73. Emil Kauder, "The Retarded Acceptance of the Marginal Utility Theory," *Quarterly Journal of Economics* (November 1953), p. 564.

74. Raymond de Roover, "Scholastic Economics: Survival and Lasting Influence from the Sixteenth Century to Adam Smith," *Quarterly Journal of Economics* (May 1955), p. 186.

75. John T. Noonan, Jr., *The Scholastic Analysis of Usury* (Cambridge, Mass.: Harvard University Press, 1957).

76. Thomas Aquinas, *Tractatus de Origine, etc., Monetarum*, ad. 2, quoted in O'Brien, *Essay on Medieval Economic Teaching*, p. 145.

77. O'Brien, *Essay on Medieval Economic Teaching*, p. 69.

78. Ibid., pp. 79–80.

79. Ibid., p. 79.

80. Charles L. Schultze, *The Public Use of Private Interest* (Washington, D.C.: Brookings, 1977).

Chapter 2

1. Tom Wolfe, *The Right Stuff* (New York: Farrar, Straus, and Giroux, 1979).

2. James M. Buchanan, *What Should Economists Do?* (Indianapolis, Ind.: Liberty Press, 1979), p. 229.

3. Ibid., p. 228.

4. Ibid., pp. 228–29.

5. Ibid., pp. 110–11.

6. Ibid., pp. 90–91, 216, 88, 121.

7. Ibid., pp. 98–99.

8. Ibid., pp. 109, 94.

9. Ibid., pp. 283, 126, 125.

10. Karl R. Popper, *The Open Society and Its Enemies,* vol. 1, *The Spell of Plato* (Princeton, N.J.: Princeton University Press, 1971; first ed. 1962). Another philosopher writes of Plato's "highly authoritarian political doctrines" and that "a modern liberal will certainly find these suggested institutions extremely repellant." See R. M. Hare, *Plato* (New York: Oxford University Press, 1982), pp. 58, 61.

11. Popper, *The Open Society and Its Enemies,* pp. 87, 83, 171.

12. Ibid., pp. 199, 94, 39, 48, 38, 165, 164.

13. Augustine, *Confessions,* J. G. Pilkington, trans. (New York: Liveright Publishing, 1942), p. 163.

14. For example, Plato's famous allegory of the cave is readily interpreted as a depiction of humanity alienated from its surroundings, whose existence is one of ignorance and falsehood. The lives of ordinary men make them "prisoners" who can see nothing but "shadows thrown by the fire-light on the wall," all amounting to "meaningless illusion." All their lives men have been "prevented from moving their heads." If they could but once see the truth, men would "endure anything rather than go back." But men in their ignorance and darkness know no better; indeed, a teller of the truth could only expect that in their current sinful condition men would "laugh at him" and "if they could lay hands on the man, . . . they would kill him." If Plato meant by this statement the fate of Socrates, it was easy for the Christian world later to envision Jesus Christ. See Plato, *The Republic,* F. M. Cornford, trans. (New York: Oxford University Press, 1945), pp. 228, 230, 231.

15. Paul Tillich, *A History of Christian Thought: From Its Judaic and Hellenistic Origins to Existentialism* (New York: Simon and Schuster, 1967), p. 6.

16. Ibid., pp. 108, 4.

17. Martha C. Nussbaum, *The Fragility of Goodness: Luck and Ethics in Greek Tragedy and Philosophy* (New York: Cambridge University Press, 1986), pp. 151–52.

18. Albert Augustus Trever, *A History of Greek Economic Thought* (Philadelphia: Porcupine Press, 1978; first ed. 1916), p. 22.

19. Plato, *Republic,* pp. 60–61.

20. Plato, *Republic,* quoted in Popper, *The Open Society and Its Enemies,* vol. 1, p. 41.

21. Plato, *Republic,* pp. 60, 61, 56, 57.

22. Ibid., p. 61.

23. Ibid., pp. 280–81.

24. Ibid., pp. 121, 166, 165.

25. Ibid., p. 160.

26. Ibid., p. 105.

27. Plato's influence on the development of Christianity is described in Paul Elmer More, *Platonism* (New York: Greenwood Press, 1969; first ed. 1917).

28. Carl Stephenson, *Mediaeval Feudalism,* (Ithaca, N.Y.: Cornell University Press, 1963; first ed. 1942).

29. Peter Brown, *Augustine of Hippo* (New York: Dorset Press, 1986; first ed. 1967).

30. John Herman Randall, Jr., *Hellenistic Ways of Deliverance and the Making of the Christian Synthesis* (New York: Columbia University Press, 1970), p. 199.

31. See Martha E. Stortz, "The Inscrutability of God and the Possibility of Political Community: Augustine's Political Theology," *Halcyon/1988: A Journal of the Humanities* 10 (1988).

32. Romans 11:33; Romans 7:19, 24.

33. See William L. Petersen, "All Things Made New: Augustine and the Past," *Halcyon/1988: A Journal of the Humanities* 10 (1988).

34. Augustine, *The City of God,* in vol. 2 of *Basic Writings of Saint Augustine,* Whitney J. Oates, ed. (New York: Random House, 1948), p. 490 (bk. 19, ch. 14).

35. Peter Brown explains that Augustine's triumph meant "a mentality of dependence; an emphasis on the absolute necessity of humility, on the idea of a 'general collapse' of the human race above which no man might dare to claim to raise himself by his own merits. . . . The Pelagian movement had . . . rested firmly on a bed rock of the old ethical ideals of paganism, especially of Stoicism. Its moral exhortations had appealed to a classical sense of the resources and autonomy of the human mind." See Brown, *Augustine of Hippo,* p. 367.

36. Randall, *Hellenistic Ways of Deliverance,* p. 192.

37. Augustine, *City of God,* quoted in Ernest L. Fortin, "St. Augustine," in Leo Strauss and Joseph Cropsey, eds., *History of Political Philosophy* (Chicago: University of Chicago Press, 1981; first ed. 1963), p. 175.

38. Augustine, *City of God,* p. 279 (bk. 15, ch. 5).

39. Ibid., pp. 51–52 (bk. 4, ch. 4).

40. Augustine, *In Psalm,* quoted in Justo L. Gonzalez, *Faith and Wealth: A History of Early Christian Ideas on the Origin, Significance, and Use of Money* (San Francisco: Harper and Row, 1990), p. 219.

41. Gonzalez, *Faith and Wealth,* p. 219.

42. Lactantius, *The Divine Institution,* quoted in George O'Brien, *An Essay on Medieval Economic Thinking* (New York: Augustus M. Kelley, 1967; first ed. 1920), pp. 56–57.

43. Richard Schlatter, *Private Property: The History of an Idea* (New York: Russell and Russell, 1973; first ed. 1951), p. 35.

44. Augustine, *City of God,* p. 492 (bk. 19, ch. 15).

45. Augustine, *City of God,* p. 274 (bk. 14, ch. 28).

46. Fortin, "St. Augustine," p. 158.

47. Robin Lane Fox, *Pagans and Christians* (San Francisco: Harper and Row, 1987).

48. Augustine, *City of God,* quoted in Jaroslav Pelikan, *Jesus through the Centuries: His Place in the History of Culture* (New Haven, Conn.: Yale University Press, 1985), p. 29.

49. Steven Ozment, *The Age of Reform, 1250–1550: An Intellectual and Religious History of Late Medieval and Reformation Europe* (New Haven, Conn.: Yale University Press, 1980).

50. James Atkinson, *Martin Luther and the Birth of Protestantism* (London: Penguin Books, 1968); and Heiko A. Oberman, *Luther: Man between God and the Devil* (New Haven, Conn.: Yale University Press, 1989; first ed. 1982).

51. Quoted in William Ebenstein, *Great Political Thinkers: Plato to the Present* (New York: Holt, Rinehart, and Winston, 1962; first ed. 1951), p. 214.

52. See Owen Chadwick, *The Reformation,* Pelican History of the Church no. 3 (New York: Penguin Books, 1986; first ed. 1964), p. 42.

53. Martin Luther, *The Bondage of the Will,* quoted in Ozment, *Age of Reform,* p. 299.

54. *D. Martin Luthers Werke,* quoted in Oberman, *Luther,* p. 159.

55. E. Harris Harbison, *The Age of Reformation* (Westport, Conn.: Greenwood Press, 1982; first ed. 1955), p. 130.

56. G. K. Chesterton, *Saint Thomas Aquinas: "The Dumb Ox"* (Garden City, N.Y.: Doubleday, 1956; first ed. 1933), pp. 195, 193.

57. Ernst Troeltsch, *Protestantism and Progress: A Historical Study of the Relation of Protestantism to the Modern World* (Boston: Beacon Press, 1958; first English ed. 1913), pp. 82–83.

58. Martin Luther, *Temporal Authority: To What Extent It Should Be Obeyed,* reprinted in *Luther's Works,* vol. 45, *The Christian in Society,* Walter I. Brandt, ed. (Philadelphia: Muhlenberg Press, 1962), p. 113.

59. Martin Luther, *Whether Soldiers, Too, Can Be Saved,* quoted in Duncan B. Forrester, "Martin Luther and John Calvin," in Strauss and Cropsey, eds., *History of Political Philosophy,* p. 311.

60. Martin Luther, *Commentary on Psalm 101,* quoted in Forrester, "Martin Luther and John Calvin," p. 322.

61. Ibid., p. 300.

62. R. H. Tawney, *Religion and the Rise of Capitalism: A Historical Study* (New York: Harcourt, Brace, 1926), pp. 89, 90.

63. Ernst Troeltsch, *The Social Teaching of the Christian Churches,* 2 vols. (Chicago: University of Chicago Press, 1981; first ed., 1931), vol. 2, p. 556.

64. Harbison, *Age of Reformation,* ch. 3.

65. Pelikan, *Jesus through the Centuries,* p. 169.

66. See Matthew 5:9; John 18:36. Luther quoted in Pelikan, *Jesus through the Centuries,* pp. 171, 170.

67. Pelikan, *Jesus through the Centuries,* p. 175.

68. John Nef, *The Conquest of the Material World* (Chicago: University of Chicago Press, 1964), pp. 63, 62, 116.

69. Ibid., p. 116.

70. Max Weber, *The Protestant Ethic and the Spirit of Capitalism* (New York: Charles Scribner, 1958; first ed. 1905).

71. Troeltsch, *Protestantism and Progress,* p. 87.

72. Forrester, "Martin Luther and John Calvin," p. 308.

73. Troeltsch, *Protestantism and Progress,* p. 125.

74. Tawney, *Religion and the Rise of Capitalism,* p. 104.

75. Ibid., p. 105.

76. Troeltsch, *Protestantism and Progress,* pp. 133, 84, 136.

77. John Calvin, *Institutes of the Christian Religion,* quoted in Ozment, *Age of Reform,* p. 378.

78. Weber, *Protestant Ethic and the Spirit of Capitalism,* p. 115.

79. Ibid., p. 163.

80. See, for example, S. N. Eisenstadt, ed., *The Protestant Ethic and Modernization: A Comparative View* (New York: Basic Books, 1968); H. M. Robertson, *Aspects of the Rise of Economic Individualism: A Criticism of Max Weber and His School* (New York: Kelley and Millman, 1959); David Little, *Religion, Order, and Law: A Study in Pre-revolutionary England* (New York: Harper and Row, 1969); and Kurt Samuelsson, *Religion and Economic Action* (London: William Heinemann, 1961).

81. Samuelsson, *Religion and Economic Action,* p. 115.

82. Tillich, *History of Christian Thought,* p. 285.

83. Carl L. Becker, *The Heavenly City of the Eighteenth-Century Philosophers* (New Haven, Conn.: Yale University Press, 1968; first ed. 1932), pp. 64–65.

Chapter 3

1. In *Science and the Modern World,* the distinguished 20th-century philosopher Alfred North Whitehead explained that the fundamental assumptions of modern science were derived from the Greeks and their belief that the universe has an order and a meaning to be discovered. This belief was carried into the Roman era and then into the Middle Ages, which were "preeminently an epoch of orderly thought, rationalist through and through." In reaction to the excesses, inflexibility, and "unguarded rationalism" of the late medieval period, a counterreaction had produced the "anti-rationalist trend of thought" of the Protestant Reformation. Nevertheless, this period was only a temporary interlude before the rationalist tradition was reasserted once again in the form of modern science. As Whitehead explains, "the faith in the possibility of science, generated antecedently to the development of modern scientific theory, is an unconscious derivative from medieval theology." Alfred North

Whitehead, *Science and the Modern World* (New York: Free Press, 1967; first ed. 1925), pp. 12, 10, 13.

2. Christopher Dawson, *Christianity and the New Age* (Manchester, N.H.: Sophia Institute Press, 1985; first ed., 1931), pp. 94–95.

3. Isaiah Berlin, *The Age of Enlightenment: The Eighteenth Century Philosophers*, in *Great Ages in Western Philosophy* (Boston: Houghton Mifflin, 1962), p. 16.

4. Carl L. Becker, *The Heavenly City of the Eighteenth-century Philosophers* (New Haven, Conn.: Yale University Press, 1968; first ed. 1932), pp. 102, 58, 60.

5. Ernst Cassirer, *The Philosophy of the Enlightenment* (Princeton, N.J.: Princeton University Press, 1979; first ed. 1932), p. vi.

6. Yvon Belaval, "La crise de la géometrisation de l'univers dans la philosophie des lumières," *Revue International de Philosophie* (1952), quoted in Jean Starobinski, *Jean-Jacques Rousseau: Transparency and Obstruction* (Chicago: University of Chicago Press, 1988; first ed. 1971), p. 112.

7. Amos Funkenstein, *Theology and the Scientific Imagination: From the Middle Ages to the Seventeenth Century* (Princeton, N.J.: Princeton University Press, 1986), p. 357.

8. Cassirer, *Philosophy of the Enlightenment*, p. 99.

9. R. R. Palmer, *A History of the Modern World* (New York: Alfred A. Knopf, 1960), p. 285.

10. John Courtney Murray, *We Hold These Truths: Catholic Reflections on the American Proposition* (New York: Sheed and Ward, 1960), p. 313.

11. John Locke, *An Essay concerning Human Understanding*, Alexander Campbell Fraser, ed. (Oxford, U.K.: Clarendon Press, 1894), vol. 2, p. 306 (bk. 4, ch. 10, para. 1).

12. John Locke, *Two Treatises of Government*, Peter Laslett, ed. (New York: Cambridge University Press, 1967), pp. 289, 304.

13. Locke, *Essay concerning Human Understanding*, vol. 2, p. 208 (bk. 4, ch. 3, para. 18).

14. Locke, *Two Treatises of Government*, p. 287.

15. Locke, *Essay concerning Human Understanding*, vol. 1, p. 122 (bk. 2, ch. 1, para. 2).

16. Ibid., vol. 2, p. 67 (bk. 1, ch. 2, para. 3).

17. Locke, *Two Treatises of Government*, p. 312.

18. Ibid., p. 308.

19. Berlin, *Age of Enlightenment*, p. 19.

20. Kenneth Scott Latourette, *A History of Christianity*, vol. 2, *Reformation to the Present* (New York: Harper and Row, 1975; first ed. 1953), p. 838.

21. Michael Walzer, *The Revolution of the Saints: A Study in the Origins of Radical Politics* (New York: Atheneum, 1974), pp. 301, 214.

22. Locke, *Two Treatises of Government*, pp. 370, 368.

23. Latourette, *History of Christianity*, p. 826.

24. Walzer, *Revolution of the Saints*, pp. 212, 214.

25. Locke, *Two Treatises of Government*, pp. 314.

26. See Joyce Oldham Appleby, *Economic Thought and Ideology in Seventeenth-century England* (Princeton, N.J.: Princeton University Press, 1978) and C. B. Macpherson, *The Political Theory of Possessive Individualism: Hobbes to Locke* (New York: Oxford University Press, 1989; first ed. 1962).

27. Ernst Troeltsch, *Protestantism and Progress: A Historical Study of the Relation of Protestantism to the Modern World* (Boston: Beacon Press, 1958; first ed. 1912), pp. 125–26.

28. Quoted in John C. Cort, *Christian Socialism* (Maryknoll, N.Y.: Orbis Books, 1988), p. 9.

29. Cort, *Christian Socialism*, p. 9.

30. Milton L. Myers, *The Soul of Modern Economic Man: Ideas of Self-interest, Thomas Hobbes to Adam Smith* (Chicago: University of Chicago Press, 1983).

31. See Istvan Hont and Michael Ignatieff, eds., *Wealth and Virtue: The Shaping of the Political Economy in the Scottish Enlightenment* (New York: Cambridge University Press, 1983).

32. Earl of Schaftesbury, *Characteristics of Men, Manners, Opinions, Times* (New York: Bobbs-Merrill, 1964), vol. 1, pp. 243, 75, 289, 282.

33. Joseph Butler, *Sermons*, quoted in Myers, *Soul of Modern Economic Man*, p. 59.

34. Alexander Pope, *The Poetical Works*, quoted in Myers, *Soul of Modern Economic Man*, p. 61.

35. J. L. Talmon, *The Origins of Totalitarian Democracy* (New York: Norton, 1970), p. 31.

36. Louis I. Bredvold, *The Brave New World of the Enlightenment* (Ann Arbor: University of Michigan Press, 1961), p. 50.

37. L. A. Selby-Bigge, ed., *British Moralists*, quoted in Myers, *Soul of Modern Economic Man*, p. 69.

38. C. Gide and C. Rist, *History of Economic Doctrines*, quoted in John Herman Randall, Jr., *The Making of the Modern Mind* (New York: Columbia University Press, 1976; first ed. 1926), p. 323.

39. Dupont de Nemours, *Maximes du Docteur Quesnay* and *Origines et Progrès d'une Science Nouvelle*, quoted in Randall, *Making of the Modern Mind*, pp. 323–24.

40. Claude Adrien Hélvetius, *De l'Esprit*, quoted in Randall, *Making of the Modern Mind*, p. 317.

41. Randall, *Making of the Modern Mind*, p. 317.

42. Myers, *Soul of Modern Economic Man*, pp. 83, 87.

43. Paul Tillich, *A History of Christian Thought: From Its Judaic and Hellenistic Origins to Existentialism* (New York: Simon and Schuster, 1967), p. 338, 334. Another distinguished theologian, Arend Van Leeuwen, comments that "Adam Smith . . . declared economic liberty to be an axiomatic principle

of the natural order, regulating economic life; and behind it he saw at work the invisible hand which through economic self-interest fulfills a providential plan.'' See Arend T. Van Leeuwen, *Christianity in World History: The Meeting of the Faiths of East and West* (New York: Charles Scribner's, 1964), p. 317.

44. Adam Smith, *An Inquiry into the Nature and Causes of the Wealth of Nations* (Indianapolis, Ind.: Liberty Press, 1981), p. 13 (I.I.1).

45. See Richard F. Teichgraeber, *''Free Trade'' and Moral Philosophy: Rethinking the Sources of Adam Smith's* Wealth of Nations (Durham, N.C.: Duke University Press, 1986).

46. Karl Polanyi, *The Great Transformation: The Political and Economic Origins of Our Times* (Boston: Beacon Press, 1957; first ed. 1944), pp. 139, 135.

47. Jerry Evensky, ''The Two Voices of Adam Smith: Moral Philosopher and Social Critic,'' *History of Political Economy* (Fall 1987), p. 447.

48. Joseph A. Schumpeter, *History of Economic Analysis* (New York: Oxford University Press, 1954), pp. 185, 184.

49. Ibid., p. 186.

50. Talmon, *Origins of Totalitarian Democracy*, p. 31.

51. Schumpeter, *History of Economic Analysis*, p. 182.

52. Ibid., pp. 91–92.

53. Jacob Viner, *Religious Thought and Economic Society: Four Chapters of an Unfinished Work*, Jacques Melitz and Donald Winch, eds. (Durham, N.C.: Duke University Press, 1978), p. 112.

54. Smith, *Wealth of Nations*, p. 343 (II.III.31).

55. Joseph Cropsey, ''Adam Smith,'' in Leo Strauss and Joseph Cropsey, eds. *History of Political Philosophy* (Chicago: University of Chicago Press, 1981; first ed. 1963), p. 626.

56. See A. W. Coats, ''Adam Smith's Conception of Self-interest in Economic and Political Affairs,'' *History of Political Economy* (Spring 1975).

57. Smith, *Wealth of Nations*, pp. 422, 456 (II.IV.17 and IV.II.9).

58. Ibid., p. 456 (IV.II.9).

59. Adam Smith, *The Theory of Moral Sentiments* (Indianapolis, Ind.: Liberty Press, 1982), pp. 185, 182, 183 (III.IV.10.8).

60. Appleby, *Economic Thought and Ideology*, pp. 248, 115, 176.

61. Albert O. Hirschman, *The Passions and the Interests: Political Arguments for Capitalism before Its Triumph* (Princeton, N.J.: Princeton University Press, 1977).

62. See John Dinwiddy, *Bentham* (New York: Oxford University Press, 1989); and James Steintrager, *Bentham* (Ithaca: Cornell University Press, 1977).

63. Anthony Quinton, *Utilitarian Ethics* (Lasalle, Ill.: Open Court, 1989).

64. Jeremy Bentham, *An Introduction to the Principles of Morals and Legislation*, Philip Wheelwright, ed. (Garden City, N.Y.: Doubleday Goran, 1935), p. 31 (ch. 5, para. 5).

65. Ibid., pp. 24, 8 (ch. 3, para. 1; ch. 1, para. 2).

66. Jeremy Bentham, *Anarchical Fallacies*, quoted in Randall, *Making of the Modern Mind*, p. 362 (art. 2).

67. Bentham, *Morals and Legislation*, p. 181 (ch. 2, para. 14).

68. Jeremy Bentham, *A Fragment on Government*, F. C. Montague, ed. (Oxford, U.K.: Clarendon Press, 1891), p. 216 (ch. 4, sec. 23).

69. Jeremy Bentham, *Manual of Political Economy*, quoted in Randall, *Making of the Modern Mind*, pp. 361–62.

70. Bentham, *Morals and Legislation*, p. 32, (ch. 4, para. 8).

71. Quoted in William Ebenstein, *Great Political Thinkers: Plato to the Present* (New York: Holt, Rinehart, and Winston, 1962; first ed. 1951), p. 503.

72. Ebenstein, *Great Political Thinkers*, p. 503.

73. Emil Kauder, "Genesis of the Marginal Utility Theory: From Aristotle to the End of the Eighteenth Century," *Economic Journal* (September 1953), pp. 640, 638.

74. Talmon, *Origins of Totalitarian Democracy*, p. 4.

75. Schumpeter, *History of Economic Analysis*, p. 131.

76. Frank Edward Manuel, *The New World of Henri Saint-Simon* (Cambridge, Mass.: Harvard University Press, 1956).

77. Henri Saint-Simon, *Esquisse d'une nouvelle encyclopédie*, quoted in Frank E. and Fritzie P. Manuel, *Utopian Thought in the Western World* (Cambridge, Mass: Harvard University Press, 1979), p. 597.

78. Henri Saint-Simon, *Oeuvres de Saint-Simon et d'Enfantin*, quoted in F. A. Hayek, *The Counter-revolution of Science: Studies on the Abuse of Reason* (Indianapolis, Ind.: Liberty Press, 1979; first ed. 1952), p. 221.

79. Henri Saint-Simon, *Oeuvres*, quoted in J. L. Talmon, *Political Messianism: The Romantic Phase* (Boulder, Colo.: Westview Press, 1985; first ed. 1960), p. 51.

80. Henri Saint-Simon, *Opinions Littéraires, Philosophiques, et Industrielles*, quoted in Manuel and Manuel, *Utopian Thought in the Western World*, p. 600.

81. Albert S. Lindemann, *A History of European Socialism* (New Haven, Conn.: Yale University Press, 1983), p. 49.

82. Saint-Simon, *Oeuvres*, quoted in Hayek, *Counter-revolution of Science*, pp. 246–47.

83. Saint-Simon, *Oeuvres*, quoted in Talmon, *Political Messianism*, p. 67.

84. Manuel and Manuel, *Utopian Thought in the Western World*, p. 603.

85. Henri Saint-Simon, *New Christianity*, quoted in Talmon, *Political Messianism*, p. 70.

86. Ibid., p. 70.

87. Saint-Simon, *Oeuvres*, quoted in Talmon, *Political Messianism*, pp. 70–71.

88. Quoted in Talmon, *Political Messianism*, p. 71.

89. Thorstein Veblen, *The Engineers and the Price System* (New York: Augustus M. Kelley, 1965; first ed. 1921), pp. 138, 69.

90. Samuel Haber, *Efficiency and Uplift: Scientific Management in the Progressive Era, 1890–1920* (Chicago: University of Chicago Press, 1964), p. 43.

91. John Kenneth Galbraith, *The New Industrial State* (Boston: Houghton Mifflin, 1967).

92. Charles L. Schultze, *The Politics and Economics of Public Spending* (Washington, D.C.: Brookings Institution, 1968), p. 96.

93. Auguste Comte, *Cours de Philosophie Positive*, quoted in Hayek, *Counter-revolution of Science*, pp. 350–51.

94. Talmon, *Political Messianism*.

95. Auguste Comte, *Système de Politique Positive*, quoted in Manuel and Manuel, *Utopian Thought in the Western World*, p. 733.

96. Manuel and Manuel, *Utopian Thought in the Western World*, pp. 723, 727, 728.

97. Quoted in Hayek, *Counter-revolution of Science*, p. 355.

Chapter 4

1. Jean Starobinski, *Jean-Jacques Rousseau: Transparency and Obstruction* (Chicago: University of Chicago Press, 1988; first. ed. 1971), pp. 4, 38.

2. Jean-Jacques Rousseau, *Discourse on the Origin of Equality* and *Discours sur les Sciences et les Arts*, quoted in Starobinski, *Jean-Jacques Rousseau*, pp. 27, 5.

3. Starobinski, *Jean-Jacques Rousseau*, pp. 28, 29, 27.

4. Ibid., p. 12.

5. Ibid., pp. 12, 13.

6. Alexis de Tocqueville, *The Old Regime and the French Revolution* (Garden City, N.Y.: Doubleday, 1955; first ed. 1856), pp. 12, 13, 11.

7. Karl Polanyi, *The Great Transformation: The Political and Economic Origins of Our Time* (Boston: Beacon Press, 1957; first ed. 1944), p. 39.

8. Robert C. Binkley, *Realism and Nationalism, 1852–1871* (New York: Harper and Row, 1963; first ed. 1935), pp. 93, 19.

9. J. L. Talmon, *Political Messianism: The Romantic Phase* (Boulder, Colo.: Westview Press, 1985; first ed. 1960), pp. 24, 23.

10. Quoted in Will Durant, *The Story of Philosophy* (Garden City, N.Y.: Garden City Publishing, 1943; first ed. 1926), p. 78.

11. Talmon, *Political Messianism*, p. 25.

12. Robert Nisbet, *History of the Idea of Progress* (New York: Basic Books, 1980), p. 172.

13. H. Stuart Hughes, *Consciousness and Society: The Reorientation of European Social Thought, 1890–1930* (New York: Random House, 1958).

14. One observer comments that "Darwinism deals confidence in science and rational thought in any field a potentially fatal blow." Men do not accept ideas because they are objectively true, "but are compelled by the survival urge to accept those that promote survival, be they true or not." Darwin's views "undoubtedly paved the way for the more explicit Marxian and Freudian views of reason as the unwitting agent of blind subrational drives." See R. F. Baum, *Doctors of Modernity: Darwin, Marx, and Freud* (Peru, Ill.: Sherwood Sugden, 1988), pp. 20–21.

15. R. H. Tawney, *Religion and the Rise of Capitalism: A Historical Study* (New York: Harcourt, Brace, 1926), p. 86.

16. Ibid., pp. 86, 87, 88, 92, 90.

17. Isaiah Berlin, *Karl Marx: His Life and Environment* (New York: Time Books, 1963; first ed. 1939), p. 113.

18. Karl Marx, *Capital: A Critique of Political Economy* (New York: Modern Library, 1906), p.708.

19. Karl Marx and Friedrich Engels, *The German Ideology,* R. Pascal, ed. (New York: International Publishers, 1965), p. 22.

20. Berlin, *Karl Marx,* p. 18.

21. Marx, *Capital,* pp. 836–37.

22. Talmon, *Political Messianism,* p. 224.

23. See also Alasdair MacIntyre, *Marxism and Christianity* (Notre Dame, Ind.: University of Notre Dame Press, 1984; first ed. 1968).

24. Joseph Cropsey, "Karl Marx," in Leo Strauss and Joseph Cropsey, eds., *History of Political Philosophy* (Chicago: University of Chicago Press, 1981), p. 778.

25. Paul Tillich, *A History of Christian Thought: From Its Hellenistic Origins to Existentialism* (New York: Simon and Schuster, 1967), pp. 426–27.

26. Friedrich Engels, "Ludwig Feuerbach and the End of Classical German Philosophy," in Karl Marx and Friedrich Engels, *Basic Writings on Politics and Philosophy,* Lewis S. Feuer, ed. (Garden City, N.Y.: Doubleday, 1959), pp. 227, 199.

27. Berlin, *Karl Marx,* p. 127.

28. Karl Marx, *A Contribution to the Critique of Political Economy,* in *A Handbook of Marxism* (New York: International Publishers, 1935), p.372.

29. Frederick Engels, *Herr Eugen Duhrings Revolution in Science* [Anti-Duhring], quoted in Thomas Sowell, *Marxism: Philosophy and Economics* (New York: William Morrow, 1985), p. 57.

30. Marx, *Contribution to the Critique of Political Economy,* p. 372.

31. Letter from Marx to F. A. Sorge, October 19, 1877, in Karl Marx and Frederick Engels, *Selected Correspondence* (Moscow: Progress Publishers, 1965), p. 310.

32. Karl Marx, *Critique of the Gotha Programme,* in Karl Marx and Frederick Engels, *On Reformism: A Collection* (Moscow: Progress Publishers, 1984), p. 129.

33. Letter from Engels to A. Bebel, October 28, 1882, in Marx and Engels, *Selected Correspondence*, p. 355.

34. Letter from Engels to E. Bernstein, October 20, 1882, in Marx and Engels, *Selected Correspondence*, p. 353.

35. Letter from Engels to A. Bebel, in Marx and Engels, *Selected Correspondence*, p. 355.

36. David McClellan, *Karl Marx: His Life and Thought* (New York: Harper, 1973).

37. Paul Johnson, *A History of the Jews* (New York: Harper and Row, 1987).

38. Tawney, *Religion and the Rise of Capitalism*, pp. 88–94.

39. Martin Luther, *Against the Murdering Thieving Hordes of Peasants*, quoted in Owen Chadwick, *The Reformation*, Pelican History of the Church no. 3 (New York: Penguin Books, 1964), p. 60.

40. Statement of Carl Schurz, quoted in Sowell, *Marxism*, p. 183.

41. Quoted in Frank E. Manuel and Fritzie P. Manuel, *Utopian Thought in the Western World* (Cambridge, Mass.: Harvard University Press, 1979), p. 739.

42. Tawney, *Religion and the Rise of Capitalism*, p. 89.

43. Ibid., pp. 97, 90–91, 100, 99, 98.

44. Berlin, *Karl Marx*, p. 115.

45. Tillich, *History of Christian Thought*, pp. 237–38.

46. Tawney, *Religion and the Rise of Capitalism*, p. 92.

47. Ibid., pp. 94, 98–99.

48. Ibid., p. 93.

49. Karl R. Popper, *The Open Society and Its Enemies*, vol. 2, *The High Tide of Prophecy—Hegel, Marx, and the Aftermath* (Princeton, N.J.: Princeton University Press, 1971; first ed. 1962), p. 201.

50. Friedrich Engels, *"Eulogy for Marx,"* quoted in Harry W. Laidler, *A History of Socialist Thought* (New York: Thomas Y. Crowell, 1927), p. 196.

51. Nicolas Berdyaev, *The Origin of Russian Communism* (Ann Arbor: University of Michigan Press, 1972; first ed. 1937).

52. *Lochner v. New York*, 198 U.S. 45 (1905).

53. Richard Hofstader, *Social Darwinism in American Thought* (Boston: Beacon Press, 1955; first ed. 1944), p. 44, 49.

54. Tawney, *Religion and the Rise of Capitalism*, pp. 109, 108, 106, 112.

55. Herbert Spencer, *Social Statics* (New York: Robert Schalkenbach Foundation, 1970; first ed. 1850), p. 290 (ch. 25).

56. Hofstader, *Social Darwinism in American Thought*, p. 10.

57. Spencer, *Social Statics*, pp. 288–89.

58. Hofstader, *Social Darwinism in American Thought*, p. 43–44.

59. Herbert Spencer, "The Coming Slavery," in Spencer, *The Man versus the State: With Six Essays on Government, Society, and Freedom* (Indianapolis, Ind.: Liberty Classics, 1981; first ed. 1884), pp. 69, 68, 67, 57.

60. Spencer, *Social Statics*, quoted in Hofstadter, *Social Darwinism in American Thought*, p. 41.

61. Spencer, *Social Statics*, p. 289.

62. Ibid., p. 290.

63. Robert Green McCloskey, *American Conservatism in the Age of Enterprise* (Cambridge, Mass.: Harvard University Press, 1951), pp. 27–28.

64. Spencer, *Social Statics*, pp. 289–90.

65. Ibid., pp. 290, 294.

66. Tawney, *Religion and the Rise of Capitalism*, p. 115.

67. Tillich, *History of Christian Thought*, p. 270–71.

68. Hofstader, *Social Darwinism in American Thought*, p. 10.

69. Spencer, "The Coming Slavery," pp. 67, 46–47.

70. Hofstader, *Social Darwinism in American Thought*, p. 35.

71. Thorstein Veblen, "The Preconceptions of Economic Science, Part III," *Quarterly Journal of Economics* (February 1900), p. 257.

72. Robert L. Heilbroner, *The Worldly Philosophers: The Lives, Times, and Ideas of the Great Economic Thinkers* (New York: Simon and Schuster, 1972), p. 40.

73. Sigmund Freud, *A General Introduction to Psychoanalysis* (New York: Washington Square Press, 1960; first ed. 1924).

74. Ernest Jones, *The Life and Work of Sigmund Freud*, 3 vols. (New York: Basic Books, 1953–57); and H. F. Ellenberger, *The Discovery of the Unconscious* (New York: Basic Books, 1970).

75. Sigmund Freud, *Civilization and Its Discontents*, trans. by J. Strachey (New York: Norton, 1961; first ed. 1930), pp. 64, 48.

76. Ibid., pp. 71, 65, 59.

77. Ibid., pp. 30, 79, 74, 51.

78. Michael Walzer, *The Revolution of the Saints: A Study in the Origins of Radical Politics* (New York: Antheneum, 1974), p. 168.

79. Ibid., pp. 21, 313, 20, 21, 215, 307.

80. Ibid., pp. 302, 215, 307.

81. Ibid., p. 212.

82. Freud, *Civilization and Its Discontents*, pp. 91, 44, 81.

83. Charles A. Reich, "The New Property," *Yale Law Journal* (April 1964).

84. Raymond E. Fancher, *Psychoanalytic Psychology: The Development of Freud's Thought* (New York: Norton, 1973), pp. 195–232.

85. Reuben Fine, *A History of Pschoanalysis* (New York: Columbia University Press, 1979), p. 544.

86. Freud, *Civilization and Its Discontents*, p. 58.

87. Ibid., p. 51.

88. William L. Shirer, *The Rise and Fall of the Third Reich: A History of Nazi Germany* (New York: Simon and Schuster, 1960).

89. Robert N. Proctor, *Racial Hygiene: Medicine under the Nazis* (Cambridge, Mass.: Harvard University Press, 1988), p. 50.

90. Fritz Lenz, *Die Rasse als Wertprinzip,* quoted in Proctor, *Racial Hygiene,* p. 48.

91. Fritz Lenz, "Alfred Ploetz zum 70. Geburtstag am 22. August, " quoted in Proctor, *Racial Hygiene,* p. 49.

92. Proctor, *Racial Hygiene,* pp. 60–61.

93. Ibid., p. 177.

94. Michael Straight, "Germany Executes Her 'Unfit,' " quoted in Proctor, *Racial Hygiene,* p. 182.

95. Proctor, *Racial Hygiene,* pp. 221–22.

96. Max Weinreich, *Hitler's Professors: The Part of Scholarship in Germany's Crimes against the Jewish People,* quoted in Proctor, *Racial Hygiene,* p. 222.

97. Richard Neuhaus, *In Defense of People: Ecology and the Seduction of Radicalism* (New York: Macmillan, 1971), pp. 154–55. Neuhaus comments that Hitler's world view "was responsive to the cultural and intellectual climate—as well as to economic and political realities—of the historical moment that granted him power" (p. 154).

Chapter 5

1. Walter Lippmann, *The Public Philosophy* (New Brunswick, N.J.: Transaction Publishers, 1989; first ed. 1955), p. 101.

2. Ibid., pp. 97–99.

3. John Courtney Murray, *We Hold These Truths: Catholic Reflections on the American Proposition* (New York: Sheed and Ward, 1960), pp. 31, 37, 36, 34, 42, 32.

4. Ibid., pp. 39, 41.

5. George Weigel, *Tranquillitas Ordinis: The Present Failure and Future Promise of American Catholic Thought on War and Peace* (New York: Oxford University Press, 1987), pp. 121–22.

6. Jacques Maritain, *Reflections on America* (New York: Charles Scribner's Sons, 1958), pp. 168, 35. See also Michael Novak, *Free Persons and the Common Good* (Lanham, Md.: Madison Books, 1989).

7. George Weigel, *Catholicism and the Renewal of American Democracy* (New York: Paulist Press, 1989), p. 20.

8. John C. Cort, *Christian Socialism: An Informal History* (Maryknoll, N.Y.: Orbis Books, 1988), p. 55.

9. Paul Tillich, *A History of Christian Thought: From Its Judaic and Hellenistic Origins To Existentialism* (New York: Simon and Schuster, 1967), pp. 381, 380, 299, 349.

10. Ibid., pp. 141, 191, 189, 186.

11. Ibid., pp. 139, 259.

12. Benjamin G. Rader, *The Academic Mind and Reform: The Influence of Richard T. Ely in American Life* (Lexington: University of Kentucky Press, 1966).

13. Harris E. Starr, *William Graham Sumner* (New York: Henry Holt, 1925), p. 498.

14. William Graham Sumner, *The Challenge of Facts,* quoted in Sidney Fine, *Laissez Faire and the General-welfare State: A Study of Conflict in American Thought, 1865–1901* (Ann Arbor: University of Michigan Press, 1964; first ed. 1956), p. 82.

15. William Graham Sumner, *Essays,* quoted in Fine, *Laissez Faire and the General-welfare State,* pp. 82–83.

16. Ibid., p. 84.

17. Fine, *Laissez Faire and the General-welfare State,* p. 85.

18. Charles Howard Hopkins, *The Rise of the Social Gospel in American Protestantism, 1865–1915* (New Haven, Conn.: Yale University Press, 1940), p. 88.

19. Fine, *Laissez Faire and the General-welfare State,* p. 238.

20. Richard T. Ely, *Social Aspects of Christianity and Other Essays* (New York: Thomas Y. Crowell, 1889), pp. 1, 7, 6, 7.

21. Ibid., pp. 15, 10, 10–11, 11, 17.

22. Ibid., pp. 121, 122, 123, 128, 129, 128, 129, 128.

23. Ibid., pp. 121, 127.

24. Richard T. Ely, "Fundamental Beliefs of My Social Philosophy," *Forum Magazine* (1894), quoted in Richard T. Ely, *Ground under Our Feet: An Autobiography* (New York: Arno Press, 1977; first ed. 1938), pp. 77–78.

25. Ely, *Social Aspects of Christianity,* pp. 53, 56, 72.

26. Ibid., pp. 73, 9.

27. Hopkins, *Rise of the Social Gospel,* pp. 320–21.

28. See Mary O. Furner, *Advocacy and Objectivity: A Crisis in the Professionalization of American Social Science, 1865–1905* (Lexington: University of Kentucky Press, 1975), pp. 59–80.

29. Quoted in Ely, *Ground under Our Feet,* p. 140.

30. John Rutherford Everett, *Religion in Economics: A Study of John Bates Clark, Richard T. Ely, Simon N. Patten* (Philadelphia: Porcupine Press, 1982; first ed. 1946).

31. Quoted in Hopkins, *Rise of the Social Gospel,* p. 162.

32. See Daniel M. Fox, *The Discovery of Abundance: Simon N. Patten and the Transformation of Social Theory* (Ithaca, N.Y.: Cornell University Press, 1967).

33. Quoted in Hopkins, *Rise of the Social Gospel,* p. 269.

34. Richard T. Ely, *Socialism: An Examination of Its Nature, Its Strength, and Its Weaknesses, with Suggestions for Social Reform* (New York: Thomas Y. Crowell, 1894), p. 72.

35. Ibid., pp. 350, 232, 212.

36. Ely, *Social Aspects of Christianity,* p. 60.

37. Dwight Waldo, *The Administrative State: A Study of the Political Theory of American Public Administration* (New York: Holmes and Meier, 1984; first ed. 1948), p. 20.

38. Quoted in ibid., p. 18.

39. Quoted in Hopkins, *Rise of the Social Gospel,* p. 322.

40. See A. W. Coats, "The First Two Decades of the American Economic Association," *American Economic Review* (September 1960); also A. W. Coats, "The American Economic Association and the Economics Profession," *Journal of Economic Literature* (December 1985).

41. See Richart T. Ely and G. S. Wehrwein, *Land Economics* (Ann Arbor, Mich.: Edwards Brothers, 1928).

42. Fine, *Laissez Faire and the General-welfare State,* p. 381.

43. Robert H. Weibe, *The Search for Order, 1877–1920* (New York: Hill and Wang, 1967) p. 153.

44. Quoted in Robert L. Heilbroner, *The Worldly Philosophers: The Lives, Times, and Ideas of the Great Economic Thinkers* (New York: Simon and Schuster, 1972), p. 235.

45. Quoted in Joseph Dorfman, *Thorstein Veblen and His America* (New York: Viking, 1934), p. 505.

46. Thorstein Veblen, "Why Is Economics Not an Evolutionary Science?" *Quarterly Journal of Economics* (July 1898), p. 379.

47. Thorstein Veblen, "The Preconceptions of Economic Science, I," *Quarterly Journal of Economics* (January 1899), p. 134.

48. Veblen, "Why Is Economics Not an Evolutionary Science?" p. 379, 378.

49. Ibid., pp. 382, 384.

50. Thorstein Veblen, "The Preconceptions of Economic Science, II," *Quarterly Journal of Economics* (July 1899), pp. 407, 412, 396–97.

51. Ibid., pp. 411, 413, 426.

52. Veblen, "The Preconceptions of Economic Science, I," p. 142, 143. See also Thorstein Veblen, "The Preconceptions of Economic Science, III," *Quarterly Journal of Economics* (January 1900).

53. Thorstein Veblen, *The Engineers and the Price System* (New York: Augustus M. Kelley, 1965; first ed. 1921), pp. 100, 136, 64.

54. Ibid., pp. 54–55, 115, 157–58.

55. Ibid., pp. 134, 144, 152, 79, 80.

56. Ibid., pp. 168, 132.

57. Ibid., pp. 68–70.

58. Ibid., pp. 147, 152.

59. Wiebe, *Search for Order,* pp. 113, 161.

60. Samuel P. Hays, *Conservation and the Gospel of Efficiency: The Progressive Conservation Movement, 1890–1920* (Cambridge, Mass.: Harvard University Press, 1959).

61. Waldo, *Administrative State*, pp. 19–20, 19.

62. Samuel Haber, *Efficiency and Uplift: Scientific Management in the Progressive Era, 1890–1920* (Chicago: University of Chicago Press, 1964), p. ix.

63. Raymond E. Callahan, *Education and the Cult of Efficiency: A Study of the Social Forces That Have Shaped the Administration of the Public Schools* (Chicago: University of Chicago Press, 1962), pp. 24–25.

64. William A. Schambra, "Progressive Liberalism and American 'Community,' " *Public Interest* (Summer 1985), p. 36.

65. Haber, *Efficiency and Uplift*, pp. 46–47, 10.

66. Joseph Dorfman, *The Economic Mind in American Civilization*, vol. 4 and 5, 1918–1933 (New York: Viking, 1959), p. 26.

67. Quoted in ibid., p. 62.

68. Ibid., pp. 62–63.

69. Alfred P. Sloan, Jr., *My Years with General Motors* (Garden City, N.Y.: Doubleday, 1964).

70. Alfred D. Chandler, Jr., *The Visible Hand: The Managerial Revolution in American Business* (Cambridge, Mass.: Harvard University Press, 1977).

71. Wiebe, *Search for Order*, p. 32.

72. Woodrow Wilson, "The Study of Administration," *Political Science Quarterly* (June 1887), reprinted in *Political Science Quarterly* (December 1941), pp. 483, 485, 499.

73. Frank J. Goodnow: *Politics and Administration: A Study in Government* (New York: Russell and Russell, 1967; first ed. 1900), p. 85.

74. Marver H. Bernstein, *Regulating Business by Independent Commission* (Princeton, N.J.: Princeton University Press, 1955).

75. Waldo, *Administrative State*, p. 21.

76. Stephen Skowronek, *Building a New American State: The Expansion of National Administrative Capacities, 1877–1920* (New York: Cambridge University Press, 1982), p. 288.

77. John B. Judis, "Herbert Croly's Promise," *New Republic* (November 6, 1989), p. 84.

78. Wiebe, *Search for Order*, p. 153.

79. Walter Lippmann, *A Preface to Morals* (New York: Macmillan, 1929), p. 120.

80. See Donald T. Critchlow, *The Brookings Institution, 1916–1952: Expertise and the Public Interest in a Democratic Society* (DeKalb, Ill.: Northern Illinois University Press, 1985).

81. Thurman W. Arnold, *The Folklore of Capitalism* (New Haven, Conn.: Yale University Press, 1937), pp. 16, 46, 5.

82. Ibid., pp. 77, 151, 55, 332, 19.

83. Ibid., pp. 117, 96, 66, 64.

84. Ibid., pp. 97, 96.

85. Ibid., pp. 116, 185, 58, 349, 45.

86. Ibid., pp. 376, 43, 44, 38, 39, 207, 333.

87. Ibid., p. 263.

88. Ibid., pp. 263, 264, 263.

89. Ibid., pp. 107, 110, 114.

90. Ibid., pp. 189, 191, 199.

91. Ibid., p. 9.

92. See Raymond Seidelman, *Disenchanted Realists: Political Science and the American Crisis, 1884–1984* (Albany: State University of New York Press, 1985).

93. William E. Leuchtenburg, *Franklin Roosevelt and the New Deal, 1932–1940* (New York: Harper and Row, 1963).

94. John Kenneth Galbraith, *American Capitalism: The Concept of Countervailing Power* (Boston: Houghton Mifflin, 1952), p. 200.

95. John Kenneth Galbraith, *The Affluent Society* (Boston: Houghton Mifflin, 1958), p. 11.

96. Galbraith, *American Capitalism*, p. 26.

97. Ibid., pp. 50, 51.

98. Ibid., p. 113.

99. Ibid., p. 136.

100. John Kenneth Galbraith, *The New Industrial State* (Boston: Houghton Mifflin, 1979; first ed. 1967), pp. 101, 94.

101. Ibid., pp. 168, 156, 170, 169.

102. Ibid., pp. 178, 169, 178, 182.

103. Galbraith, *Affluent Society*, p. 1.

104. As Dwight Waldo observed, the progressives sought "to extend the methods and the spirit of science to an ever-widening range of man's concerns." In so doing, they achieved "a revised and expurgated 'Religion of Humanity,' " one that bore "striking similarities" to the positivist vision of August Comte and of his mentor, Saint-Simon. See Waldo, *Administrative State,* p. 49.

105. Milton Friedman interview, conducted by Peter Brimelow, "Why Liberalism Is Now Obsolete," *Forbes* (December 12, 1988), p. 162.

106. Herbert A. Simon, "The Proverbs of Administration," *Public Administration Review* (Winter 1946).

107. David B. Truman, *The Governmental Process: Political Interests and Public Opinion* (New York: Alfred A. Knopf, 1951), pp. 50–51.

108. Charles E. Lindblom, "The Science of 'Muddling Through,' " *Public Administration Review* (Spring 1959).

109. Theodore J. Lowi, *The End of Liberalism: Ideology, Policy, and The Crisis of Public Authority* (New York: Norton, 1969), p. 101.

110. The emergence of the "public choice" school of economics offered another set of powerful criticisms of interest-group government. See Anthony Downs, *An Economic Theory of Democracy* (New York: Harper and Brothers, 1957); James M. Buchanan and Gordon Tullock, *The Calculus of Consent:*

Logical Foundations of Constitutional Democracy (Ann Arbor: University of Michigan Press, 1962); and Mancur Olson, *The Logic of Collective Action: Public Goods and the Theory of Groups* (Cambridge, Mass: Harvard University Press, 1965).

Chapter 6

1. See Robert H. Nelson, "Introduction and Summary," in Joseph A. Pechman, ed., *The Role of the Economist in Government: An International Perspective* (New York: New York University Press, 1989).

2. See Robert H. Nelson, "Economists as Policy Analysts: Historical Overview," in David L. Weimer, ed., *Policy Analysis and Economics: Developments, Tensions, Prospects* (Kluwer-Nijhoff, forthcoming); also Robert H. Nelson, "The Economics Profession and the Making of Public Policy," *Journal of Economic Literature* (March 1987).

3. Bertrand Russell, personal statement in *Living Philosophies: A Series of Intimate Credos* (New York: Simon and Schuster, 1931), p. 17.

4. Ibid., pp. 13–14.

5. Eric Hoffer, *The True Believer* (New York: Harper and Row, 1966; first ed. 1951), pp. 27, 24.

6. Ibid., p. 21.

7. Henry D. Aiken, *The Age of Ideology: The Nineteenth Century Philosophers*, in *The Great Ages of Western Philosophy* (Boston: Houghton Mifflin, 1962), p. 428.

8. See *Great Ages of Western Philosophy*.

9. Albert Einstein, *The World As I See It*, quoted in David Oldroyd, *The Arch of Knowledge: An Introductory Study of the History of the Philosophy and Methodology of Science* (New York: Methuen, 1986), p. 274.

10. Michael Ellman, *Socialist Planning* (New York: Cambridge University Press, 1979), pp. 42–43.

11. Barry Dean Karl, *Executive Reorganization and Reform in the New Deal: The Genesis of Administrative Management, 1900–1939* (Cambridge, Mass.: Harvard University Press, 1963), p. 222. See also Barry D. Karl, *The Uneasy State: The United States from 1915 to 1945* (Chicago: University of Chicago Press, 1983).

12. Raymond Seidelman, *Disenchanted Realists: Political Science and the American Crisis, 1884–1984* (Albany: State University of New York Press, 1985), p. 148.

13. Karl, *Executive Reorganization and Reform in the New Deal*, p. 261.

14. John Maynard Keynes, *The General Theory of Employment, Interest, and Money* (New York: Harcourt, Brace, and World, 1965; first ed. 1936), p. 374.

15. Ibid., pp. 380, 379, 380.

16. Ibid., pp. 380–81.

17. Ibid., pp. 381, 378.

18. Ibid., pp. 378–80.

19. Lawrence R. Klein, *The Keynesian Revolution* (New York: Macmillan, 1961; first ed. 1947), p. 153.

20. See C. A. R. Crosland, *The Future of Socialism* (New York: Schocken Books, 1970; first ed. 1956).

21. Quoted in Robert L. Heilbroner, *The Worldly Philosophers: The Lives, Times, and Ideas of the Great Economic Thinkers* (New York: Simon and Schuster, 1972; first ed. 1953), p. 272.

22. Keynes, *General Theory,* pp. 381–82.

23. John Maynard Keynes, "Economic Possibilities for Our Grandchildren," (1930) in Keynes, *Essays in Persuasion* (New York: Norton, 1963), pp. 366, 369–70, 372.

24. Albert O. Hirschman, "How Keynes Was Spread from America," *Challenge* (November/December 1988), p. 6.

25. Mark Blaug, *The Methodology of Economics—Or How Economists Explain* (New York: Cambridge University Press, 1980), pp. 221–22.

26. Paul A. Samuelson, *Economics: An Introductory Analysis,* 5th ed. (New York: McGraw-Hill, 1961), pp. 242, 403, 386, 403.

27. Ibid., p. 17.

28. Ibid., pp. 38, 41.

29. Ibid., p. 193.

30. Ibid., p. 186.

31. Ibid., pp. 21–22.

32. Ibid., pp. v, 831.

33. See Friedrich Hayek, "The Use of Knowledge in Society," *American Economic Review* (September 1945).

34. Paul Anthony Samuelson, *Foundations of Economic Analysis* (New York: Atheneum, 1965; first ed. 1947), p. 6.

35. Lloyd A. Metzler, "Review of Foundations of Economic Analysis," *American Economic Review* (December 1948), p. 905.

36. Paul A. Samuelson, "The Pure Theory of Public Expenditures," *Review of Economics and Statistics* (November 1954). In a personal vein I might note that one of the many articles spawned by Samuelson's 1954 piece was James Heckman and Robert Nelson, "A Note on Second Best Conditions for Public Goods," *Public Finance,* vol. 27, no. 1 (1972).

37. Arjo Klamer, *Conversations with Economists: New Classical Economists and their Opponents Speak out on the Current Controversy in Macroeconomics* (Totowa, N.J.: Rowman and Allanheld, 1984), p. 248.

38. Joseph A. Schumpeter, *Capitalism, Socialism, and Democracy* (New York: Harper Brothers, 1950; first ed. 1942).

39. Raaj Kumar Sah and Joseph E. Stiglitz, "The Architecture of Eco-

nomic Systems: Hierarchies and Polyarchies," *American Economic Review* (September 1986), p. 726.

40. Thorstein Veblen, "Why Is Economics Not an Evolutionary Science?" *Quarterly Journal of Economics* (July 1898), p. 382.

41. Milton Friedman, *Capitalism and Freedom* (Chicago: University of Chicago Press, 1962), p. 197. See also Milton Friedman and Rose Friedman, *Free to Choose: A Personal Statement* (New York: Avon Books, 1981).

42. Friedman, *Capitalism and Freedom,* pp. 10, 9, 18, 13, 15.

43. Ibid., pp. 14, 200.

44. Ibid., pp. 197, 199, 198.

45. Ibid., pp. 197, 200, 197.

46. Ibid., p. 38.

47. Ibid., p. 191.

48. Ibid., p. 97.

49. Ibid., p. 174.

50. Herbert Spencer, *The Man versus the State* (Indianapolis, Ind.: Liberty Classics, 1981; first ed. 1884).

51. Ibid., pp. 514–15.

52. Milton Friedman, "The Methodology of Positive Economics" (1953), reprinted in Daniel M. Hausman, ed., *The Philosophy of Economics: An Anthology* (New York: Cambridge University Press, 1984), pp. 211, 214.

53. Friedman, *Capitalism and Freedom,* p. 199.

54. Milton Friedman, "Using the Market for Social Development," *Cato Policy Report* (November/December 1988), pp. 1, 13.

55. Charles L. Schultze, *The Public Use of Private Interest* (Washington, D.C.: Brookings Institution, 1977), pp. 2, 6. A similar message from another economist at the Brookings Institution is found in Arthur M. Okun, *Equality and Efficiency: The Big Tradeoff* (Washington, D.C.: Brookings Institution, 1975).

56. Schultze, *Public Use of Private Interest,* p. 2.

57. Ibid., p. 5.

58. Ibid., p. 6.

59. Ibid., pp. 17–18, 19, 18.

60. Ibid., p. 20.

61. Ibid., p. 25.

62. Ibid., pp. 75, 72.

63. Ibid., pp. 21, 23.

64. Ibid., pp. 21, 22.

65. Ibid., pp. 30, 29, 30, 29.

66. Ibid., p. 90.

67. Charles L. Schultze, *The Politics and Economics of Public Spending* (Washington, D.C.: Brookings Institution, 1968), p. 101. See also Charles L. Schultze, "The Role and Responsibilities of the Economist in Government," *American Economic Review* (May 1982).

68. See Arnold J. Meltsner, *Policy Analysts in the Bureaucracy* (Berkeley: University of California Press, 1976); and Aaron Wildavsky, *Speaking Truth to Power: The Art and Craft of Policy Analysis* (New Brunswick, N.J.: Transaction Books, 1987; first ed. 1979), p. 413.

69. "Remarks by the President to the National Association of Manufacturers," White House press release, Washington, D.C., March 15, 1990.

Chapter 7

1. Robert Nisbet, *History of the Idea of Progress* (New York: Basic Books, 1980), pp. 352, 182, 331.

2. Ibid., pp. 353, 355, 348.

3. Ibid., pp. 334, 335, 339, 349, 351, 317. For further discussion of the historic importance of economic abundance to American beliefs, see David M. Potter, *People of Plenty: Economic Abundance and the American Character* (Chicago: University of Chicago Press, 1954).

4. See Robert N. Proctor, *Racial Hygiene: Medicine under the Nazis* (Cambridge, Mass.: Harvard University Press, 1988).

5. Erich Fromm, *The Art of Loving* (New York: Harper and Row, 1962; first ed. 1956), p. 7.

6. Michael Harrington, *Socialism* (New York: Bantam Books, 1973), p. 65.

7. Frank E. Manuel and Fritzie P. Manuel, *Utopian Thought in the Western World* (Cambridge, Mass.: Harvard University Press, 1979), pp. 788, 793–94.

8. See Michael Walzer, *The Revolution of the Saints: A Study in the Origins of Radical Politics* (New York: Atheneum, 1974).

9. Morris Kline, *Mathematics: The Loss of Certainty* (New York: Oxford University Press, 1980), pp. 331, 326.

10. Ibid., p. 326.

11. Ibid.

12. Hermann Weyl, quoted in Kline, *Mathematics*, pp. 335–36.

13. J. Robert Oppenheimer, *Science and the Common Understanding* (New York: Simon and Schuster, 1953), pp. 40–41.

14. Ibid., pp. 73–74, 61.

15. Niels Bohr, *Atomic Physics and Human Knowledge* (New York: Wiley, 1958), p. 99.

16. Robert Andrews Millikan, commentary in *Living Philosophies: A Series of Intimate Credos* (New York: Simon and Schuster, 1931), pp. 46–47.

17. Eugene G. Bewkes et al., *The Western Heritage of Faith and Reason* (New York: Harper and Row, 1963), pp. 629–30.

18. Werner Heisenberg, *Physics and Philosophy: The Revolution in Modern Science* (New York: Harper and Brothers, 1958), pp. 201–02.

19. Richard J. Bernstein, *The Restructuring of Social and Political Theory* (Philadelphia: University of Pennsylvania Press, 1978), pp. 128, 128–29, 131.

20. P. F. Strawson, *Individuals, An Essay in Descriptive Metaphysics*, quoted in Bernstein, *Restructuring of Social and Political Theory*, p. 119.

21. Thomas S. Kuhn, *The Structure of Scientific Revolutions* (Chicago: University of Chicago Press, 1962).

22. Paul K. Feyerabend, *Science in a Free Society*, quoted in David Oldroyd, *The Arch of Knowledge: An Introductory Study of the History of the Philosophy and Methodology of Science* (New York: Methuen, 1986), p. 335.

23. Oldroyd, *Arch of Knowledge*, p. 336.

24. Ibid., p. 365.

25. Richard Rorty, *Philosophy and the Mirror of Nature* (Princeton, N.J.: Princeton University Press, 1979), p. 318.

26. Ibid., p. 170.

27. Robert Nozick, *Philosophical Explanations* (Cambridge, Mass.: Harvard University Press, 1981), p. 23.

28. Ibid., pp. 18, 4.

29. Ibid., p. 21.

30. Peter L. Berger, *The Sacred Canopy: Elements of a Sociological Theory of Religion* (Garden City, N.Y.: Doubleday, 1969), pp. 21, 22.

31. Ibid., p. 7.

32. Ibid., pp. 138, 153.

33. Charles E. Lindblom, "The Science of 'Muddling Through,' " *Public Administration Review* (Spring 1959).

34. See Charles E. Lindblom, *Politics and Markets: The World's Political-Economic Systems* (New York: Basic Books, 1977); and Charles E. Lindblom and David K. Cohen, *Usable Knowledge: Social Science and Social Problem Solving* (New Haven, Conn.: Yale University Press, 1979).

35. Charles E. Lindblom, *The Intelligence of Democracy: Decision Making through Mutual Adjustment* (New York: Free Press, 1965), pp. 137–38. The rational model of public decision making was also criticized in Aaron Wildavsky, *The Politics of the Budgetary Process* (Boston: Little, Brown, 1964).

36. Lindblom, *Intelligence of Democracy*, p. 138.

37. Ibid., p. 138.

38. Ibid., pp. 139, 143.

39. Ibid., pp. 143, 144, 145, 146.

40. Ibid., pp. 149, 148, 149.

41. Ibid., pp. 3, 294.

42. Ibid., p. 142.

43. Mancur Olson, *The Logic of Collective Action: Public Goods and the Theory of Groups* (Cambridge, Mass.: Harvard University Press, 1965), pp.

111, 2. See also Mancur Olson, *The Rise and Decline of Nations: Economic Growth, Stagflation, and Social Rigidities* (New Haven, Conn.: Yale University Press, 1982).

44. Olson, *Logic of Collective Action*, pp. 7, 12, 11.

45. Ibid., pp. 165, 143.

46. Ibid., pp. 165, 166.

47. See Theodore J. Lowi, *The End of Liberalism: Ideology, Policy, and the Crisis of Public Authority* (New York: Norton, 1969).

48. Olson, *Logic of Collective Action*, p. 64.

49. Donald N. McCloskey, *The Rhetoric of Economics* (Madison: University of Wisconsin Press, 1985); see also Donald N. McCloskey, "The Rhetoric of Economics," *Journal of Economic Literature* (June 1983) and Donald N. McCloskey, *If You're So Smart: The Narrative of Economic Expertise* (Chicago: University of Chicago Press, 1990).

50. McCloskey, *Rhetoric of Economics*, pp. 6, 7, 9, 6, 4.

51. Ibid., p. 6.

52. Ibid., pp. 5, 4, 8, 7.

53. Ibid., pp. 7, 16.

54. Ibid., p. 16.

55. Ibid., pp. 182, 139, 96.

56. Ibid., pp. 52, 184.

57. Ibid., pp. 185, 174.

58. Ibid., p. 6.

59. James M. Buchanan and Gordon Tullock, *The Calculus of Consent: Logical Foundations of Constitutional Democracy* (Ann Arbor: University of Michigan Press, 1962); and James M. Buchanan, *The Limits of Liberty: Between Anarchy and Leviathan* (Chicago: University of Chicago Press, 1975).

60. James M. Buchanan, *What Should Economists Do?* (Indianapolis, Ind.: Liberty Press, 1979), pp. 24, 145.

61. Ibid., pp. 157, 173.

62. Ibid., p. 281.

63. Ibid., pp. 281, 280, 279.

64. Ibid., pp. 211, 213.

65. Ibid., p. 211.

66. Ibid., p. 226.

67. Ibid., p. 228.

68. Ibid., pp. 228, 229.

69. Alfred North Whitehead, *Science and the Modern World* (New York: Free Press, 1967; first ed. 1925).

70. Bill Devall and George Sessions, *Deep Ecology* (Salt Lake City, Utah: Peregrine Smith Books, 1985), p. 48.

71. Neil Everndon, "Beyond Ecology," quoted in Devall and Sessions, *Deep Ecology*, p. 48.

72. Stephen Fox, *The American Conservation Movement: John Muir and*

His Legacy (Madison: University of Wisconsin Press, 1985; first ed. 1981), p. 373.

73. Ernest Callenbach, *Ecotopia* (New York: Bantam, 1977; first ed. 1975), p. 5.

74. Robert Wright, *Three Scientists and Their Gods: Looking for Meaning in an Age of Information* (New York: Times Books, 1988).

75. Kenneth E. Boulding, *Beyond Economics: Essays on Society, Religion, and Ethics* (Ann Arbor: University of Michigan Press, 1970), pp. 275, 186, 212.

76. Ibid., pp. 107, vi, vii.

77. Ibid., p. 296.

78. Ibid., pp. 296–97.

79. Ibid., pp. 204, 106, 105.

80. Ibid., p. 248.

81. Ibid., pp. 294, 127, 263, 127.

82. Ibid., pp. 9, 300, 299, 125.

83. Ibid., pp. 230, 173.

84. Ibid., pp. 28, 29, 28, 13.

85. Ibid., pp. 210 211, 210, 108.

86. Ibid., pp. 210, 211, 210, 211.

87. Ibid., p. 195.

Chapter 8

1. Dave Foreman, "The Destruction of Wilderness," *Earth First: The Radical Environmental Journal* (December 21, 1989), p. 20. See also Robert H. Nelson, "Unoriginal Sin: The Judeo-Christian Roots of Ecotheology," *Policy Review* (Summer 1990).

2. Foreman, "Destruction of Wilderness," p. 20.

3. Barbara Ward and Rene Dubos, *Only One Earth: The Care and Maintenance of a Small Planet* (New York: Norton, 1972), p. 195.

4. Ibid., pp. 218, 219–20.

5. Ibid., pp. xviii, 189, 19, 189, xviii.

6. Jonathan Schell, *The Fate of the Earth* (New York: Avon Books, 1982), pp. 226–27, 219, 187, 210.

7. Norman Macrae, *The 2025 Report: A Concise History of the Future, 1975–2025* (New York: Macmillan, 1984), p. 124.

8. Ibid., pp. 141, 141–42, 142.

9. Ibid., pp. 132, 124.

10. Ibid., p. 115.

11. Ibid., pp. 136, 139.

12. Ibid., p. 51.

13. *Miller v. California,* 413 U.S. 15 (1973).

14. Joel Garreau, *The Nine Nations of North America* (New York: Avon Books, 1982), pp. 1, 8.

15. See Richard Cummings, *Proposition Fourteen: A Secessionist Remedy* (New York: Grove Press, 1981).

16. The text of Havel's speech to Congress was printed in the *Washington Post*, February 22, 1990, p. A28.

Index

About the Author

Economist Robert H. Nelson has been a Visiting Scholar with the Brookings Institution, the Woods Hole Oceanographic Institution, and the Political Economy Research Center. He has written widely on economic and environmental issues including *Zoning and Property Rights: An Analysis of the American System of Land Use Regulation* (MIT Press), *The Making of Federal Coal Policy* (Duke University Press), and recent articles in *Forbes, The Wall Street Journal, The Journal of Economic Literature, Policy Review,* and other publications. He resides in Chevy Chase, Maryland.